Fuchsia Lexicon

Fuchsia Lexicon

Ron Ewart

BLANDFORD PRESS
Poole Dorset

First published in the U.K. 1982 by
Blandford Press, Link House, West
Street, Poole, Dorset, BH15 1LL

ISBN 0 7137 1078 0

Typeset by Polyglot Pte Ltd, Singapore

Printed by South China Printing Co. Hong Kong

CONTENTS

Preface 7
Acknowledgements 9

Introduction 11
Cultivation 12
Trained Types 12
Pest and Disease Control 15
Key to Plant Sizes used in the Text 15
Notes on the Descriptions 16

Fuchsia Species 17
Section Quelusia 17
Section Fuchsia 18
Section Kierschlegeria 21
Section Skinnera 21
Section Hemsleyella 22
Section Schufia 22
Section Encliandra 22
Natural Variants etc 24

Alphabetical List of Cultivars 25
Colour Plates 193
Glossary 329
Bibliography 331
Appendix-Principal Fuchsia Societies 333
Index of Colour Plates 335

PREFACE

The *Fuchsia Lexicon* was written with the purpose of providing the amateur and professional fuchsia grower alike with a much more detailed description than is normally available to them of the plants they grow, or would like to grow, and taking into account their individual likes and dislikes, coupled with recommendations as to the best type of growth for each one. It is the product of over 25 years spent in growing fuchsias, studying other collections, visiting shows and specialist nurseries and talking with growers and hybridisers in Britain and overseas; collecting information on many thousands of the species and cultivars of which over 2000 are described and 192 illustrated in the *Lexicon.*

The descriptive text is arranged alphabetically to enable quick reference to be made to any name required, and plate numbers are given where applicable. The illustrations are laid out in such a way as is hoped will aid identification: the species are shown first, followed by the triphylla types, then the cultivars arranged according to colour. Thus the differences which may not be immediately apparent from a written description are more easily distinguished.

Hybridisers in many countries are striving to improve the quality and colour range of the cultivars, and there are few colours which remain elusive. Yellow, although found in several of the species, has not as yet been successfully bred into a hybrid. The late Cliff Gadsby of Derby produced several cultivars with pale buttercup yellow corollas, but he discarded them. Herman de Graaf of Lisse in Holland is presently working on similar lines; so the advent of the yellow fuchsia may not be so far off. Selectivity is of prime importance in hybridisation, not only in choosing carefully both seed and pollen parents to ensure that the progeny bear the best qualities of each, but also in the eventual release into commerce of these seedlings, to ensure that only the best of them are retained, and then only after rigorous trials. It is unfortunate that so many amateur hybridisers of today are not selective, and a large number of insignificant and worthless fuchsias, many of them identical to cultivars already in existence, are finding their way into commerce. This makes positive identification difficult in many cases, and a more stringent control over the introduction of new fuchsias is required. The naming of new fuchsias is another area where a greater measure of control should be exercised. The *International Code of Nomenclature for Cultivated Plants 1969*, which lays down the rules to be followed when naming all new plants, is too often ignored by fuchsia growers.

The heyday of the fuchsia was undoubtedly the Victorian era, when every cottage garden sported several plants, and growers like James Lye were exhibiting 8-foot specimen pillars and pyramids at Reading and Trowbridge, but the advent of the Great War led to a decline in their popularity. The formation of the American Fuchsia Society in 1929 and the British Fuchsia Society (then the Fuchsia Society) in 1938 started what has now become a worldwide chain of fuchsia societies embracing Holland, Belgium, France, Germany, Denmark, South Africa, Zimbabwe, Australia and New Zealand, each country with its own climatic problems to contend with, but all succeeding in making the fuchsia more popular today than it has ever been before.

R. EWART
1982

ACKNOWLEDGEMENTS

Grateful thanks are due to all of the following for their assistance in the preparation of this book: Robin Fletcher, who took all of the photographs in the colour section; Steve Head of High Trees Nurseries, Reigate, Surrey, Ruth and Reg Witts of Chippenham, Wiltshire, and Brenda and Harry Hemmings of Stubbington, Hampshire, all of whom allowed their fuchsia collections to be photographed.

I would also like to acknowledge the help of the numerous hybridisers who sent me details of their introductions; my daughter Pat, who did most of the typing of the manuscript; and Jean, Alison and Robert, who spent a considerable amount of time helping with the research.

INTRODUCTION

The first printed reference to the fuchsia was in Father Charles Plumier's *Nova Plantarum Americanarum Genera*, published in 1703. This was an account of plants which he had discovered in the course of four voyages to Central America in the late seventeenth and early eighteenth centuries. Plumier was a Jesuit monk in the Order of Minims, and a botanist of repute. It was in this latter capacity that he was invited by Fagon, physician to King Ludwig XIV, to take part in these expeditions, the primary function of which was to seek out further sources of the cinchona tree from which quinine was obtained.

The fuchsia, which Plumier called 'Fuchsia triphylla flore coccineo', was named in honour of Leonhart Fuchs (1501–66), for some 30 years Professor of Medicine at the University of Tubingen, a famous herbalist of his time. The precise location of the discovery was not stated in Plumier's book, but it is generally believed to have been Santo Domingo. This was confirmed in 1873 when Thomas Hogg, an American, sent seeds of *F. triphylla* which he had collected there to the Botanic Gardens in New York.

In the years between the discovery by Plumier and Hogg's rediscovery of *F. triphylla*, many other species were collected by other plant-hunting expeditions and introduced to the Western world. These included: *F. coccinea* (1788); *F. magellanica* (1768); *F. lycioides* (1796); *F. arborescens* (1824); *F. excorticata* (1824); *F. microphylla* (1827); *F. fulgens* (1830); *F. corymbiflora* (1840); *F. denticulata* (*F. serratifolia*) (1844) and *F. boliviana* (1873).

With the introduction of so many species it was only a matter of time before the first hybrids appeared. Mr Harrison, director of the 'Floricultural Cabinet', Mr Smith of Dalton and Mr Standish of Bagshot were amongst the early hybridisers in England; and M. Salter of Versailles was one of Europe's most prolific breeders of fuchsia hybrids at that time. Red and purple were the dominant colours and most of the early hybrids bore these in varying shades. The first real breakthrough came in 1842 with the introduction of 'Venus Victrix'. This was an accidental seedling, found by Mr Gulliver, gardener to the Rev. Marriott of Hurstmonceaux, and it was the first to have a white tube and sepals. It is still widely used by hybridisers today.

From there it was a short step to the white-corolla fuchsia, and Mr Story, a nurseryman of Newton Abbot in Devon, was the pioneer with several varieties in 1850, including 'Mrs Story' and 'Queen Victoria', both double-flowered. He later brought out the first fuchsia with a striped corolla. James Lye, who was head gardener to the Hon. Mrs Hay at Clyffe Hall, Market Lavington in Wiltshire, was one of the most productive of the British fuchsia hybridisers in the second half of the nineteenth century with over 60 varieties to his credit, many of which are still grown today. His hallmark of a creamy white tube and sepals gave his hybrids a distinctive appearance.

The first of the triphylla hybrids as we now know them was 'Thalia', introduced by Turner in 1855. Messrs. Veitch of Exeter brought out 'Superba' in 1882 from a *F. triphylla–F. boliviana* cross; but the main work on the triphylla hybrids was being done in Germany. Between 1904 and 1906 Carl Bonstedt of the Gottingen Botanic Gardens introduced 'Gartenmeister Bonstedt', 'Mary' and 'Koralle', while Rehnelt of the Giessen Botanic Gardens raised 'Andenken an Heinrich Henkel'. Several years later, in 1928, another German, Hartnauer, introduced the variety 'Leverkusen'.

The number of new varieties has been on the increase every year since then with hybridisers, both amateur and professional, in Britain, America, Holland, France and Germany, working, some scientifically and others haphazardly, on increasing the varieties available to the grower. Some 6000 fuchsias have been introduced over the past 150 years, but only slightly more than 2000 of them are still currently in cultivation. Red, purple and white are the predominant colours, with a multitude of pastel shades in between; and presently work is continuing on producing a blue which does not fade, together with the elusive yellow.

CULTIVATION

The main method of propagation is by cuttings and this is usually done in the early spring when plentiful supplies of young growth are available. Although cuttings can be virtually any length, the smaller they are the more quickly they will root as there is less leaf area to use up the energy required for this purpose. Two pairs of leaves and the growing tip make the ideal cutting (see Fig 1), which should be removed from the parent plant with a sharp knife to avoid damaging the tissue. It is then trimmed to immediately below a leaf joint before insertion in the rooting compost of equal parts of sharp sand and peat. They may be placed in pots, boxes or in a propagating frame and after watering in should be covered with glass or polythene to conserve moisture, and shaded from direct sunshine until they are rooted. From the rooted cutting stage fuchsias should be potted on progressively through each pot size, never over-potted. There are so many types of potting compost available nowadays, both soil-based and soil-less, that choosing the best for one's particular situation is just a matter of trial and error. Feeding must be done on a regular basis, altering the ratio gradually from a high nitrogen content in the early stages to a high potash content as the plant matures.

Seed

Fuchsia seed should be sown in heat in January in a good seed compost. Seedlings are pricked out when they have made two pairs of leaves and then potted on gradually as required. Seed saved from hybrid fuchsias will not, of course, come true.

TRAINED TYPES

The basic shape for a fuchsia plant is either that of the *bush* (see Fig 2) or the *shrub* (see Fig 3); the former is grown with a single stem of no more than 1½in (4 cm) in length, and the latter has multiple growths from below soil level. Training starts at the cutting stage by pinching out the growing tip after two or three pairs of leaves have been formed, and continuing this process on every resulting sideshoot until the required size and shape have been attained.

Fig 1

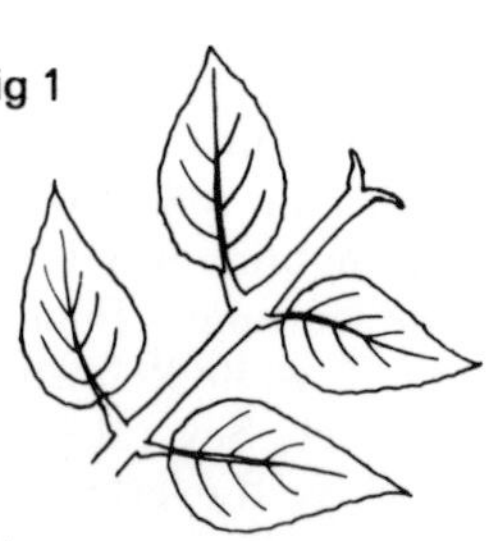

Fig 2

Fig 3

The formation of a *standard* (see Fig 4) demands a different approach, in that the growing tip is left intact and all sideshoots removed. The main leaves on the stem are left until the head has been formed. When the stem length is about 12 in or 30 cm (5–6 in or 15–20 cm for quarter and half standards) under the total height required, pinching out of the sideshoots stops, and four or five pairs are left to develop before removing the growing tip. Training from then on to form the head of the standard is the same as for a bush or shrub.

Plants used in making up a *basket* or *half-basket* (see Fig 5) are normally grown in pots up to 3½ in (9 cm) before planting. Care must also be taken to use suitable cultivars. In a full basket the plants are spaced at equal intervals round the basket, with one plant in the centre to give the basket height. Pinching out of the growing tips is done after three or four pairs of leaves have been formed, and the end result should be growth cascading down over the basket to hide the framework completely when viewed from eye level. For a half-basket the procedure is similar; in this instance the growth covering the top, front and sides of the structure.

These are the simpler trained forms of the fuchsia, but there are several other more ambitious types requiring greater attention to shaping and training and in most cases more space in which to grow them. These are the *pyramid*, *conical*, *pillar*, *fan* and *espalier*. For each of them a strong growing variety is essential and the plant staked or the framework inserted from the start.

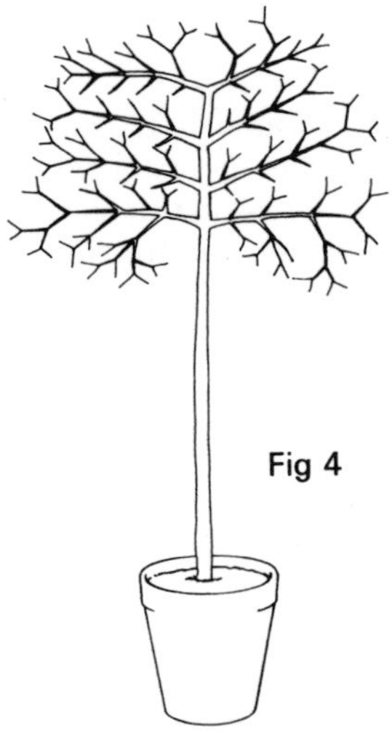

Fig 4

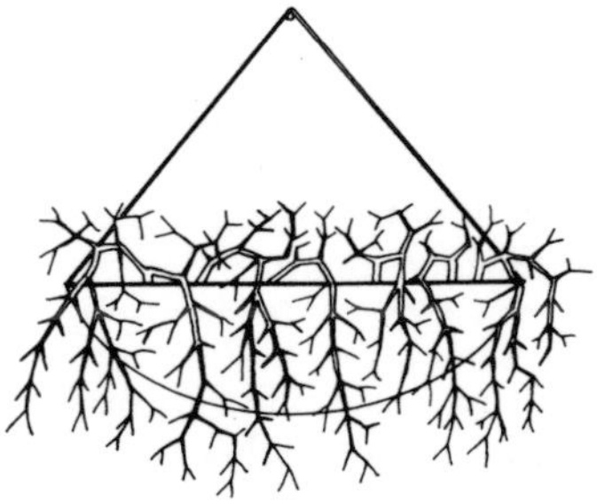

Fig 5

Pyramid (see Fig 6) **and Conical** (see Fig 7)
Grow the cutting until it has developed four or five pairs of leaves, then remove the growing tip. Once the sideshoots have started to grow remove the weaker of the two leading shoots and tie the other in to the stake. Allow this shoot to make a further four or five pairs of leaves before removing its growing tip, and repeat this procedure until the desired height is reached. Pinching out of the tips and secondary growths on the sideshoots is done as necessary to keep the plant in shape.

The conical is similar in all respects to the pyramid except that the taper to the apex is more gradual.

Pillar (see Fig 8)
The cutting is grown until three pairs of leaves have been formed before the growing tip is removed. Of the two leading shoots which result one is treated as a standard, by

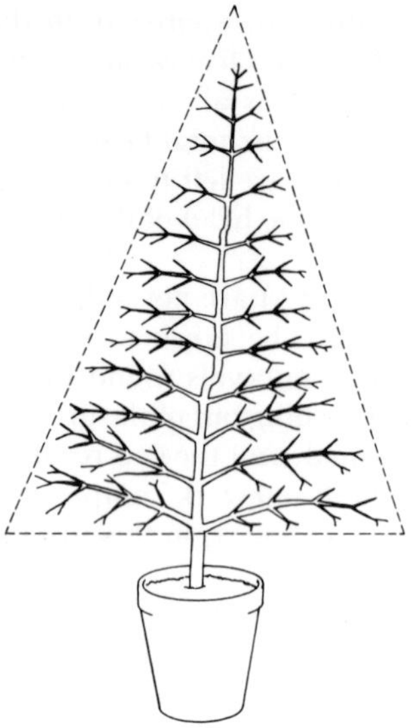

Fig 6

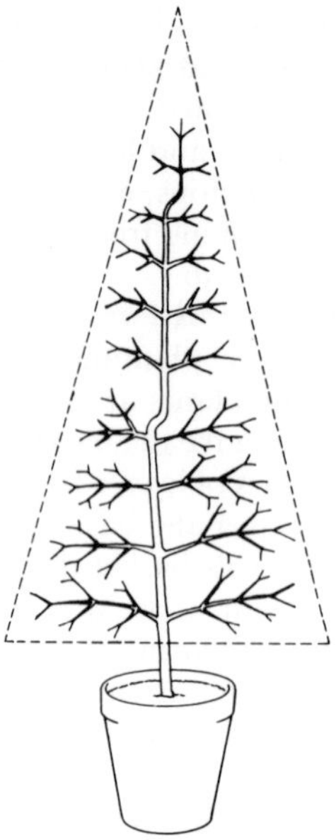

Fig 7

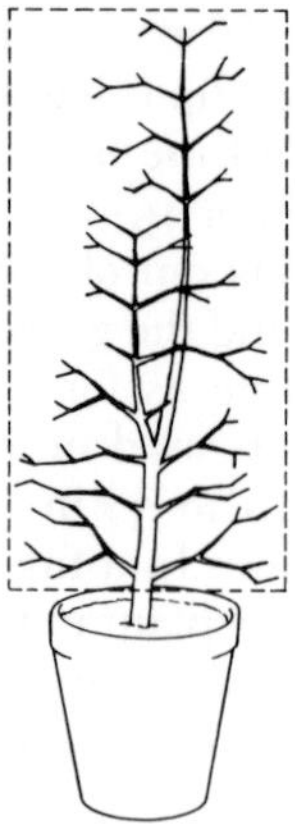

Fig 8

removing all the sideshoots as they form, and the other as a bush, growing it up to half the eventual height of the whole plant before removing the tip, leaving the sideshoots to grow and pinching them out regularly. The idea of this is that the part treated as a standard, once it has reached the desired height and having had the tip removed, will form the top half of the plant, while the growth from the other tip will form the lower part of the finished plant.

Fan (see Fig 9)
When the cutting has made four or five pairs of leaves, remove the growing tip. This should result in 8–10 sideshoots which are tied in to a previously made framework. These are allowed to grow to a further four or five pairs of leaves before their growing tips are removed and again all the resulting side growths are tied in until the framework is completely clothed.

Espalier (see Fig 10)
This differs from the fan in that, while the fan framework is made up of vertical stakes, the espalier framework is a series of horizontals. The leading shoot is left to grow until

Fig 9

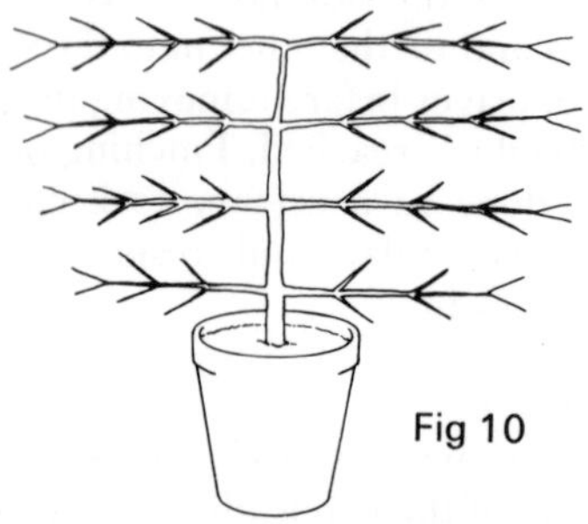

Fig 10

the top of the frame is reached, but the sideshoots are tied in to the horizontals and pinched out as they reach the extremities. It will often be found that trailing types of fuchsia lend themselves best to fan and espalier cultivation as the growths are more pliable and less sturdy.

One point which must be borne in mind regardless of the mode of training is that pinching out of the growing tips retards flowering by anything from 8 to 12 weeks on the resultant growths; therefore, if the plant is required to be in bloom for a particular time, care must be taken to discontinue pinching out in plenty of time beforehand.

PEST AND DISEASE CONTROL

The main pests attacking fuchsias are Aphid, White Fly, Thrips, Leaf Hopper, Capsid Bug and Red Spider Mite. A regular programme of spraying with a good all-purpose insecticide will do much to keep the plants clean and pest free. Diseases of fuchsias are few, only two being generally encountered. These are Grey Mould (*Botrytis cinerea*) and Fuchsia Rust (*Pucciniastrum epilobii*). *Botrytis* is usually the result of cold, damp conditions and poor ventilation. Good air circulation and periodic spraying with a good fungicide, combined with greater attention to the provision of clean growing conditions are important. Fuchsia Rust is spread by means of air-borne spores and can also be carried in the soil from infected plants. Its hosts are plants of the *Epilobium* spp; and removal of those from the immediate area where fuchsias are grown can be of assistance in combating the disease. Control is by burning all leaves which show the symptomatic orange-coloured pustules on the underside, then by spraying the plants with zineb (zinc ethylene bis-dithio carbamate).

KEY TO PLANT SIZES USED IN THE TEXT

Blooms are divided into four categories:

- Very small
- Small
- Medium
- Large

The 'type' cultivars for each category are:

- Very small—flowers from the Section Encliandra
- Small—'Tom Thumb'
- Medium—'Eva Boerg'
- Large—'Pink Marshmallow'

Foliage is classified as:

- Small—for leaves up to $\frac{3}{4} \times \frac{1}{2}$ in (2 × 1 cm)
- Medium—for leaves up to $2\frac{3}{4} \times 1\frac{3}{4}$ in (7 × 4.5 cm)
- Large—for leaves over 3 × 2 in (7.5 × 5 cm)

Tubes are classified as:

Thin	Short
Medium thickness	Medium length
Thick	Long

These sizes are relative to the over-all size of the bloom, and 'medium size' denotes that the tube is in proportion to the flower as a whole.

Sepals are classified as:

Short	Narrow/slender
Medium length	Medium width
Long	Broad

and these are again in relation to the over-all size of the flower, medium length or width denoting that it is in direct proportion to the bloom as a whole.

NOTES ON THE DESCRIPTIONS

The colours used in the descriptions are generally those given by the raiser, although where the Royal Horticultural Society's Colour Chart has been used the Chart Numbers are given as an additional aid to identification.

The AFS Registration Numbers are those allocated by the American Fuchsia Society in its role as International Registrar. Registration is not mandatory and only a very small percentage of new cultivars are in fact registered.

As far as the size of bloom is concerned, the size given in the plant description is for one grown in optimum conditions.

Numbers in bold type in brackets after the name refer to colour illustrations.

FUCHSIA SPECIES

The genus *Fuchsia* is divided into seven sections.

1) Quelusia. Tube usually not longer than the sepals. Stamens long, exserted.
2) Fuchsia. Formerly called Eufuchsia. Tube several times as long as the sepals. Stamens not much extended beyond the sepals.

In both of these sections the flowers are perfect, the stamens more or less exserted, erect, and the berries are many-seeded. They are mostly South American species.

3) Kierschlegeria. Leaves with a thickened persistent petiole base which becomes spine-like. Petals almost as long, or the same length, as the sepals. Sepals reflexed, leaves mostly opposite or in whorls, flowers small. Chilean species.
4) Skinnera. Leaves alternate, petals lacking or very small, sepals reflexed, separate. Tube funnel-shaped, not more than ½ in (1.5 cm) in length. New Zealand and Tahitian species.
5) Hemsleyella. None believed in cultivation.
6) Schufia. Flowers erect in terminal cymose (where the central flowers open first) panicles. Found from Mexico to Panama.
7) Encliandra. Flowers mostly pendulous, not in cymes, small and inconspicuous. Stamens short. Berry with few seeds.

1) SECTION QUELUSIA

F. magellanica

Tube deep red, short and slender.
Sepals deep red, short, medium width, held well out.
Corolla opening bright purple, fading as the bloom matures.
Stamens reddish. Compact, small bloom.
Foliage darkish-green, usually with reddish veins. Leaves opposite or in threes (ternate), lanceolate to ovate, serrated and with short petioles.
Growth shrubby, up to 12 ft (3.5 m) in height. Free-branching with slender, reddish shoots.
Chile and Argentina.

F. magellanica var. **magellanica**

Similar to *F. magellanica* except that the leaves are slightly smaller, and the corolla not such a bright shade of purple. Chile and Argentina.

F. magellanica var. **macrostema**

Syn. *F. coccinea* (Curtis)
F. gracilis var. *macrostema* (Lindley)
F. gracilis (Lindley)
F. magellanica var. *gracilis* (Bailey)
Tube red, short and slender.
Sepals red.
Corolla purplish. Small blooms, fairly compact.
Foliage darkish green, small and usually serrated.
Growth upright and bushy.
Chile and Argentina.

F. magellanica var. ***molinae***
Syn. *F. magellanica* var. *alba*
Tube and sepals pink.
Corolla lilac-pink.
Stamens and style pink.
Foliage pale to medium green, small, serrated leaves.
Growth upright and bushy, to 12 ft (3.7 m).
Chile.

F. regia
Tube deep red.
Sepals red, long and narrow, held well out.
Corolla purplish, short and compact.
Foliage darkish green with red veins. Leaves small, narrow, opposite or in threes. Not serrated. Often hairy.
Growth shrubby, upright, free-branching with slender, reddish branches. Ultimate height 20 ft (6 m).
Brazil.

F. regia var. ***regia***
Tube, sepals and corolla as for *F. regia.*
Foliage and branches devoid of hair.
Growth as for *F. regia.*
Brazil.

F. regia var. ***alpestris***
Tube, sepals and corolla as for *F. regia.*
Leaves and young branches covered in fine hairs.
Foliage and growth as for *F. regia.*
Fairly hardy.
Brazil.

2) SECTION FUCHSIA

F. splendens
Tube rose to bright red, compressed in the middle.
Sepals green, sometimes reddish at the base, ovate-lanceolate.
Corolla green, ovate.
Filaments and anthers pale yellow.
Foliage medium green, paler on the underside. Opposite, ovate to ovate-cordate. Stems and branches greenish to reddish.
Growth shrubby upright.
Mexico, Guatemala, Costa Rica.

***F. cordifolia* (3)**
Tube full red, swollen at the base, narrowing, then broader at the end.
Sepals green except for the base which is reddish.
Corolla green to olive-green.
Anthers yellow.
Foliage medium green, paler on the underside. Opposite, ovate to ovate-cordate, medium-sized and slightly serrated.
Growth shrubby, upright, straggling, up to 3 ft (1 m) high.

Young branches reddish. Flowers solitary in leaf axils.
Guatemala.

F. denticulata (11)
Syn. *F. serratifolia*
Tube red, longish, hairy.
Sepals red with green tips.
Corolla crimson to scarlet.
Anthers and stigma white.
Foliage dark green, reddish on the underside. Opposite or in threes, large leaves. Young branches green to red.
Growth shrubby upright. Flowers solitary in leaf axils.
Peru, Bolivia.

F. loxensis
Tube deep red, to 1 in (25 mm) in length.
Sepals scarlet, $\frac{1}{3}$ in (10 mm) long, $\frac{1}{10}$ in (4 mm) wide.
Corolla dull red, ovate.
Foliage deep shiny green, veins reddish on the underside.
Leaves opposite or in threes, large (up to $2\frac{3}{4} \times 1$ in—7×3 cm), hairy on the underside.
Growth upright, stiff and bushy. Flowers solitary in axils.
Ecuador.

F. jahnii
Tube red, tubular.
Sepals red, lanceolate, spreading.
Corolla light red.
Foliage dark green, lighter on the underside. Small, narrow leaves, slightly hairy.
Growth shrubby upright with purplish young branches.
Flowers in terminal clusters.
Venezuela.

F. simplicicaulis
Tube bright red, tinged purple, hairy.
Sepals red, tinged purple
Corolla red. Long flowers.
Foliage medium green. Leaves in whorls of four, very long (to 6 in—15 cm) and narrow.
Growth tall and shrubby. Flowers solitary in axils.
Peru.

F. corymbiflora
Tube scarlet, up to $2\frac{1}{2}$ in (6 cm) long.
Sepals scarlet.
Corolla deeper shade of red. *Filaments and anthers* reddish.
Foliage medium green, opposite, large (up to 4×2 in—11×5 cm) with soft hairs on both upper and lower surfaces.
Growth shrubby upright, with greyish, hairy branches. Flowers in terminal racemes.
Ecuador and Peru.

F. corymbiflora var. **alba**
As *F. corymbiflora* except for a white tube and sepals.

F. boliviana (2)
Tube dark red, long, up to 2½ in (6 cm).
Sepals dark red, reflexed.
Corolla varying from light to dark red.
Foliage light to medium green, paler on the underside.
Leaves opposite, ternate or alternate, 6 × 4 in (15 by 10 cm), serrated and with soft hairs on both surfaces.
Growth upright, shrubby. Flowers in terminal racemes. Can be distinguished from *F. corymbiflora* by the reflexing sepals.
Bolivia.

F. boliviana var. **boliviana**
Shorter tube and sepals than *F. boliviana* but of the same colours.
All new growth hairy.
Bolivia, Peru, Argentina.

F. boliviana var. **luxurians (4)**
Same size as *F. boliviana.* Foliage large, hairy.

F. boliviana var. **luxurians** 'Alba' **(5)**
Tube and sepals white. In other respects similar to *F. boliviana.*
Colombia, Venezuela, Guatemala.

F. fulgens
Tube dull scarlet, 2 in (5 cm) long
Sepals yellowish to greenish with pale yellow or red base.
Corolla bright red.
Foliage sage green, lighter on the underside. Ovate, large, up to 7 × 5 in (17 by 12 cm), finely serrated and with a tinge of red. Fine hairs on both surfaces.
Growth shrubby, upright with thickened tuberous roots. Flowers in short racemes.
Mexico.

F. sanctae-rosea
Tube deep to bright red, ½–¾ in (13–18 mm) long.
Sepals scarlet, short and narrow.
Corolla orange-red to scarlet.
Foliage deep green on top, lighter on the underside and with fine hairs on both surfaces. Leaves mostly in threes or fours, medium-sized.
Growth shrubby upright. Young shoots purplish-red.
Bolivia and Peru.

F. macrophylla
Tube scarlet, ¾–⅘ in (18–20 mm) in length.
Sepals red with green tips.
Corolla bright red.
Foliage dark green on top, paler underneath. Large leaves up to 6 × 2 in (15 × 5 cm).
Growth upright, shrubby with the young branches tinged red or purplish.
Peru.

F. sessilifolia
Tube scarlet, $\frac{1}{2}$–$\frac{3}{5}$ in (13–16 mm) in length.
Sepals greenish-red.
Corolla scarlet. Small flower, length 1 in (2.5 cm).
Foliage glossy green, paler on the underside. Leaves in whorls of three or four, large (3–6 by 1–1$\frac{1}{2}$ in—8–15 by 2.5–4 cm), long and fairly narrow, faintly serrated.
Growth shrubby upright, branches purplish-red. Flowers in terminal racemes.
Colombia and Ecuador.

F. lampadaria
Tube bright orange-red, purplish at the base.
Sepals bright orange with green tips.
Corolla bright orange-red. Flower length 2 in (5 cm).
Foliage dark green, medium to large, slightly serrated and with purplish veins. Normally in threes.
Growth shrubby, upright. Flowers solitary in axils.
Colombia.

F. triphylla
Tube red, hairy on the outside, length 1$\frac{1}{4}$ in (3 cm).
Sepals red.
Corolla red at the tips, slightly lighter at the base.
Foliage darkish greeny bronze with reddish veins. Long and narrow (3 × 1$\frac{1}{4}$ in—8 by 3 cm). Leaves in threes or fours.
Growth shrubby, low-growing. Young stems reddish.
Haiti.

3) SECTION KIERSCHLEGERIA

F. lycioides
Tube red, very small.
Sepals red, small and slightly reflexed.
Corolla purplish, short.
Foliage alternate, very small, darkish green, paler on the underside. When the leaves are shed the thickened woody bases of the petioles form spines $\frac{1}{20}$–$\frac{1}{10}$ in (1.5–2 mm) long.
Growth shrubby, upright. Flowers solitary in the axils.

4) SECTION SKINNERA

F. excorticata
Tube green, becoming dark reddish purple, short.
Sepals green, becoming reddish purple, reflexing slightly.
Corolla dark purple. Anthers blue, stigma yellowish.
Foliage alternate, green on top, whitish on the underside with small hairs along the veins and margins. Medium-sized leaves.
Growth upright, bushy and spreading with light brown, papery bark. Flowers solitary in the axils.
New Zealand.

F. colensoi
Tube red.
Sepals greenish to reddish, spreading and reflexing slightly.

Corolla purple, short. Small flowers.
Foliage green on top, whitish on the underside with fine hairs on the main veins. Small leaves.
Growth shrubby upright.
New Zealand.

F. perscandens
Tube red.
Sepals greenish to reddish, not reflexed.
Corolla purple. Small blooms.
Foliage green on the upper surface, whitish underneath. Small ovate leaves.
Growth climbing shrub. Dark purple berries.
New Zealand.

***F. procumbens* (10)**
Tube yellowish-green, red at the base.
Sepals chocolate brown. No corolla.
Foliage very small, darkish green, lighter on the underside.
Growth trailer, long thin stems, flowers held upright. Large berries maturing to plum-purple.
New Zealand.

5) SECTION HEMSLEYELLA

None known in cultivation.

6) SECTION SCHUFIA

***F. arborescens* (1)**
Tube rose-red to magenta.
Sepals reddish to wine-purple, spreading and reflexing.
Corolla lilac-lavender.
Flowers in corymbose panicles, erect.
Foliage leaves opposite or in threes, shiny bright green on top, paler on the underside. Reddish veins. Large leaves, oblong-elliptic in shape.
Growth shrubby upright.
Mexico.

F. paniculata
Similar to *F. arborescens* except that the flowers are somewhat darker in colour and the panicles less compact. The flowers are also slightly smaller.
Mexico and Guatemala.

7) SECTION ENCLIANDRA

F. thymifolia
Tube white, reddening with age.
Sepals white, spreading.
Corolla white, becoming purplish-red as it matures.
Foliage very small, medium green on top, paler underneath. Elliptic-ovate in shape.
Growth shrubby upright with slender branches, reddish and with small hairs.
Mexico.

F. minimiflora
Tube whitish to reddish $\frac{1}{20}$–$\frac{1}{10}$ in (1–2 mm) long.
Sepals whitish to reddish, reflexed and spreading.
Corolla white to red.
Foliage similar to *F. thymifolia.*
Growth upright, bushy, slender branches, reddish. Small flowers.
Mexico.

F. bacillaris
Tube red, $\frac{1}{5}$–$\frac{1}{4}$ in (5–6 mm) long.
Sepals rose, spreading and reflexing slightly.
Corolla rose. Very small flowers.
Foliage small, finely serrated, medium green with a line of minute hairs on the veins of the upper surface.
Growth upright, bushy.
Mexico.

F. minutiflora
Tube reddish, $\frac{1}{8}$–$\frac{1}{7}$ in (3–4 mm) long.
Sepals reddish, spreading.
Corolla whitish. Very small blooms.
Foliage very tiny, serrated. Medium green, leaves opposite.
Growth shrubby upright with slender branches.
Mexico.

F. microphylla
Tube deep red.
Sepals deep red (three or four).
Corolla rose, slightly serrated petals. Very small flower.
Foliage deep green on the upper surface, paler on the underside. Small and serrated.
Growth shrubby upright with slender branches.
Mexico.

F. hemsleyana (7)
Tube rose, $\frac{1}{5}$–$\frac{1}{3}$ in (5–7 mm) long.
Sepals rose, spreading and slightly reflexed.
Corolla rose with a purplish tinge. Very small flowers.
Foliage deep green, paler on the underside, serrated. Very small leaves.
Growth upright, bushy.
Panama and Costa Rica.

F. michoacanensis
Tube red, $\frac{1}{7}$–$\frac{1}{4}$ in (4–6 mm) long.
Sepals red, spreading, slightly hairy.
Corolla coral red, very small flowers.
Foliage darkish green, small 1 × $\frac{3}{4}$ in (25 × 20 mm), opposite, serrated, slightly hairy on the underside.
Growth shrubby, upright, with slender, hairy branches.
Mexico, Guatemala and Costa Rica.

F. encliandra
Tube red, $\frac{1}{4}$–$\frac{1}{3}$ in (6–8 mm) long.
Sepals reddish.
Corolla reddish. Small flowers.
Foliage very small, medium green, slightly serrated. Leaves opposite.
Growth upright, bushy, fairly vigorous with slender branches.
Mexico.

F. tetradactyla
Tube rose-orchid to deep red, $\frac{1}{3}$–$\frac{1}{4}$ in (7–10 mm) long.
Sepals red to orchid.
Corolla rose-scarlet or pale rose-scarlet. Small flowers.
Foliage dark green on top, paler on the underside, slightly hairy on both surfaces, faintly serrated. Leaves broadly ovate.
Growth shrubby, low growing, slender branched, with reddish young branches.
Guatemala and Mexico.

NATURAL VARIANTS ETC

F. fulgens gesneriana
Tube orange-scarlet.
Sepals green.
Corolla orange-scarlet.
Foliage and growth as for *F. fulgens.*

F. fulgens 'Rubra Grandiflora' (**6**)
Tube orange-scarlet.
Sepals green.
Corolla orange-scarlet. Very long blooms.
Foliage and growth as for *F. fulgens.*

F. magellanica var. ***macrostema*** 'Tricolor' (**23**)
Similar to *F. magellanica* var. *macrostema* except for the foliage which is variegated red, white and green. A very good hedging plant.

F. magellanica var. ***macrostema*** 'Variegata' (**9**)
Foliage is variegated green and silvery shades. *F.* 'Riccartonii' is a hybrid of *F. magellanica.* This is the plant seen in hedges on the West Coast of Scotland, Ireland and in Cornwall.

'A-1'
ROBERT CASTRO 1969
AFS Registration No 837
Double
Tube pale pink, medium length and thickness. *Sepals* pale pink, broad. *Corolla* pale blue in the centre, fading to lavender. Petaloids pink and blue. Very full. *Foliage* medium green. *Growth* trailer, self-branching, vigorous and free-flowering. A very showy plant. Basket.

'Abbé Farges' (152)
LEMOINE 1901
Semi-double
Flower length $1\frac{1}{2}$ in (4 cm)
Tube light cerise, short and medium thickness. *Sepals* light cerise, held horizontal. *Corolla* rosy lilac, small. *Foliage* medium green, small and shiny, slightly serrated. *Growth* upright, vigorous, self-branching and very free-flowering. Branches are very brittle and easily broken off. It will make an excellent exhibition plant, and is equally at home in the garden as a hardy when established. Will withstand very low winter temperatures. Bush or quarter standard.

'A Bit of Red'
SOO YUN FIELD 1969
AFS Registration No 850
Double
Tube bright red, short and medium thickness. *Sepals* bright red, slightly upturned. *Corolla* white, flushed red, with dark red variegations at the base of the petals and dark red veining, very large bloom. *Foliage* medium to dark green. *Growth* trailer, not very floriferous. Trailer, not quite good enough for a basket.

'Abundance'
TODD 1870
Single
Tube rich cerise, medium length and thickness. *Sepals* rich cerise, longish and pointed, slightly upturned at the tips. *Corolla* deep purple, fading a little on maturity. Petaloids are small, cerise-coloured. *Foliage* medium to darkish green. *Growth* upright, bushy, self-branching and free-flowering. Very vigorous grower, but tends to spread. Does well out of doors, permanently planted and will withstand quite low winter temperatures. Bush.

'Abundance'
NIEDERHOLZER 1944
Single to semi-double
Tube rose pink, medium thickness and length. *Sepals* rose pink. *Corolla* pale bishop-blue, with the base of the petals almost white. Very compact. *Foliage* medium green. *Growth* very lax, vigorous, free-flowering. Basket.

'Accent'
KENNETT 1969
AFS Registration No 862
Single to semi-double
Tube pink, long and medium thickness. *Sepals* pink, longish, medium width. *Corolla* deep purple, fading to deep magenta, small. *Foliage* medium green, medium-sized leaves. *Growth* rather lax, free-flowering. Bush (if staked early) or basket.

'Achievement' (173)
MELVILLE 1886
Single
Tube carmine cerise, medium length and thickness. *Sepals* carmine cerise, long and slender, slightly upturned. *Corolla* reddish purple, turning to scarlet at the base of the petals. *Foliage* yellowish green, medium size. *Growth* upright, vigorous, self-branching and free-flowering. Responds well to pinching, and will make an excellent exhibition plant with medium to large blooms freely produced. Beautifully shaped bloom in the classic fuchsia shape. Can be grown as a garden hardy in favourable districts. Total length of bloom 3 in (7.5 cm).

'Adagio'
H. TIRET 1961
AFS Registration No 485
Double

Tube white, medium length and thickness, pink flush. *Sepals* rosy-red with green tips, slightly curled upwards. *Corolla* claret red, white at the base of the petals. *Filaments and style* pink. *Foliage* medium green, slightly serrated, largish. *Growth* very lax, free-flowering, bushy. Basket.

'Admiration'
W.P. WOOD 1940
Single
Tube bright cherry red, approx. $2\frac{1}{2}$ in (6 cm) in length. *Sepals* bright cherry red, yellowish-green tips, slightly upturned. *Corolla* Indian Lake, longish but compact. *Foliage* medium green, slightly reddish at the growing tips. *Growth* lax, spreading bush. Free-flowering. *Parentage* Seedling × 'Mrs Rundle'.

'After Five'
ROBERT CASTRO 1972
AFS Registration No 1028
Single to semi-double
Tube white, very thin and short. *Sepals* white, completely upturning when they mature. *Corolla* opens a deep burgundy red shade, fading to a lighter shade of red, short and compact. *Foliage* medium to dark green, small. *Growth* upright, self-branching, bushy and free-flowering. Bush.

'Aileen'
SOO YUN 1972
Double
Tube light green, short and of medium thickness. *Sepals* pale green with darker green tips. *Corolla* cerise, lighter at the base of the petals, medium size. *Foliage* medium size, dark green. *Growth* upright, bushy, self-branching and free-flowering. Prefers shade. Dwarf plant. Bush.

'Aintree' (41)
NEED 1964
Single
Tube ivory white, thin. *Sepals* ivory, slightly tinted rose pink, green tips, upswept. *Corolla* vivid rose madder, with touches of white at the base of the petals. *Filaments and style* pink. *Foliage* medium green, slightly serrated. *Growth* upright, vigorous, self-branching and free-flowering, which sometimes tends to grow to the horizontal. Good exhibition plant. Named after Liverpool's racecourse. Bush or standard.

'Airy Fairy'
HAZARD AND HAZARD (date unknown)
Single
Tube red, long and thin. *Sepals* red, long and narrow, slightly upturned. *Corolla* dark bluish-violet, compact. *Foliage* medium green, slightly serrated. *Growth* upright, bushy, self-branching and free-flowering. Bush.

'Alameda'
NIEDERHOLZER-WALTZ 1950
Double
Tube dark red, medium length and thickness. *Sepals* dark red. *Corolla* white, crimson veining at the base of the petals, very full and compact. *Foliage* dark green. *Growth* upright, bushy, self-branching and free-flowering. Bush.

'Alaska'
ROTH 1956
Double
Tube white, short and of medium thickness. *Sepals* white, tinted very pale blue at the tips. *Corolla* white, pale blue on the edges of the petals, medium-sized. *Foliage* medium green to pale green. *Growth* lax, trailing, bushy and free-flowering. Basket.

Do not confuse with the following cultivar.

'Alaska' (29)
SCHNABEL 1963
AFS Registration No 585
Double
Tube white, medium length and thickness. *Sepals* white with green tips, slightly upturned at the tips. *Corolla* white, very full and fluffy. *Filaments* pale pink, style white. *Foliage* dark green, very slight

serrations. *Growth* vigorous, self-branching, low growing upright, free-flowering. The number and weight of the blooms make staking a necessity if this cultivar is to be grown as a bush. It does best in the shade and must be protected from the rain which spoils the blooms. Bush.

'Albion'

GADSBY 1972
AFS Registration No 1049
Single
Tube neyron rose, long and of medium thickness. *Sepals* neyron rose, pointed and held back close against the tube. *Corolla* hyacinth blue RHS 91A passing to spectrum violet RHS 82B and fading to mallow purple RHS 72D. Medium-sized, saucer-shaped. *Foliage* medium green. *Growth* upright, bushy, free-flowering and self-branching. Bush. Prefers shaded conditions. *Pollen parent* 'Lady Isobel Barnett'.

'Al Castro'

ROBERT CASTRO 1971
AFS Registration No 948
Semi-double
Tube white, medium length and thickness. *Sepals* white, long and slightly upturned. *Corolla* peachy pink marbled with white on the outer petals which flare out as the flower matures. *Foliage* medium green, slightly serrated. *Growth* trailer, self-branching, bushy, free-flowering. Basket.

'Aldham'

H. DUNNETT 1979
AFS Registration No 1514
Double
Tube white, medium length and thickness. *Sepals* white, showing slight pink tinges as they age, reflexing. *Corolla* white, full. *Stamens and pistil* red. *Foliage* dark green with red veins. Serrated. *Growth* vigorous, free-flowering, bushy and trailing. Holds its colour best when grown in the shade. Basket. *Parentage* 'Shelley Lyn' × self.

'Alfred Rambaud'

LEMOINE 1896
Double
Tube rich scarlet, medium length and thickness. *Sepals* rich scarlet slightly upturning. *Corolla* violet-purple, fading as the bloom matures. *Foliage* darkish green. *Growth* vigorous, upright, bushy, self-branching and free-flowering. With judicious pinching it will make a good exhibition plant. Bush.

'Alf's Pet'

R. HOLMES 1980
AFS Registration No 1555
Single
Tube white, long and thin. *Sepals* blush white with green tips, azalea pink RHS 41C on the underside. Of medium length and width, held slightly below horizontal and reflexing. *Corolla* scarlet RHS 43B, mandarin red RHS 40B at the base. *Pistil* very long, pink with a yellow stigma. *Anthers* short, blush white. *Foliage* mid-green, RHS 137B with pale green veins. *Growth* small self-branching upright which will make a nice bush or standard.

'Alice'

HAZARD AND HAZARD
Semi-double
Tube rich pink, medium length and thickness. *Sepals* pink, longish, slightly reflexed. *Corolla* purple, fading slightly as it matures. *Foliage* medium green. *Growth* lax, self-branching and reasonably free-flowering. Half-basket.

'Alice Ashton' (102)

HORACE TIRET 1971
AFS Registration No 991
Double
Tube pale pink, medium length and thickness. *Sepals* pink, with pale pink tips, darker on the undersides. Completely reflexed against the tube. *Corolla* porcelain blue, with pink shading at the base of the petals. *Filaments* pale pink. *Style* pale pink. *Foliage* medium green, longish leaves. *Growth* trailer, very lax, but free-flowering for its size. Basket.

'Alice Eastwood'
HAZARD AND HAZARD
Semi-double
Tube white, medium length and thickness. *Sepals* crepe-white, longish, with a pale rose tint. *Corolla* white with rose-red veins, large and full. *Foliage* medium green. *Growth* upright, free-flowering, self-branching and bushy. Bush. Named after Miss Alice Eastwood, one of the founder members of the American Fuchsia Society.

'Alice Hoffman' (125)
KLEVE 1911
Semi-double
Tube rose pink, smallish. *Sepals* rose, slightly upturned. *Corolla* white with rose veins, very compact. *Style and filaments* rose. *Foliage* dark bronze green, small and slightly serrated. *Growth* upright, vigorous, bushy and very free-flowering. Hardy in most areas and does exceptionally well when planted outside in a border. Bush or quarter standard.

'Alice Travis' (154)
JAMES TRAVIS 1956
Semi-double to double
Tube carmine cerise, medium length and thickness. *Sepals* carmine cerise, broad and completely reflexed. *Corolla* deep lavender blue with reddish veining at the base of the petals. *Style* pink. *Filaments* pink. *Foliage* medium green, serrated. *Growth* rather lax but can be grown upright, bushy, and free-flowering. Bush or basket.

'Alison Ewart' (100)
GEORGE ROE 1976
Single
Tube neyron rose, small and medium thick. *Sepals* neyron rose, tipped green, small and pointed. *Corolla* mauve with a pink flush, small. *Foliage* darkish green with red veining, and bronzy sheen. *Growth* upright, bushy, self-branching and very free-flowering. Excellent exhibition plant in pots from $3\frac{1}{2}$ in (9 cm) upwards. Bush or quarter standard. *Parentage* 'Eleanor Leytham' × 'Pink Darling'.

'Alison Ryle'
M. RYLE 1967
AFS Registration No 112 (Registered 1973)
Semi-double
Tube fuchsia pink, short and of medium thickness. *Sepals* pink with paler tips, with crepe undersides, rather broad and upturned. *Corolla* deep lavender blue, flushed pale mauve and with rose pink veins, the whole fading with age. Flares when fully open. *Style* pink. *Filaments* red. *Foliage* medium green, medium-sized, serrated. *Growth* upright, vigorous, bushy, self-branching, and very free-flowering. Bush. *Parentage* 'Lena Dalton' × 'Tennessee Waltz'.

'Allegra'
SCHABEL-PASKESEN 1960
AFS Registration No 416
Double
Tube rose pink, medium length and thickness. *Sepals* rose pink, reflexing. *Corolla* rose bengal, very loose petalled, flaring. *Foliage* medium green, slightly serrated. *Growth* natural trailer, free-flowering. Requires pinching to get it into shape. Basket.

'Aloha'
NIEDERHOLZER 1947
Single
Tube white, medium length and thickness. *Sepals* white with green tips. *Corolla* light purple, medium-sized. *Foliage* medium green. *Growth* upright, vigorous, free-flowering, needs careful pinching to shape. Bush.

'Alpestris Reevesi'
EVANS AND REEVES 1937
Tube scarlet, medium length, rather thin. *Sepals* scarlet, slightly upturned. *Corolla* deep blue purple. *Foliage* medium to dark green, smallish. *Growth* very vigor-

ous, upright, self-branching and free-flowering. Eminently suitable for growing as a hedge. *Parentage F. alpestris* × 'Virgata' seedling.

'Alsa Garnet'
T. THORNE 1965
Double
Tube white, long and of medium thickness. *Sepals* white on top, pink on the undersides, tipped green, and upturned. *Corolla* garnet red, very compact shape. *Style and filaments* pale pink. *Foliage* medium green, smallish. *Growth* bushy, vigorous, self-branching, bushy and free-flowering. Basket.

'Al Stettler'
PENNISI 1968
AFS Registration No 746
Double
Tube white with a pink flush, medium length and thickness. *Sepals* white, flushed pink, slightly recurved. *Corolla* deep rose pink with shades of salmon pink, large blooms. *Foliage* medium green. *Growth* upright, bushy, self-branching and free-flowering. Requires heat for best growth. Bush.

'Alwin' (128)
MRS I. CLYNE 1976
Semi-double
Tube neyron rose, short and thick. *Sepals* neyron rose, recurving. *Corolla* white, with red veins, tightly fluted and of medium size. *Foliage* bright green, smallish. *Growth* bushy, vigorous, short-jointed and very floriferous. Excellent exhibition plant. *Parentage* 'La Campanella' × 'Liebriez'.

'Alyce Larson'
H. TIRET 1972
AFS Registration No 1070
Double
Tube white, short and thick. *Sepals* white, green tips, broad and held upwards of the horizontal. *Corolla* white with pale pink veining, very full and fluffy. *Style and filaments* pale pink. *Foliage* medium green. *Growth* natural trailer, very vigorous and free-flowering. Basket or half-basket.

'Amapola'
DALE 1950
Semi-double
Tube dark pink, medium length and thickness. *Sepals* dark pink. *Corolla* rose purple, very large, rather loose. *Foliage* medium green, largish-sized. *Growth* natural trailer, free-flowering. Basket or half-basket.

'Amazing Grace'
CHESELDINE 1975
AFS Registration No 1288
Double
Tube candy pink, medium length and thickness. *Sepals* candy pink, tipped leaf green, upturned. *Corolla* wedgewood blue, flushed candy pink at the base, and maturing to lilac, flaring. *Foliage* dark green, large. *Growth* vigorous, upright, bushy and free-flowering. An interesting colour combination, and a plant which does best when grown in the shade. Bush or standard.

'Amazing Mary'
J.A. WRIGHT 1980
AFS Registration No 1596
Semi-double
Tube longish, light red. *Sepals* light red, recurving. *Corolla* dark red. *Foliage* dark green, medium size. *Growth* vigorous, self-branching upright. Will make a good standard. *Parentage* 'Marinka' ×.

'Ambassador'
JONES/MACHADO 1962
AFS Registration No 502
Single
Tube white, with pink flush, medium length and thickness. *Sepals* white on top, pink on the undersides. *Corolla* violet purple, changing to peony purple with age. *Style* pink. *Filament* pink. *Foliage* medium green. *Growth* upright, self-branching, vigorous and bushy. Bush. Good exhibition plant if pinched at every

first or second pair of leaves. Equally good as a summer bedder.

'Amelie Aubin'
EGGBRECHT 1884
Single
Tube white, long and of medium thickness. *Sepals* white, green tips, drooping at first but coming to the horizontal as the flower grows. *Corolla* rosy-cerise, white at the base of the petals. *Style* white. *Filaments* pale pink. *Foliage* light green, large and serrated. *Growth* very vigorous, willowy, free-flowering. Needs a lot of pinching to get it into shape. Blooms large and beautifully shaped. Bush or can be tried as a pyramid.

'America'
NIEDERHOLZER 1941
Single
Tube rose madder, medium length and thickness. *Sepals* rose madder, crimson on the undersides with green tips. *Corolla* deep crimson, very large and well shaped. *Foliage* medium green. *Growth* natural trailer, free-flowering and bushy. Basket. *Parentage* 'Golondrina' × 'Mrs Rundle'.

'Americana Elegans'
Raiser and date unknown
Single
Tube cerise, small and thin. *Sepals* cerise, small and narrow. *Corolla* purple, compact. *Foliage* medium green, small to medium size. *Growth* vigorous, upright, bushy, self-branching and very free-flowering. Makes an excellent hedging plant, reaching up to 4 ft (1.3 m) each year in early July. Hedge.

'American Beauty'
R. HODGES 1958
Double
Tube pale pink, long and medium thickness. *Sepals* rose bengal, longish, and curled. *Corolla* rich rose red, with tinges of white at the base of the petals. *Foliage* dark green. *Growth* trailing, bushy, free-flowering. Basket.

'American Prelude' (sometimes known as 'Prelude')
KENNETT AND ROSS 1958
Double
Tube white, long and of medium thickness. *Sepals* white, broad and reflexing completely against the tube. *Corolla* purple, with the outer petals splashed with white, pink and purple. Royal purple centre petals surrounded by smaller white petals, stays compact. *Style* white. *Filaments* pink. *Foliage* medium green, broad and slightly serrated. *Growth* natural trailer, very vigorous, and free-flowering. It is apt to get rather straggly if not tightly pinched in its early stages. A very showy cultivar. Basket.

'Amethyst'
TIRET 1941
Double
Tube pale red, medium length and thickness. *Sepals* pale red, outswept. *Corolla* purple, very full and showy. *Foliage* medium green, medium to large leaves. *Growth* upright, vigorous, bushy and free-flowering. Bush.

'Amigo'
KENNETT 1969
AFS Registration No 863
Single to semi-double
Tube white, long and medium thickness. *Sepals* pale salmon pink, with deeper pink shade underneath, green tips, completely reflexed against the tube. *Corolla* dark purple with deep salmon and pink splashes, white at the base of the petals. *Style* pale pink. *Filaments* pale pink. *Foliage* medium green with red margins. *Growth* upright, free-flowering, bushy and vigorous. Very easy to grow. Bush.

'A.M. Larwick'
SMITH (New Zealand) 1940
Single
Tube carmine red, long and medium thick. *Sepals* carmine, long and arching backwards towards the tube. *Corolla* purplish mauve with carmine veining, remaining very compact. *Style* carmine red.

Filaments carmine red. *Foliage* medium green with red veins. *Growth* vigorous, bushy, self-branching and free-flowering upright. Bush, standard, or summer bedder.

'Amy Lye'
LYE 1885
Single
Tube creamy white, thick and of medium length. *Sepals* white, with green tips and slight pink flush, broad and slightly upturned at the tips. *Corolla* coral orange-cerise. *Filaments* pink. *Style* white. *Foliage* bronzy green when young, changing to a medium dark green with crimson veins. *Growth* upright, bushy, and vigorous, but needs pinching to get any sort of shape. Bush or standard.

'Andenken an Heinrich Henkel' (18)
REHNELT 1897
Triphylla type.
Tube light rose pink, long and thin. *Sepals* slightly deeper rose, small. *Corolla* deep rose pink. *Foliage* dark olive green with dark magenta veins. *Growth* vigorous, spreading, and free-flowering. Bush.

'Andre le Nostre'
LEMOINE 1909
Double
Tube cerise, medium length and thickness. *Sepals* cerise, broad and held immediately on top of the corolla with slight upturn at the tips. *Corolla* violet purple, with cerise veining and a lighter shade at the base of the petals, very full and fluffy. *Style* cerise. *Filaments* cerise. *Foliage* dark green, broad and with a reddish veining. *Growth* upright, vigorous, bushy, free-flowering. Bush.

'Andrew'
WATSON 1967
Single
Tube creamy white with a pink flush, medium length and thickness. *Sepals* pale rose madder, deeper pink on the undersides, and pale green tips. *Corolla* pale Tyrian purple, pink at the base of the petals, very compact. *Foliage* medium green, slightly serrated. *Growth* upright, bushy, vigorous and free-flowering. Equally at home in a pot or bedded out. Easy to grow. Bush.

'Andrew Carnegie'
DEMAY
Double
Tube crimson, medium length and thickness. *Sepals* crimson, broad and held immediately over the top of the corolla, tips slightly upturned. *Corolla* white with cerise veining, very full and frilly. *Style* pink. *Filaments* cerise. *Foliage* medium green, serrated. *Growth* vigorous, self-branching, lax upright, free-flowering. Grows best if kept in cool conditions. Bush.

'Andrew Ryle' (118)
RYLE 1976
Single
Tube crimson, short and stubby. *Sepals* crimson with green tips, held well out from the corolla and upturned at the tips. *Corolla* white with crimson veins. *Style and filaments* red. *Foliage* dark bluish-green with purple veining, smallish. *Growth* upright, self-branching, bushy and vigorous, very free-flowering, although the flowers are rather small. Easy to grow. Bush.

'Andromeda' (96)
DE GROOT (Netherlands)
Single
Tube pale red, small, medium thickness. *Sepals* pale red, short, held well out from the corolla. *Corolla* lilac with reddish veining. Small to medium-sized bloom. *Foliage* medium green, small to medium-sized leaves, serrated. *Growth* upright, vigorous, bushy and free-flowering. *F. regia* var. *typica* × 'Upward Look'. Bush.

'Angel'
GORMAN 1970
AFS Registration No 928
Semi-double

Tube white, medium length and thickness. *Sepals* white with pink flush as the blooms age. *Corolla* white, compact shape. *Foliage* medium pale green, new branches are reddish. *Growth* lax bush, reasonably vigorous and free-flowering. Quite an attractive flower which needs to be grown in the shade to keep its colour. Bush, half-basket.

'Angela Gallegos'
TONY ARAUJO
Double
Tube white. *Sepals* white. *Corolla* plum royal blue. *Foliage* medium green. *Growth* upright, self-branching, easy to shape. Bush.

'Angela Leslie' (69)
TIRET 1959
AFS Registration No 382
Double
Tube pink, medium length and thickness. *Sepals* pink, deeper pink underneath and green tips, fully recurving over the tube. Rather broad. *Corolla* pink, splashed and veined deeper shade of pink. *Filaments and style* pink. *Growth* upright and bushy, self-branching and free-flowering. Strong growing. *Foliage* medium green, largish to medium. Needs staking to support the weight of the blooms. A beautiful cultivar best grown as a bush, and prefers cool conditions.

'Angela Rippon'
CLIFF GADSBY 1977
AFS Registration No 1423
Single
Tube china rose, medium length and thickness. *Sepals* china rose, RHS 58D with green tips. *Corolla* wistaria blue RHS 92A, medium size. *Foliage* dark green. *Growth* self-branching, bushy, upright. Will make a good bush or standard. Very free-blooming, flowers carried horizontal to the foliage. Grows best in the shade, does not like full sun. *Parentage* 'Christine Clements' × 'Forward Look'.

'Angeline'
DUNNETT 1979
AFS Registration No 1515
Double
Tube long, thin, white. *Sepals* white, flushed pink, with green tips. Long, thin, recurving. *Corolla* campanula violet RHS 82C, flecked with pink RHS 65D. *Foliage* medium green, long and slender, serrated, with red veins. Self-branching trailer, makes a good basket. Best colour develops if grown in the shade. *Parentage* 'Shelley Lyn' × self.

'Angel's Dream'
MRS ANNABELLE STUBBS 1973
AFS Registration No 1079
Double
Tube fuchsia pink, short, medium thickness. *Sepals* brilliant fuchsia pink, medium width, crepe undersides, flaring from the tube. *Corolla* white, pink markings towards the centre, serrated petals, bloom flares when mature, lacy and frilly. Petaloids pale pink. *Foliage* medium dark green, veined red, red stems. *Growth* trailer, it will make a good basket. Very free-flowering and self-branching. It is a very heavy bloomer, with blooms all the way along the branches. Larger and more double than 'Angel's Flight'. The best colour develops in the shade.

'Angel's Flight'
GEORGE MARTIN 1957
AFS Registration No 320
Tube long, white. *Sepals* pink, slightly deeper colour at the base, curling right over against the tube. *Corolla* white with pale pink veining. *Foliage* medium green. *Growth* trailer or lax bush, self-branching, and very vigorous. Grows best in cool conditions, will make a nice basket. Needs staking if grown as a bush.

'Anita'
NIEDERHOLZER 1946
Double
Tube red. *Sepals* red. *Corolla* violet, splashed red. Large flowers and a very vigorous upright habit of growth. Has

been known to reach 8 feet (2.6 m) tall in California, and could well be worth trying as a greenhouse climber. Awarded the American Fuchsia Society Certificate of Merit in 1948.

'Anna'

VICTOR REITER 1945
Double
Tube carmine. *Sepals* carmine. *Corolla* magenta, carmine at the base. Large flowers. *Foliage* large, medium green. *Growth* trailer. Awarded AFS Certificate of Merit 1948.

'Annabel' (31)

M. RYLE 1978
AFS Registration No 1476
Double
Tube white, flushed neyron rose, medium length and width. *Sepals* slightly curved down from the horizontal, white flushed neyron rose RHS 58C at the base with the underside faintly blushed pink RHS 62A. Bright pink stamens and pistil. *Foliage* light green RHS 146A. *Growth* bushy. Will make a good bush or standard. The colour develops best in the shade. Free-flowering, and the pale foliage contrasts well with the white blooms. Awarded the BFS Silver Certificate of Merit 1977.

'Anna Marie'

MUNCKNER 1952
Double
Tube scarlet. *Sepals* scarlet. *Corolla* violet, outer petals splashed pink. *Blooms* large, free-flowering. *Growth* upright and vigorous. Bush.

'Anna Roth'

NIEDERHOLZER 1946
Tube red. *Sepals* red. *Corolla* dark red. Large double flowers, free-flowering, self-branching. *Growth* upright bush.

'Anne'

HARRIS 1974
AFS Registration No 1211
Single
Tube long and thin, very pale cerise. *Sepals* pale cerise, long and spreading. *Corolla* mauve cerise, long and tight. *Foliage* medium green, serrated. Prefers sun for best growth. Upright. Very similar to many other better cultivars available.

'Annie Earle'

JAMES LYE 1887
Single
Tube waxy cream. *Sepals* waxy cream with green tips. *Corolla* carmine scarlet, flushed orange at the base. Very free-flowering. *Growth* upright bush, vigorous.

'Annie Laurie'

HAZARD AND HAZARD
Double
Tube and sepals red. *Corolla* deep violet with petaloids. *Foliage* medium green. *Growth* lax bush, will trail if weights are used. Free-flowering.

'Anniversary'

ROY WALKER — introduced by
MRS A. STUBBS 1969
AFS Registration No 836
Tube short, pink. *Sepals* deep coral pink. *Corolla* variegations of red, purple and orange. *Flowers* large, free-flowering. *Foliage* medium-sized, dark green. Makes a showy bush or can be used as a trailer.

'Ann Pacey'

CLIFF GADSBY 1978
AFS Registration No 1479
Double
Tube short, thick and white. *Sepals* broad, pink tipped green with neyron rose underside. *Corolla* phlox pink at the base shading to pale neyron rose. Self-branching medium upright. Medium to large flowers. A good bush or standard. Colour develops best in the shade.

'Ann's Delight'

GAGNON 1962
AFS Registration No 507
Double

Tube long, bright pink, crepy texture. *Sepals* long, bright pink, crepy texture. *Corolla* large and loose orchid pink. The petals are spoon-shaped. *Foliage* leathery green, strong growth. *Growth* upright, self-branching. Will make a good bush or standard.

'Anthea Bond'
C. GADSBY 1975
AFS Registration No 1311
Single
Tube short, medium thick, spiraea red. *Sepals* long, slender and recurving at the tips, measuring 4 in (10 cm) across. Spiraea red RHS 63C. *Corolla* long, tapering, rolled petals and coloured wisteria blue RHS 92A, lighter at the base. *Foliage* dark green lanceolate. Self-branching, bushy medium upright. Makes a good bush for exhibition purposes and will trail if weights are used. Short-jointed. Very free-flowering. *Parentage* 'Upward Look' ×.

'Antigone'
BANKS 1887
Single
Tube white, with pink blush. *Sepals* white, with pink blush. *Corolla* pinkish orange. Medium-sized blooms, free-flowering. *Foliage* dark green. Upright habit of growth. Bush.

'Antonia'
HARRIS 1974
AFS Registration No 1213
Single
Tube pale pink, medium length and thickness. *Sepals* pale pink flushed with cerise, deeper on the inside, spreading. *Corolla* cerise, bell-shaped. *Stamens* cerise, short. *Pistil* long. *Foliage* medium green, finely serrated. Self-branching and free-flowering. Makes a good bush. Shows best colour in sun.

'Aphrid'
HARRIS 1974
AFS Registration No 1212
Double
Tube striped pink and white, medium length and thickness. *Sepals* short, spreading, deep pink. *Corolla* white with pink veins, tight. *Petaloids* white (4). *Foliage* medium green. Free-flowering, self-branching. Bush.

'Aphrodite'
DR O. COLVILLE 1964
Double
Tube pink. *Sepals* pink, deeper pink at the edges, green tips. *Corolla* white veined pink. *Foliage* medium green, crimson margins. *Growth* upright and vigorous. Self-branching and free-flowering. Bushy growth. Prefers to be grown in cool conditions. A very nice, light coloured fuchsia. Bush.

'Applause'
MRS A. STUBBS 1978
AFS Registration No 1440
Double
Tube short, thick, pale carmine. *Sepals* pale carmine to deeper carmine, very broad, up to 1 in (2.5 cm) across. Sepals have a paler streak down the middle and curve slightly when mature. *Corolla* deep orange red — very large, wide spreading with many petals. *Foliage* medium size, dark green. Very vigorous upright growth, but because of the size of the blooms will require staking if grown as a bush. Can also be grown as a basket but must be trained early. Best colour develops if the plant is grown in shaded conditions.

'Apple Blossom'
SCHNABEL-PASKESEN 1953
AFS Registration No 417 (1960)
Single
Tube shell pink. *Sepals* shell pink. *Corolla* shell pink, flaring. Very small flower. *Foliage* dark green. *Habit of growth* low spreading bush. Will tolerate heat. Bush.

'Apricose'
NIEDERHOLZER 1944
Single
Tube shrimp pink. *Sepals* shrimp pink.

Corolla rose pink, lighter at the base of the petals. *Flowers* medium size. *Foliage* medium green. Vigorous and upright growth. Free-flowering. Bush.

'Aquarius'
SOO YUN 1971
AFS Registration No 946
Single
Tube medium length, pale pink. *Sepals* light pink, darker pink on the underside, green tips. *Corolla* pink, medium size, bell-shaped. *Foliage* green, medium size, serrated edges. *Growth* upright. Bush.

'Arabella Improved'
LYE 1871
Single
Tube waxy creamy-white. *Sepals* waxy creamy white, slightly reflexed. *Corolla* rosy cerise. *Flowers* medium size, free-flowering, vigorous growth. *Growth* upright, will make a good bush.

'Arcadia'
TOLLEY/FUCHSIAVALE 1979
AFS Registration No 1520
Single
Tube reddish cerise, thick and medium length. *Sepals* red cerise, upturned, long and broad. *Corolla* magenta, long compact petals which do not flare. *Stamens and pistil* magenta. *Foliage* pale green, oval, serrated. *Growth habit* lax, bushy, upright. Stems are long and thin. Will tolerate heat if shaded. Bush.

'Arcady'
DR O. COLVILLE 1968
Single
Tube and sepals pink, suffused salmon; sepals have green tips. *Corolla* deep rose, edged salmon. *Foliage* medium green. *Growth* upright. Bush.

'Archie Owen'
ANNABELLE STUBBS 1977
AFS Registration No 1410
Double
Tube soft pink, medium length and width. *Sepals* soft pink, medium length, slightly tapering, reflexing on maturity. *Corolla* soft pink, many petalled. *Foliage* dark green with reddish tinges and red veins, leaves medium to small. Natural trailer which will make a good basket without weights. A very adaptable and easy to grow cultivar. Basket.

'Arctic Night'
FUCHSIA-LA NURSERY 1964
Double
Tube deep red. *Sepals* deep red. *Corolla* petunia purple. *Growth* upright, self-branching. *Foliage* medium to dark green. Bush.

'Ariel'
JAMES TRAVIS 1973
AFS Registration No 1136
Single, breviflora type
Tube magenta, medium length, thick. *Sepals* magenta with green tips, very pointed, spreading and not reflexed. *Corolla* deep magenta pink, petals reflexed. *Foliage* deep green, deeply cut serrated margin, glossy. *Growth* upright vigorous, self-branching and will make a good bush or quarter standard. This type is also very suitable for small pot culture or bonsai. It is happy in full sun but colours best in shade. Very floriferous. Black berries about $\frac{1}{2}$ in (1 cm) in diameter in the autumn.

'Army Nurse'
HODGES 1947
Semi-double
Tube carmine. *Sepals* carmine. *Corolla* bluish violet, flushed pink at the base, and veined pink. *Foliage* medium green. *Growth* upright, bushy, very vigorous grower. Free-flowering, easy to grow as a pot plant or as a garden hardy in sheltered areas. Bush.

'Artemis'
JAMES TRAVIS 1975
AFS Registration No 1317
Single, Encliandra type
Tube long, thin, white. *Sepals* white with very pale green tips. *Corolla* white, typical

Encliandra type, flared. *Foliage* small, serrated, dense. Self-branching, bushy, medium upright. Natural trailer, which will make a good basket, bush or small standard. Prefers shade, where best colour develops. Very floriferous. Large purple to black berries follow the flowers.

'Arthur Cope'
C. GADSBY 1968
AFS Registration No 982 (1971)
Semi-double
Tube long and white.
Sepals waxy white. *Corolla* large, spiraea red, flushed rose red and splashed white. Prefers shade. Free-flowering, vigorous growth, spreading habit. Bush.

'Arthur Fritz'
MIKE PENNISI 1967
AFS Registration No 712
Double
Tube Chinese red. *Sepals* Chinese red. *Corolla* deep burgundy, variegated orange and pink. Large blooms, very free-flowering. Upright, vigorous habit of growth. Bush.

'Athela'
WHITEMAN 1942
Single
Tube creamy pink. *Sepals* creamy pink. *Corolla* salmon pink, darker at the base of the petals and with pale pink edges. *Flowers* medium and very free. *Growth* upright. Will shape well for exhibition. Bush. *Parentage* 'Rolla' × 'Mrs Rundle'.

'Athene'
WARREN 1947
Single
Tube white. *Sepals* white with Tyrian rose shading. *Corolla* rose. Medium size bloom, free-flowering. Lax habit of growth. Bush.

'Atlantis'
HANDLEY 1974
AFS Registration No 1170
Semi-double
Tube white, short and thick. *Sepals* white, flushed pale pink RHS 56D, inside, broad and thick. *Corolla* lilac RHS 68B and RHS 68C, with deeper shade RHS 72C at edges, petals of even length. *Foliage* dark green, serrated. Self-branching, will make a good bush or standard, and, with weights, a reasonable basket. Bush.

'Atomic Glow'
MACHADO 1963
AFS Registration No 561
Double
Tube coral pink, thin, medium length. *Sepals* pale orange, completely recurving over the tube. *Corolla* bright pink with orange tint. *Filaments and style* pink. *Foliage* dark green with a light brown tinge in the centre of the leaves. Medium size early bloomer. *Growth* lax. Self-branching, free-flowering. Will make a good basket — trailing habit; but can also be trained as a bush plant.

'Audrey Thill'
PRENTICE 1975
AFS Registration No 1299
Double
Tube small, deep pink. *Sepals* pink with lighter tips, turning to rose, long and curling over the tube. *Corolla* Alice Blue, changing to rose orchid when mature, flaring and rather loose. *Foliage* small, dark green, branches very wiry. *Stamens and pistil* long. *Growth* natural trailer without weights. Blooms very small but a very heavy bloomer. Makes a good basket. *Parentage* 'Flash' ×.

'Aunt Chloe'
EWING 1953
AFS Registration No 150
Double
Tube deep phlox pink. *Sepals* deep phlox pink, curved. *Corolla* purple-blue, deep phlox pink at the base. *Foliage* bright green with serrated edges. Heat-tolerant. Vigorous grower, upright or trailing. Bush.

'Auntie Elsie'
J.A. WRIGHT 1980
AFS Registration No 1597
Single
Tube violet. *Sepals* smoky violet, recurving. *Corolla* cherry red. *Foliage* light green, large-sized. *Growth* vigorous, tall growing upright. Will make a good bush. Seedling of 'Barbara'.

'Auntie Jinks' (57)
J.W. WILSON 1970
Single
Tube pinkish red. *Sepals* white, edged cerise. *Corolla* purple with white shading. *Foliage* mid-green, small. *Blooms* small, but very floriferous. Habit — pendulous type, will make a good basket.

'Auntie Maggie'
TOLLEY 1974
AFS Registration No 1228
Single
Tube flesh pink, medium length and thickness. *Sepals* pink on the upper side, pale geranium pink underneath with paler tips, coiled right back. *Corolla* Indian red, close barrel-shaped. *Stamens and pistil* Indian red. *Foliage* pale green, oval, serrated. *Habit* upright, vigorous grower. Will make a good bush or standard. Medium-sized bloom, floriferous. Seedling of 'Mrs Marshall'.

'Aunt Juliana'
HANSON 1951
Double (Sport of 'Uncle Jules')
Tube carmine. *Sepals* carmine, reflexing to almost hide the tube. *Corolla* pale lavender blue, veined carmine. *Filaments and style* carmine. *Foliage* medium green, medium-sized. *Growth* very lax, and possibly best used as a basket, but with support could be trained to a very nice bush. It is very free-flowering for such a large bloom, is self-branching, and a very easy cultivar to grow. Basket/bush.

'Aunt Ruth'
C. HANSON 1960
AFS Registration No 1321 (1976)
Double
Tube red, short, medium length, thick. *Sepals* red, long and curved. *Corolla* violet, streaked red and white. *Foliage* dark green. Free-flowering, upright, bushy growth. Self-branching. Will make a good bush or standard.

'Aurora Superba' (177)
Raiser and date unknown
Single 5 in (12.5 cm) long
Tube pale apricot. *Sepals* pale apricot, droop but go horizontal as flower matures. *Corolla* deep orange, peach. *Flowers* medium size, free-flowering. *Foliage* soft, light green, serrated, tendency to curl. One of the characteristics of this cultivar is the pronounced leaf curl, often mistaken for some disease or deficiency. Not an easy cultivar to grow as the growth is rather lax, and not easy to pinch to shape. Prefers heat for best results. Standard/pyramid.

'Australia Fair'
RAWLINS 1954
Double
Tube bright red. *Sepals* bright red, recurving slightly. *Corolla* white flushed and veined red. *Style* red. *Filaments* red. *Foliage* medium green. *Growth* upright and bushy. Blooms large and very free, requires staking because of the size and weight of the flowers.

'Autumnale' (22)
METEOR 1880
Single
Tube scarlet. *Sepals* scarlet. *Corolla* purple. *Flowers* medium-sized. *Foliage* variegated — starting yellow and green, changing to coppery red. *Growth* stiff and almost horizontal, very difficult to train into any shape, but when well grown makes a most attractive and eyecatching pot plant. Has been known grown as a standard, but the horizontal branches do not lend themselves to this type of growth. Often confused with, and probably the same cultivar as, 'Burning Bush'.

'Autumn Red'
DE FRANCISCO/SOO YUN 1979
AFS Registration No 1496
Single
Tube rose bengal RHS 57B, medium length. *Sepals* rose bengal RHS 57B. *Corolla* beetroot purple RHS 71A fading to Tyrian purple RHS 61C. Beetroot purple petaloids. *Foliage* light green, red veined, $3\frac{1}{4}$ in (8 cm) long and $1\frac{1}{2}$ in (4 cm) wide, with red stems. Natural trailer without weights. Can be grown as a bush; prefers shade, where the best colour develops.

'Ava Ellen'
VEE JAY 1978
AFS Registration 1464
Single
Tube rose pink, medium length and thickness. *Sepals* rose, with pale rose tips. *Corolla* fluorescent fuchsia colour with slight orange shading at the base. Stamens rose pink. *Foliage* medium size, mid-green. Self-branching, free-flowering, upright growth. Needs sunshine for best colour. Will make a good bush or standard. Very fast growing. Requires very little pinching and will make a large bush in one year.

'Avalanche'
HENDERSON 1869
Double $3\frac{1}{2}$ in (9 cm)
Tube short, scarlet, medium thickness. *Sepals* scarlet, recurving, completely over the tube. Carmine filaments and style. *Corolla* purple violet, shaded and splashed carmine. *Foliage* yellowish green. *Growth* lax bush or trailer. Self-branching and very free-flowering. Needs careful staking and pinching to make a good bush, or standard; otherwise it will tend to spread and trail. Does equally well in a pot or as a garden hardy in sheltered areas. Prefers shade.

'Avalon'
EVANS AND REEVES 1946
Single
Tube white. *Sepals* white, held horizontally. *Corolla* rose-lilac. Upright, vigorous habit of growth. Bush.

'Ave Maria'
VICTOR REITER 1945
Double
Tube white. *Sepals* white. *Corolla* white. Must be grown in the shade to keep its colour, otherwise shows pinkish markings on the sepals and tube and veinings on the corolla. Free-flowering. Habit—bushy, stiff upright.

'Aviator'
R. DENIER
Single
Tube red. *Sepals* red, twisted. *Corolla* long and white. Large blooms, strong upright habit of growth. A very attractive and unusually shaped flower, but striking colour contrast. Bush.

'Avocet'
JAMES TRAVIS 1958
AFS Registration No 1137 (1973)
Single
Tube crimson, longish and medium thickness. *Sepals* crimson, crepe-like, long and pointed. Reflexed. *Corolla* white, veined red at base of petals, neatly rolled. *Foliage* dark green, glossy, red-veined, slightly serrated. Self-branching and very free-flowering. A most beautiful cultivar which will make an excellent show plant either as a bush or standard. The bloom keeps its shape and the corolla remains tightly rolled. *Parentage* 'Jules Daloges' × 'Elizabeth Travis'.

'Azalea'
NIEDERHOLZER 1944
Now renamed, *see* 'Electra'.

'Aztec'
EVANS AND REEVES 1937
Double
Tube rich red. *Sepals* rich red. *Corolla* vivid violet. *Foliage* deep green with a touch of red. *Growth* very vigorous upright — will reach up to 6 ft (2 m) in California. Large blooms, free-flowering. Bush. *Parentage* 'Graphic' × unknown seedling.

'Baby Ballerina'
SOO YUN FIELD 1980
AFS Registration No 1545
Single
Tube pale green to pale pink, short and thin. *Sepals* pale ivory, green on top, bright pink on the underside, tipped green. Long, turning straight up. *Corolla* short, dark purple fading to rosy magenta on maturity, Petals are concave, giving the corolla a full effect. *Foliage* small, dark green. *Growth* self-branching upright, bushy. It will make a nice bush and can be trained as a basket using weights.

'Baby Belle'
DE FRANCISCO/SOO YUN FUCHSIA GARDENS 1980
AFS Registration No 1565
Single
Tube Light bengal red medium size. *Sepals* light bengal red on the underside, slightly paler shade on top, long. *Corolla* white with pink veins. *Stamens* pink, pistil light pink. *Foliage* light green medium size. *Growth* upright, bushy and self-branching. Best colour develops in the shade. Bush.

'Baby Blue Eyes' (160)
JOE PLUMMER 1952
Single
Tube and sepals red. *Corolla* dark lavender. *Growth* upright. Free-flowering. Makes a good pot plant.

'Baby Bunting'
DR J.B. LANGEN 1938
Tube pale rose pink. *Sepals* pale rose pink. *Corolla* pale lavender blue. Small flowers. *Foliage* golden yellow, small. *Habit of growth* semi-trailer. *Parentage* 'Rolla' × 'Venus Victrix'.

'Baby Chang'
Raiser and date unknown
Single
Tube orange-red. *Sepals* orange-red, with green tips. *Corolla* orange. Flowers very small, but floriferous. *Foliage* mid-green, small. Untidy habit with rather trailing growths.

'Baby Dark Eyes'
MRS FRANCESKA STASKO 1975
AFS Registration No 1289
Single
Tube red, short. *Sepals* red, incurving. *Corolla* purple with pink centre, small with four distinct cups. *Stamens and pistil* pinkish red. *Foliage* dark green. *Habit* semi-trailer, which will trail with weights, but will normally grow upright. Self-branching, and will make a good bush or standard. Will tolerate heat if shaded. An unusual bloom, small but distinct. The buds and blossoms are like small dark eyes, hence the name.

'Baby Doll'
REITER 1949
Double
Tube white. *Sepals* white. *Corolla* amethyst violet. Medium-sized blooms. *Growth* not very vigorous. Bush.

'Baby Face'
WILF TOLLEY 1973
AFS Registration No 1154
Double
Tube short, thin baby pink. *Sepals* baby pink, green tips, reflexed. *Corolla* creamy white, full and fluffy, with eight petaloids. *Stamens and pistil* pink. *Foliage* pale green, medium size and slightly crimped. Self-branching, and will make a nice bush, or quarter standard. Colours best in the shade.

'Baby Lilac'
MIKE PENNISI 1970
AFS Registration No 889
Double
Tube white, short. *Sepals* white with green tips. *Corolla* light pinkish-lilac, flaring. *Foliage* mid-green. Box type blooms. Bush.

'Babylon'
MRS E. HANDLEY 1973
AFS Registration No 1131

Single
Tube pale pink RHS 55D, thick, medium length. *Sepals* pale pink RHS 55D, long, reflexing right back to the stem. *Corolla* Magenta-rose RHS 57C, long and bell-shaped. Small. *Foliage* bright green. *Habit of growth* natural trailer. Large flowers. Gives the best colour in shaded conditions.

'Baby Pink'
SOO YUN 1975
AFS Registration No 1355
Double
Tube white, long and thin with green tinge. *Sepals* light pink with green tips, curving. *Corolla* light pink with dark pink veins, darker pink at the base, petals flaring slightly. Stamens pink, pistil white. *Foliage* dark green, light veining and red stems. Leaves serrate when mature. *Growth* semi-trailer, will make a good basket. Self-branching, very floriferous.

'Bachelor Girl'
SCHMIDGT-TIRET 1952
AFS Registration No 141
Semi-double
Tube white. *Sepals* white with green tips and flushed pale pink inside. *Corolla* pale mallow purple. Self-branching, free-flowering. Sport of 'Bewitched', with the same growth habits.

'Bagworthy Water'
ENDICOTT 1972
Single
Tube medium long, salmon orange. *Sepals* salmon-orange, curling right up round. *Corolla* claret rose fading to neyron rose. Blooms of medium size, free-flowering. *Habit of growth* semi-trailer, with arching branches.

'Baker's Tri'
BAKER/DUNNETT 1974
AFS Registration No 1197
Single
Triphylla type
Tube short for a triphylla, medium thick, geranium lake RHS 47D. *Sepals* venetian pink RHS 49B, green tips, pointed. *Corolla* spinel red RHS 54C. *Foliage* green RHS 137C, leaves small. *Growth* natural trailer which will make a good basket. Not a very fast grower.

'Balalaika'
FOSTER 1973
AFS Registration No 1083
Double
Tube deep bright red, lighter near the ovary, long and thin. *Sepals* deep bright red with green tips, long and slender, reflexed to the tube. Pale. *Corolla* deep purple with irregular red streaks which give it a painted effect. The corolla turns deep lavender on maturity, and flares slightly. *Stamens and pistil* deep bright red. *Foliage* light green, small to medium size, slightly serrated. *Habit* natural trailer which will make a good basket. Very heavy bloomer. Best colour in shaded conditions. In hot conditions it requires heavy watering.

'Bali Hi'
TIRET 1955
AFS Registration No 234
Double
Tube white. *Sepals* white, tipped green, upturned. *Corolla* blue-violet fading to rose-violet. *Habit* trailer, will make a good basket. Very floriferous, medium-sized flowers.

'Balkonkonigin'
NEUBRONNER 1896
Single
Tube pale pink, medium length and thickness. *Sepals* pale pink, tipped green, deeper pink underneath, held down from the horizontal. *Corolla* pink, small and compact. Filaments pale pink, style white. *Foliage* small, medium green, red veined. *Growth* willowy, not self-branching, trailing habit. Very thin stems which would need careful and frequent pinching to produce a decent shaped plant, but is very floriferous.

'Ballerina'
NIEDERHOLZER 1939
Single
Tube and sepals ivory pink. *Corolla* clear pink with rose pink edges. *Blooms* medium-sized. *Growth* very vigorous and tall growing, but branches very brittle, so care is needed.

'Ballet Girl'
VEITCH 1894
Double
Tube bright cerise. *Sepals* bright cerise, reflexed. *Corolla* large white, with cerise veining. Very free-flowering, will make a nice bush with careful pinching. Upright, vigorous habit.

'Ball of Fire'
REEDSTROM 1957
Double
Tube and sepals red. *Corolla* fiery red with orange-red shading. *Foliage* dark green with red veining. *Habit of growth* trailer. Will make a nice basket without weights.

'Bambi'
SOO YUN 1978
AFS Registration No 1449
Double
Tube short, rose bengal. *Sepals* short, rose pink, slightly cup-shaped. *Corolla* dark mallow purple veined rose bengal, loose petalled. *Foliage* light green, medium size. *Stamen and pistils* rose bengal. *Growth* upright, free-flowering. Will make a good small bush plant.

'Barbara'
WILF TOLLEY 1973
AFS Registration No 1155
Single
Tube pale pink, short and medium thick. *Sepals* pale pink, slightly upturned. Short. *Corolla* tangerine pink, semi-flared, shortish. *Foliage* pale dull green, medium size. Self-branching, flowers of medium size but very prolific. Will make a good bush, standard. Will take full sun and gives the best colour in the sun. An excellent exhibition variety which grows well in most types of growth.

'Baron Baron'
THORNLEY 1978
AFS Registration No 1465
Single
Tube claret rose RHS 50B. *Sepals* claret rose RHS 50B with green tips and held horizontal. *Corolla* claret rose RHS 50A. Flowers small to medium. Growth medium upright, will make a good bush, but needs careful pinching from the cutting stage as it is not self-branching. *Parentage* 'Liver Bird' × 'Chang'.

'Baron von Ketteler' or 'Baron de Ketteler'
LEMOINE 1901
Double
Tube and sepals waxy scarlet red. *Corolla* deep purple, with lighter flesh pink centre petals. A large flower, fairly free and vigorous habit of growth. Will make a good bush plant with careful pinching.

'Barrington'
REITER 1947
Double
Tube rose red. *Sepals* rose red. *Corolla* pink. Medium-sized blooms. *Growth* upright, slow-growing.

'Basket Strawberry Festival'
HAAG 1956
Tube bright red. *Sepals* bright red. *Corolla* light rose pink. *Foliage* medium green. *Habit* trailer, suitable for a basket. Sometimes known as 'Trailing Strawberry Festival'.

'Bay Fair'
KUECHLER 1961
AFS Registration No 488
Double
Tube pink. *Sepals* pink, darker at the base. Green tips to the sepals. *Corolla* creamy white, flushed pink at the base. *Habit of growth* trailer. Free-flowering and medium-sized blooms.

'Bayou Blue'
KENNETT 1967
AFS Registration No 738

Double
Tube pale pink. *Sepals* pale pink, long and curling upwards. *Corolla* lavender blue. *Growth* trailer.

'Beacon' (140)
BULL 1871
Single
Tube scarlet. *Sepals* scarlet. *Corolla* bright mauvish pink. *Foliage* darkish green, slightly serrated. Upright bushy growth which is self-branching and makes a good exhibition plant. Equally does very well as a garden hardy on sheltered areas. Blooms early in the season and continuously.

'Beacon Rosa'
BURGI-OTT 1972
Single
Tube rose red. *Sepals* rose red, longish. *Corolla* rose pink with pale red veining. *Foliage* dark green, similar to 'Beacon'. Medium large bloom. Upright growth, self-branching.

'Beauty 'n' Blue'
SOO YUN 1979
AFS Registration No 1491
Double
Tube medium to short, rose red, thick. *Sepals* smooth, rose red on top, crêped rose bengal underneath. Medium length, curving up tight against the stem. *Corolla* amethyst violet tipped, fading to roseine purple at the base, wavy and open. Short. Petaloids attached to the sepals. Stamens dark pink, pistil white. *Foliage* medium green with red stems and red veins. Self-branching trailer which will make a good basket with a little pinching. Early, heavy and prolonged bloomer.

'Beauty 'n' Red'
DE FRANCISCO/SOO YUN 1980
AFS Registration No 1560
Double
Tube medium length, pinkish white. *Sepals* long (2 in or 5 cm) cardinal red, RHS 53A, on the upper surface, and carmine rose RHS 52D on the underside, recurving back to the tube. *Corolla* beetroot purple RHS 71A, with eight or more petaloids of the same colour but smaller than the petals. *Foliage* dark green with red stems—large foliage $4\frac{1}{2}$ in (11 cm) long and $2\frac{5}{8}$ in (7 cm) wide. *Growth* can be grown either as an upright or as a trailer, prefers shaded conditions.

'Beauty of Bath'
COLVILLE 1965
Semi-double
Tube pale pink. *Sepals* pale pink, with deeper pink base and green tips. *Corolla* white, long oval shape. Self-branching, upright vigorous growth.

'Beauty of Clyffe Hall'
Although there is some controversy regarding the raiser, it is generally believed to be JAMES LYE, who was for many years Head Gardener at Clyffe Hall, at Market Lavington, Wiltshire.
Raised 1881
Single
Tube waxy white. *Sepals* waxy white. *Corolla* pink. Smallish flowers and foliage, growth rather lax, but will make a nice bush plant with careful pinching early.

'Beauty of Exeter'
LETHEREN 1890
Semi-double 4 in (10 cm) long
Tube and sepals pale rose-salmon. *Corolla* rosy salmon, slightly darker than the sepals. *Foliage* yellowish green. *Growth* vigorous, straggly. *Habit of growth* semi-trailer, but will bush if staked. Standard.

'Beauty of Swanley'
JAMES LYE 1875
Single 3 in (7.5 cm) long
Tube waxy white. *Sepals* waxy white, long, slight pink tinges. *Corolla* pale rose-pink. *Foliage* pale to medium green, dull. Free-flowering, medium blooms. *Growth* lax bush type, needs pinching to form any shape. Spreading habit.

'Beauty of Trowbridge'
JAMES LYE 1881
Single 4 in (10 cm) long
Tube thick, creamy white, waxy texture. *Sepals* creamy white recurving. *Corolla* rose-cerise. Very vigorous cultivar which grows upright and bushy, but straggly, free-flowering. *Foliage* light to medium green. Needs careful pinching to produce a good plant, and also requires attention to feeding as it has a tendency to yellowing leaves and subsequent leaf drop.

'Beauty Queen'
SOO YUN 1974
AFS Registration No 1181
Double
Tube red with lighter red veins (3–4 in or 7-5–10 cm long). *Sepals* light red with dark red veining and green tips, folding back around the tube. *Corolla* violet purple, light red at the base, fading to mallow purple, medium size. The foliage is dark green with red stems and branches. Large leaves up to $3\frac{1}{4}$ in (8 cm) long by 2 in (5 cm) wide. Needs weighting to make it trail properly, but will make an excellent basket with care.

'Bee Keesey'
PENNISI 1972
AFS Registration No 1045
Double
Tube white, short and thick. *Sepals* long, thick and held horizontal, white. *Corolla* wisteria blue with white variegations, large, full, box type. *Foliage* medium green. *Habit* semi-trailer, but will make a good upright bush.

'Bella Forbes'
FORBES 1890
Double
Tube cerise. *Sepals* cerise, held back against the tube. *Corolla* creamy white, veined cerise, very full and fluffy. *Foliage* medium green. *Growth* vigorous, but still upright. Not suitable for exhibition as the growth is too stiff and it dislikes pinching. Self-branching, one of the best red and white cultivars.

'Bella Mia'
MACHADO 1963
AFS Registration No 562
Single
Tube short, flesh coloured. *Sepals* flesh with white tips. *Corolla* ochre red, very firm. *Foliage* large, spear-shaped. *Growth* vigorous upright, tall growing.

'Bellbottoms'
CASTRO 1972
AFS Registration No 1029
Single
Tube light salmon, medium length and thickness. *Sepals* pale orange to salmon, long and thin and curling back. *Corolla* opens purple with a coral base, fading to smoky orange, bell-shaped. *Foliage* very light green, turning dark green as the plant ages, and serrated. *Growth* upright, tall growing.

'Bell Buoy'
SMALLWOOD 1973
AFS Registration 1073
Single
Tube bright red, medium length. *Sepals* bright red, broad and thick. *Corolla* dark blue purple, flared. *Foliage* medium green. *Growth* self-branching upright, colours best in the sun. Makes a good bush or standard. Hardy in sheltered areas.

'Belle de Lisse'
DE GRAFF 1977
Double
Tube white with pink flush. *Sepals* white with pink flush, with green tips. *Corolla* rosy-lilac, outside petals shorter than the inside ones. Large blooms. Upright growth or semi-trailer. *Parentage* 'Trailblazer' ×.

'Belle of Salem'
RAYMOND HODGES 1957
AFS Registration No 304
Single
Tube bright rose red. *Sepals* bright rose red. *Corolla* bell-shaped in an unusual shade of pink, heavily veined rose-red. *Foliage* dark green, small. *Growth* can be

trained either as a basket or upright. Very floriferous.

'Bellisima'
NIEDERHOLZER 1957
Single
Tube bright red. *Sepals* bright red. *Corolla* deep purple. *Foliage* medium to dark green. *Growth* upright, vigorous. Large blooms.

'Bells of Rozelle'
JOHN PRENTICE 1969
AFS Registration No 854
Single
Tube rose pink. *Sepals* rose pink. *Corolla* light pink, streaked rose pink, and bell-shaped. *Foliage* smallish. *Growth* trailer.

'Belmont'
NIEDERHOLZER 1946
Single
Tube turkey red. *Sepals* turkey red. *Corolla* purple. *Blooms* medium-sized. *Growth* Upright, free-flowering.

'Belsay Beauty'
M. RYLE 1975
AFS Registration No 1240
Semi-double
Tube Rhodamine pink RHS 62A, short and medium thickness. *Sepals* Rhodamine pink RHS 62A underneath, whitish with rhodamine pink shading on top, short and fat. *Corolla* violet RHS 86A fadint to cyclamen purple RHS 74A. Old blooms hold their colour well. *Buds* short and plump. *Anthers* light pink. *Foliage* mid to light green, smooth. *Growth* bushy, natural trailer. The best colour develops in the sun. A few small petaloids RHS 86A (violet) with rhodamine pink streaks.

'Belvedere'
REEDSTROM 1960
AFS Registration No 421
Tube thick and heavy, dark reddish pink. *Sepals* dark pink to red, curling back over the tube. *Corolla* very large, pale blue mottled with dark pink, with many short pink petaloids. Corolla fades to pale purple with age. *Foliage* medium green. *Growth* vigorous upright bush.

'Belvoir Beauty'
GADSBY 1975
AFS Registration No 1279
Semi-double
Tube short and medium thickness, white flushed green. *Sepals* white with green tips. *Corolla* white at the base shading through pale wisteria RHS 92D with distinct bluebird blue edge to each petal. *Foliage* light green. *Growth* short-jointed, medium upright bushy. Colours best in the shade. Neat and attractive pastel-coloured blooms.

'Ben Hill'
ALF THORNLEY 1966
Double
Tube short, rose madder. *Sepals* white, tipped green, underside shell pink. *Corolla* shell pink, flushed rose at the base of the petals. *Foliage* light to mid-green. *Growth* upright bush. Large flowers.

'Ben Hur'
MARTIN 1963
AFS Registration No 571
Double
Tube coral pink. *Sepals* coral pink. *Corolla* purple marbled with contrasting shades of pink and white. Very large blooms. *Growth* either trailer or bush, but needs staking for the latter owing to the weight of the blooms. Rather a stiff basket.

'Berkeley'
REITER 1955
Double
Tube rose pink. *Sepals* rose pink, recurving. *Corolla* tyrian rose, edged and marbled deeper shades. *Growth* upright and fairly vigorous, but will make a basket in warmer areas.

'Berliner Kind'
EGGBRECHT 1882
Double
Tube scarlet-cerise. *Sepals* scarlet-cerise.

Corolla pure white, with pink veining at the base. Flowers small, but very prolific. Makes a small bush.

'Bernadette'
SCHNABEL 1950
AFS Registration No 52
Double
Tube pale rose pink. *Sepals* pale rose pink. *Corolla* veronica blue. *Foliage* small, dark green. Flowers of medium size. *Growth* medium upright, with stiff laterals.

'Bernard Rawdin'
GADSBY 1968
AFS Registration No 982 (1971)
Single
Tube rose red. *Sepals* rose red. *Corolla* cyclamen purple, wide bell-shaped. *Growth* medium bush, upright. Prefers partial shade.

'Bernard Rawlings'
T. THORNE 1959
Tube long, white with pink flush. Petals are bright orange. Upright growth and free-flowering, triphylla type. *Parentage F. triphylla* ×.

'Bertha Lee'
LEE 1945
Single
Tube dark pink. *Sepals* dark pink. *Corolla* irregular pink, streaked red. *Foliage* dark green, small, holly-shaped. Flowers long. *Growth* trailer.

'Beryl's Choice'
RICHARDSON (Australia) 1980
AFS Registration No 1531
Double
Tube pink, short. *Sepals* pink on top, dark crepe pink on the underside, with green tips, broad and 1 in (2.5 cm) long, reflexing. *Corolla* light mauve-pink, becoming deeper pink as the flower matures, with deep rose blotching at the base of the petals. Outer petals streaked rose pink and inner petals slightly deeper colour and overlapping. *Stamens* long, rose red. *Pistil* mauve pink. *Foliage* lighter green and twice the size of that of its parent 'Georgana' of which it is a sport.

'Bessie Royle'
ROYLE 1979
AFS Registration No 1523
Single
Tube light red, long and of medium thickness. *Sepals* pink, curling slighly upwards. *Corolla* blue shading to pink near the sepals, wavy petals. *Stamens and pistil* pink. *Foliage* dark green, oval-shaped. *Growth* medium bushy upright. Needs stopping early to make a good bush.

'Best Wishes'
DE FRANCISCO/SOO YUN FUCHSIA GARDENS 1980
AFS Registration No 1544
Single
Tube deep bengal red, small. *Sepals* deep bengal red reflexing completely over the tube. *Corolla* white with deep rose bengal veining. *Stamens and pistil* bengal red. *Foliage* light green 1 in (2.5 cm) wide × 2 in (5 cm) long. *Growth* medium bushy upright which will make a good bush. Grows best in warm climate, best colour develops in the shade. Will sometimes produce double blooms with petaloids.

'Beth Robley'
TIRET 1971
AFS Registration No 992
Double
Tube salmon. *Sepals* salmon. *Corolla* orange salmon. *Foliage* medium green. *Growth* trailer.

'Betty'
HAZARD 1946
Semi-double
Tube rose red. *Sepals* rose red. *Corolla* rich creamy white, veined rose red. *Flowers* small. *Growth* trailer.

'Beverley'
RON HOLMES 1976
AFS Registration No 1378
Single
Tube short, medium and thick, empire

rose RHS 48D, striped empire rose RHS 48C. *Sepals* neyron rose RHS 55A, with green tips, curving upwards. *Corolla* fuchsia purple RHS 67A with neyron rose RHS 55A at the base. Bell-shaped. Flowers medium size. *Foliage* mid-green, serrated. *Growth* upright and vigorous. *Parentage* 'Percy Holmes' ×.

'Beverley Hills'
EVANS AND REEVES 1936
Single
Tube and sepals shell pink, sepals long with white strip and tipped white. *Corolla* vivid Burgundy red. *Flowers* large. *Foliage* medium green. *Growth* very vigorous, upright. *Parentage* 'Santa Monica' × 'Grenadine'.

'Beverley Wilson'
PRENTICE 1967
AFS Registration No 720
Double
Tube pink. *Sepals* light rose. *Corolla* light blue, with outer petals marbled with light rose. *Foliage* small. *Growth* basket type.

'Bewitched'
TIRET 1951
AFS Registration No 94
Double
Tube white outside, pink inside. *Sepals* white outside, pink inside. *Corolla* deep purple with white base. Large flowers, free-flowering. *Growth* basket type, but very willowy growth.

'Bianca'
PENNISI 1967
AFS Registration No 715
Double
All white. Short tube. *Foliage* light to mid-green. *Growth* upright, free-flowering. Colours best in the shade.

'Bicentennial'
PASKESEN 1976
AFS Registration No 1344
Double
Tube white, thin. *Sepals* Indian orange RHS 32A, underneath, salmon orange on top. *Corolla* outside petals Indian orange RHS 32A, inside magenta RHS 51A. *Petaloids* Indian orange. Blooms medium-sized. *Growth* will make either an upright bush or a basket with weights. Free-flowering. Colours best in the sun.

'Big Blue Boy'
GORMAN 1970
AFS Registration No 935
Double
Tube white. *Sepals* white above, pale pink underneath, with green tips, standing horizontal until mature then curling upwards. *Corolla* deep purple fading to dark burgundy purple. *Foliage* dark medium green. *Growth* upright bush type.

'Big King'
GORMAN 1970
AFS Registration 936
Double
Tube dark red. *Sepals* dark red. *Corolla* very dark purple, very large blooms. *Foliage* mid to dark green. *Growth* upright, very vigorous.

'Billy Green' (12)
Raiser unknown (about 1966)
Blooms long, pinkish salmon. Triphylla type. Very heavy bloomer. *Foliage* olive green. *Growth* upright, very vigorous, needs careful pinching from the cutting stage and will make a first class exhibition plant.

'Bingo'
CASTRO 1971
AFS Registration No 949
Semi-double to double
Tube white. *Sepals* white. *Corolla* reddish pink with white marbling. Long petals. *Growth* can be grown either as a trailer or bush.

'Bishop's Bells'
GADSBY 1970
AFS Registration No 869
Semi-double
Tube rose red. *Sepals* rose red, very long.

Corolla bishop's violet. *Growth* medium bush, prefers partial shade. Very large blooms.

'Bishop's Robe'
MACHADO 1960
AFS Registration No 448
Double
Tube light pink. *Sepals* light pink, with white stripe running through. *Corolla* large, campanula violet with a row of bishop's violet petaloids. Very free-flowering, vigorous upright growth.

'Bittersweet' (179)
KENNETT 1971
AFS Registration No 953
Double
Tube pale pink. *Sepals* pale pink underneath, white. *Corolla* purple in the centre fading to rose, outer petals rose pink with salmon to orange marbling. *Growth* can be grown as either a trailer or bush.

'Black Beauty'
FAIRCLO 1952
Double
Tube dark red. *Sepals* dark red. *Corolla* deep purple. *Foliage* medium to dark green. *Growth* upright. *Flowers* medium-sized, prolific.

'Black Eyes'
BROWN AND SOULES 1953
Double
Tube short and *sepals* rose pink. *Corolla* white. *Growth* vigorous bushy upright. One unusual fact is that it produces black pollen.

'Black Pearl'
NIEDERHOLZER 1946
Single
Tube turkey red. *Sepals* turkey red. *Corolla* deep purple. *Foliage* medium to dark green. *Habit* trailer, medium-sized flowers. Will make a decent basket.

'Black Prince'
BANKS 1861
Single
Tube red. *Sepals* red. *Corolla* dark purple. *Growth* will make a small pot plant, or can be trained in a basket with weights.

'Black Princess'
NIEDERHOLZER 1940
Single
Tube red. *Sepals* red. *Corolla* deep purple, opens out wide. *Habit* vigorous arching growth, has been known to grow to 8 ft (2.5 m) tall in California. Grows best in heat.

'Blanche Regina'
MRS IVY CLYNE 1974
AFS Registration No 1175
Double
Tube white, medium length and thickness. *Sepals* white, medium length, reflexed, crepe inside. *Corolla* amethyst violet ageing to rhodamine purple, petals flared and fluted, medium size. Long stamens and pistil. *Foliage* spinach green, small and narrow. *Growth* self-branching, natural trailer, but with pinching will form a bush. Best colour in shade. Prolific flowering, vigorous grower. *Parentage* 'La Campanella' × 'Flirtation Waltz'.

'Bland's New Striped' (141)
BLAND 1872
Single 4 in (10 cm)
Tube cerise, medium length and thickness. *Sepals* cerise recurving as flower matures. *Filaments and style* cerise. *Corolla* purple with a red streak on each petal. Flowers medium size, free-flowering. *Foliage* dark green, longish. *Growth* upright and bushy, self-branching, fairly vigorous. One of the best of the 'striped' cultivars. Will make a very good pot plant, bush or standard.

'Blaze'
HANDLEY 1977
AFS Registration No 1413
Single
Tube light coral RHS 43D. *Sepals* light coral RHS 43D, deeper coral inside. Long and held well out. *Corolla* coral

RHS 44C at the base, blending to flame RHS 46D. *Foliage* mid-green flushed bronze. *Growth* self-branching trailer which will make a good basket plant. Early flowering, flowers very free, medium to large blooms. Best colour will develop in the shade.

'Blondine'
BROWN AND SOULES 1953
Single
Tube white. *Sepals* pink upturned. *Corolla* pale lilac. *Growth* vigorous, bushy upright.

'Bloomer Girl'
WALTZ 1951
AFS Registration No 105
Double
Tube (short) bright carmine. *Sepals* (long) bright carmine. *Corolla* bell-shaped, palest pink, carmine at the base, overlaid with extra pleated petals of the same colour, and carmine veining. *Growth* trailer.

'Blossom Time'
TIRET 1952
AFS Registration No 142
Single
Tube waxy white. *Sepals* white, long and upturned. *Corolla* pink. *Growth* vigorous, pendant branches. Free-flowering.

'Blue Adonis'
HAAG 1949
Double
Tube shell pink. *Sepals* shell pink. *Corolla* light orchid blue. Strong upright growth.

'Blue Beauty'
BULL 1864
Double
Tube dark red, short. *Sepals* dark red, large, held horizontal with the tips upturned. *Corolla* violet-blue, short petals, puckered and spread out, some of the petals completely violet. Full double. Erect growth.

'Blue Bells'
BROWN AND SOULES 1952
AFS Registration No 135
Semi-double
Tube short, rose pink. *Sepals* upturned, pink. *Corolla* light blue with red base and veining, bell-shaped. *Foliage* mid-green. *Growth* upright, bush, free-flowering.

'Blue Bird'
WALTZ 1957
AFS Registration No 309
Semi-double
Tube pure white. *Sepals* pure white. *Corolla* rich parma violet, with scalloped and slightly folded petals. Large blooms, free-flowering. *Growth* cascade.

'Blue Bonnet'
HODGES 1950
AFS Registration No 69
Single
Tube red. *Sepals* red, broad and turned up. *Corolla* purple-blue, flaring, with red veins. *Growth* trailer.

'Blue Boy'
PASKESEN 1971
AFS Registration No 958
Double
Tube white, tinted pink, short. *Sepals* short, white, tinted pink. *Corolla* deep violet blue with pink shading at the base. *Growth* upright, bushy.

Do not confuse with the following.

'Blue Boy'
FRY 1889
Single
Tube deep rose pink. *Sepals* deep rose pink. *Corolla* clear violet blue. Small flower, very free. *Growth* upright bush.

'Blue Bush'
GADSBY 1970
AFS Registration No 1120 (1973)
Single
Tube rose red, medium length and thickness. *Sepals* rose red RHS 724/3, long, held out from the corolla. *Corolla*

bluebird blue RHS 042/1, fading to bishop's violet RHS 34/1 with rose veins. Medium size. *Stamens and pistil* pink. Self-branching, vigorous upright, suitable for growing as a hedging fuchsia and will make up to 4 ft (1.2 m) in a year when established.

'Blue Butterfly'
WALTZ 1960
AFS Registration No 438
Semi-double
Tube short and white. *Sepals* white. *Corolla* deep violet blue splashed with white. Bloom medium to large. As the bloom matures the inner petals open wide, orchid with blue undertones. *Foliage* small, dark green. *Growth* willowy, trailer.

'Blue Elf'
MRS MARGARET HALL 1968
AFS Registration No 1116 (1973)
Single
Tube rose pink RHS 58D. *Sepals* rose pink RHS 58D, with crepe effect on the undersides, curling back to the tube, short and narrow. *Corolla* light blue with violet edges, flushed very pale blue at the base, fading to pale mauve with brighter edges. Rose pink RHS 81D veins. Medium size, bell-shaped. *Foliage* olive green with red RHS 137A veins and serrated edges. *Growth* very free-flowering, upright and bushy. Colours best in the sun. Makes an excellent exhibition plant.

'Blue Eyes'
REEDSTROM 1954
Double
Tube clear pink. *Sepals* clear pink. *Corolla* bright blue. Free-flowering, medium to large blooms. *Growth* upright, bushy.

'Blue Flame'
NIEDERHOLZER 1948
Single
Tube crimson. *Sepals* crimson. *Corolla* rich violet, veined blue and pink. Medium to large flower. *Growth* upright, bushy and free-flowering.

'Blue Gown'
MILNE
Double
Tube scarlet. *Sepals* scarlet. *Corolla* blue, changing to purple, splashed carmine and pink. *Foliage* medium green, slightly serrated. *Growth* upright, largish blooms, free-flowering. Vigorous growth which will need staking in the greenhouse due to the weight of the blooms.

'Blue Lagoon'
JAMES TRAVIS 1958
Double
Tube short, bright red. *Sepals* bright red, broad and recurving. *Corolla* blue with deep purple cast on the petals. Large blooms, spreading out as they open. *Growth* upright, bushy.

Do not confuse with the following.

'Blue Lagoon'
TIRET 1961
AFS Registration No 482
Double
Tube rosy red. *Sepals* rosy red. *Corolla* medium blue. Very large flowers. *Growth* upright and bushy, but needs careful pinching.

'Blue Mink'
RON HOLMES 1976
Single
Tube and sepals bright carmine pink. *Corolla* deep bluish purple, veined carmine and pink at the base. *Foliage* medium green with red veins. *Growth* upright, very floriferous and bushy, makes a good plant for pots or bedded out.

'Blue Moon'
NIEDERHOLZER 1938
Semi-double
Sepals bright red. *Tube* short. *Corolla* bluish. *Growth* vigorous, upright, stiff branches. *Parentage* 'Rolla' × 'Heron'.

'Blue 'n' White'
BRAND 1960
AFS Registration No 420

Double
Tube short, wavy, white. *Sepals* white tinted blush, with green tips. Long and broad. *Corolla* lilac blue, spreading. Smaller outer petals overlaid with phlox pink. *Flowers* large. Free-flowering, trailing habit.

'Blue Pearl'
MARTIN 1957
AFS Registration No 325
Double
Tube pink. *Sepals* pink, arching and tipped green. *Corolla* violet blue. Large blooms. *Growth* vigorous upright, can be made to trail. Very easy to grow, flower opens flat.

'Blue Pendant'
BROWN 1949 (USA)
Double
Tube pale tyrian rose. *Sepals* pale tyrian rose, tipped white. *Corolla* campanula violet with a blue cast. *Foliage* small, medium green. *Flowers* medium size, growth lax, semi-trailer.

'Blue Petticoat'
EVANS AND REEVES 1954
AFS Registration No 216
Double
Tube white. *Sepals* white, tinted pink on the undersides. *Corolla* lilac lavender ageing to orchid pink. Trailing growth, fairly free-flowering.

'Blue Pinwheel'
MRS A. STUBBS 1970
AFS Registration No 902
Single
Tube and sepals rose pink. *Sepals* curled. *Corolla* lavender blue, pale pink at the base. *Foliage* medium green. *Growth* basket type. Very free-flowering, self-branching, easy to grow. Will make a good half-basket.

'Blue Ranger'
GADSBY 1975
AFS Registration No 1312
Semi-double
Tube crimson RHS 52A, long and thick. *Sepals* crimson RHS 52A, board and waxy, slightly curved back. *Corolla* bluebird blue, shading to hyacinth blue RHS 91A, fading to violet. *Foliage* medium green. *Growth* self-branching and bushy upright which will trail with weights.

'Blue Rhythm'
LEE 1953
AFS Registration No 153
Semi-double
Tube dawn pink, peach on the top. *Sepals* dawn pink, peach on the top, recurved. *Corolla* dauphine's violet shading to peach white at the base with overlaying petaloids of the same colour. Free-flowering, upright vigorous growth.

'Blue Ribbon'
FUCHSIA-LA NURSERIES 1967
AFS Registration No 695
Double
Tube pale pink. *Sepals* pale pink. *Corolla* white, square. *Growth* lax bush, will make a basket. Free-flowering, largish blooms.

'Blue Satin'
WALKER 1969
AFS Registration No 835
Tube short and white. *Sepals* long and white. *Corolla* indigo blue shading to white at the base, giving it a satiny sheen, flares after opening. *Foliage* medium size, dark green. *Growth* will make a good bush or trailer.

'Blue Skies'
NESSIER 1948
Single
Tube rose pink. *Sepals* rose pink. *Corolla* bluish violet. Flowers small, free-flowering. *Growth* upright and bushy.

'Blue Waves' (144)
WALTZ 1954
AFS Registration No 201
Double
Tube pink. Sepals pink. *Corolla* bluish violet, splashed rose pink and veined carmine. *Foliage* light green. *Growth* vigor-

ous upright, very easy to grow and makes a lovely exhibition plant.

'Blushing Beauty'

DE FRANCISCO/SOO YUN 1980
AFS Registration No 1559
Double
Tube Bengal red, $\frac{3}{8}$ in (1 cm) long. *Sepals* Bengal red, $1\frac{1}{4}$ in (3 cm) long. *Corolla* pale pink $1\frac{1}{2}$ cm (4 cm) wide by $\frac{3}{4}$ in (2 cm) long. Four pale pink petaloids $\frac{1}{2}$ in (1.5 cm) long. *Pistil and stigma* pink. *Foliage* light green, 1 in (2.5 cm) long. *Growth* medium upright, bush. Prefers shade.

'Blush of Dawn' (53)

MARTIN 1962
AFS Registration No 516
Double
Tube white. *Sepals* white, waxy with green tips. *Corolla* silver grey blue, very full, medium size. *Foliage* medium green. Very free-flowering and long-lasting blooms. *Growth* bush or semi-trailer. Will make a very nice pot plant.

'Bobby Boy'

FUCHSIA FOREST 1965
AFS Registration No 625
Double
Tube pink, short and of medium thickness. *Sepals* reddish rose, recurving slightly. *Filaments and style* pale pink. *Corolla* small, bluish rose fading to rose, with touches of orange on the outer petals. *Growth* bush type, free-flowering. *Foliage* medium green, small serrations. Must be well pinched to get a decent shape.

'Bobby Shaftoe'

RYLE 1970
AFS Registration No 1113 (1973)
Semi-double
Tube clear frosty white flushed pale pink, short, medium thick. *Sepals* clear frosty white, pink underside with lemon tips, short, broad and fairly thick textured. *Corolla* clear frosty white, flushed palest pink, with pink veins, flared and ruffled to form four flutes. *Foliage* mid to light green, medium size, oval. Self-branching upright bush, will trail with weights. Prolific bloomer, short-jointed, good show plant.

'Bobby Wingrove'

WINGROVE 1966
Single
Tube short, medium thickness. *Sepals* pinkish red, tipped green, held down from horizontal. *Filaments and style* pale pink. *Corolla* turkey red. Medium green foliage, serrated slightly. *Growth* self-branching and compact bush. Very easy to grow, makes an excellent exhibition variety and blooms throughout the season almost non-stop.

'Bob Kennedy'

PENNISI 1969
AFS Registration No 812
Double
Tube white. *Sepals* white with green tips. *Corolla* white. *Foliage* light to medium green, small. Will stand very hot conditions. *Growth* trailer, and will make a nice basket. Large blooms.

'Bo Bo'

ADKINS 1980
AFS Registration No 1587
Double
Tube short, red, medium thickness. *Sepals* red. *Corolla* purple, shaded magenta at the base. Small to medium. *Foliage* dark green, orate, slightly serrated. Veins partially red. *Growth* upright, bush.

'Bobolink'

EVANS 1953
AFS Registration No 182
Tube flesh pink. *Sepals* flesh pink, upturned. *Corolla* blue-violet. Upright growth, vigorous and free-flowering, but blooms apt to be rather loose.

'Boerhave'

VAN WIERINGEN 1970
(Netherlands)

Single
Tube deep red, long. *Sepals* deep red. *Corolla* deep rose-pink to rose-purple. *Foliage* mid-green. Upright growth, largish bloom. A very easy-growing cultivar which flowers profusely.

'Bolero'
NIEDERHOLZER 1942
(probably earlier)
Double
Tube bright red. *Sepals* bright red. *Corolla* very dark plum purple. Large blooms and upright growth though the weight of the flowers makes the branches tend to droop.

'Bon Accorde' (54)
CROUSSE (FRANCE) 1861
Single
Tube short and medium thickness, white. *Sepals* white, slightly downpointing at tips. *Corolla* pale purple with white flush. *Foliage* medium green, medium size. *Filaments* pink, style white. *Growth* bushy, stiff upright. This cultivar was perhaps the first to hold its flowers erect instead of hanging down in the usual fashion, and does not, as a result, make a good plant for use as a standard. It is not self-branching and needs much careful pinching in its early stages to make a nice shaped bush. Very free-flowering, and attractive as a garden plant where the flowers can be seen to their best advantage. Known in the USA as 'Erecta Novelty'.

'Bonanza'
FUCHSIA-LA NURSERIES 1963
Double
Tube spinel pink. *Sepals* spinel pink. *Corolla* spectrum-violet, fading to petunia purple as the flower matures. Free-flowering, rather lax habit.

'Bon Bon'
KENNETT 1963
AFS Registration No 592
Double
Tube greenish-white, long, and thin turned up at the ends. *Sepals* short and broad, pale pink, deeper pink underneath. *Corolla* very pale pink, tight. Medium size. Filaments pink, style white. *Foliage* small, medium green, glossy, slightly serrated. *Growth* self-branching, long arching stems, very vigorous and prolific bloomer. Needs careful pinching, does well in a half-basket.

'Bonita'
FUCHSIA-LA NURSERIES 1972
AFS Registration No 1021
Double
Tube light pink. *Sepals* light pink, shading to white on top, china rose on the underside. *Corolla* orchid purple. *Foliage* dark green, medium size. *Growth* trailer, very vigorous, and makes a very good basket.

'Bonnie Lass'
WALTZ 1962
AFS Registration No 522
Single
Tube clear frosty white. *Sepals* white outside, pale pink on the underside, reflexed. *Corolla* clear lilac fading to rose pink. Medium-sized blooms. *Foliage* dark green, small. Very free-flowering, vigorous self-branching growth, makes an excellent pot plant.

'Bonnie Sue'
ADKINS 1980
AFS Registration No 1550 (Introduced 1965)
Double
Tube medium length and thickness, pink. *Sepals* rose pink with green tips, horizontal. *Corolla* rosy red, petals edged dark rose, paler at the base. Medium size. *Foliage* dark green, small to medium size, ovate serrated edges. *Habit* trailer, lax growth, will make a good basket.

'Bo Peep'
SCHNABEL 1948
Semi-double
Tube white, tinged pale pink. *Sepals* white, tinged pale pink. *Corolla* orchid blue.

Foliage small, medium green. *Growth* slow growing, will make a small bush.

'Bora Bora'
TIRET 1966
AFS Registration No 688
Double
Tube white, medium length and thickness. *Sepals* white, tipped green, and pink on the undersides, almost completely reflexed. *Corolla* purplish blue, full and frilly. *Filaments* pink, style white. *Foliage* medium green, rather long. *Growth* vigorous, very bushy trailer, self-branching. Free-flowering, prefers shaded conditions. Bush with support.

'Border Queen' (97)
RYLE 1972
Registered with the AFS in 1974 No 1167
Single
Tube short, thin, pale pink. *Sepals* rhodamine pink RHS 62A, tipped pea green RHS 149A, neyron rose RHS 55B, on the underside with darker rose veining, flaring outwards and, as the bloom matures, reflexing almost to the tube. *Corolla* amethyst violet, flushed pale pink fading to white at the base, darker pink veins and bell-shaped. *Foliage* medium green, reddish stems. *Growth* self-branching, vigorous, free-flowering upright which will make a very good bush or standard exhibition plant. *Parentage* 'Leonora' × 'Lena Dalton'.

'Border Reiver'
RYLE 1980
AFS Registration No 1574
Single
Tube neyron rose, medium length and thickness. *Sepals* neyron rose on top, vermilion underneath, semi-reflexed. *Corolla* cardinal red, medium size. *Filaments* pink. *Anthers* ruby red. *Foliage* dark green, orate, serrate margins, medium to large. *Growth* upright, bushy, vigorous. Bush.

'Boudoir'
REITER 1954
Double
Tube creamy white, pink at the base, medium length and thickness. *Sepals* cream with green tips, upturned at tips. *Filaments* pale pink, style white. *Corolla* violet-blue, fading to pink at the base and with pale cerise veins. *Foliage* bright green with red veining. *Growth* rather lax bush, not very free-flowering. Bush.

'Bouffant' (13)
TIRET 1949
Single
Tube long and thin, red. *Sepals* red, long and narrow, slightly turned up at the tips. *Corolla* white with red veins, petals tightly rolled. *Style and filaments* red. *Foliage* medium green, medium to large size. *Growth* trailer, will make an excellent basket. Self-branching and very free-flowering, but needs pinching to obtain a good shape. A very easy cultivar to grow.

'Bountiful' (84)
MUNKNER 1963
AFS Registration No 564
Double
Tube white, long, medium thickness. *Sepals* pale pink, deeper pink on the undersides, green tips upturned. *Corolla* milky white with pink veining at the base of the petals. *Foliage* medium green, slightly serrated. *Growth* vigorous upright, very free-flowering and will make a good bush if pinched well from its early stages. A superb variety. Good bush if staked.

'Bouquet'
LEMOINE 1893 or ROZAIN-BOUCHARLET 1893
Single
Tube carmine. *Sepals* carmine. *Corolla* purple, ageing to reddish purple. *Foliage* small, medium green. *Growth* upright, bushy, low growing, dwarf. Makes a very good plant for a rockery, prolific-flowering, and self-branching.

'Bow Bells' (45)
HANDLEY 1972
AFS Registration No 1051
Single
Tube white, short and thick. *Sepals* white,

reflexed, green tips. *Corolla* magenta RHS 66B, white at the base. *Foliage* mid-green, largish and serrated. *Growth* upright, self-branching, makes a good spreading bush. Early bloomer, large flowers, very prolific. Very easy to grow, equally good as a garden plant.

'Brandt's 500 Club'
BRAND 1955
Single
Tube pink. *Sepals* long, upturned at the tips, pale pink with deeper colouring underneath. *Corolla* pinkish cerise, pink at the base with an orange flush. *Foliage* medium green, serrated. *Growth* upright, bushy growth. An easy cultivar to grow.

'Bravado'
CASTRO 1960
AFS Registration No 425
Double
Tube red. *Sepals* red. *Corolla* periwinkle blue splashed at the base with rose red, and fading to Spanish red. *Foliage* medium green. *Growth* semi-trailer, which will also make a good bush if well pinched and staked in the early stages.

'Brazier'
REITER 1947
Semi-double
Tube carmine red. *Sepals* carmine red. *Corolla* deep carmine, almost a self colour. Medium-sized flowers. *Growth* trailer with rather stiff branches.

'Breeder's Dream'
JONES 1961
Double
Tube white with pinkish flush. *Sepals* white with pinkish flush, with green tips. *Corolla* phlox purple. Free-flowering, upright growth.

'Brenda'
RYLE 1980
AFS Registration No 1575
Double
Tube pale pink, thick and short. *Sepals* white, tinged pink, reflexing. *Corolla* shades of pink. *Foliage* dark green, ovate to cordate, slightly crinkled, medium to large. *Growth* vigorous, self-branching, bushy upright. Bush.

'Brenda Lee Peterson'
VEEJAY GREENHOUSE 1980
AFS Registration No 1590
Double
Tube flesh-coloured, short, medium thickness. *Sepals* light rose. Green tips on upper surface, sepals lie across the corolla. *Foliage* medium green with red stems. Medium size. *Growth* natural trailer. Basket.

'Brentwood'
EVANS AND REEVES 1936
Semi-double
Almost a self white, with the sepals having green tips. *Growth* not very vigorous, low grower and compact. Must be grown in the shade if the white colour is to be kept, otherwise it colours slightly pinkish. *Parentage* 'Rolla' × 'Duchess of Albany' seedling.

'Brian Young'
YOUNG 1980
AFS Registration No 1566
Semi-double
Tube pale greenish-white (*eau de nil*), short and thin. *Sepals* white (RHS 159D) on top, flushed pale pink, undersides at the base and white to the tips, green tips, recurving completely. *Corolla* purple (RHS 93C), medium-sized, flaring, with two purple petaloids on each petal. *Stamens* rose. *Pistil* white. *Foliage* green (RHS 137A) long and narrow. *Growth* trailer or upright, will make a good bush. Standard or basket. *Parentage* 'Susan Young' × 'Arthur Young'.

'Bridal Veil'
WALTZ 1963
AFS Registration No 586

Double
Tube white. *Sepals* white with green tips, slightly upturned. *Corolla* large, full white. *Foliage* small, dark green and glossy. *Growth* self-branching trailer.

'Bridesmaid'
TIRET 1952
AFS Registration No 143
Double
Tube white, thick. *Sepals* broad white with light carmine flush, phlox pink on the underside and recurving. *Corolla* pale lilac orchid, deepening toward the edge of the petals. *Growth* upright, bushy.

'Brigadoon'
ERICKSON 1957
AFS Registration 322
Double
Tube rose pink. *Sepals* rose pink, recurved, crepe inside and with light green tips. *Corolla* violet blue with pink marbling at the base. *Foliage* medium green. *Growth* upright, willowy bush. Large flowers, free-flowering and vigorous.

'Bright Eyes'
SOO YUN 1973
AFS Registration No 1093
Double
Tube light red, medium thick, short. *Sepals* light red with green tips, reflexing back to the tube. *Corolla* blue with four swirls in the centre, outer petals flaring. *Foliage* medium green, smallish, with serrated edges. *Growth* semi-trailer which will make a basket with weights, but otherwise a good bush if pinched and staked early. Prolific bloomer.

'Brilliant'
BULL 1865
Single 4 in (10 cm) long
Tube $1\frac{3}{4}$–2 in (4.5–5 cm) long. Medium thickness. *Sepals* scarlet, recurving slightly. *Style and filaments* pink. *Corolla* violet magenta with red veining. *Foliage* medium green, finely serrated. *Growth* upright, very vigorous and needs pinching back early to form a good shape, otherwise it will send out long arching branches. Does best as a garden plant, and is hardy in sheltered areas. Standard/pyramid.

'British Sterling'
FOSTER 1973
AFS Registration No 1084
Semi-double
Tube short, white, medium thickness. *Sepals* white on top, rosy pink on the underside, greenish white tips, short, broad and reflexed to the tube. *Corolla* lavender with faint rose cast, veined pink, small with a slight flair. *Foliage* light green with deep rose stems, fairly slender. *Growth* upright, bushy.

'Bronte Belle'
FOSTER 1972
AFS Registration 1039
Double
Tube short, medium thickness, variegated pink and white. *Sepals* variegated pink, and white, with faint green tips, horizontal with crinkled appearance. *Corolla* white, small, ruffled, full and flared. *Foliage* small and slender, light to medium green. *Growth* upright but will trail with weights. Best colour develops in the shade.

'Brutus' (161)
LEMOINE 1897
Single $2\frac{1}{2}$ in (6 cm)
Tube short, crimson-cerise. *Sepals* crimson-cerise. *Corolla* deep purple, shading to carmine at the base, and ageing to wine; purple. *Foliage* medium green, dark veins. *Growth* vigorous, bushy upright. Brutus will make an excellent plant either in a pot or planted in the open garden. Very free-flowering. Standard, pyramid or bush.

'Bubble Hanger'
NIEDERHOLZER 1946
Single
Tube pale pink. *Sepals* pale pink. *Corolla* rose madder. Large blooms, free-flowering cascade, vigorous growth. The large fat buds give the plant its name.

'Buddha'
FUCHSIA-LA NURSERIES 1968
Semi-double
Tube white, longish, medium thick. *Sepals* white, flushed pink and tipped green. Underside of the sepals pale pink. Sepals reflexing. *Corolla* deep wine red with pink splashes. *Foliage* dark green, large. *Growth* upright, lax growth which needs staking to take the weight of the blooms.

'Bunker Boy'
TIRET 1952
AFS Registration No 144
Double
Tube thick and waxy white. *Sepals* broad, white, upturned and flushed pale carmine. *Corolla* white at the base, deepening to geranium lake at the petal edges, smaller outer petals marbled fuchsia pink. *Corolla* long and fluted. *Foliage* medium green. *Growth* upright, vigorous and self-branching.

'Burning Bush'
COURCELLES
Single
Tube red. *Sepals* red. *Foliage* variegated reddish, yellow and cream. *Corolla* reddish purple. *Growth* rather stiff and usually tends to the horizontal making it a difficult variety to train. A very good foliage variety which is slow to flower but worth growing for the foliage alone. Some confusion exists between this cultivar and 'Autumnale' (q.v.).

'Buttercup' (49)
PASKESEN 1976
AFS Registration No 1345
Single
Tube short, soft rose pink. *Sepals* soft rose, orange shading underneath, held horizontal. *Corolla* bright orange. Medium-sized bloom which colours best in the shade. Upright, bushy growth.

'Butterfly'
VICTOR REITER 1942
Single
Tube rose bengal. *Sepals* rose bengal, recurving. *Corolla* rose bengal, crimson at the base, almost a self colour. Large flowers. *Growth* trailer.

'Buttermere'
TRAVIS 1973
AFS Registration No 1137
Single
Tube short, medium thickness. Rose with greenish vein stripes, glossy. *Sepals* rich rose pink, tips eau-de-nil, long and narrow, reflexing and spiralling in older flowers. *Corolla* lavender purple with a silver sheen at the base of the petals. Deep purple edge to the petals which open almost flat, and overlap. *Foliage* deep green, dullish with a red mid-vein, serrated. *Growth* self-branching, upright, bushy growth. Colours best in the shade. *Parentage* 'Opalescent' × 'Citation'.

'Buttons & Bows'
MACHADO 1962
AFS Registration No 499
Double
Tube red. *Sepals* red. *Corolla* white, very full, opens in a cup shape, veined cerise. *Foliage* darkish green. *Growth* upright, bushy and dwarf. A small flower which is a slow grower, and not an easy cultivar.

'Caballero'
KENNETT 1965
AFS Registration No 638
Double
Tube salmon pink. *Sepals* salmon pink. *Corolla* large, bluish purple to violet with splashes of salmon pink on outer petals. Petaloids red and white. Can be grown as a bush, but is rather lax and is best as a trailer.

'Cabaret'
MRS E. HANDLEY 1971
AFS Registration No 948
Double
Tube medium length and thickness, white. *Sepals* white with pale pink flush on the undersides. *Corolla* large, bright magenta RHS 66B streaked with pink RHS 49A from the base. Each petal has a

vermilion edge. The bloom holds its shape well as it matures. *Foliage* small to medium size. *Growth* trailer, self-branching, early flowering. Very prolific. Basket.

'Cable Car'
TED PASKESEN 1968
AFS Registration No 762
Double
Tube short, white. *Sepals* pale pink, tips darker pink. *Corolla* orchid and various shades of rose. *Foliage* dark green with red veining. *Growth* upright, vigorous, will make a good standard. Bush/standard.

'Cadmus'
ROZAIN-BOUCHARLAT 1928
Single
Tube cerise. *Sepals* cerise. *Corolla* white, slightly veined cerise.

'Caesar'
FUCHSIA FOREST (CASTRO) 1967
AFS Registration 722
Double
Tube red. *Sepals* red. *Corolla* large, purple fading to burgundy. The petals curl up, making the bloom rose-shaped. *Foliage* medium green. *Growth* upright and will make a good bush but requires staking early to support the weight of the blooms. Can be trained as a basket with weights. Bush.

'Caledonia'
LEMOINE 1899
Single
Tube cerise, long and thin. *Sepals* cerise, pointing down from the horizontal. *Corolla* crimson, small. *Style and filaments* red. *Foliage* medium green. *Growth* upright, dwarf, will make a good small pot plant or equally at home in the garden in sheltered areas. Bush.

'Calico'
NESSIER 1952
AFS Registration 116
Single
Tube Tyrian rose. *Sepals* Tyrian rose. *Corolla* cobalt violet, white in the centre, flaring. *Foliage* medium green, smallish. *Growth* upright bush, not very vigorous.

'California'
EVANS AND REEVES 1936
Single
Tube orange pink. *Sepals* orange pink. *Foliage* light green. *Corolla* bright orange. *Growth* very vigorous, tall growing upright. Will make a good standard. Bush. *Parentage* 'Fireflush' × unnamed seedling.

'California Beauty'
FIELD 1980
AFS Registration No 1546
Single
Tube rhodamine purple (RHS 68D), short, $\frac{1}{4}$in (5 mm) long, by $\frac{1}{8}$ in (2.5 mm) wide. *Sepals* rhodamine purple (RHS 68D) on top with green tips, underside off white. Medium length ($1\frac{1}{8}$ in – 28 mm). *Corolla* fuchsia purple (RHS 67B), medium size. *Stamens* pink. *Pistil* white, long, with yellow tip. *Foliage* light green, leaves 1 in (25 mm) long × $\frac{3}{8}$ in (10 mm) wide. *Growth* natural trailer. Basket.

'California Centennial'
WALKER AND JONES 1949
Double
Tube rose red. *Sepals* long, rose red. *Corolla* violet and dark purple, very large. *Growth* will make a good basket, the large blooms being too heavy to form a good bush plant. Basket.

'California Queen'
PENNISI 1971
AFS Registration No 1013
Tube medium size, orange. *Sepals* light orange with darker tips. *Corolla* medium red. *Foliage* medium green. *Growth* trailer, will make a small basket. Unusual colour combination.

'Callaly Pink'
RYLE 1974
Tube white, flushed pink. *Sepals* white,

upturned. *Corolla* pale pink with pink veining. *Foliage* medium green. *Growth* upright, will make a good bush plant if pinched regularly. Not an outstanding cultivar, rather too like many others of the same colour. Bush.

'Calypso'
REITER 1956
AFS Registration No 275
Double
Tube rose. *Sepals* rose, Tyrian rose underneath, recurved. *Corolla* pink, marbled and flecked cyclamen purple, amethyst violet and white, opening wide. *Foliage* medium green, largish. *Growth* best grown as a basket because of the weight of the blooms.

'Cambridge Louie'
NAPTHEN 1978
AFS Registration No 1473
Single
Tube thin pinkish-orange. *Sepals* stand out, and are pinkish-orange with green tips, and darker on the underside. *Corolla* rosy pink. *Foliage* smallish, light green. *Growth* upright, self-branching and moderately vigorous. Will make a very good exhibition plant up to 6½ in (16 cm) pot. Short-jointed, very floriferous. Bush.

'Cameo'
SCHNABEL 1950
AFS Registration No 53
Semi-double
Tube pale rose madder. *Sepals* pale rose madder. *Corolla* delicate pink. *Foliage* medium green. *Growth* not very vigorous, self-branching upright. Will make a small pot plant. Bush.

'Cameron Ryle'
RYLE 1971
AFS Registration 1972 No 1024
Semi-double
Tube short pale pink. *Sepals* frosty white with pink to red overcast, green tips. The sepals reflex over the tube. *Corolla* very dark bluish-purple outside, pale pink inside, maturing to magenta. *Stamens* pink, anthers red. *Foliage* medium green. *Growth* self-branching upright, prolific bloomer. Medium size blooms. Bush. *Parentage* 'Lena Dalton' × 'Citation'.

'Camille'
SCHNABEL 1956
AFS Registration No 264
Double
Tube crimson. *Sepals* crimson, reflexed, short. *Corolla* rose bengal. Large blooms, spreading growth, will make a good basket.

'Can Can'
MRS E. HANDLEY 1973
AFS Registration No 1132
Double
Tube short, medium thick, pink RHS 55B. *Sepals* pink RHS 55B, broad and reflexed. *Corolla* short, white veined pink, full and fluffy. *Stamens* pink. *Foliage* dark green with bronze flush in the centre of the leaves, and veined red. Dark red stems. *Growth* vigorous upright, will make a good bush, best colour in shaded conditions.

'Candelabra'
CASTRO (FUCHSIA FOREST) 1962
AFS Registration No 512
Semi-double
Tube greyish white. *Sepals* greyish white, long, curling up tight at the base of the corolla. *Corolla* very long dark blue with streaks of white and reddish pink. *Foliage* light green. *Growth* trailer, very prolific bloomer. Basket.

'Candlelight'
WALTZ 1959
AFS Registration No 391
Double
Tube white. *Sepals* pure white on top, slightly flushed pink on the underside. *Corolla* rose pink with overlapping petals of very dark purple-lilac fading to bright carmine. *Foliage* medium green. *Growth* upright, vigorous, self-branching.

'Candy Floss'
BARTON 1970
AFS Registration No 916
Double
Tube short, pink. *Sepals* pink. *Corolla* pink with deeper pink markings, almost a self colour. Large fluffy blooms, upright bushy growth.

'Candy Rose'
GAGNON 1964
AFS Registration No 600
Double
Tube short, bright red. *Sepals* red, crepe texture. *Corolla* pale pink with deep pink stripes. *Stamen and pistil* deep pink. Bloom resembles a small rose bud. *Foliage* is bronzy green with medium large leaves. *Growth* upright, vigorous, self-branching. The bloom lasts well and will stand heat and sunshine.

'Candy Stripe'
ENDICOTT 1965
Single
Tube pale pink with deep pink stripes, short and thick. *Sepals* upturned, pink with deeper colouring underneath. *Corolla* pale purple changing to pale pink at the base of the petals. *Foliage* medium green with red veining. *Growth* vigorous, self-branching upright which will make a nice bush with little pinching.

'Capitola'
ANTONELLI 1971
AFS Registration No 1003
Double
Tube pale pink to white. *Sepals* pale pink to white, green tipped. *Corolla* orange rose. *Foliage* medium green. *Growth* trailer.

'Capri'
SCHNABEL PASKESEN 1960
AFS Registration No 418
Double
Tube short, thick, white. *Sepals* broad, white. *Corolla* deep rich blue-violet, very large petals. *Foliage* medium green. *Growth* arching, will make a good bush or trailer. Beautiful colour combination.

'Caprice'
NIEDERHOLZER 1944
Single
Tube long, pale rose madder. *Sepals* pale rose madder. *Corolla* short, petunia purple. *Flowers* small. *Growth* trailer.

'Capricorn'
PASKESEN 1970
AFS Registration 872
Double
Tube short, pale pink. *Sepals* white, upturned. *Corolla* rich blue-white, flushed white at the base, long petals. *Foliage* medium green, largish. *Growth* vigorous trailer, needs to be grown in the shade for best results.

'Cara Mia'
SCHNABEL 1957
AFS Registration No 288
Semi-double
Tube greenish white, thin. *Sepals* pale pink with green tips, long and reflexed. *Corolla* deep crimson. *Foliage* medium green. *Growth* cascading, free-flowering and vigorous. Makes a superb half-basket.

'Cardinal'
EVANS AND REEVES 1938
Single
Tube long, medium thickness. *Sepals* red, long, narrow, upturned. *Corolla* red, compact. *Style and filamenis* pink. Very large flowers. *Foliage* light to medium green, large, serrated. *Growth* very vigorous upright, not self-branching, so will require a lot of pinching if it is to be grown as a pot plant. Has been known to reach 12 ft (4 m) so can be recommended as a greenhouse climber. Long jointed.

'Cardinal Farges'
Sport from 'Abbé Farges', introduced by RAWLINS 1959
Semi-double
Tube short, medium thickness. *Sepals* pale

cerise. *Style and filaments* pale cerise. *Corolla* white, lightly veined cerise. *Foliage* medium green, small, brittle. *Growth* upright, self-branching and vigorous. It makes a very good show plant in pots up to 6½ in (16 cm), also good for a 3½ in (9 cm) pot class. Hardy in sheltered areas.

'Cargundy'
REEDSTROM 1952
AFS Registration No 108
Double
Tube cardinal red. *Sepals* cardinal red. *Corolla* burgundy red. *Foliage* dark green, large. *Growth* vigorous upright, will make a good bush or standard.

'Carioca'
SCHMIDT 1951
AFS Registration No 98
Single
Tube pale rose red. *Sepals* pale rose red, green tips. *Corolla* rose red with purplish markings, spreading. Petals serrated. *Foliage* medium green. *Growth* upright, very vigorous, can be made to trail.

'Carla'
NIEDERHOLZER 1943
Single
Tube pale flesh pink. *Sepals* pale flesh pink. *Corolla* carmine. *Flowers and foliage* smallish. *Growth* trailer, will make a small basket.

'Carl Drude'
GADSBY 1975
Semi-double
Tube cardinal red. *Sepals* cardinal red. *Corolla* white, veined red. *Foliage* golden bronze, medium size. *Growth* upright, vigorous and bushy. *Parentage* 'Strawberry Delight' ×.

'Carlotta'
HOWARTH 1980
AFS Registration No 1577
Single
Tube pale pink. *Sepals* bright red, tipped green, 1¼ in (3 cm) long. *Corolla* cerise, flushed pink, bell-shaped. *Stamens* deep pink. *Foliage* mid-green, serrated, small. *Growth* upright, bushy. Bush/standard. *Parentage* 'Display' × 'Gay Fandango'. BFS Bronze Certificate 1979.

'Carmel Blue'
HODGES 1956
Single
Tube white, long and thin. *Sepals* white, pink tinged and reflexed. *Corolla* blue, ageing to purplish blue. Medium green foliage, small to medium. *Growth* upright, vigorous, self-branching. Prolific bloomer. One of the finest blue and white cultivars which will make a good exhibition plant with the minimum of pinching.

'Carmen'
JOHN BLACKWELL 1966
Double
Tube medium length carmine.
Sepals carmine, recurved completely against the tube. *Corolla* bluish purple ageing to cerise purple. Base of the petals carmine pink, cerise veining. *Foliage* medium green. *Growth* upright, vigorous, bushy. Full double, opens up on maturity.
Do not confuse with the following.

'Carmen'
LEMOINE 1893
Semi-double to double 3 in (7.5 cm)
Tube cerise. *Sepals* cerise. *Corolla* purple. *Foliage* small, medium to dark green. *Flowers* small, very free-flowering, dwarf growth. Does well as a garden hardy, particularly as a rockery plant. Hybrid from *F. myrtifolia*.

'Carmen Maria'
Sport of 'Leonora'
Introduced by BREITNER 1970
AFS Registration No 907
Single
Tube pink. *Sepals* long narrow pink, reflexed, green tips. *Corolla* baby pink with deeper pink veins, petals overlapping. *Stamens* pink. *Foliage* medium green.

Growth upright, self-branching and vigorous. Will make a good exhibition plant, free-flowering.

'Carnival'
TIRET 1956
Double
Tube long, medium thickness, crimson. *Sepals* white, green tips, curling right back to the tube. *Filaments* pink. *Style* white. *Corolla* long, thin, bright red, petals overlapping. *Foliage* medium green, largish. *Growth* not self branching, needs a lot of pinching to get it into shape, but will make a good half-basket.

'Carol Elizabeth'
SHAW 1972
AFS Registration No 1035
Single
Tube short, medium thickness, dusky pink. *Sepals* dusky pink with green tips, horizontal to fully reflexed over the tube as it matures. Long, narrow. *Corolla* royal purple fading slightly with age, lavender-mauve tinge at the base. Short petals flare out into bell shape with maturity. *Foliage* medium green, small to medium. Self-branching. Green stems changing to reddish as the plant matures. *Flower* very small. *Growth* vigorous, tall upright. Does not usually bloom in its first year but prolific afterwards.

'Carole Pugh'
PUGH 1975
AFS Registration No 1235
Double
Tube Orient pink RHS 36C. *Sepals* orchid pink RHS 62C, frosted inside. *Corolla* amethyst violet RHS 81C, base of the petals mallow purple RHS 72D. *Foliage* RHS 137C. Self-branching natural trailer. Best colour develops in the shade.

'Caroline'
V.V. MILLER 1967
Single
Tube pink. *Sepals* pale pink with green tips, and deeper pink undersides. *Corolla* pale lavender shading to pale pink at the base. *Foliage* medium green, slightly serrated. *Growth* vigorous upright which will make a good bush if well pinched in its early stages.

'Carol Peet'
GEORGE ROE 1976
Single
Tube neyron rose. *Sepals* neyron rose, tipped green. *Corolla* pink, small. *Foliage* smallish, dark green. *Growth* upright, bushy. Very strong and vigorous. Will make a superb exhibition plant, either as a $3\frac{1}{2}$ in (9 cm) pot plant or quarter standard. *Parentage* 'Eleanor Leytham' × 'Pink Darling'.

'Carol Roe'
GEORGE ROE 1976
Single
Tube short, thick, creamy white. *Sepals* light pink above, pale above, pale rose underneath, tipped green and held almost horizontal. *Corolla* rosy pink, pale pink style, white stigma. Small flowers but profuse. *Growth* upright, very bushy and self-branching, flowers over a very long period. *Parentage* 'Eleanor Leytham' × 'Pink Darling'.

'Carousel'
EVANS 1954
Double
Tube crimson red. *Sepals* crimson red. *Corolla* white. *Growth* upright, bushy, vigorous. Flowers of medium size.

'Cascade' (48)
DR J.B. LAGEN 1937
Single
Tube white, flushed carmine, medium length, thin. *Sepals* long, slim, white flushed carmine, down-pointing. *Corolla* rose bengal. *Foliage* light to medium green, finely serrated. *Growth* cascading. Self-branching, makes a superb basket. *Parentage* 'Rolla' × 'Amy Lye'.

'Cassandra'
NIEDERHOLZER 1946
Single

Tube turkey red. *Sepals* turkey red. *Corolla* purple. *Foliage* medium green, medium to large size. *Growth* upright, bushy.

'Catalina'
Sport of 'Gypsy Queen'
EVANS AND REEVES 1937
Double
Tube crimson. *Sepals* crimson. *Corolla* white-veined cerise. *Foliage* medium green, reddish margins. *Growth* upright, vigorous, bushy.

'Catherine Claire'
MRS I. CLYNE
Double
Tube carmine. *Sepals* carmine. *Corolla* rose madder. Large blooms, very free-flowering. Dark green foliage. *Growth* upright, and bushy, self-branching. Makes a good standard or bush.

'Cathie Macdougall'
THORNE 1960
AFS Registration No 454
Double
Tube cerise. *Sepals* cerise, upturned. *Corolla* medium-sized, petals marbled and striped blue and pink. *Foliage* medium green. *Growth* naturally trailing. Very prolific bloomer.

'Cavalier'
SCHNABEL 1953
AFS Registration No 188
Single
Tube pale pink. *Sepals* pale carmine pink, long and twisted. *Corolla* petunia purple, long and bell-shaped, shading to rhodamine at the base of the petals. *Foliage* medium green. *Growth* trailer, free-flowering. Long cascading branches.

'Cecil Glass'
JAMES LYE 1887
Single
Tube white with a pink flush. *Sepals* white with a pink flush. *Corolla* rich magenta. *Foliage* medium to light green. *Growth* rather lax but will make a good bush if staked early.

'Celebrity'
FUCHSIA-LA NURSERIES 1967
AFS Registration No 696
Double
Tube red. *Sepals* red. *Corolla* white, very large bloom. *Growth* basket variety.

Celia Smedley' (44)
GEORGE ROE 1970
Single
Tube neyron rose, tube of medium length and thickness. *Corolla* vivid currant red. *Sepals* neyron rose, upturned. *Foliage* medium green, large leaves, crimson veins. *Growth* upright, self-branching and very vigorous. Needs careful pinching to form a good bush, but is an ideal cultivar for a standard. An unusual colouring in the corolla which makes this a most outstanding cultivar. *Parentage* 'Joy Patmore' × 'Glitters'.

'Centrepiece'
CASTRO 1964
AFS REGISTRATION No 604
Semi-double
Tube red. Sepals red. *Corolla* opens with four pink petaloids over the lavender blue petals. The petaloids flare out and the centre lengthens, making a longish bloom. *Foliage* medium green. *Growth* will make a good bush plant or basket.

'Century 21'
KEIFFER 1962
AFS Registration No 496
Semi-double
Tube coral rose. *Sepals* coral rose. *Corolla* two shades of orchid, large blooms. *Foliage* medium green. *Growth* basket, natural trailer. Sport of 'Amapola' (q.v.).

'Ceri'
MRS E.HOLMES 1980
Single
Tube white. *Sepals* white. *Corolla* white, medium size. *Foliage* light to mid-green. *Growth* upright, vigorous, bushy. *Flowers* early and prolific.

'Cerrig'
HOWARTH 1979
AFS Registration No 1529
Single
Tube pale pink, medium length. *Sepals* clear rose pink. *Corolla* deep rose, 1¼ in (3 cm) long, slightly flared. *Stamens and pistil* purple. *Foliage* medium green with red rib, closely serrated, leathery and with pronounced veining. *Growth* tall growing upright, vigorous. Best colour develops in the sun. Will make a good bush or standard.

'Chance Encounter'
SCHNEIDER 1980
AFS Registration No 1589
Single
Tube pink, maturing to darker pink, very long. *Sepals* white, oral. *Corolla* white. *Foliage* dark green, short jointed, fernlike. *Growth* natural trailer, self-branching. Basket. *Parentage* Encliandra ×.

'Chandelier'
W. JONES/MACHADO 1962
AFS Registration No 501
Single
Tube white with faint pink flush. *Sepals* white with faint pink flush. *Tube* long, sepals slender and long. *Foliage* medium green. *Corolla* lilac purple. *Growth* upright, makes a good exhibition plant.

'Chandlerii'
CHANDLER 1839
Single
Tube creamy white. *Sepals* creamy white. *Corolla* rich orange scarlet, medium-sized bloom. *Foliage* medium green. *Growth* upright, vigorous bush, self-branching. *Parentage* 'Globosa' ×.

'Chang' (191)
HAZARD 1946
Single
Tube orange red. *Sepals* orange red, green tipped. *Corolla* brilliant orange (described by hybridiser as 'rose'). *Foliage* smallish, medium green. *Growth* very vigorous, upright. Difficult to grow to any recognised shape unless pinched carefully from the small plant stage, but will make a tall, arching standard in a relatively short time. *F. cordifolia* hybrid.

'Chantilly'
KENNETT 1962
AFS Registration No 538
Double
Tube reddish pink. *Sepals* white, reflexed up to the tube. *Corolla* white, many short petaloids touched with pink, giving the flower a lacy look, hence the name. Corolla full and spreading. *Foliage* large, palish green, red veining. *Growth* a very vigorous upright grower which needs careful pinching to bring it into shape, as it is not self-branching.

'Charlie Girl'
TANFIELD 1975
AFS Registration No 1277
Double
Tube pink, short and thick. *Sepals* rose pink, opening right out and covering the tube. *Corolla* lilac blue, paler at the base, veined rose. Petals open out. *Foliage* medium green, outstanding veins. *Growth* upright, bushy, vigorous and self-branching. Will make a very good exhibition plant.

'Charlie S. Field'
PALKO/SOO YUN FUCHSIA GARDENS 1980
AFS Registration 1564
Double
Tube light pink, short, thin. *Sepals* rose Bengal (RHS 61D), with green tips, long. *Corolla* white, medium size, with pink variegations. Eight rose bengal petaloids. ⅛ in (3 mm) shorter than the petals. *Pistil* pink. *Stigma* white. *Foliage* dark green, medium to long. *Growth* natural trailer. Develops best colour in the shade. Basket.

'Charming'
JAMES LYE 1895
Single 3¼ in (8 cm)
Tube carmine. *Sepals* carmine, recurving. *Corolla* purple, changing to reddish

purple as it matures, cerise at the base of the petals. *Foliage* yellowish green. *Growth* upright, vigorous and self-branching. Will make an excellent pot plant, and is equally at home in the garden as a hardy in sheltered areas.

'Chartwell'
GADSBY 1977
AFS Registration No 1424
Single
Tube white, medium length and width. *Sepals* recurving, rhodamine pink RHS 62A, green tips. *Corolla* medium-sized, wistaria blue RHS 92A, on a lighter base. *Foliage* medium green, medium size. *Growth* upright, self-branching, bushy. Makes a good pot plant and will also do well as a summer bedder.

'Chatsworth'
GADSBY 1975
AFS Registration No 1280
Single
Tube crimson RHS 52A, length 1 in (2.5 cm). *Sepals* neyron rose RHS 55A, on the underside, crimson on the top, green tips. Waxy, crepe effect, 2 in (5 cm) long. *Corolla* magenta rose RHS 64B, large, open bell-shaped, diameter of opening 1½ in (4 cm). *Foliage* medium green. *Growth* medium upright, self-branching bush. Best colour develops in the shade. *Parentage* 'Magenta Flush' × 'Derby Belle'.

'Checkerboard'
WALKER AND JONES 1948
Single
Tube deep red, long. *Sepals* white, red at the base, reflexing slightly. *Corolla* is red, white at the base and compact. *Foliage* medium to darkish green, finely serrated. Growth very vigorous, upright, makes long jointed growth and unsuitable for close-pinched type of training. It will make a very good standard in one season, although the stiffness of the branches gives the appearance of being out of proportion with the stem. Very prolific bloomer.

'Checkers'
EASTWOOD 1971
AFS Registraion No 988
Single
Tube red. *Sepals* white, reflexed with crepe appearance. *Corolla* magenta at the edge of the petals and shading to white at the base. *Foliage* medium green. *Growth* upright, not quite so vigorous as 'Checkerboard', will train to a trailer with weights. Blooms small, but prolific. Sport of 'Checkerboard'.

'Checkmate'
TOLLEY/FUCHSIAVALE 1980
AFS Registration No 1540
Single
Tube pale striped pink, short. *Sepals* pale magenta pink, short, slightly upturned. *Corolla* Indian magenta, short, semi-flared. *Stamens and pistil* Indian magenta. *Foliage* medium to dark green, orate. Slightly serrate leaf margins. Medium size. *Growth* upright, self-branching, lax. Will make a good weeping standard. Very floriferous. Sport of 'Checkerboard'.

'Cheerio'
KENNETT 1967
AFS Registration No 739
Double
Tube white. *Sepals* white with green tips. *Corolla* deep pink, compact. *Foliage* medium green, smallish to medium. *Growth* upright, small bush.

'Cheers'
MRS A. STUBBS 1979
AFS Registration No 1499
Double
Tube light coral pink, of medium length and thickness. *Sepals* broad, sharply pointed, coral pink streaks along the centre. *Corolla* orange red RHS 44B, mixed with poppy red RHS 40D, quite short but very full, with over 40 petals. *Foliage* medium-sized, dark green with large serrations. *Growth* vigorous upright bush, but can be made to trail with weights.

'Cherie'
HODGES 1952
AFS Registration No 124
Single
Tube rose red. *Sepals* rose red, long and upturned. *Corolla* blue-purple, almost white at the base of the petals which are rolled in at the edges and have prominent veins. *Foliage* medium green *Growth* upright, bushy, free-flowering. Blooms medium size.

'Cherry Jubilee'
MRS A. STUBBS 1970
AFS Registration No 908
Double
Tube short, white. *Sepals* white. *Corolla* burgundy cherry to flaming cherry red, large size. *Foliage* dark green, medium size. *Growth* vigorous bushy upright. Large blooms; will require staking because of the weight if grown as a bush plant. Very striking colours.

'Chessboard'
DR O. COLVILLE 1975
Single
Tube pink. *Sepals* long, starting pink and turning to white in the centre, with green tips. *Corolla* magenta with crimson edges. Medium to large blooms, similar to 'Checkerboard', as is the vigorous upright growth habit. The blooms are larger than those of 'Checkerboard', and rather brighter in colouring.

'Cheviot Princess'
RYLE 1977
AFS Registration No 1433
Single
Tube short, white. *Sepals* long, held almost horizontal, white with green tips. *Corolla* ruby red RHS 61A, shading to spiraea red, long. *Foliage* medium green. *Growth* vigorous, self-branching, bushy upright. Very prolific bloomer. *Parentage* 'Athela' × seedling from 'Pink Cloud' × 'Lena Dalton'. Bears a striking resemblance to 'Athela', though the flower is longer and slightly larger.

'Chic'
FUCHSIA FOREST 1964
AFS Registration No 605
Single
Tube light pink to coral pink. *Sepals* light pink to coral pink. *Corolla* long burgundy red, compact. *Foliage* medium green. *Growth* vigorous, bushy upright which will trail with weights.

'Chillerton Beauty' (107)
BASS 1847
Single
Tube pale pink. *Sepals* pale pink, deeper pink undersides, and green tips, held horizontal. *Corolla* purple with pink veins. Ages to magenta, stays quite compact as it matures. *Foliage* medium green, smallish, leathery shiny appearance. *Growth* self-branching, vigorous upright. Blooms freely, easy to grow, and hardy in most areas.

'Chillingham Countess'
RYLE 1975
AFS Registration No 1241
Single
Tube long and thin, rhodamine pink RHS 62A. *Sepals* long, medium width, slightly upturned, phlox pink RHS 62B. *Corolla* long and compact, violet blue RHS 90A, fading to purple violet RHS 80A, turning to pink near the base of the petals. *Stamens and pistil* reddish purple. *Foliage* medium green, medium-sized. *Growth* vigorous, medium upright, bushy, will make a good bush or standard. Best colour develops in the shade.

'China Doll'
WALKER AND JONES 1950
Double
Tube cerise with darker stripes, medium length and thickness. *Sepals* cerise, slightly upturned. *Corolla* white, heavily veined and blotched red. *Foliage* medium green. *Growth* rather lax, best grown as a trailer.

'China Lantern'
Raised 1953, believed American
Single
Tube shiny reddish pink. *Sepals* white with

green tips, reflexed. *Corolla* rose pink, white at the base, reddish pink on the edges of the petals. *Foliage* dark green, slightly serrated. *Growth* vigorous upright, tends to be rather lax.

'Christine Gatske'
PRENTICE 1967
AFS Registration No 721
Double
Tube pale pink. *Sepals* pale pink. *Corolla* deep blue splashed with pale pink, maturing to rosy lavender. *Foliage* light green turning to medium green. Growth basket variety. Very free-flowering, medium-sized flowers.

'Christine Pugh'
PUGH 1975
AFS Registration No 1236
Double
Tube phlox pink RHS 62B, medium length and thickness. *Sepals* rhodamine pink RHS 62A, frosted inside, green tips, recurving, length 1 in (2.5 cm), width ½ in (1.5 cm). *Corolla* phlox purple RHS 75C, twelve petals up to 1 in (2.5 cm) length and 1 in (2.5 cm) wide, four petaloids. *Foliage* medium green, leaves 4 in (10 cm) by 2½ in (60 cm). *Growth* upright, self-branching, will make a good bush or standard and can be trained to a basket. Best colour develops in the shade.

'Christmas Elf'
GENTRY 1972
AFS Registration No 1027
Single
Tube bright red. *Sepals* bright red, fully reflexed. *Corolla* almost pure white, with red veins. *Foliage* dark green, small. *Growth* self-branching, dwarf growth, very small flowers but very profuse. Suitable for use as a bonsai or miniature basket. 'Jingle Bells' seedling.

'Christmas Holly'
MRS A. STUBBS 1977
AFS Registration No 1411
Double
Tube red, thin, medium length. *Sepals* bright red, opening straight but turning up as the flower matures. *Corolla* deep purple streaked with crimson. Petaloids uneven deep purple. *Foliage* medium to small deep green leaves, holly-like, deeply serrated edges. *Growth* bushy, self-branching upright, which will trail if weights are used. Requires staking when grown as a bush.

'Christmas Ribbons'
FOSTER 1974
AFS Registration No 1170
Double
Tube rhodonite red, medium length and thickness. *Sepals* rhodonite red, short, medium width, curling upwards towards the tube. *Corolla* campanula violet with rhodonite red veining, small and fairly compact. *Stamens and pistil* rhodonite red. *Foliage* medium green, small to medium size. *Growth* upright, self-branching, will make a good bush or small standard. Best colour develops in the shade.

'Christopher Hammett'
HAMMETT 1966
Registered 1972
AFS Registration No 1025
Double
Tube scarlet, ½ in (13 mm) long. *Sepals* scarlet, reflexing, 2¼ in (57 mm) long. Filament and style scarlet. *Corolla* scarlet turning to purple. *Foliage* deep green, large — 3½ in (9 cm) long. *Growth* very vigorous upright, self-branching, suitable for a bush or standard.

'Christy'
ANTONELLI 1963
AFS Registration No 559
Double
Tube short, pink. *Sepals* pink, short and upturned. *Corolla* salmon pink mottled with white. Centre petals creamy white. *Foliage* dark green, stems reddish. *Growth* vigorous self-branching upright and bushy.

'Chrysanthea'
NIEDERHOLZER 1945
Double
Tube red. *Sepals* red. *Corolla* purple. *Foliage* medium to dark green. *Growth* basket, very large, loose blooms.

'Cicely Ann'
RON HOLMES 1977
AFS Registration No 1418
Single
Tube crimson RHS 52A, long and thin. *Sepals* crimson RHS 52A, on the outside, crimson inside, and with yellowish-green tips. Crepe appearance, upturned, medium length and width. *Corolla* mallow purple RHS 42A, crimson RHS 52A at the base, veined crimson with a fine crimson edging. The four petals of the corolla form a short semi-flared bell. *Foliage* medium to large, medium green, young stems are red, and there is some red veining on the leaves. *Growth* self-branching, natural trailer which will make a good basket; can also be trained as a bush but requires staking.

'Cinderella'
HAZARD
Single
Tube red. *Sepals* red. *Corolla* white. *Foliage* bronzy, small. *Flowers* small but quite vigorous. *Growth* upright and bushy.

'Circe'
KENNETT 1965
AFS Registration No 639
Semi-double
Tube pale pink. *Sepals* pale pink. *Corolla* light blue, fading to lavender, with pink petaloids opening and spreading almost flat. *Foliage* medium green. *Growth* self-branching upright, very prolific bloomer.

'Circus'
FUCHSIA FOREST (CASTRO) 1967
AFS Registration No 723
Single
Tube coral pink. *Sepals* coral pink. *Corolla* coral pink shading to bright magenta orange. *Foliage* medium green. *Growth* upright, self-branching, very vigorous and tall. Profuse bloomer.

'Citation' (129)
HODGES 1953
AFS Registration No 153
Single
Tube light pink to rose pink. *Sepals* light pink to rose pink. *Sepals* long and turned up against the tube. *Corolla* white, veined light pink at the base, flaring wide, saucer-shaped. *Growth* upright, vigorous, bushy. *Foliage* light to medium green. Prolific bloomer, but one which is not easy to grow. Tendency to leaf drop.

'City of Derby'
GADSBY 1978
AFS Registration No 1480
Single
Tube crimson, medium length and width. *Sepals* crimson, waxy and curved, showing a spiky effect. *Corolla* campanula violet on a lighter base, opening wide and giving a saucer effect. *Foliage* medium green, small and narrow. *Growth* self-branching bushy medium upright, will make a good bush. Best colour develops in the shade. Free-flowering.

'City of Millbrae'
GEORGE MARTIN 1958
AFS Registration No 365
Double
Tube rose pink, medium length and width. *Sepals* rose pink with green tips. *Corolla* orchid blue, pink at the base of the petals. Bloom opens rather square-shaped. *Foliage* medium green. *Growth* lax, will make a good basket.

'City of Pacifica'
REEDSTROM 1962
AFS Registration No 546
Double
Tube white. *Sepals* white. *Corolla* pale blue. *Foliage* medium green. *Growth* vigorous upright. Large blooms, free-flowering, will make a good bush if pinched early.

'City of Portland'
SCHNABEL 1950
AFS Registration No 51
Double
Tube carmine. *Sepals* carmine, broad. *Corolla* petunia purple, shaded light carmine. *Foliage* medium green, roundish. *Growth* vigorous self-branching upright, free-flowering, large blooms. Will make a good bush but may require staking.

'C.J. Howlett'
HOWLETT 1911
Single
Tube light scarlet, short. *Sepals* light scarlet, green tips, slightly upturned. *Corolla* pale cerise purple, pink at the base, slight carmine veining. *Foliage* medium green. *Growth* self-branching, upright and bushy, quite vigorous. *Flowers* smallish but very prolific. Will make a good bush plant either in a pot or in the garden.

'Clair de Lune' (188)
ROZAIN-BOUCHARLAT 1880
Single
Tube salmon pink. *Sepals* salmon pink. *Corolla* salmon orange. *Foliage* light to medium green. *Growth* upright, bushy.

'Claire Evans'
EVANS AND REEVES 1951
AFS Registration No 102
Double
Tube white. *Sepals* white on top, shell pink undersides. *Corolla* opens light blue, fading to rosy mauve. *Foliage* medium green. *Growth* bushy and compact upright.

'Clara'
BROWN AND SOULES 1952
Double
Tube rose pink. *Sepals* rose pink. *Corolla* blue to purple with short red veins at the base of each petal. *Foliage* medium green. *Growth* upright, bush, self-branching, will make a good bush.

'Clara-Beth'
GAGNON 1965
AFS Registration No 621
Double
Tube short, white. *Sepals* heavy white crepe effect, green tips, short and pointed. *Corolla* medium blue fading to lavender. *Foliage* medium light reddish shade, with red veins. *Growth* trailer.

'Claret Cup'
J.B. LAGEN 1940
Single
Tube creamy pink. *Sepals* creamy pink. *Corolla* deep Tyrian rose. *Foliage* medium green. *Growth* trailer, will make a good basket. *Parentage* 'Rolla' × 'Amy Lye'. A sister seedling to 'Cascade' and 'Hallowe'en'.

'Clarion'
REITER 1949
Tube crimson. *Sepals* crimson. *Corolla* rose bengal. *Foliage* medium green. *Growth* vigorous upright and bushy. Large blooms and free-flowering.

'Classy'
CASTRO 1973
AFS Registration No 1102
Double
Tube white, medium length and thickness. *Sepals* pure white, reflexed. *Corolla* opens deep red, changing to bright red as it matures, with white marbling, very full with petals curved inwards and outwards. *Stamens* pink. *Foliage* dark green with red veins. *Growth* vigorous and upright, will make a good pillar or pyramid. Very heavy bloomer, holding its colour well.

'Cleopatra'
MARTIN 1964
AFS Registration No 607
Double
Tube red. *Sepals* red. *Corolla* blue on opening, fading to lavender on maturity, very full, and flaring. *Foliage* medium green. *Growth* bushy but lax, better grown as a basket. Flowers very large, but profuse.

'Clevedon'
J.A. WRIGHT 1980
AFS Registration No 1598
Single

Tube pink, medium length and thickness. *Sepals* bright pink, arching back. *Corolla* lilac, with red veins, large. *Foliage* medium green, large. *Growth* upright, vigorous, self-branching. Bush or standard. 'Snowcap' seedling.

'Cliff's Hardy'
GADSBY 1971 (raised 1966)
AFS Registration No 983
Single
Tube crimson, thick. *Sepals* crimson with green tips. *Corolla* campanula violet, lighter at the base with scarlet veins. *Foliage* darkish green, small to medium size. *Growth* upright and bushy, very free-flowering. Flowers held upright, stand out well from the foliage. It will make a nice pot plant, but has been proved hardy in most areas.

'Cliff's Own'
GADSBY 1977
AFS Registration No 1425
Single
Tube white, medium length and thickness. *Sepals* waxy white with pale pink undersides, and green tips. *Corolla* hyacinth blue RHS 91A becoming a delicate pale violet. Flower small to medium. *Foliage* light green, small. *Growth* medium bushy upright and free-flowering.

'Cliff's Unique' (104)
GADSBY 1976
AFS Registration No 1392
Double
Tube light pink, short and thick. *Sepals* waxy white, with a pink flush and green tips. Short and broad, reflexing. *Corolla* gentian blue maturing to pale violet-pink. A very attractive, medium-sized bloom. *Foliage* medium green, medium-sized, serrated leaves. *Growth* upright, bushy, self-branching and free-flowering. Bush.

'Clifton Beauty'
MRS E. HANDLEY 1975
AFS Registration No 1272
Double
Tube white, thick and of medium length. *Sepals* creamy pink. *Corolla* rosy purple RHS 66B with crimson edges, outer petals streaked with salmon RHS 41C. *Foliage* medium green. *Growth* vigorous semi-trailer which will make a good pot plant if staked, and is equally at home in a basket. It will take full sun, which it requires for its best colour.

'Clifton Belle'
MRS E. HANDLEY 1974
AFS Registration No 1191
Double
Tube white, long and of medium thickness. *Sepals* white, tinged pink on the undersides, long and reflexed right back to the stem. *Corolla* brilliant magenta RHS 66A and RHS 67B, even length of petals. *Foliage* medium green. *Growth* upright and bushy. Colours best in the shade.

'Clipper'
JAMES LYE 1897
Single $3\frac{3}{4}$ in (9.5 cm)
Tube scarlet cerise. *Sepals* scarlet cerise, recurving. *Corolla* rich claret red. *Foliage* medium green. *Growth* upright, bushy and quite vigorous. It makes a good bush or standard.

'Close Call'
GORMAN 1970
AFS Registration No 926
Double
Tube bright red. *Sepals* bright red. *Corolla* dark bluish purple. *Foliage* dark green, medium-sized. *Growth* self-branching upright bush, which will trail with the use of weights.

'Cloth of Gold' (21)
STAFFORD 1863
Single
Tube red. *Sepals* red. *Corolla* purple. *Foliage* golden yellow, ageing to green and with a bronzy flush, undersides reddish. *Growth* upright and bushy, not a

very tall growing plant. Like many of these foliage cultivars, it is late to come into bloom and not very prolific. Sport of 'Souvenir De Chiswick' (BANKS 1855).

'Cloverdale'

GADSBY 1972
AFS Registration No 1050
Single
Tube short and thin, crimson. *Sepals* crimson. *Corolla* cornflower blue fading to cyclamen purple. Flowers are small and open. *Foliage* small, medium green. *Growth* upright but dwarf. The flowers are held horizontal, well out from the plant. Makes a neat, compact bush and is suitable for border edging or small pot exhibition classes. Free-flowering and long-lasting.

'Cloverdale Delight'

GADSBY 1977
AFS Registration No 1426
Semi-double
Tube pink, of medium length and width. *Sepals* soft pink, held back against the tube. *Corolla* wistaria blue RHS 92A, fading to violet, bell-shaped. *Foliage* medium green. *Growth* upright, self-branching and bushy. Will make a good bush, or can be trained as a cordon or pillar. Very easy to grow and train. *Parentage* 'Rosedale' × 'Forward Look'.

'Cloverdale Jewel'

GADSBY 1974
AFS Registration No 1218
Semi-double
Tube neyron rose RHS 55B, medium length and thickness. *Sepals* neyron rose, held well back to the tube. *Corolla* wisteria blue RHS 92B with rose pink veins, maturing to violet blue RHS 90D. Blooms of medium size. *Foliage* medium green, small. *Growth* upright, vigorous and bushy. Very floriferous, and blooms over a long period. Easy to grow. It will make a good bush plant, either in a pot or in the open garden as a summer bedder. Excellent 3½ in (9 cm) exhibition plant. *Parentage* 'Cloverdale' × 'Lady Isobel Barnett'.

'Cloverdale Joy'

GADSBY 1979
Registered by FUCHSIAVALE NURSERIES
AFS Registration No 1518
Single
Tube white. *Sepals* white with a tinge of pink, held well out. *Corolla* violet RHS 84A. *Foliage* medium green. *Growth* upright, vigorous, bushy. Strong-growing and floriferous over a long period. *Parentage* 'Cloverdale Pearl' × 'Christine Clements'.

'Cloverdale Pearl' (167)

GADSBY 1973
AFS Registration No 1219 (1974)
Single
Tube white, medium length and thickness. *Sepals* rhodamine pink RHS 62A, shading to white, green tips, held well out and curving back towards the tube. *Corolla* white, pink veins. *Foliage* small, darkish green. *Growth* upright self branching bush, easy to grow and shape. *Parentage* un-named seedling × 'Grace Darling'.

'Cloverdale Pride'

GADSBY/FUCHSIAVALE 1979
AFS Registration No 1519
Single
Tube pale pink, medium length and thickness. *Sepals* rose bengal RHS 61D, upturned and curving back. *Corolla* cyclamen RHS 74B. *Foliage* medium green. *Growth* self-branching, medium, upright. It will make a good bush plant. Best colour develops in the shade. *Parentage* seedling × 'Grace Darling'.

'Cloverdale Star'

GADSBY 1976
Single
Tube white. *Sepals* white, underside, flushed pink, held well back. *Corolla* wisteria blue RHS 92B on a lighter base. *Foliage* medium green. *Growth* self-branching medium upright which will make a good bush.

'Coachman' (190)
BRIGHT (date unknown)
Single
Tube salmon pink. *Sepals* salmon pink, slightly below horizontal. *Corolla* orange vermilion. *Foliage* light green, of good size. *Growth* self-branching medium upright which can also be trained into a basket. Very free-flowering and easy to grow.

'Cocky'
NIEDERHOLZER 1946
Single
Tube dark geranium lake. *Sepals* dark geranium lake. *Corolla* petunia purple. *Foliage* medium green to dark green. *Growth* upright self-branching bush. Smallish blooms but free-flowering.

'Coconut Ice'
D. BURNS 1978
AFS Registration No 1513
Single
Tube white, medium length and thickness. *Sepals* rose RHS 56B outside, RHS 56D, inside, reflexed. *Corolla* rose pink RHS 56D veined RHS 55C. *Foliage* smallish mid-green RHS 147A. *Growth* bushy, self-branching medium upright. It will make a very good bush and responds well to pinching. Normally has three leaves at each node. *Parentage* 'Iced Champagne' × 'Cloverdale Pearl'.

'Coed'
ERICKSON 1962
AFS Registration No 539
Double
Tube white, long. *Sepals* white, broad and spreading out well. *Corolla* smoky rose with orange undertone, white marbling on some of the petals. *Foliage* medium green. *Growth* not very vigorous, inclined to be lax and can best be used as a basket plant.

'Colleen'
SOO YUN 1970
AFS Registration No 911
Double
Tube pale greenish white. *Sepals* light green with darker green tips. *Corolla* orchid, medium size. *Foliage* medium green. *Growth* upright, self-branching, bushy.

'Collingwood' (40)
NIEDERHOLZER 1945
Double
Tube pale pink, medium length and thickness. *Sepals* pale pink, slightly upturned. *Corolla* pure white, full. *Foliage* medium green. *Growth* self-branching, bushy upright. Makes a very good pot plant, and also does well as a summer bedder.

'Colombine'
REITER 1949
Double
Tube white. *Sepals* white. *Corolla* rhodamine purple, flaring. *Foliage* medium green. *Growth* medium bushy upright, self-branching.

'Come Dancing'
MRS E. HANDLEY 1972
AFS Registration No 1052
Double
Tube deep pink RHS 55A, short and thick. *Sepals* deep pink, long and broad, greenish yellow tips. *Corolla* magenta-rose RHS 57C, salmon rose at the base. *Foliage* bright green, leaves rounded and crinkled. *Growth* vigorous, self-branching spreading bush which will make a good basket using weights, and can also make a nice bush. Large flowers, and blooms over a long period.

'Comet'
BANKS 1862
Single
Tube red. *Sepals* large, bright red, reflexed. *Corolla* violet-blue, bell shaped when first open then opening up to become almost horizontal, measuring up $1\frac{3}{4}$ in (4.5 cm) across. *Foliage* medium green. *Growth* vigorous upright self-branching bush which flowers early and continues throughout the summer. Described by Porcher as one of the finest introductions of the period.

'Comet'
TIRET 1963
AFS Registration No 579
Double
Tube red. *Sepals* red. *Corolla* purplish blue. *Foliage* medium to dark green. *Growth* upright, bushy.

'Commander in Chief'
REITER 1942
Double
Tube carmine red. *Sepals* carmine red. *Corolla* purple. *Foliage* medium green. *Growth* arching stems, long jointed. Sister seedling of 'Reiter's Giant'.

'Companion'
PALKO/SOO YUN 1978
AFS Registration No 1443
Double
Tube rose bengal, long and thin. *Sepals* rose bengal, medium length, slight downward curve. *Corolla* marshmallow white with spiraea red stripe. *Foliage* olive green, medium-sized. Stems are reddish brown on top and light green on the underside. *Growth* tall, vigorous upright which will make a good standard. Heavy bloomer which prefers heat for best results.

'Conchilla'
NIEDERHOLZER 1941
Single to semi-double
Tube short, pink. *Sepals* pale pink. *Corolla* amethyst violet changing to rhodamine purple. *Foliage* medium green. *Growth* vigorous, upright bushy which makes rapid, sturdy growth.

'Confetti'
MARTIN 1965
AFS Registration No 629
Semi-double to double
Tube short, pink. *Sepals* pink. *Corolla* centre petals bright violet blue, outer petals shorter, and shades of red, pink and white. Many petaloids. *Foliage* medium green. *Growth* medium upright bushy, profuse bloomer.

'Coniston Water'
TRAVIS 1959
Registered 1973
AFS Registration 1139
Single
Tube soft rose pink, thick and of medium length. *Sepals* soft rose pink, very long, lanceolate and recurving. *Corolla* deep lavender blue, large, stiff, cone-shaped. *Foliage* deep green, medium size, ovate. *Growth* self-branching, vigorous upright which will make a good bush or standard, and can also be trained to a pillar etc. Large blooms, free-flowering and will take full sun although the best colour develops in the shade.

'Connie'
DAWSON 1961
Double
Tube cerise red. *Sepals* cerise red, broad, hang down over corolla. *Corolla* white with deep pink veining, petals folded. *Foliage* medium green, slightly serrated. *Growth* upright, vigorous and tall growing, self-branching.

'Conspicua'
SMITH 1863
Single
Tube crimson. *Sepals* crimson, recurving back almost against the tube. *Corolla* white with cerise veins. *Foliage* dark green. *Growth* vigorous upright, very free-flowering and equally at home in a pot in the greenhouse or bedded out in the garden where it is hardy in sheltered areas. Described by Porcher as one of the most beautiful single-flowered fuchsias.

'Constance'
BERKELY HORT NURSERIES 1935
Double
Tube pale pink. *Sepals* pale pink with green tips. Deeper pink undersides. *Corolla* rosy-mauve with pink tints at the base of the petals. *Foliage* medium green. *Growth* free-flowering, bushy upright which will make an excellent bush or standard, or is almost trainable to any shape except basket. Easy to grow. *Parentage* 'Pink Pearl' ×.

'Constellation'
SCHNABEL 1957
AFS Registration No 289
Double
Tube white, medium length, thin. *Sepals* white with green tips, upturned slightly. *Corolla* creamy white. *Foliage* darkish green serrated. *Growth* upright, free-flowering and bushy. It will make a very good exhibition plant if pinched at an early stage. Prefers shaded conditions if the true white colour is to be retained. Like many of the white cultivars it is subject to *Botrytis* if extreme care is not taken.

'Contessa'
MRS E. HANDLEY 1972
AFS Registration No 1053
Double
Tube pale green, short and medium thick. *Sepals* white, thick and reflexed back to the stem. *Corolla* orchid rose RHS 67C, flecked white and pink, very full. *Foliage* mid-green. *Growth* vigorous upright bush. Will make a good bush plant. Large, free-flowering.

'Coos Bay'
PRENTICE 1971
AFS Registration No 989
Double
Tube short, dark red. *Sepals* dark red. *Corolla* deep blue fading to rosy purple. Petals have a nice folded look. Very large blooms, but quite free-flowering. *Foliage* medium green. *Growth* bushy upright or trailer. Best as a basket plant as the weight of the blooms makes it difficult to grow upright unless well staked.

'Coos Bay Pirate'
VEE JAY 1979
AFS Registration No 1510
Single
Tube rose, short, medium thickness. *Sepals* dark rose with green tips, wide, flaring up towards the stem on maturity. *Corolla* purple, fading to violet-red, flaring up to saucer shape. Some of the petals twist giving it an unusual appearance. *Foliage* medium green. *Growth* a natural basket plant which will trail without the use of weights. Sport of 'Nonpareil'.

'Coos Cutie'
GAGNON 1963
AFS Registration No 556
Double
Tube pink, medium length and thickness. *Sepals* pink and white, with green tips. *Corolla* white in the centre, outer petals pink and white. *Foliage* medium green with a nice texture. *Growth* natural trailer which makes an excellent basket. Prolific bloomer, flowering continuously throughout the summer.

'Coppelia'
JOHN BLACKWELL 1964
Single
Tube reddish pink. *Sepals* reddish pink. *Corolla* purple, ageing to plum purple. Pale green foliage. *Growth* lax bush, or can be grown as a trailer.

'Coquet Bell' (101)
RYLE 1973
AFS Registration No 1114
Single
Tube deep rose madder, medium length and thickness. *Sepals* deep rose madder with green tips, longish. *Corolla* pale mauve flushed rose-mauve at the base with distinctive red veins, bell shape with slightly waved edges which fade on maturity. *Stamens* pale red, pistil pale pink. *Foliage* medium green, longish with serrated edges. *Growth* self-branching, bushy upright, vigorous and free-flowering. It makes a good exhibition bush plant. *Parentage* 'Lena Dalton' × 'Citation'.

'Coquet Dale' (98)
RYLE 1976
AFS Registration No 1397
Double
Tube pinkish white, short. *Sepals* neyron rose RHS 55B, short and broad, held well up. *Corolla* lilac RHS 76A with a few

petaloids, slightly flared. *Foliage* medium green. *Growth* vigorous self-branching upright and bushy. *Parentage* 'Joe Kusber' × 'Northumbrian Belle'.

'Coquet Gold'
RYLE 1976
AFS Registration No 1398
Single
Tube pinkish white. *Sepals* white with pink flush on top, pink undersides, held horizontally. *Corolla* violet purple RHS 77B, opens square and matures to a bell shape. *Foliage* lettuce green RHS 144A with some leaves citron-green RHS 151A and most with yellow edges. *Growth* self-branching upright bush which can be trained as a basket also, with the use of weights. Prefers unshaded conditions for the foliage to be seen at its best. Sport from 'Belsay Beauty'.

'Coquette'
NIEDERHOLZER 1943
Single
Tube white, short, medium thickness. *Sepals* red, slightly upturned. *Corolla* purple. *Foliage* medium green. *Growth* basket type, small flowers, bushy.

'Cora-Belle'
GAGNON 1965
AFS Registration No 623
Double
Tube long, white. *Sepals* long, white, tipped chartreuse. *Corolla* blue turning to orchid, white at the base. *Foliage* light green, largish. *Growth* natural trailer, very heavy bloomer. Makes a good basket.

'Cora Brandt'
NIEDERHOLZER 1941
Single
Tube crimson, thick and short. *Sepals* crimson short and spreading. *Corolla* rose madder tinged with geranium lake, flaring. *Foliage* medium green. *Growth* vigorous, self-branching, upright and bushy. Free-flowering, large blooms. *Parentage* 'Aviator' × 'Sunset' × 'Libuse'.

'Cora Elsey'
COPLEY GARDENS 1967
AFS Registration No 743
Semi-double
Tube short, pink. *Sepals* pink, upturned. *Corolla* blush pink with darker pink veining, bell-shaped. *Foliage* medium green, medium size. *Growth* vigorous upright, will trail with heavy pinching and the use of weights.

'Coralle'
Correctly named 'Koralle' (q.v.).

'Corallina'
PINCE 1843
Single
Tube carmine. *Sepals* carmine, drooping. *Corolla* purple, pink at the base of the petals. *Foliage* darkish green, medium length. *Growth* vigorous spreading bush, rather lax and hardy in sheltered areas. Inclined to spread rather than grow upwards and needs some early staking. *Parentage F. cordifolia* × 'Globosa'.

'Coral Seas'
GEORGE MARTIN 1966
AFS Registration No 672
Single
Tube salmon. *Sepals* salmon to orange. *Corolla* burnt orange. *Foliage* medium green. *Growth* natural trailer, free-flowering.

'Core'ngrato'
JOHN BLACKWELL 1964
Double
Tube pale coral pink, long. *Sepals* pale coral outside, frosty salmon pink inside. *Corolla* opens burgundy purple, changing to salmon burgundy with salmon pink splashes. *Foliage* medium green. *Growth* vigorous upright, self-branching. Makes a good pot plant, free-flowering.

'Coronation'
TIRET 1953
AFS Registration No 154
Double

Tube short, white, waxy. *Sepals* long and narrow, waxy white on top, pinkish below. *Corolla* rosy-raspberry, wide and spreading. *Foliage* medium green. *Growth* tall vigorous upright, free-flowering.

'Corpus Christie'
WALKER AND JONES 1953
Double
Tube rose red. *Sepals* rose red, turned up. *Corolla* soft lilac lavender overlaid with flesh pink petals at the base. *Foliage* medium green. *Growth* bushy, free-flowering upright.

'Corsage'
MR A. STUBBS 1979
AFS Registration No 1500
Double
Tube ivory pink, medium length and thickness. *Sepals* ivory pink to pale salmon outside, salmon on the inside, short, medium width, standing straight out until fully mature then going straight up against the tube. *Corolla* short but very full, orange coral, rosette-like with 30 or more petals. *Foliage* medium green with red stems on new growth. *Growth* is semi-trailer, or lax bush type. Will make a good basket with the use of weights. Prefers heat to obtain the best colour.

'Corsair'
KENNETT 1965
AFS Registration No 640
Double
Tube white. *Sepals* white. *Corolla* opens sky blue, fading to light purple on maturity. Centre petals are white and other petals white at the base. Outer petals white with purple marbling, a very striking colour contrast. *Foliage* darkish green with red vein through the centre. *Growth* upright but tends to be rather lax. Makes a beautiful exhibition plant if well pinched from an early stage.

'Cosmopolitan'
FUCHSIA FOREST/CASTRO 1960
AFS Registration No 426
Double
Tube pink. *Sepals* deep rose pink, broad and completely recurved. *Corolla* white with pale pink flush, veined and splashed rose pink towards the base. *Foliage* medium green. *Growth* lax, best suited to a basket but will make a pleasing bush if staked and pinched well.

'Cotton Candy' (34)
TIRET 1962
AFS Registration No 529
Double
Tube white with pink veins. *Sepals* white on top, pink underneath, green tips, recurving and curling towards the tube. *Corolla* pale pink with cerise veining, full and fluffy. *Foliage* dark to medium green. *Growth* upright, bushy and vigorous. A beautiful flower, easy to grow and shape.

'Countess of Aberdeen'
DOBBIE FORBES 1888
Single
Tube creamy white, short. *Sepals* white, upturning slightly. *Corolla* white, small. *Foliage* medium green, smallish. *Growth* upright, bush and self-branching. Best grown in the shade otherwise the whole flower takes on a pink tint. Makes an excellent exhibition variety, but not one of the easiest to grow, being subject to *Botrytis* if kept on the damp side.

'Country Cousin'
HODGES 1952
AFS Registration No 125
Semi-double
Tube short, deep red. *Sepals* deep red, upturned. *Corolla* violet purple, almost white at the centre, spreading saucer-shaped. *Foliage* medium green. *Growth* free-flowering, medium upright bush.

'Country Girl'
TOLLEY/FUCHSIAVALE 1979
AFS Registration No 1521
Single
Tube flesh pink, of medium length and thickness. *Sepals* flesh pink, longish and

thin, twisting. *Corolla* rose bengal, rolled effect. *Stamens and pistil* rose bengal. *Foliage* light green, medium to large, longish. *Growth* vigorous, short-jointed upright bush. Will make a good bush or standard.

'County Fair'
HUBBARD 1967
AFS Registration No 703
Double
Tube red. *Sepals* red. *Corolla* white, very small flower. *Foliage* light green, small. *Growth* self-branching trailer. Needs no pinching.

'Court Jester' (151)
FUCHSIA FOREST/CASTRO 1960
AFS Registration No 427
Double
Tube rose red, short. *Sepals* rose red, crepe effect. *Corolla* royal purple with pink-coral petals overlaying the centre. *Foliage* medium green. *Growth* vigorous upright bushy, very free-flowering and easy to grow and shape.

'Cover Girl'
HAAG AND SON 1953
Semi-double
Tube bright red. *Sepals* bright red. *Corolla* rich blue, with white at the base of the petals. *Foliage* medium green. *Growth* vigorous tall growing upright.

'Coxeen'
1936
Single
Tube reddish pink. *Sepals* white with green tips. *Corolla* bluish pink, white at the base. *Foliage* medium green. *Growth* natural trailer, bushy growth, very floriferous.

'Coza'
CARLSON 1971
AFS Registration No 941
Double
Tube white, tinged pink. *Sepals* white with a pink tinge underneath, crepe-like texture, wide, tapered and upturning. *Corolla* rosy violet. *Foliage* light green, long and oval-shaped. *Growth* natural trailer.

'Crackerjack'
FUCHSIA-LA NURSERIES 1961
Single
Tube white. *Sepals* white with pink flush, completely recurved round the tube. *Corolla* pale mauve-blue, white at the base, with pink veins. *Foliage* light green with crimson vein, large leaves. *Growth* natural cascade, very vigorous, self-branching and free-flowering. An excellent basket variety.

'Crater Lake Blue'
PRENTICE 1970
AFS Registration No 883
Single
Tube white, short, with pink shading. *Sepals* white with green tips, pink blush on top and underside. *Corolla* Crater Lake blue. *Foliage* medium green, small. *Blooms* star-shaped, growing the full length of the branches. *Growth* vigorous bushy upright or can be made to trail with weights.

'Cream Puff' ('Creampuff')
KENNETT 1960
AFS Registration No 428
Double
Tube long and slender, slightly curved, pale pink. *Sepals* pale pink becoming white at the tips. *Corolla* creamy white with delicate pink overlay on the outer folded petals, large and frilled. *Blooms* large and borne on long pedicels. *Foliage* medium green and medium-sized. *Growth* natural trailer, fine stemmed, free-flowering.

'Creole'
SCHNABEL 1949
Semi-double
Tube bright red. *Sepals* bright red. *Corolla* ox-blood red and maroon. *Foliage* medium green. *Growth* natural trailer, short-stemmed.

'Crescendo'
REITER 1942
Double
Tube turkey red. *Sepals* turkey red. *Corolla* peony purple and turkey red, margins turkey red. *Foliage* medium to darkish green. *Growth* vigorous, bushy upright, good bloomer. *Parentage* 'Mme Danjoux' × 'Mrs Victor Reiter'.

'Crinoline' (35)
REITER SR 1950
AFS Registration No 58
Double
Tube rosy white tipped green. *Sepals* rosy white tipped green. *Corolla* clear pale rose pink. *Foliage* medium green. *Growth* upright, bushy, tends to make very heavy wood. AFS Certificate of Merit.

'Crown Derby'
GADSBY 1970
AFS Registration No 962 (1972)
Double
Tube waxy crimson. *Sepals* waxy crimson. *Corolla* centre petals are white with the outer petaloids crimson. *Foliage* medium green. *Growth* medium upright bush, very floriferous over a long period.

'Crown Jewel'
SCHMIDT 1953
AFS Registration No 151
Double
Tube flesh pink. *Sepals* white with faint pink blush, long and broad. *Corolla* glowing rose, ruffled and spreading. *Foliage* medium green. *Growth* vigorous, tall willowy upright.

'Crusader'
TIRET 1967
AFS Registration No 733
Double
Tube frosty white. *Sepals* frosty white. *Corolla* deep purple. *Foliage* medium green. *Growth* natural trailer, good bloomer, makes a nice basket.

'Crystal Blue'
KENNETT 1962
AFS Registration No 537
Single to semi-double
Tube greenish white. *Sepals* white with green tips, recurving right back against the tube. *Corolla* violet blue, white at the base of the petals. *Foliage* medium green, medium size. *Growth* upright, self-branching but benefits from some judicious pinching, very free-flowering. One of the best of the blue and white cultivars. Easy to grow. Bush.

'Crystal Stars'
MRS IVY CLYNE 1974
AFS Registration No 1362
Semi-double
Tube short, thick, greenish white, flushed red. *Sepals* white, reflexed. *Corolla* white. *Foliage* medium to small spinach-green leaves, ovoid. *Growth* self-branching, upright and bushy. BFS Silver Certificate 1975. Bush. *Parentage* 'Ting a Ling' × ('La Campanella' × 'Flirtation Waltz').

'C. T. Lehew'
KENNETT 1965
AFS Registration No 653
First introduced in 1953
Semi-double
Tube white. *Sepals* white to pale pink. *Corolla* violet blue. *Foliage* medium green. *Growth* self-branching, upright bush which will make a basket if weighted.

'Cunning'
VERNON BRAND 1956
Double
Tube rose pink. *Sepals* rose pink. *Corolla* pale orchid, with petals scalloped and edged with a deeper shade of orchid. *Foliage* medium green. *Growth* vigorous upright and bushy. Very free-flowering. Bush.

'Cupertino'
SHAW 1972
AFS Registration No 1033
Single
Tube white, long and thin with a tinge of pink. *Sepals* white with pale green tips, medium length and thickness, held slightly below the horizontal. *Corolla*

reddish with mauve overtones, tight petals, bell-shaped. *Foliage* light to medium green, medium size. *Growth* self-branching, lax habit but will make a good bush if pinched hard. Smallish to medium size flowers. Will stand the sun, but the best colour develops in shaded conditions. Resembles its parent, 'Checkerboard', except in its habit of growth.

'Cupid'
W.P. WOOD 1946
Single
Tube pale scarlet cerise. *Sepals* pale scarlet cerise. *Corolla* pale bluish-magenta. *Foliage* medium to darkish green. *Growth* self-branching, vigorous upright bush.

'Curlew'
EVANS AND REEVES 1951
AFS Registration No 104
Double
Tube white. *Sepals* white, with pink flush, long. *Corolla* white, medium size. *Foliage* medium green. *Growth* semi-trailer. Will make a good wall basket.

'Curly Locks'
HAZARD AND HAZARD
Single
Tube deep pink. *Sepals* deep pink. *Corolla* purple. *Foliage* smallish, medium green. *Growth* dwarf, upright. Small flowers.

'Curly Q'
KENNETT 1961
AFS Registration No 474
Single
Tube whitish carmine. *Sepals* pale carmine, reflexing or curling back against the tube. *Corolla* violet-purple, four rolled petals. *Foliage* small, medium green with dark purple stems. *Growth* self-branching, lax trailer, which can also be trained to a bush with careful pinching. Free-flowering, very unusual and attractive bloom.

'Curly Wurly'
NIEDERHOLZER 1941
Tube turkey red. *Sepals* turkey red, longish and curled. *Corolla* dark violet purple with red streaks and lighter colour at the base of the petals. *Foliage* medium green, medium size. *Growth* vigorous, shrubby upright. Makes a good bush. *Parentage* '1915' × 'Aviator'.

'Curtain Call' (91)
MUNKNER 1961
AFS Registration No 479
Double
Tube pale carmine to white. *Sepals* pale carmine to white. *Sepals* white, flushed pink on the underside, reflexing. *Corolla* rosy cerise, white at the base of the petals, serrated. *Foliage* medium green, medium-sized. *Growth* trailer, very lax, but will make a bush or upright plant if staked. Very free-flowering, producing four blooms from each pair of leaf axils instead of the normal two.

'Cutie'
NIEDERHOLZER-WALTZ
Single
Tube thick, white. *Sepals* broad, small, white. *Corolla* deep purple. *Foliage* small, medium green. *Growth* dwarf, upright, bushy. Very small flowers, but profuse. Bush.

'Cymru'
ALF THORNLEY 1966
Double
Tube short wild silk. *Sepals* ivory-white, reflexed and broad. *Corolla* shell pink, very compact with long narrow cylindrical petals. *Foliage* medium green. *Growth* upright, bushy. Bush. *Parentage* 'Nightingale' ×.

'Dainty'
Date of introduction and raiser unknown
Single
Tube cerise. *Sepals* cerise. *Corolla* bluish-mauve, flaring. *Foliage* medium green. *Growth* upright, bushy. Bush.

'Dainty Damosel'
SCHNABEL 1953
AFS Registration No 187
Semi-double

Tube waxy pink, short. *Sepals* clear white, short and sturdy. *Corolla* deep cobalt violet, fading to mallow purple. *Foliage* medium green. *Growth* upright, self-branching and bushy. Bush.

'Dainty Dinah'
DYE 1974
AFS Registration No 1164
Single
Tube creamy pink, medium length and thickness. *Sepals* white, flushed pink, slightly upturned. *Corolla* creamy pink shading to cyclamen pink towards the edges of the petals, veined deep orange, conical open shape with rounded petals. *Stamens and pistil* cyclamen pink. *Foliage* mid-green, leaves long and pointed, crinkled form, serrated edges. *Growth* upright, self-branching, will make a good bush or standard. Very free-flowering, blooms medium-sized. Best colour produced in the shade. Bush or standard.

'Dainty Lady'
LOWE (date unknown)
Semi-double
Tube cerise, medium length and thickness. *Sepals* cerise, recurving completely against the tube. *Corolla* white, veined cerise. *Foliage* darkish green. *Growth* upright, self-branching, bush. Will make a good summer bedder. Bush.

'Daisy Bell' (184)
Raiser unknown, introduced by MIESCKE 1977
AFS Registration No 1420
Single
Tube white, long, with an orange cast, shading to green at the base. *Sepals* pale orange, shading to apple green at the tips. Held straight out at right angles to the tube. *Corolla* vermilion, shading to orange at the base of the petals. *Stamens and pistil* pink. *Anthers and stigma* cream. *Foliage* medium green on top, lighter underneath, smallish in size, with reddish main vein and petiole. New growth is light green, darkening with age. *Growth* natural trailer which makes a good basket, and an excellent half-basket. Develops its best colour in the sun. Vigorous self-branching and very free-flowering cultivar.

'Dalliance'
Raised by LEHDER? (date unknown)
Single
Tube waxy rose. *Sepals* waxy rose, deeper shade underneath. *Corolla* rosy-cerise. *Foliage* medium green. *Growth* upright, free-flowering and self-branching. Will make a good low growing bush plant, and does well as a summer bedder.

'Dalton'
ALF THORNLEY 1971
AFS Registration No 1008
Single
Tube flesh pink RHS 49C and D, sepals have green tips. *Corolla* described by the raiser as soft pink (Venetian pink RHS 74D). *Foliage* medium green. *Growth* upright, self-branching, compact and bushy. Will make a good exhibition plant, and also does well as a summer bedder. *Parentage* 'Hawkshead' × 'Other Fellow'.

'Dandy Lady'
PENNISI 1969
AFS Registration No 861
Tube short, pink. *Sepals* pink, medium length and thickness. *Corolla* white, with petaloids around the base. *Foliage* medium green, medium size. *Growth* natural trailer with large blooms which will make a nice half-basket.

'Daniel Lambert'
LEE 1857
Single $3\frac{1}{2}$ in (9 cm)
Tube short, sepals recurving completely on maturity — light cerise. *Corolla* bluish pink, paler at the base of the petals. Medium size. *Foliage* light green. Vigorous and free-flowering. Bush or standard. Hardy.

'Danish Pastry'
FUCHSIA FOREST 1968
AFS Registration No 771

Single
Tube coral pink. *Sepals* coral pink with green tips. *Corolla* salmon red to lavender shading, large blooms. *Foliage* medium green, medium size. *Growth* rather lax growing. Will make a nice bush if staked and well pinched, but better as a half-basket.

'Danny Boy'
TIRET 1961
AFS Registration No 483
Double
Tube pale reddish. *Sepals* pale reddish. *Corolla* red, very large size. *Foliage* medium green, largish. *Growth* upright, self-branching, bushy, but requires staking and hard pinching to keep upright due to the weight of the blooms.

'Daphne Arlene'
PUTLEY 1979
Single
Tube waxy white, tinged pink. *Sepals* waxy white, tinged pink. *Corolla* coral pink. *Flowers* small, very free-flowering. *Foliage* small, medium to dark green. Sport from 'Countess of Aberdeen', and identical to 'Shuna' (q.v.).

'Dariway'
ADKINS 1980
Introduced 1965
AFS Registration No 1551
Single
Tube pale pink, short and of medium thickness. *Sepals* pale pink, held slightly below horizontal. *Corolla* mauve, pink at the base, small. *Foliage* dark green, medium size, new stems reddish. *Growth* medium, self-branching upright, which will make a small bush.

'Dark Eyes'
ERICKSON 1958
AFS Registration No 351
Tube deep red. *Sepals* deep red, slightly upturned. *Corolla* deep violet blue. *Foliage* medium to darkish green. *Growth* upright, free-flowering, bushy.

'Dark Night'
CROCKETT 1967
AFS Registration No 823
Double
Tube currant red RHS 46A. *Sepals* currant red RHS 46A. *Corolla* spectrum violet RHS 82A, heavily flushed with cherry RHS 45C. *Foliage* small, dark green. *Growth* upright, very free-flowering, self-branching, very large bloom. Will make a good garden hardy in sheltered areas. Bush or standard.

'Dark Secret'
HODGES 1957
AFS Registration No 300
Double
Tube greenish white, short. *Sepals* waxy white on the upper side, pinkish on the undersides, crepe textured, slightly upturned. *Foliage* green, medium size. *Corolla* deep violet purple, splashed phlox pink. *Growth* upright, self-branching, bushy growth. Bush or standard.

'Darlene'
SCOTT 1952
Semi-double
Tube white, long. *Sepals* white, flushed pink. *Corolla* purple, white at the base and fading to orchid on maturity. *Foliage* medium green. *Growth* upright, self-branching, free-flowering, makes a good bush. Bush or standard.

'David'
W.P. WOOD 1949
Single
Tube cerise. *Sepals* cerise. *Corolla* rich, purple. *Foliage* medium to darkish green, slightly larger than 'Pumila'. *Growth* low growing, bushy and free-flowering—dwarf. Will make a good summer bedder. Bush. *Parentage* 'Pumila' × seedling.

'David Alston' (133)
FORBES 1906
Double
Tube crimson, medium length and thickness. *Sepals* crimson, crepe effect on the underside, broad and turned up almost to the tube. *Corolla* white, veined carmine

and with carmine flushing near the base of the petals. Very full, large blooms. *Filaments* medium green, broad and very slightly serrated. *Growth* upright but rather lax, bushy and free-flowering. Will require staking to support the weight of the blooms, but is a very striking colour and showy plant. Bush.

'David Lockyer'
MRS E. HOLMES 1968
Double
Tube white, medium length and thickness. *Sepals* white on top, white with pink flush on the undersides, green tips. Semi-reflexing. *Corolla* bright crimson red with some of the petals splashed and striped with white. Unusual shape with long petals in the centre, surrounded by folds of shorter petals. *Filaments* red. *Style* white. *Foliage* medium green, large leaves. *Growth* very vigorous, bushy, self-branching upright. Very striking colour combination. Bush.

'David Perry' (162)
RON HOLMES 1976
Single
Tube crimson, short and medium thickness. *Sepals* crimson, held horizontal. *Corolla* magenta, veined crimson, pink at the base of the petals and deep magenta on the edges. Small bell-shaped. *Filaments and style* crimson. *Foliage* dark green wtih crimson veins, slight serrations. *Growth* upright, bushy, self-branching and vigorous. Very free-flowering. Bush.

'Dawn'
BAKER 1970
Single
Tube white with pink flush, long and rather thin. *Sepals* white with green tips, medium length, held downwards from the horizontal. *Corolla* pale lavender blue, with paler shade of lavender at the base of the petals, remaining compact. *Style* white, filaments pale pink. *Foliage* upright, vigorous, bushy and free-flowering, easy to grow. Bush.

'Dawn Sky'
CROCKETT 1967
Double
Tube neyron rose, RHS 55B, thick and of medium length. *Sepals* dark rose pink on top, paler rose on the undersides and with pale pink tips. Broad, very slightly upturned at the tips. *Corolla* heliotrope, with neyron rose RHS 55B at the base of the petals, fading to petunia purple with age. Pink veining on the petals. Very full and fluffy double bloom. *Style and filaments* pink. *Foliage* medium green, large leaves. *Growth* vigorous, upright, bushy and free-flowering. Bush or standard.

'Dawn Thunder'
STUBBS 1975
AFS Registration No 1257
Double
Tube flesh pink, thin and of medium length. *Sepals* pink, long and broad, slightly upturned. *Corolla* various shades of purple and pink, fading to coral and rose. Very large bloom with serrated petals. *Foliage* dark green, leaves medium to large sized. *Growth* semi-trailer, rather lax habit, vigorous and free-flowering. Basket or can be trained as bush if pinched early and staked.

'Day by Day'
WAGTAILS NURSERY 1971
Single
Tube scarlet, short and of medium thickness. *Sepals* scarlet, slightly paler at the tips which turn up. *Corolla* reddish purple, small and neatly shaped. *Filaments and style* pink. *Foliage* cream, green and cerise variegated, medium-sized leaves. *Growth* upright, vigorous and bushy. Sport of 'Emile Zola'.

'Day Dream'
BROWN AND SOULES 1952
AFS Registration No 133
Semi-double
Tube rose pink, thin, and of medium length. *Sepals* pink, slightly reflexed. *Corolla* light blue with white mottling and some petals of pink and white. *Foliage*

medium green, slightly serrated. *Growth* upright, bushy, vigorous, self-branching and free-flowering. Bush.

'Deane le Baron'

TIRET 1969
AFS Registration No 828
Double
Tube rose pink, medium length and thickness. *Sepals* rose pink, slightly paler on the undersides, upturned at the tips. *Corolla* violet purple, full and compact. *Foliage* medium green, medium to large leaves. *Growth* trailer, bushy, vigorous, free-flowering. Basket.

'Debbie "C"'

COPLEY 1966
AFS Registration No 693
Semi-double to double
Tube bright rose red, medium length and thickness. *Sepals* rose red, long and slightly upturned. *Corolla* pink with red veining. Bell-shaped, rather loose. *Foliage* medium green, small leaves. *Growth* trailer, vigorous, free-flowering, and early. Basket or bush if carefully pinched in its early stages.

'Debby'

NESSIER 1952
AFS Registration No 117
Double
Tube rose bengal, medium length and thickness. *Sepals* rose bengal, wide and recurving. *Corolla* heliotrope blue, fading to cobalt violet, full. *Foliage* medium green, medium-sized, upright, and free-flowering. Needs careful pinching to shape. Bush.

'Deben Rose'

DUNNETT 1979
AFS Registration No 1516
Single
Tube azalea pink RHS 38B, medium length and thickness. *Sepals* spinel red RHS 54C, green tips, recurving slightly, long and slender. *Corolla* mallow purple RHS 72C, petals edged spinel red RHS 54A. *Stamens and pistil* red. *Foliage* medium green RHS 137A. *Growth* vigorous, self-branching, bushy trailer which can be pinched to train it to most other shapes. Free-flowering. Bush or basket. *Parentage* 'La Campanella' × 'Shady Lady'.

'Debonair'

KENNETT 1964
AFS Registration No 611
Double
Tube pale pink, medium length and thickness. *Sepals* pale pink, broad and green tips. *Corolla* various shades of lilac and rose pink. *Foliage* medium green, small to medium size, serrated. *Growth* vigorous, upright, free-flowering and self-branching. Bush or can be trained to a basket.

'Debono's Pride'

DEBONO 1980
AFS Registration No 1535
Double
Tube ivory white, overlaid and veined pink, short and thin. *Sepals* pink on the upper side, shading to white at the tips. Pink on the underside with green (RHS 150A) tips, flaring. *Corolla* reddish purple RHS 72A at the outer edges of the petals fading to rose bengal RHS 61D at the base. Four small petaloids of the same colour. *Stamens* crimson. *Pistil* long, pink. *Foliage* dark green, small, serrated edges. *Growth* upright, bushy, self-branching and very free-flowering. Bush or standard.

'Deborah'

TIRET 1970
AFS Registration No 897
Double
Tube white with pale pink flush. *Sepals* white, flushed rose pink. *Corolla* orange red, full and fluffy. *Foliage* medium green, medium to large-sized leaves. *Growth* trailer, vigorous, bushy, free-flowering. Basket.

'Debutante'

SCHNABEL 1949
Double

Tube pink, medium length and thickness. *Sepals* pink, long and slightly upturned. *Corolla* pink, medium size, full. *Foliage* medium green, medium-sized leaves. *Growth* low growing, bushy, self-branching and free-flowering. Low bush.

'Dee Copley'
COPLEY GARDENS 1964
AFS Registration No 617
Double
Tube bright red, medium length and thickness. *Sepals* bright red, broad and upturned. *Corolla* deep purple, mottled red at the base of the petals. Very large bloom of unusual shade. *Foliage* deep green, medium to large size. *Growth* very vigorous, upright, self-branching and free-flowering. Bush standard pyramid.

'Dee Dee'
WALKER 1974
AFS Registration No 1179
Double
Tube white, medium length and thickness. *Sepals* white, long and recurved, medium length, green tips. *Foliage* light green, medium-sized leaves. *Corolla* rose purple RHS 75B. *Growth* natural trailer, self-branching, bushy and free-flowering. Basket.

'De Ell'
EASTWOOD/YANCY 1980
AFS Registration No 1568
Semi-double
Tube dawn pink RHS 49A, short and thin. *Sepals* carmine rose RHS 52C on top, dawn pink RHS 49A on the undersides, green tips. *Corolla* Bishop's violet RHS 81A fading to cyclamen purple RHS 74A as it matures. Petaloids of the same colour. Corolla flares open. *Foliage* dark green RHS 136A with red stems, large leaves. *Growth* natural trailer, bushy, vigorous, and free-flowering. Basket.

'Deepdale'
A. THORNLEY 1961
Registered 1973
AFS Registration No 1099
Double
Tube rose bengal RHS 61D, medium length and thickness. *Sepals* ivory white, flushed pink, green tips. Medium length, and thickness, held horizontal. *Corolla* spectrum violet RHS 82B, changing to campanula violet RHS 82C when grown in the shade. *Foliage* medium green, medium to large sized, ovate. *Growth* upright, vigorous, bushy and free-flowering. Needs careful pinching to form a good shape. *Parentage* 'White Spider' × 'Blue Gown'.

'Delaval Lady'
RYLE 1975
AFS Registration No 1242
Single
Tube rose pink with carmine stripes, medium length and thickness. *Sepals* white on top with pink shading, neyron rose RHS 55B on the underside, sepals slightly twisted. *Corolla* rhodamine pink RHS 62A, very compact, keeping its shape as the bloom matures and does not fade. *Foliage* medium green, medium to large-sized leaves. *Growth* upright, free-flowering, bushy and vigorous. Bush.

'Delightful'
NIEDERHOLZER 1946
Single
Tube pink, medium length and thickness. *Sepals* pink, longish and slightly upturned. *Corolla* white with violet cast. *Foliage* medium green, medium-sized. *Growth* upright, bushy, self-branching and vigorous. Bush.

'Delilah'
HANDLEY 1974
AFS Registration No 1192
Double
Tube rose pink RHS 55A, medium length and thickness. *Sepals* rose pink RHS 55A, fully reflexing over the tube. *Corolla* violet RHS 82A, flecked with pink and white and maturing to rosy magenta RHS 74A, short and full. *Foliage* medium green, slightly serrated. *Growth* upright, bushy,

short-jointed and very free-flowering. It keeps its colour best if grown in shaded conditions. Bush.

'Del's Spring King'
DEL BROWN 1964
AFS Registration No 618
Double
Tube red, medium length and thickness. *Sepals* red, slightly upturned. *Corolla* milky white, full and fluffy. *Foliage* variegated, medium size. *Growth* natural trailer, very lax, vigorous and free-flowering. Basket.

'Delta Rae'
ADKINS 1980
AFS Registration No 1552
(Introduced 1965)
Single
Tube rose pink, short and of medium thickness. *Sepals* rose pink, light green tips, held downwards from the horizontal. *Corolla* rosy red with dark red borders to the petals, medium size. *Foliage* dark green with red stems and veins, and the new growth tinged bronze-red. *Growth* natural trailer, bushy, vigorous and free-flowering. Basket.

'De Pleiaden'
DE GROOT 1974 (Holland)
Single
Tube rose pink, short and medium thickness. *Sepals* rose pink. *Corolla* rose pink, small. *Foliage* medium green, small and slightly serrated. *Growth* upright, bushy, free-flowering. Small flowers, held upright. *Parentage* 'Saturnus' × 'Bon Accorde'.

'Derby Belle'
CLIFF GADSBY 1970
AFS Registration No 876
Single
Tube white with pink flush, medium length and thickness. *Sepals* white, flushed rose pink, held slightly above the horizontal. *Corolla* cyclamen purple with magenta flush, slightly paler at the base of the petals, bell-shaped. *Foliage* pale green, slightly serrated. *Growth* upright, bushy, self-branching and vigorous. Free-flowering. Prefers to be grown in the shade. *Parentage* 'Upward Look' × 'Caroline'. Bush.

'Derby Countess'
CLIFF GADSBY 1973
AFS Registration No 1121
Single
Tube white, long and thick. *Sepals* white, slightly twisted but held almost horizontally. *Corolla* violet purple RHS 77A, with pink at the base of the petals. *Style* white. *Filaments* pink. *Foliage* medium green, medium to large size with small serrations. *Growth* upright, very vigorous, free-flowering, but needs very careful pinching in its early stages to keep it to shape. One to bloom late in the season. Bush. *Parentage* 'Pepi' × 'Sleigh Bells'.

'Derby Imp' (169)
CLIFF GADSBY 1974
AFS Registration No 1220
Single
Tube crimson red, thin and short. *Sepals* crimson RHS 52A, on top, rose red RHS 58B on the underside, slightly arching. *Corolla* violet blue RHS 93A, maturing to violet purple RHS 97A as the bloom ages, pink at the base of the petals and with cerise veining. Small. *Style and filaments* cerise. *Foliage* medium green, small and serrated. *Growth* bushy, self-branching, vigorous and very free-flowering. Easy to grow and train. Basket, bush or quarter standard. *Parentage* 'Sleigh Bells' ×.

'Derby Star'
CLIFF GADSBY 1975
Single
Tube white, flushed pink, medium length and thickness. *Sepals* white, flushed pink, longish and narrow. *Corolla* wisteria blue RHS 92A blending into violet blue with white at the base of the petals. *Foliage* medium green, medium-sized leaves. *Growth* upright, spreading, bushy, vigorous and self-branching. Very free-flowering, with flowers held well out from

the foliage. Bush. *Parentage* 'Cliff's Hardy' × 'Shy Look'.

'Derwentwater'

JAMES TRAVIS 1961

Double

Tube white with pale pink flush, medium length and thickness. *Sepals* pale pink, paling to white, tips shaded green. *Corolla* soft lilac shade with very pale pink at the base of the petals, very full and compact. *Foliage* medium green, serrated slightly. *Growth* upright, bushy, vigorous and free-flowering. Bush.

'Desert Rose'

TIRET 1946

Double

Tube pale pink, medium length and thickness. *Sepals* carmine red, longish and slightly upturned. *Corolla* rosy purple, splashed with carmine, large. *Foliage* medium green, medium to large size. *Growth* vigorous, upright, bushy, free-flowering. Blooms large and heavy and require support if the plant is to be grown as a bush. Bush or basket.

'Deutsche Kaiserin'

WEINRICH 1870

Semi-double

Tube crimson red, short and of medium thickness. *Sepals* carmine with green tips, held downwards from the horizontal. *Corolla* carmine purple, red at the base of the petals, very compact. Smallish flower. *Style and filaments* crimson. *Foliage* medium green with red veins and stems, very slightly serrated. Large leaves, broad. *Growth* upright, bushy, free-flowering. Bush.

'Diablo'

TIRET 1961

AFS Registration No 484

Double

Tube greenish white with a pink flush, short and thick. *Sepals* white, flushed carmine at the tips, pointing downwards and curled up at the ends. Broad and creped effect on the undersides. Corolla burgundy purple with splashes of red on the outer petals, slightly paler at the base. *Style and filaments* white. *Foliage* pale greenish yellow with red veining, large and long. *Growth* natural trailer which produces a fair number of very large blooms if pinched early, but needs staking if to be grown as a bush. Basket or bush.

'Diadem'

REITER 1946

Semi-double

Tube white, medium length and thickness. *Sepals* white, longish and narrow. *Corolla* peony purple, medium size, full and compact. *Foliage* medium green, large-sized leaves. *Growth* upright, bushy, free-flowering and very attractive. Bush.

'Diana'

KENNETT 1967

AFS Registration No 740

Double

Tube greenish-white with tinges of pink, short and thick. *Sepals* pale pink on top, darker pink underneath, and with green tips. Broad and completely reflexing around the tube. *Corolla* mauve pink with the outer petals cerise and splashed pink. Very full but rather loose. *Style* white. *Filaments* pale pink. *Foliage* pale green, medium to large-sized leaves, slightly serrated. *Growth* natural trailer, vigorous, bushy and free-flowering. Basket.

'Diana Wills'

GADSBY 1971

AFS Registration No 976

Double

Tube greenish-white, medium length, thick. *Sepals* white with green tips, horizontal then turned up at the tips. *Corolla* bluish purple, turning to reddish purple as the bloom matures, petals splashed pink and white. *Filaments* pink. *Style* pink. *Foliage* medium green, medium to large-sized, serrated. *Growth* upright, but rather lax grower. Free-flowering, bushy and self-branching, needs staking to grow best as a bush or otherwise will sprawl. Bush (if staked) or basket.

'Diane'
HAZARD (date unknown)
Single
Tube waxy white, medium length and thickness. *Sepals* waxy white, longish and slightly upturned. *Corolla* dusky pink, medium size, compact. *Foliage* medium green. *Growth* upright, bushy, self-branching and free-flowering. Rather an attractive colour combination. Bush.

'Diawillis'
NIEDERHOLZER 1947
Single
Tube pale rose pink, medium length and thickness. *Sepals* pale rose pink. *Corolla* Tyrian rose, medium size, compact. *Foliage* medium green. *Growth* upright, bushy, free-flowering. Bush.

'Dickie Doo'
ARAUJO/BISHOP 1975
AFS Registration No 1304
Semi-double
Tube pink, long and of medium thickness. *Sepals* pink, long, flaring. *Corolla* Bishop's violet with white marbling towards the top and sweeping down the centre of the petals. *Foliage* bright green. *Growth* natural trailer, very vigorous, bushy, exceptionally free-flowering. Basket.

'Dilly Dilly'
TIRET 1963
AFS Registration No 577
Double
Tube white, medium length and thickness. *Sepals* pale pink on top, darker pink on the undersides, green tips. Broad and upturned. *Corolla* lilac, with pink at the base of the petals, large and full. *Style and filaments* pink. *Foliage* medium green, large with slight serrations. *Growth* upright, tends to be rather lax, mainly due to the weight of the blooms. Easy to grow. Bush or basket.

'Dipton Dainty'
RYLE 1975
AFS Registration No 1243
Semi-double
Tube rhodamine pink RHS 62A, short, medium thickness. *Sepals* rhodamine pink RHS 62A, medium-sized, curving slightly upwards. *Corolla* wisteria blue RHS 92A with lighter shading. Petaloids flecked and striped phlox pink RHS 62B. *Foliage* medium green, medium-sized. *Growth* upright, self-branching and bushy, free-flowering. Bush or standard. Best colour in shaded conditions.

'Display' (136)
SMITH 1881
Single
Tube pink, medium length and thickness. *Sepals* deep rose pink, arching upwards. *Corolla* deep cerise pink, opening bell-shaped. *Style and filaments* pink. *Foliage* medium full green, slightly serrated. *Growth* upright, bushy, self-branching, free-flowering. Excellent exhibition variety. Bush or standard.

'Doctor Brendan Freeman'
GADSBY 1977
AFS Registration No 1427
Single
Tube pale pink, medium length and thickness. *Sepals* rhodamine pink (RHS 62A) shading to phlox pink (RHS 62B) *Corolla* white, medium size. *Foliage* medium green. *Growth* upright, bushy, very free-flowering. Bush or standard. Excellent exhibition plant. Superior to 'Cloverdale Pearl.' *Parentage* 'Cloverdale Pearl' × 'Grace Darling'.

'Doctor Jill'
PUGH 1978
AFS Registration No 1457
Double
Tube red purple RHS 65B, short and thin. *Sepals* phlox pink RHS 62B, completely reflexing on to the tube, medium length and width. *Corolla* red purple RHS 65C, veined magenta RHS 66A, medium size. *Stamen and pistil* roseine purple RHS 68A. *Foliage* darkish green RHS 146A, $2\frac{1}{2}$ in (6 cm) long and $1\frac{1}{2}$ in (4 cm) wide.

Growth upright, self-branching, bushy. Bush or standard.

'Doctor O'Connor'
SOO YUN FIELD 1965
AFS Registration No 644
Double
Tube bright red, medium length and thickness. *Sepals* bright red, long and broad. *Corolla* deep purple, opens flat and compact, very large and full. *Foliage* light to medium green, medium-sized leaves. *Growth* upright, bushy, vigorous and free-flowering, heavy bloomer. Bush.

'Dodie'
STORVICK 1980
AFS Registration No 1543
Double
Tube bright red, medium length and thickness. *Sepals* bright red, narrow and completely reflexed. *Corolla* deep purple, splashed cerise, small and compact but spreading out as the bloom matures. *Foliage* dark green, narrow and slightly serrated. *Growth* lax bush, self-branching, bushy and free-flowering. Bush or basket.

'Dollar Princess' (172)
LEMOINE 1912
Double
Tube cerise, small, medium, thickness. *Sepals* cerise, quite broad, reflexing almost to the tube. *Corolla* purple, cerise at the base of the petals, small. *Filaments* cerise. *Style* cerise. *Foliage* medium green, small to medium size, serrated. *Growth* upright, self-branching, bushy, vigorous and very free-flowering. Easy to grow, early bloomer. Bush or garden hardy.

'Dollie Pausch'
OLSEN 1962
AFS Registration No 495
Double
Tube rose red, medium length and thickness. *Sepals* deep rose red, broad and upturned. *Corolla* creamy white with red veining at the base of the petals, large and full. *Style and filaments* pink. *Foliage* dark green, medium-sized leaves. *Growth* lax bush, vigorous, self-branching, bushy, free-flowering. Bush or basket.

'Dolly Varden'
MARTIN SOULES 1953
AFS Registration No 174
Semi-double
Tube white with a pink flush, short. *Sepals* white, narrow and upturned. *Corolla* lilac blue, ageing to lavender pink, medium-sized. *Foliage* medium green. *Growth* lax bush, vigorous, free-flowering. Bush or basket.

'Dolores'
NIEDERHOLZER 1944
Single
Tube carmine rose, medium length and thickness. *Sepals* carmine rose, longish and upturned. *Corolla* carmine rose, compact, medium-sized. *Foliage* medium green. *Growth* trailer, not self-branching, but makes long, slender branches. Needs careful pinching to shape. Basket or half-basket.

'Dominiana'
DOMINY 1852
Flowers long, triphylla type, rosy scarlet, rather loose corolla. *Foliage* dark greenish bronze. *Growth* upright, bushy, vigorous and free-flowering. This is a plant best grown in the heated greenhouse as it is a very late bloomer—normally between October and January. *Parentage F. serratifolia* × *F. spectabilis*.

'Donna Marie'
TIRET 1969
AFS Registration No 829
Single
Tube pale pink, medium length and thickness. *Sepals* pale, long and reflexing slightly, pink. *Corolla* salmon pink, long and fairly compact. *Foliage* medium green, serrated. *Growth* trailer, fairly vigorous, free-flowering. Attractive bloom. Basket.

'Don Peralta'
TIRET 1950
AFS Registration No 62

Single to semi-double
Tube red, medium length and thickness. *Sepals* red, upturned. *Corolla* red, large and full. *Foliage* medium green, medium to large-sized leaves. *Growth* upright, vigorous, bushy and free-flowering. Needs careful pinching early to make a good plant. Bush.

'Dorothea Flower'
THORNLEY 1969
Registered 1971
AFS Registration No 1009
Single
Tube white, long and thin. *Sepals* white with pink flush, long, narrow and reflexed. *Corolla* opens a deep lavender blue with shades of pink and white at the base of the petals. Very compact. *Style* white. *Filaments* pink. *Foliage* medium green, longish. *Growth* upright, self-branching, bushy and vigorous. Very free-flowering. Excellent exhibition plant. Bush or standard.

'Dorothy'
W.P. WOOD 1949
Single
Tube bright crimson, short and of medium thickness. *Sepals* crimson, spreading out from the corolla. *Corolla* violet purple with red veining and red at the base of the petals, medium size. *Foliage* medium green. *Growth* vigorous, bushy, upright, self-branching and free-flowering. Hardy in protected districts. Bush.

'Dorothy Louise'
SCHNABEL 1952
Double
Tube, *sepals*, *corolla* pale pink. Medium-sized flowers. *Foliage* medium green. *Growth* upright, bushy, vigorous and free-flowering. Bush.

'Dorothy Woakes'
DUBB/GAY 1973
AFS Registration No 1153
Double
Tube rosy carmine, short and thick. *Sepals* rosy carmine, long and arching. *Corolla* pale rose pink with darker rose veining on the petals. *Foliage* medium to dark green, small and narrow. *Growth* upright, vigorous, self-branching, and free-flowering with large blooms. Good exhibition variety. Bush.

'Dotti'
STORVICK 1978
AFS Registration No 1485
Double
Tube red, short. *Sepals* rosy red, completely reflexed. *Corolla* deep purple, flecked pink at the base, maturing to rose. Flaring, smallish. *Stamens* rosy red. *Pistil* pink, shading to rosy red at the tip. *Foliage* dark green, medium size. *Growth* upright, bushy and self-branching, very profuse bloomer. Will trail with weights and can be grown to most other shapes. Bush, standard, basket, pyramid, etc. *Parentage* 'Dollar Princess' × 'Jingle Bells'.

'Dragonfly'
CROCKETT 1965
AFS Registration No 819
Double
Tube cherry red, medium length and thickness. *Sepals* cherry red on top, rose madder on the undersides, long and upturned. *Corolla* dauphin's violet (RHS 86) with rose madder veins and flush, large and full. *Foliage* light green, medium-sized leaves. *Growth* upright, vigorous, self-branching and free-flowering. Bush or standard.

'Dr A.M. De Cola'
PENNISI 1969
AFS Registration No 814
Double
Tube white with pink flush, medium length and thickness. *Sepals* white on top, pink on the undersides, green tips. *Corolla* various shades of pink with orange variegations, long and very full double. *Foliage* medium green, small. *Growth* lax

bush, self-branching, vigorous, free-flowering. Bush or basket.

'Drame'
LEMOINE 1880
Semi-double
Tube scarlet, medium length and thickness. *Sepals* scarlet, broad, held horizontally and turning up at the tips. *Corolla* purplish red, red at the base of the petals, medium size. *Filaments* red. *Style* scarlet red. *Foliage* medium green when mature, yellowish-green new growth. Small to medium-sized leaves, slightly serrated. *Growth* upright, self-branching, bushy, vigorous and free-flowering. Bush. Good garden hardy. Hybrid of *F. m.* var. *riccartonii*.

'Dr Bowman'
FRANCESCA 1973
AFS Registration No 1098
Single
Tube deep pink, thick, medium length. *Sepals* pale pink with a blue tinge, and edged deeper blue. *Corolla* orchid pink, compact. Smallish blooms. *Foliage* long and broad, medium green. *Growth* upright, self-branching, vigorous and bushy. Free-flowering. Bush.

'Dr Davis'
HAZARD
Double
Tube pink, medium length and thickness. *Sepals* pale pink, long and upturned. *Corolla* light creamy white, medium-sized. *Foliage* medium green. *Growth* upright, vigorous, free-flowering and bushy. Bush.

'Dream'
MUNKNER 1952
Single
Tube pink, medium length and thickness. *Sepals* deep pink with green tips, long and upturned. *Corolla* rose pink, medium-sized. *Foliage* medium green. *Growth* exceptionally vigorous, upright and bushy—will do well as a greenhouse climber. Bush, standard or greenhouse climber.

'Dr Ennis'
GAGNON 1964
AFS Registration No 601
Tube pale carmine red, medium length and thickness. *Sepals* carmine, long and broad with crepe appearance. *Corolla* violet blue, touches of carmine on the petals, brightening as the flower matures, large bloom, very full. *Foliage* dark green, medium to large-sized leaves. *Growth* trailer, very vigorous, not self-branching, so it requires careful pinching. Very free-flowering. Basket.

'Dresden'
NIEDERHOLZER 1946
Semi-double
Tube neyron rose, medium length and thickness. *Sepals* neyron rose, upturned. *Corolla* mauve purple with neyron rose outer petals, medium-sized blooms. *Foliage* medium green, slightly serrated. *Growth* upright, vigorous, bushy. Bush.

'Dr Foster'
LEMOINE 1899
Single
Tube scarlet, medium length and thickness. *Sepals* scarlet, broad and pointed. *Corolla* violet purple, large and full. *Foliage* medium green, medium-sized leaves. *Growth* upright, vigorous, self-branching and bushy. Very free-flowering and generally hardy. Bush or garden hardy.

'Dr John Gallwey'
REITER 1940
Double
Tube rose madder, long and of medium thickness. *Sepals* rose madder, long and upturned. *Corolla* white, full and large blooms. *Foliage* medium green, medium to large sized leaves. *Growth* upright, self-branching, bushy and vigorous. *Parentage* 'Mrs Gladstone' × 'Amy Lye'. Bush.

'Dr Jules Welch'
EVANS AND REEVES 1946
Double

Tube dark red, medium length and thickness. *Sepals* dark red, long and broad, upturned. *Corolla* violet blue, very full, large flowers. *Foliage* medium green, medium-sized leaves. *Growth* upright, vigorous, self-branching and bushy. Bush.

'Dr Kelly'
SOO YUN FIELD 1966
AFS Registration No 682
Double
Tube light pink, medium length and thickness. *Sepals* light pink, long and upturned. *Corolla* orchid pink, large, with serrated petals. *Foliage* medium green, large and serrated. *Growth* upright, vigorous, bushy and free-flowering. Bush.

'Dr Olson'
OLSON 1959
Double
Tube rose pink, medium length and thickness. *Sepals* rose pink, reflexed almost to the tube. *Corolla* white with pink flush and splashed rose. Cerise veining, very loose. Medium to large. *Style and filaments* pink. *Foliage* medium green, large, broad, serrated. *Growth* trailer, vigorous, bushy and free-flowering. Basket.

'Dr S.A. Appel'
STEEVENS 1968
Single
Tube red, medium length and thickness. *Sepals* red with green tips. *Corolla* violet purple, medium-sized blooms. *Foliage* medium green. *Growth* upright, self-branching, bushy and free-flowering. Bush.

'Dr Topinard'
LEMOINE 1890
Single 3 in (7.5 cm)
Tube deep rose red, short and thick. *Sepals* rose red, short and upswept. *Corolla* pure white with rose veining, small and compact. *Foliage* dark green, longish and very slightly serrated. *Growth* free-flowering, upright, bushy, self-branching. Quarter standard, bush.

'Dr Vance'
EVANS AND REEVES 1935
Double
Tube red, medium length and thickness. *Sepals* vivid red, long and upturned. *Corolla* dark violet and cerise, large and very loose-petalled. *Foliage* dark green, medium to large-sized leaves. *Growth* upright, vigorous, self-branching, bushy. Very strong grower. Bush.

'Dr Wm.R. Vizzard'
CHILES 1953
AFS Registration No 163
Double
Tube deep red, medium length and thickness. *Sepals* deep red, long, broad and upturned. *Corolla* pure white with red veining and red at the base of the petals. *Foliage* medium green, medium to large leaves. *Growth* very lax, longish growths, vigorous and free-flowering. Basket or half-basket.

'Du Barry'
TIRET 1950
Double
Tube soft pink, medium length and thickness. *Sepals* soft pink, long and reflexed. *Corolla* varying from purple to fuchsia purple inside petals with the smaller outside petals having flesh pink marbling. Medium to large blooms. *Foliage* medium to dark green, leathery-look leaves. *Growth* vigorous, upright, bushy and free-flowering. Bush or standard.

'Duchess of Albany'
RUNDLE 1891
Single
Tube creamy wax, thick and of medium length. *Sepals* white with pink flush, long and recurving. *Corolla* pale cerise, compact. *Foliage* medium green, medium to large-sized leaves. *Growth* upright, vigorous, bushy and free-flowering. A very attractive flower, not an exhibition plant but worth growing. Bush or standard.

'Dulcie Elizabeth'
CLYNE 1974
AFS Registration No 1227

Double
Tube rose pink, short and thick. *Sepals* rose pink, short, broad and completely recurving over the tube. *Corolla* lavender blue, with pink flecks on the petals, medium size. *Foliage* medium green, long and narrow. *Growth* self-branching, vigorous, upright and bushy. Very free-flowering. Makes an excellent exhibition plant, but tends to bloom late. Bush.

'Dulcinea'
EDWARDS 1948
Double
Tube red, medium length and thickness. *Sepals* red, very long and upturned. *Corolla* pure white, with light red at the base of the large petals. *Foliage* medium green, medium to large-sized leaves. *Growth* upright, vigorous, bushy and free-flowering. Bush.

'Dunrobin Bedder'
MELVILLE 1890
Single
Tube bright red, small and thin. *Sepals* scarlet, long and upturned. *Corolla* violet purple, small and compact. *Style and filaments* red. *Foliage* medium green, small with slight serrations. *Growth* bushy, vigorous, dwarf, spreading habit. Bush or garden hardy.

'Dusky Rose'
WALTZ 1060
AFS Registration No 439
Double
Tube deep reddish pink, long and of medium thickness. *Sepals* pink with green tips, broad, held horizontal and turning up at the tips. *Corolla* rose red, ageing to raspberry pink, petals splashed coral pink, very full and ruffled. *Style and filaments* pink. *Foliage* medium green, large and smooth. *Growth* lax, vigorous, bushy, self-branching, and very free-flowering. Basket or half-basket.

'Dutch Mill' (143)
Single
Tube rose pink, medium length and thickness. *Sepals* rose pink, long, twisting and reflexing towards the tube. *Corolla* pale violet purple, pale violet at the base of the petals and with rose veining. Medium-sized. *Style and filaments* pink. *Foliage* medium green, broad and serrated. *Growth* upright, bushy, self-branching, vigorous and very free-flowering. Good exhibition plant. Bush.

'Dutch Shoes'
PENNISI 1970
AFS Registration No 895
Double
Tube rose pink, short and of medium thickness. *Sepals* rose pink with pink tips, in the form of little Dutch shoes. *Corolla* rose pink, medium-sized. *Foliage* medium green. *Growth* trailer, vigorous, bushy and free-flowering. Half-basket.

'Dynamic'
KUECHLER 1962
AFS Registration No 506
Double
Tube white with pink flush, medium length and thickness. *Sepals* white with green tips on top, rose pink on the underside, long and broad. *Corolla* blue with pink marbling, large and full. *Foliage* bright green, medium to large size. *Growth* upright, bushy, vigorous, self-branching and free-flowering. A very attractive bloom. Bush.

'Earl of Beaconsfield'
LAING 1878
Single $4\frac{1}{2}$ in (11 cm)
Tube salmon pink, long medium thickness. *Sepals* salmon pink, broad and upturned, green tips. *Corolla* vermilion, medium size. *Foliage* light to medium green, large, serrated. *Growth* spreading, vigorous, upright, not self-branching. Free-flowering, a very attractive flower, but not an exhibition variety. Bush/pyramid.

'East Anglian'
THORNE 1960
Single

Tube pale pink, thick and of medium length. *Sepals* pinkish white with deeper stripes, long, downward pointed with the tips turned up. *Corolla* rose pink with an orange flush to the petals, and with white shading at the base. *Style and filaments* white. *Foliage* medium to dark green, large and broad, with red veins and serrated. *Growth* vigorous, bushy, lax upright. Bush.

'Easter Bonnet'
WALTZ 1955
Double
Tube pink, short and of medium thickness. *Sepals* pink, with green tips, broad and turned up at the tips. *Corolla* dark rose-pink, slightly darker at the base of the petals, very full and fluffy, medium size. *Foliage* darkish green, medium-sized leaves. *Growth* upright, bushy, self-branching, free-flowering. A most beautiful cultivar. Bush.

'Ecstasy'
TIRET 1948
Double
Tube rose pink, medium length and thickness. *Sepals* neyron rose with green tips, long and upswept. *Corolla* hyacinth blue with splashes of phlox pink, large. *Foliage* medium green. *Growth* lax, spreading, bushy and vigorous. Bush, if staked, or half-basket.

'Edale'
GADSBY 1975
AFS Registration No 1281
Single
Tube light pink, thick and of medium length. *Sepals* rhodamine pink RHS 62A, slightly upswept. *Corolla* spectrum violet RHS 82B, shading to imperial purple RHS 78B, very compact. Medium size. *Foliage* medium green. *Growth* upright, bushy, self-branching and free-flowering. *Parentage* 'Joan Pacey' × 'Miss Great Britain'.

'Eden Beauty'
R. HOLMES 1974
AFS Registration No 1201
Single
Tube carmine RHS 52B, medium length and thickness. *Sepals* carmine RHS 52B, on top, crimson RHS 52A on the underside medium length, curving upwards. *Corolla* fuchsia purple RHS 67A with red veins. Crimson RHS 52A at the base of the petals, fading to magenta rose, large and bell-shaped. *Foliage* medium green with lighter green veins and red stems, small. *Growth* vigorous, trailer, bushy, self-branching and very free-flowering. Basket.

'Eden Lady'
RYLE 1978
AFS Registration No 1478
Single
Tube pale rose pink, short and thin. *Sepals* Amaranth rose RHS 65A, with a deeper shade on the undersides, shading to white at the tips. *Corolla* hyacinth blue RHS 91A, rose shade at the base of the petals, medium-sized bloom. *Stamens* ruby red RHS 61A, pistil pale rose pink. *Foliage* medium green, small to medium-sized. *Growth* upright, self-branching, bushy, short-jointed and very free-flowering. Good exhibition variety. Bush or standard.

'Edith Emery'
CLYNE 1975
AFS Registration No 1284
Semi-double
Tube waxy white, short and thick. *Sepals* white with crepe reverse, reflexed. *Corolla* amethyst violet RHS fading to rhodamine purple. RHS 81C fading to RHS 68C. Short, compact shape, medium-sized. *Foliage* spinach green, small to medium-sized, broad. *Growth* upright, bushy, self-branching and free-flowering. Good exhibition plant. Short-jointed. Bush. *Parentage* 'La Campanella' × 'Flirtation Waltz'.

'Edith Pohley'
BROWN AND SOULES 1951
AFS Registration No 75
Semi-double

Tube pale salmon pink, short and of medium thickness. *Sepals* salmon pink, short and upturned. *Corolla* pinkish blue, medium size, loose petalled. *Foliage* light to medium green, medium-sized leaves. *Growth* upright, bushy, self-branching and free-flowering. Bush.

'Edith Russell'
YORK 1953
AFS Registration No 137
Double
Tube salmon pink, short and thin. *Sepals* salmon pink, small and upturned at the tips. *Corolla* salmon pink with tinges of violet purple at the base of the petals which fold over each other. Small and very compact. *Foliage* medium green, small. *Growth* semi-trailer, bushy, free-flowering. Bush or half-basket.

'Ed Lagarde'
PENNISI 1967
AFS Registration No 713
Double
Tube white, short and of medium thickness. *Sepals* white, broad and held immediately over the corolla. *Corolla* very deep purplish blue shade, very full and frilly large bloom. *Stamens* pink. *Pistil* white. *Foliage* medium green, large, slightly serrated. *Growth* natural trailer, bushy and free-flowering. A most beautiful fuchsia, not an exhibition plant, but well worth growing. Basket.

'Eileen Saunders'
RON HOLMES 1974
AFS Registration No 1202
Single
Tube carmine RHS 52B, striped crimson RHS 52A, long and of medium thickness. Slightly curved. *Sepals* crimson RHS 52A, with green tips, long and reflexing to completely cover the tube. *Corolla* fuchsia purple RHS 67B, with carmine RHS 52B at the base of the petals, and crimson veining. Bell-shaped, medium-sized. *Stamens and pistil* carmine RHS 52B. *Foliage* medium green paler on the underside, small and serrated. Red stems. *Growth* upright, self-branching, vigorous and bushy, free-flowering. Bush or summer bedder. *Parentage* 'Percy Holmes' × 'Prodigy'.

'Elaine Allen'
ALLEN 1974
AFS Registration No 1214
Semi-double
Tube neyron rose, medium length and thickness. *Sepals* neyron rose, long and held horizontally. *Corolla* magenta rose, pale rose at the base of the petals. Opens saucer-shaped, large bloom. *Foliage* pale green, medium-sized leaves. *Growth* upright, bushy, self-branching, free-flowering. Bush. *Parentage* 'Albion' × 'Rosedale'.

'El Camino'
LEE 1955
Double
Tube rose red, thin and of medium length. *Sepals* rose red, broad and completely reflexed over the tube. *Corolla* pure white, flushed and veined rose red, full but loose petalled, medium size. *Stamens and pistil* red. *Foliage* medium to dark green, long. *Growth* upright, self-branching, bushy, free-flowering. Easy to grow. Bush.

'Eleanor Clark'
CLARK/FUCHSIAVALE 1980
AFS Registration No 1539
Single
Tube pale phlox pink with deeper pink stripes, medium length and width. *Sepals* pale phlox pink, fully reflexing on maturity. *Corolla* shell pink, medium size. *Foliage* light to medium green, ovate with an obtuse leaf tip, lobed leaf base and serrate margins, small to medium size. *Growth* upright, bushy. Bush. Best colour in shaded conditions. Sport of 'Symphony'.

'Eleanor Leytham' (81)
GEORGE ROE 1974
Single
Tube pinkish white, short and of medium thickness. *Sepals* pinkish white, short and

broad. *Corolla* pink, with deeper pink on the edges of the petals. *Foliage* medium green, glossy, small. *Growth* upright, bushy, free-flowering, very small blooms. *Parentage* 'Countess of Aberdeen' × 'Pink Darling'. Not an easy cultivar to grow, but very attractive. Bush or quarter standard.

'Eleanor Rawlins'
WOOD 1954
Single
Tube carmine, short and thick. *Sepals* carmine, long and upturned. *Corolla* magenta, carmine red at the base of the petals, very compact, medium size. *Stamens* pink. *Pistil* pink. *Foliage* medium green, long and slightly serrated. *Growth* upright, bushy, self-branching, free-flowering. Bush or garden hardy.

'Electra'
NIEDERHOLZER 1944
Double
Tube red, medium length and thickness. *Sepals* red, long and upturned. *Corolla* very pale pink with rose pink veining, large and full. *Foliage* medium green, medium to large-sized leaves. *Growth* vigorous, upright, bushy and free-flowering. Bush.

'Elfin'
NIEDERHOLZER 1941
Single
Tube pale pink, small, short. *Sepals* pale pink, small, spreading. *Corolla* pure white, veined very pale carmine, small, compact. *Foliage* medium green, small leaves. *Growth* upright, self-branching, bushy, free-flowering. Bush. *Parentage* 'Rolla' ×.

'Elfin Glade'
COLVILLE 1964
Single
Tube rose pink, thick, medium length. *Sepals* pink with green tips, held horizontally and with the tips upturned. *Corolla* pinkish mauve with darker edges, paler at the base of the petals and pinkish veining. *Stamens and pistil* pink. *Foliage* medium green, medium-sized leaves, slightly serrated. *Growth* upright, self-branching, bushy and vigorous. Very free-flowering. Bush or garden hardy.

'Elina'
MIKE PENNISI 1969
AFS Registration No 815
Double
Tube white, medium length and thickness. *Sepals* white with green tips, upturned. *Corolla* dark lilac purple, very full and compact. *Growth* trailer, bushy, vigorous, free-flowering. Basket.

'Elizabeth'
WHITEMAN
Single
Tube rose opal, long and slender. *Sepals* rose opal with green tips, broad and turning up at the tips. *Corolla* rose pink, very compact, small to medium-sized. *Stamens* pink. *Pistil* pink. *Foliage* medium green, large leaves, finely serrated. *Growth* vigorous, long growths, not self-branching but very free-flowering. A difficult cultivar to train to shape but nevertheless an attractive flower. Bush.

'Elizabeth'
TIRET 1970
AFS Registration No 898
Double
Tube rose pink, medium length and thickness. *Sepals* rose pink, medium length, upturned. *Corolla* pastel pink, medium-sized blooms. *Foliage* medium green. *Growth* trailer, bushy, vigorous, free-flowering. Basket.

'Elizabeth Travis'
TRAVIS 1956
Double
Tube pale pink, medium length and thickness. *Sepals* pale pink on top, deeper pink on the undersides, green tips, broad and completely reflexing around the tube. *Corolla* white, full but loose petalled, medium size. *Stamens and pistil* pink. *Foliage* dark green with red veins,

medium to large, narrow leaves, finely serrated. *Growth* upright, bushy, vigorous, self-branching and very free-flowering. Very easy to grow. Bush or quarter standard.

'Elk Horn'

BRAND 1949

Double

Tube carmine, medium length and thickness. *Sepals* deep carmine red, long and upturned. *Corolla* deep pink, very full and fluffy, large, serrated petals. *Foliage* medium green, medium to large leaves. *Growth* upright, self-branching, vigorous and bushy. Free-flowering. Bush.

'Ellen Diane'

SHAW 1973

AFS Registration No 1034

Single (Miniature)

Tube pale red, very small. *Sepals* fuchsia red, very small, and narrow. *Corolla* rose-purple, miniature, bell-shaped. *Stamens and pistil* red. *Growth* upright, bushy, free-flowering. Although classed and registered as a single this cultivar will habitually throw numerous blooms with five sepals and five petals. Bush.

'Ellen Morgan'

R. HOLMES 1976

Double

Tube salmon pink, short and thick. *Sepals* salmon pink with green tips, broad and reflexing. *Corolla* magenta with salmon pink shading at the base of the petals, medium size. *Stamens* pink. *Pistil* pink. *Foliage* medium green, small to medium-sized leaves, broad and serrated. *Growth* upright, bushy, vigorous and free-flowering. Easy to grow. Bush. *Parentage* 'Phyllis' ×.

'Elma Oliver'

KUECHLER 1962

AFS Registration No 503

Double

Tube pale pink, medium length and thickness. *Sepals* pale pink on top, deeper pink on the undersides, long and twisting. *Corolla* dusky rose shade, very full, medium size. *Foliage* bright green, medium-sized leaves. *Growth* trailer, vigorous, free-flowering. Basket.

'El Matador'

KENNETT 1965

AFS Registration No 641

Semi-double

Tube pink, long, thin. *Sepals* pale salmon pink, long and narrow, upturned at tips. *Corolla* shades of dark purple and burgundy with numerous salmon pink streaks on the petals which flare out wide. Medium to large blooms. *Foliage* medium green, medium to large leaves. *Growth* natural trailer, vigorous, free-flowering. Very attractive flower. Basket.

'Elsa'

Raiser and date unknown

Single $3\frac{1}{2}$ in (9 cm)

Tube flesh pink, medium length and thickness. *Sepals* flesh pink, deeper on the underside. *Corolla* bluish magenta fading to pale purple. *Foliage* light green, medium-sized leaves. *Growth* upright, bushy, self-branching, free-flowering, very vigorous. Bush.

'Elsie Mitchell'

RYLE 1980

AFS Registration No 1576

Double

Tube pink, medium length and width. *Sepals* pink at the base, shaded to white and tipped green, semi reflexing. *Corolla* sea lavender with pink blush, medium size. *Foliage* medium green, ovate, small to medium size. *Growth* upright, self-branching, bushy. Bush.

'Embarcadero'

SCHNABEL PASKESEN 1962

AFS Registration No 532

Double

Tube pale pink, long and of medium thickness. *Sepals* pale pink with deeper pink tips, long and narrow. *Corolla* pale purple, fading to dusky rose, very large and flaring. *Foliage* medium green, medium-sized leaves. *Growth* natural trailer, vigorous, bushy, free-flowering. Very large flowers. Basket.

'Emile de Wildeman'
(syn. 'Fascination')
LEMOINE 1905
Double
Tube carmine red, short and thick. *Sepals* carmine red, broad and completely reflexing over the tube. *Corolla* pink with cerise veining and flushed pink, very full, medium size. *Stamens and pistil* cerise. *Foliage* medium green, medium-sized leaves, slightly serrated. *Growth* upright, bushy, vigorous, self-branching and free-flowering. An easy cultivar to grow. Bush.

'Emile Zola'
LEMOINE 1910
Single
Tube red, thick, medium length. *Sepals* red, slightly turned up at the tips. *Corolla* rosy magenta, compact, medium size. *Foliage* medium green, medium-sized leaves, serrated. *Growth* upright, bushy, vigorous, free-flowering. Bush or garden hardy.

'Emilie'
NESSIER 1948
Semi-double
Tube coral pink, medium length and thickness. *Sepals* coral pink, upturned. *Corolla* fuchsia pink and peach shades, medium size. *Foliage* medium green. *Growth* lax, trailing, long stems, vigorous and free-flowering. Bush or half-basket.

'Emma O'Neill'
SCHNABEL 1952
AFS Registration No 110
Semi-double
Tube ivory white, flushed neyron rose, medium length and thickness. *Sepals* ivory white, flushed neyron rose. *Corolla* phlox pink, darker pink at the edges, and with white at the base of the petals. Medium size. *Foliage* medium green, medium-sized leaves. *Growth* upright, bushy, vigorous, self-branching and free-flowering. Bush.

'Empress of Prussia (12)
HOPPE 1868
Single
Tube scarlet, short and thick. *Sepals* scarlet, broad, held slightly above the horizontal of the petals, very compact, medium size. *Foliage* medium to dark green, medium-sized, broad leaves, slightly serrated. *Stamens and pistil* pink. *Growth* upright, bushy, self-branching, and free-flowering. Makes very sturdy growth with thick stems. Bush or garden hardy.

'Enchanted'
TIRET 1951
AFS Registration No 95
Double
Tube short, rose red. *Sepals* rose red, long and broad, reflexing. *Corolla* campanula blue, with fuchsia pink overlay on the outer petals. Very loose and open, large bloom. *Foliage* medium green, medium-sized leaves, serrated. *Growth* trailing, willowy branches, free-flowering. Basket.

'Encore'
REEDSTROM 1960
AFS Registration No 422
Double
Tube white, medium length and thickness. *Sepals* white. *Corolla* amethyst with pink mottling, fading to white at the base of the petals, large blooms. *Foliage* medium green, medium-sized leaves. *Growth* natural trailer, self-branching, vigorous and free-flowering. Basket.

'Enfante Prodigue'
(sometimes known as 'Prodigy')
LEMOINE 1887
Double
Tube crimson, long, medium thickness. *Sepals* crimson, reflexing. *Corolla* bluish purple turning to magenta as the bloom matures, pink at the base of the petals

and scarlet veining. *Stamens and pistil* cerise. *Foliage* medium to dark green, small to medium-sized leaves, serrated. *Growth* upright, very vigorous, bushy and free-flowering. Easy to grow. Bush or garden hardy. *F. riccartonii* hybrid.

'Eos'

TRAVIS 1975
AFS Registration No 1318
Single, breviflora type
Tube white, long and thin. *Sepals* phlox pink RHS 62B, reflexing. *Corolla* tyrian purple RHS 61C. *Foliage* mid-green, serrated, ovate, small. *Growth* self-branching, bushy, and lax, but can be trained to most shapes—bush, basket, etc. Very free-flowering, with black berries, following.

'Eppsii'

EPPS 1840
Single $3\frac{1}{2}$ in (9 cm)
Tube light pink, long, medium thickness. *Sepals* cerise, horizontal. Green tips. *Corolla* rosy magenta, compact. *Foliage* light green. Vigorous, upright growth. Free-flowering. Bush, standard or pyramid.

'Eris'

TRAVIS 1980
AFS Registration No 1581
Single
Tube deep rose, thin $\frac{1}{4}$ in (6 mm) in length. *Sepals* deep rose on top, lighter on the underside, recurving slightly, $\frac{2}{5}$ in (10 mm) in length. *Corolla* light rose, very small petals pressed against the sepals. *Stamens* short. *Pistil* prominent with rose stigma, spreading. Total length of the flower is $\frac{3}{10}$ in (11 mm). *Foliage* light green, fernlike, diamond-shaped and deeply toothed. *Berries* large, black. *Growth* upright, tall and self-branching, will make a good bush. *Parentage* Encliandra ×.

'Eroica'

HOWARTH 1979
AFS Registration No 1530
Single
Tube salmon pink, short and thick. *Sepals* red, upswept at tips. Held well out from corolla $1\frac{1}{2}$ in (4 cm) long. *Corolla* $1\frac{1}{2}$ in (4 cm) long, opens claret, changing to red, very bright. *Stamens and pistil* pink. *Foliage* light green, serrated, lanceolate, medium-sized leaves. *Growth* upright, medium-jointed, vigorous, free-flowering, bushy. *Flowers* large. Bush.

'Errol'

BRAND 1949
Double
Tube scarlet, medium length and thickness. *Sepals* scarlet, long, broad upturned *Corolla* pink, full and compact, large. *Foliage* medium green. *Growth* upright, bushy, self-branching and free-flowering. Bush or standard.

'Eschott Elf'

RYLE 1976
AFS Registration No 1400
Single
Tube white, flushed pink, short and thin. *Sepals* white flushed pink, long, thin and completely reflexed. *Corolla* white, bell-shaped. *Foliage* medium green, small to medium-sized leaves. *Growth* trailer, bushy, vigorous and free-flowering. Very small flower, useful for small pot culture. *Parentage* 'Pink Cloud' × 'Lena Dalton' seedling × 'Sonata' × 'Lakeside'.

'Escondilo'

EVANS AND REEVES 1952
Double
Tube pale pink, long and medium thickness. *Sepals* light pink with green tips, long and flaring. *Corolla* light violet, fading to lilac on maturity, very loose petalled, medium size. *Foliage* medium green, medium to large leaves. *Growth* upright, vigorous, bushy and free-flowering. Bush.

'España'

FOSTER 1973
AFS Registration No 1085

Single
Tube white with a pink cast, short, medium thickness. *Sepals* white, flushed pale pink on top, undersides pink with green tips, long narrow and tapering. *Corolla* rosy pink, pink at the base of the petals and a deeper colour on the petal edges, compact, medium-sized bloom. *Stamens and pistil* pink. *Foliage* bright medium green, broad, medium-sized leaves with pinkish stems. *Growth* trailer, vigorous, free-flowering. Basket.

'Esperanza'
REITER 1942
Single
Tube dark rose madder, short and medium thickness. *Sepals* dark rose madder, small. *Corolla* pale fuchsia purple, compact, medium-sized blooms. *Foliage* medium to dark green, medium-sized leaves. *Growth* upright, bushy, vigorous and free-flowering. Bush. *Parentage F. lycioides* ×.

'Estelle Marie' (59)
NEWTON 1973
AFS Registration No 1082
Single
Tube greenish-white, short and thick. *Sepals* white with green tips, completely recurving. *Corolla* pale violet purple, darkening on maturity, with white at the base of the petals. *Foliage* darkish green, oval, medium-sized leaves. *Stamens and pistil* pink. *Growth* upright, self-branching, vigorous, bushy and free-flowering. Blooms are held upright, well out from the foliage; reminiscent of the cultivar from which this one must be descended—'Bon Accorde'. Excellent exhibition variety. Bush.

'Esther'
PUGH 1974
AFS Registration No 1188
Double
Tube white, short and thick. *Sepals* white with green tips, crepe effect on the underside recurving. *Corolla* purple violet RHS 81C, shading to 82C, full medium to large size. *Stamens and pistil* red. *Foliage* medium green, medium-sized leaves. *Growth* upright, bushy, self-branching, vigorous, and free-flowering. Bush or standard.

'Esther Nelson'
NELSON 1951
AFS Registration No 175
Double
Tube deep red, medium length and thickness. *Sepals* red, long and reflexing slightly. *Corolla* orchid purple shading to pink, full and compact, medium-sized blooms. *Foliage* medium green. *Growth* willowy branches, trailer, free-flowering, but needs careful pinching. Basket.

'Estrella'
NIEDERHOLZER 1941
Single
Tube rose pink, medium length and thickness. *Sepals* rose pink, upturned. *Corolla* violet purple, compact. *Foliage* medium green. *Growth* upright, vigorous, bushy, free-flowering. Bush.

'Estrellita'
TIRET 1950
AFS Registration No 67
Single
Tube white with pink flush, medium length and thickness. *Sepals* pink, long and upturned. *Corolla* white with pale pink veining, long and compact, medium-sized blooms. *Foliage* medium green. *Growth* upright, bushy, free-flowering. Bush.

'Eternal Flame'
PASKESEN 1971
AFS Registration No 959
Semi-double
Tube salmon orange, medium length and thickness. *Sepals* salmon orange, held outwards. *Corolla* smoky rose with salmon streaks at the base of the petals, medium-sized blooms. *Foliage* medium green, medium-sized leaves, serrated. *Growth* upright, vigorous, bushy and free-flowering. Bush.

'Ethel'
MARTIN 1967
AFS Registration No 726
Semi-double
Tube white with pink flush, medium length and thickness. *Sepals* white on top with green tips, pale pink on the underside. *Corolla* lavender in the centre with pink petaloids, fading to pale orchid and spreading. Medium to large blooms. *Foliage* medium green. *Growth* upright, vigorous, bushy and free-flowering. Bush.

'Ethel Wilson'
J. WILSON 1967
Single
Tube pink, short and thick. *Sepals* pale pink with white tips. *Corolla* cerise with pink at the base of the petals, medium-sized blooms. *Foliage* medium green, medium-sized leaves. *Growth* upright, bushy, vigorous and free-flowering. Bush or garden hardy.

'Eva Boerg'
YORKE 1943
Semi-double
Tube greenish white, short and thick. *Sepals* white with pink flush on top and with green tips, pink crepe effect on the underside, broad and reflexed. *Corolla* pinkish purple, splashed pink, with paler colour at the base of the petals. Fairly loose petalled. *Stamens* pink. *Pistil* pink. *Foliage* pale to medium green, oval, serrated, medium-sized leaves. *Growth* upright, tending to be rather lax, self-branching, bushy, vigorous and free-flowering. Very easy to grow. Bush.

'Evelyn Kern'
KUECHLER 1962
AFS Registration No 504
Double
Tube deep rose pink, short and thick. *Sepals* rose pink, broad and upturned. *Corolla* violet blue, marbled pink at the base of the petals. Large bloom, very compact and full. *Foliage* dark green, medium to large leaves. *Growth* natural trailer, vigorous, free-flowering. Basket.

'Evelyn Steele Little'
GREEN 1930
Single
Tube rose red, short, medium thickness. *Sepals* rose red, held over the corolla. *Corolla* lavender pink with magenta markings on the petals, small to medium-sized blooms. *Stamens and pistil* pink. *Foliage* medium green, long and slightly serrated. *Growth* trailer, bushy, self-branching, vigorous and free-flowering. Basket or half-basket.

'Evening Sky'
TRAVIS 1957
Registered 1973
AFS Registration No 1140
Double
Tube eau-de-nil flushed rose bengal, long and thin. *Sepals* eau-de-nil flushed rose bengal, long, reflexing. *Corolla* violet flushed ruby when the bloom opens, with paler flushes of orange, pink and ruby. Full and compact. Large blooms. *Foliage* dark green, obovate, red veining, serrated. *Growth* natural trailer, vigorous, self-branching, bushy and free-flowering. Basket.

'Evensong' (26)
DR O. COLVILLE 1968
Single
Tube pink, medium length and thickness. *Sepals* white with green tips, long, broad and completely reflexed against the tube. *Corolla* white, loose bell-shaped. *Stamens* pink. *Foliage* pale green, medium-sized, serrated leaves. *Growth* upright, bushy, vigorous, self-branching and free-flowering. Bush.

'Eyecatcher'
JACKSON 1977
AFS Registration No 1416
Double
Tube rose pink (RHS 55A) medium length and thickness. *Sepals* rose pink (RHS 55A) on the outside, deep rose

(RHS 55B) on the underside. Short and broad. *Corolla* white, deep rose (RHS 58B), veined lighter rose (RHS 55C) at the base of the petals. Very full. *Stamens* rose pink RHS 55A. *Foliage* mid-green, close-jointed. *Growth* upright, self-branching and bushy. Free-flowering, four at each leaf joint, and early bloomer. Bush or standard. Good exhibition plant.

'Fabulous'
PALKO/SOO YUN 1978
AFS Registration No 1444
Double
Tube Tyrian purple, long, medium thickness. *Sepals* Tyrian purple, with white and yellow tips, medium length and width, curving upwards. *Corolla* spiraea red fading to magenta rose at the sepals. *Stamens and pistil* Tyrian purple with yellow tips. *Foliage* olive green, $3\frac{1}{4}$ m (8 cm) long by $1\frac{3}{4}$ in (4.5 cm) wide. *Growth* natural trailer, bushy and self-branching, very floriferous.

'Fair Cop'
PUGH 1974
AFS Registration No 1189
Semi-double
Tube white, short and of medium thickness. *Sepals* pure white, flushed pink on maturity, crepe effect on the undersides, reflexed slightly. *Corolla* purple RHS 78B, full, medium-sized bloom. *Foliage* medium green, medium-sized leaves. *Growth* upright, bushy, vigorous, free-flowering. Prefers heat. Bush.

'Fairyland'
SOO YUN 1975
AFS Registration No 1405
Double
Tube white, long. *Sepals* pink with green tips, flaring upwards. *Corolla* variegated amethyst violet, maturing to variegated magenta, tight and very full. Medium size. *Stamens* magenta pink, stigma chrome yellow. *Foliage* medium green and slightly serrated. *Growth* upright, vigorous, and very floriferous. Bush or standard.

'Fairytale'
LOCKERBIE 1972
AFS Registration No 1047
Semi-double
Tube pink, short, medium thickness. *Sepals* candy pink, reflexing against the tube. *Corolla* candy pink, medium size. *Foliage* medium green. *Growth* vigorous, trailing, bushy, free-flowering. Basket. Seedling from 'Pink Galore' and 'Pink Cloud.'

'Falling Stars' (117)
REITER SR 1941
Single
Tube pale pink, longish, thick. *Sepals* deep reddish pink on top, pale pink on the undersides. Medium length, held downwards from the horizontal. *Corolla* dark orange red, very compact and neat. *Stamens and pistil* pink. *Foliage* light green, medium-sized leaves, serrated. *Growth* upright, tends to be rather lax, bushy if pinched at an early stage, otherwise throws long, arching branches. Bush or summer bedder.

'Fancy Flute'
HANDLEY 1972
AFS Registration No 1054
Single
Tube greenish white, medium length, thickish. *Sepals* white with green tips, completely recurving. *Corolla* magenta, RHS 57B with red RHS 44B edges to the petals which are velvety and fluted (hence the name). *Foliage* medium green, medium to large-sized leaves, serrated. *Growth* upright, bushy, free-flowering and self-branching. Bush.

'Fancy Pants'
REEDSTROM 1961
AFS Registration No 489
Double
Tube red, medium length and thickness. *Sepals* bright red, recurving. *Corolla* opens purple and fades to reddish purple, very full. *Foliage* medium green, medium-sized leaves, serrated. *Growth* upright, vigorous, bushy, free-flowering, very easy to

grow. Bush or can be trained to basket with weights.

'Fan Dancer'
CASTRO 1962
AFS Registration No 513
Double
Tube carmine, medium length, rather thick. *Sepals* carmine, very broad and short, reflexing. *Corolla* lavender blue in the centre, outer petals splashed with pink, and with reddish pink veins. *Stamens* pink, pistil reddish pink. *Foliage* medium green, long leaves, very slight serrations. *Growth* vigorous, bushy, rather lax, very free-flowering. Bush (requires staking).

'Fanfare'
REITER SR 1941
Single
Tube pink with carmine stripes, long and thin. *Sepals* carmine pink with green tips, short and held downwards from the horizontal. *Corolla* scarlet, small and compact. *Foliage* darkish green, large leaves. *Growth* very vigorous, tall grower with drooping stems, very long (3 in–7.5 cm) flowers, blooming late in the season into winter. A very striking flower, but one with a most untidy habit of growth.

'Fan Tan'
PASKESEN 1973
AFS Registration No 1110
Double
Tube pale pink, short, medium thickness. *Sepals* white with pale pink tips, reflexing. *Corolla* reddish-orange, marbled at the base of the outside petals. *Foliage* medium green, medium-sized leaves, serrated. *Growth* upright, bushy, very vigorous and free-flowering. Bush or standard.

'Fantasy'
WALTZ 1951
AFS Registration No 106
Semi-double
Tube white, short, medium thickness. *Sepals* white with pink flush on the outside, fuchsia pink on the underside, long and upturned. *Corolla* pale orchid pink at the base of the petals, shading to deep purple at the edges and overlaid with small petaloids of the same colour. Opens almost flat. *Foliage* medium green, medium to large-sized leaves. *Growth* upright, vigorous, bushy and self-branching. Very free-flowering.

'Fascination'
LEMOINE 1905
Double 5 in (13 cm)
English name for 'Emile de Wildeman' (q.v.).

'Fashion'
NEIDERHOLZER-WALTZ 1951
AFS Registration No 91
Semi-double
Tube white, medium length and thickness. *Sepals* rose pink on top, flushed deeper shades, pink on the undersides. *Corolla* deep violet purple with mauve marbling and rose pink petaloids. Medium-sized blooms. *Foliage* medium green, medium-sized leaves. *Growth* upright, bushy, vigorous, and free-flowering. Bush.

'Favourite'
BLAND 1868
Single $3\frac{1}{2}$ in (9 cm) long
Tube white, flushed carmine pink. *Sepals* white, flushed carmine, medium width, horizontal and curling slightly, rosy red, white at the base of the petals, very compact. *Foliage* medium green. Medium-sized and serrated. *Growth* lax bush, free-flowering, long stems. Standard/pyramid. A good old variety.

'Fenrother Fairy'
RYLE 1979
AFS Registration No 1527
Single
Tube thin, medium length, pinky white. *Sepals* horizontal, curving upwards, white with pink flush and green tips. *Corolla*

pale pink RHS 62D, tube-like. *Stamens* magenta. *Stigma* white. *Leaves* medium green. *Growth* small, upright. Bushy, dwarf growth. Bush.

'Festival'
SCHNABEL 1948
Semi-double
Tube pale pink, medium length and thickness. *Sepals* pink, long and upturned. *Corolla* claret rose, medium to large blooms. *Foliage* medium green, medium-sized leaves. *Growth* upright, vigorous, bushy and free-flowering. Bush.

'Fiddlesticks'
CASTRO 1973
AFS Registration No 1103
Single
Tube white with a pale pinkish flush, long and thin. *Sepals* very pale pink, paler at the tips, long, narrow and slightly twisted. Sepals held horizontally. *Corolla* deep rose red with darker edge to the petals, and pink at the base, keeping fairly compact. *Foliage* dark green, medium-sized leaves. *Growth* semi-trailer, bushy, self-branching and fairly vigorous. Bush or basket with weights.

'Fiery Spider'
MUNKNER 1960
AFS Registration No 452
Single
Tube pale carmine, long and thin. *Sepals* pale salmon pink, long and narrow, arching upwards, and with green tips. *Corolla* crimson, flushed orange, small and tight. *Foliage* pale to medium green, medium-sized leaves, very slightly serrated. *Growth* natural trailer, very vigorous and free-flowering. Basket.

'Fiona' (58)
W.D. CLARK 1962
Single
Tube white, long and thin. *Sepals* white with green tips, long, narrow and completely recurving to the tube, twisting slightly. *Corolla* opens a beautiful shade of blue, which matures to reddish purple, white markings at the base of the petals. *Stamens* pink. *Foliage* medium green, medium-sized leaves, finely serrated. *Growth* upright, vigorous, very free-flowering, not self-branching. A very beautiful flower, but this cultivar is prone to *Botrytis*. Bush or standard.

'Firebird'
DE GRAAF 1976
Single
Tube light red, long and medium thickness. *Sepals* light red, long and spidery. *Corolla* red with purple shading. Large blooms. *Stamens and style* pink. *Foliage* medium green. *Growth* lax, free-flowering, self-branching and vigorous. Basket or climber. *Parentage* 'Mevr Goyaerts' ×.

'Fireglow'
NELSON 1953
AFS Registration No 180
Double
Tube white, thin, medium length. *Sepals* pale rose pink, slender and upturned. *Corolla* rosy red, shorter outer petals pale rose, medium-sized blooms. *Foliage* medium green, medium-sized leaves. *Growth* natural trailer, self-branching, free-flowering. Basket.

'Firelite'
WALTZ 1965
AFS Registration No 654
Double
Tube white medium length and thickness. *Sepals* white, long and pointed, curling slightly. *Corolla* brilliant carnival red, very full and fluffy, large bloom. *Foliage* light green, medium-sized leaves. *Growth* upright, self-branching, bushy and vigorous. Bush.

'Fire Marshal Parker'
HAZARD
Double
Tube red, medium length and thickness. *Sepals* red, reflexing slightly. *Corolla* deep

purple streaked with flame red, large and full. *Foliage* medium to dark green, medium-sized leaves. *Growth* vigorous, bushy, upright, self-branching and very free-flowering. Bush or standard.

'Fire Mountain'
STUBBS 1980
AFS Registration No 1536
Double
Tube flesh-coloured medium length and width. *Sepals* pale orange pink, slightly curving. *Corolla* large orange carmine, shaded orange on the outer petals. Opens compact but spreads as the bloom ages. *Foliage* medium green, 3 in (7.5 cm) long by 2 in (5 cm) wide, new growth shows some red veining. *Growth* semi-trailer which will trail with weights and will make a good basket. Immature plants show single and semi-double blooms.

'Fire Opal'
GAGNON 1963
AFS Registration No 552
Single to semi-double
Tube red, medium length and thickness. *Sepals* red, long and broad. *Corolla* deep blue, maturing to a rosy blue, petals veined red. *Foliage* medium bronzy green, large leaves. *Growth* trailer, bushy, vigorous, self-branching. Basket.

'First Kiss' (89)
DE GRAAF 1978
Semi-double
Tube creaming white, medium length and thickness. *Sepals* creamy white, becoming reddish if grown in full sun. *Corolla* pale rose pink, medium-sized blooms. *Foliage* medium green, medium-sized leaves. *Growth* self-branching, bushy, vigorous, free-flowering. A very attractive flower. Bush. *Parentage* 'La Campanella' ×.

'First Lady'
STUBBS 1973
AFS Registration No 1080
Double
Tube pinkish white, long and rather thick. *Sepals* pale pink on top with green tips, salmon pink on the undersides, long, narrow and held well out. *Corolla* coral pink, loose petalled. *Stamens* pinkish. *Foliage* medium green, medium to large-sized leaves, finely serrated. *Growth* natural trailer, very lax, bushy, free-flowering. Basket.

'First Love'
KENNETT 1957
Double
Tube greenish white, medium length and thickness. *Sepals* white with pinkish flush on top, green tipped, pink on the undersides. *Corolla* pale lavender blue with pink marbling on the outer petals and pink veining. Medium-sized flowers. *Foliage* pale to medium green, medium-sized leaves, finely serrated. *Growth* natural trailer, bushy, free-flowering, vigorous. Basket.

'Flair'
TIRET 1961
AFS Registration No 486
Double
Tube white, thick, medium length. *Sepals* white, broad and curling up and round the tube. *Corolla* raspberry pink, very full, medium-sized blooms. *Foliage* trailer, vigorous, self-branching and very free-flowering. Half-basket.

'Flame'
NIEDERHOLZER
Single
Tube white, long and of medium thickness. *Sepals* white, flushed pink, on top. Undersides pink, long, narrow and upturned. *Corolla* reddish orange, very compact. *Foliage* medium green, medium-sized, broad leaves, finely serrated. *Growth* upright, bushy, self-branching and free-flowering. Bush.

'Flame of Bath'
COLVILLE 1967
Single
Tube salmon pink, short and thick. *Sepals*

salmon pink, broad and completely reflexed. *Corolla* orange-cerise, long and compact. *Stamens and style* pink. *Foliage* medium green with red veining, medium to large-sized leaves, serrated. *Growth* upright, bushy, free-flowering. Bush.

'Flaming Beauty'
SOO YUN 1972
AFS Registration No 1041
Double
Tube pale crimson, long and of medium thickness. *Sepals* pale crimson, broad, slightly reflexing. *Corolla* light crimson red, full, medium-sized blooms. *Foliage* dark green, large-sized leaves, serrated. *Growth* upright, bushy, self-branching and free-flowering. Bush.

'Flaming Glory'
MARTIN 1962
AFS Registration No 517
Double
Tube white with greenish tinge, long and thin. *Sepals* pale pink on top with green tips, darker pink on the undersides, broad and reflexed. *Corolla* purple to bright red in the centre, outer petals orange and pink, medium-sized bloom. *Foliage* pale green, medium-sized leaves, very finely serrated. *Growth* trailer, self-branching, vigorous, bushy. Basket.

'Flamingo'
DE GRAAF 1976
Single
Tube salmon pink, long and of medium thickness. *Sepals* salmon pink, paler towards the tips, which are green. *Corolla* salmon-pink, small. Almost a self-coloured bloom. *Filaments and style* pink. *Foliage* medium green, small leaves. *Growth* upright, self-branching, free-flowering. A very attractive flower. Bush. *Parentage* 'Duke of York' ×.

'Flash'
HAZARD
Single
Tube light magenta red, thin, medium length. *Sepals* light magenta, short and broad, pointing downwards. *Corolla* red, small. *Foliage* light green, small to medium-sized leaves, finely serrated. *Growth* upright, bushy, self-branching, very vigorous. Bush or garden hardy. Prone to attack by red spider mite.

'Flashlight'
GADSBY 1968
Registered 1971
AFS Registration No 977
Single
Tube pale pink, very short and thin. *Sepals* pale pink with green tips, turning up from the centre. *Corolla* pinkish purple, small. *Stamens* pink. *Foliage* pale green. *Growth* upright, bushy, self-branching, and free-flowering. Bush or garden hardy. *Parentage* 'Flash' × *F. magellanica* var *molinae*.

'Flavia'
TIRET 1971
AFS Registration No 993
Double
Tube pink, medium length and thickness. *Sepals* pink, long, upturned. *Corolla* deep lilac blue, full and compact, medium-sized bloom. *Foliage* medium green, medium-sized leaves, serrated. *Growth* natural trailer, bushy, free-flowering. Basket.

'Flek'
MUELLER 1975
AFS Registration No 1308
Double
Tube light pink, medium length and thickness. *Sepals* light pink with rose tips, medium size, pointed and standing straight outwards. *Corolla* pink, tipped rose, medium size. *Foliage* medium-sized, dark green leaves. *Growth* bushy, upright. Bush.

'Flim Flam'
DE GRAAF 1976
Single
Tube creamy white with pink flush, long

and of medium thickness. *Sepals* creamy white, flushed deep pink. *Corolla* deep salmon pink with darker, orangey edges to the petals. *Stamens* pink. *Style* white. *Foliage* medium to dark green, smallish leaves. *Growth* upright, bushy, self-branching and free-flowering. Bush.

'Flirtation'
LEITNER 1946
Double
Tube pale pink, medium length and thickness. *Sepals* pale pink on top, darker pink on the undersides, long and reflexing around the tube. *Corolla* pale pinkish mauve, rather loose, darker edge to the petals. *Foliage* medium green, longish leaves, finely serrated. *Growth* upright, bushy, self-branching and free-flowering. Bush.

'Flirtation Waltz' (39)
WALTZ 1962
AFS Registration No 523
Double
Tube white, short and thick. *Sepals* white on top with green tips, pink on the underside. *Corolla* pale pink, very full and compact. *Stamens* pink. *Foliage* pale to medium green, medium-sized leaves, serrated edges. *Growth* upright, bushy, self-branching, free-flowering and very vigorous. An excellent exhibition plant, though the blooms tend to mark easily.

'Flocon de Neige'
LEMOINE 1884
Semi-double to double
Tube bright red, short and thick. *Sepals* red, short and broad, curling upwards towards the tube. *Corolla* white with scarlet veins, medium-sized. *Foliage* medium green, small to medium-sized leaves, serrated. *Growth* upright, self-branching, bushy, vigorous and free-flowering. Easy to grow and train. Bush.

'Flora'
TOLLEY 1973
AFS Registration No 1156
Semi-double
Tube bright cerise red, medium length and thickness. *Sepals* bright cerise, long and narrow, upturned. *Corolla* pale violet purple, veined pink and with pale violet petaloids. Large and bell-shaped. *Foliage* yellowish green with red veins, medium to large leaves. *Growth* vigorous, bushy, upright, self-branching and free-flowering. Bush. *Parentage* 'Tennessee Waltz' ×.

'Floradora'
WALTZ 1951
AFS Registration No 107
Double
Tube neyron rose, short and medium thick. *Sepals* neyron rose, broad and arching. *Corolla* deep violet, flushed rose pink at the base of the petals. Medium blooms. *Foliage* medium green, medium-sized leaves. *Growth* upright, vigorous, bushy, free-flowering. Bush or standard.

'Flora Rugh'
GAGNON 1963
AFS Registration No 554
Single
Tube carmine red, medium length and thickness. *Sepals* carmine red, slightly reflexed. *Corolla* orchid blue, medium-sized blooms. *Foliage* medium to dark green, medium-sized leaves, serrated. *Growth* upright, bushy, self-branching and free-flowering. Bush.

'Florence Turner'
TURNER 1955
Single
Tube pale pink, short and thick. *Sepals* white, short and broad, held just below the horizontal. *Corolla* pale pinkish mauve, very compact. *Foliage* medium green, medium-sized foliage, serrated edges. *Stamens* pink. *Growth* upright, bushy, self-branching, free-flowering. Bush.

'Florentina'
MARTIN-TIRET 1960
AFS Registration No 432
Double

Tube greenish white, short and of medium thickness. *Sepals* white with green tips, curling upwards towards the tube, crepe effect on the undersides. *Corolla* burgundy red, very full and fluffy, white at the base of the petals. *Foliage* medium green with red veins, medium size, longish leaves. *Growth* natural trailer, bushy and free-flowering. Basket.

'Flossie Fant'
GAGNON 1964
AFS Registration No 599
Double
Tube white, flushed pale pink, medium length and thickness. *Sepals* white with pale pink lines, undersides splashed pink. *Corolla* white with pink veins, attractive bloom which opens up to resemble an orchid. *Foliage* medium green to dark green, willowy branches. *Growth* natural trailer, long arching branches, free-flowering. Basket.

'Flossie Mae'
FOSTER 1973
AFS Registration No 1086
Double
Tube red, short and thin. *Sepals* red, long and narrow, reflexed to the tube. *Corolla* white with red veins, compact and full. *Stamens and pistil* red. *Foliage* light to medium green with red stems, and finely serrated. *Growth* natural trailer, bushy, free-flowering. Basket.

'Fluffy Ruffles'
COPLEY 1966
AFS Registration No 692
Double
Tube rose pink, medium length and thickness. *Sepals* rose red, long and upturned. *Corolla* white, full but rather loose petalled. Medium-sized bloom. *Foliage* medium green, medium to large leaves. *Growth* natural trailer, long branches, free-flowering. Basket.

'Fluorescent'
WALKER AND JONES 1952
Double
Tube white, medium length and thickness. *Sepals* white with green tips, long and arching. *Corolla* orchid pink, white at the base of the petals, with short outer petals shaded roseine purple, medium blooms. *Foliage* medium green, medium-sized leaves. *Growth* upright, vigorous, bushy and free-flowering. Bush or basket with weights.

'Flyaway'
CROCKETT 1969
AFS Registration No 820
Double
Tube white with pink flush, short and of medium thickness. *Sepals* white on top, rose madder crepe effect on the undersides completely reflexing over the tube. *Corolla* spectrum violet fading to orchid purple, with rose madder flush at the base of the petals, large blooms. *Foliage* medium green with red veining, medium to large-sized leaves, long and pointed. *Growth* upright, bushy, self-branching, free-flowering. Bush.

'Fly by Night'
CROCKETT 1965
AFS Registration No 821
Double
Tube cherry red, medium length and thickness. *Sepals* cherry red, recurving. *Corolla* fuchsia purple shaded cherry red at the base of the petals, and with deep purple edges. Large blooms. *Foliage* medium green, medium-sized leaves. *Growth* upright, vigorous, free-flowering and bushy. Bush.

'Flying Cloud'
REITER 1949
Double
Tube white, short and of medium thickness. *Sepals* white with green tips, pink on the undersides, completely reflexing over the tube. *Corolla* white, with splashes of pink at the base of the petals, full but rather loose-petalled. *Foliage* medium to dark green, medium-sized leaves, serrated. *Growth* upright, bushy, vigorous,

but tending to be rather lax, prefers to be grown in shade to keep its colour. Bush.

'Folies Bergère'
FUCHSIA FOREST 1968
AFS Registration No 769
Double
Tube pinkish white, short and thick. *Sepals* pink with green tips, short, broad and upturned. *Corolla* pale lavender blue with pink splashes, very full and fluffy, but rather loose-petalled, and open. *Foliage* medium to darkish green, medium-sized, broad leaves with very fine serrations. *Growth* natural trailer, bushy and free-flowering. Basket.

'Fondant'
HOWARTH 1980
AFS Registration No 1578
Double
Tube pink. *Sepals* frosty candy pink, held horizontally. *Corolla* pure white, no veining, medium size. *Stamens* deep red. *Pistil* pink, very long. *Foliage* dark green, small and glossy. *Growth* upright, self-branching, small. *Parentage* 'Swingtime' × 'Seventeen'.

'Forest King'
TOLLEY 1978
AFS Registration No 1471
Single
Tube magenta, medium length and thickness. *Sepals* magenta with green tips, broad, medium length and not upturned. *Corolla* magenta violet. *Foliage* dark green with red central vein, long, oval and very slightly serrated. *Growth* natural semi-trailer which will make a good basket or bush/standard.

'Forget-me-not'
NIEDERHOLZER 1940
Single
Tube pale pink, long and thin. *Sepals* pale pink, long, narrow, and completely recurved. *Corolla* pale blue, maturing to pale mauve, small and compact. *Foliage* pale green, small to medium-sized leaves. *Growth* upright, self-branching, vigorous and bushy. Very free-flowering. Bush.

'Fort Bragg'
WALTZ 1957
AFS Registration No 314
Double
Tube pink, short and thick. *Sepals* pink, broad and upturned. *Corolla* pale lavender with rose-pink veins, rather an untidy, loose petalled flower. *Foliage* medium green, medium-sized leaves. *Growth* vigorous, bushy, rather lax growing, self-branching and free-flowering. Basket.

'Forward Look'
GADSBY 1973
AFS Registration No 1122
Single
Tube pink, short and thick. *Sepals* pink with green tips, broad, short and upturned almost to the tube. *Corolla* violet-blue, small to medium-sized. *Foliage* medium green, medium to large-sized leaves, slightly serrated. *Growth* upright, bushy, vigorous, self-branching and free-flowering with blooms held at right angles to the foliage. A good exhibition variety. Bush.

'Foxtrot'
TOLLEY 1974
AFS Registration No 1229
Semi-double
Tube pale cerise, short and of medium thickness. *Sepals* pale cerise with green tips, held well out from the corolla. *Corolla* pale lavender blue, pink at the base of the petals, open and semi-flared. *Stamens and pistil* pink. *Foliage* pale green, small to medium-sized leaves, serrated. *Growth* upright, bushy, self-branching, vigorous and free-flowering. Very easy to grow and shape. Bush or standard. *Parentage* 'Tennessee Waltz' ×.

'Frances Keizer'
GAGNON 1967
AFS Registration No 709
Double

Tube rose red, medium length and thickness. *Sepals* red, crepe effect on the underside. *Corolla* deep rose red, very full and compact. *Foliage* medium green, medium to large-sized leaves. *Growth* natural trailer, bushy and free-flowering. This cultivar invariably has five sepals. Basket.

'Frances Lo Bue'
PENNISI 1969
AFS Registration No 860
Double
Tube white with pink flush, short and thick. *Sepals* white on top with pink on the undersides, short and upturned. *Corolla* fuchsia pink with pink petaloids, medium-sized blooms. *Foliage* pale green, small and serrated. *Growth* upright, vigorous, bushy, self-branching and free-flowering. Bush.

'François Devos'
COENE 1869
Double
Tube pink, thick and of medium length. *Sepals* pink, slightly paler at the tips, held well out from the corolla and sweeping upwards. *Corolla* reddish purple with splashes of pink on the outer petals, and pale reddish at the base. *Foliage* medium to dark green with scarlet veining, very large leaves, slightly serrated. *Growth* upright, vigorous, bushy, self-branching and free-flowering. Bush.

'Frankie'
J.A. WRIGHT 1980
AFS Registration No 1599
Double
Tube light pink, longish. *Sepals* light pink, arching back towards the tube. *Corolla* mottled blue and red, small. *Foliage* dark green, medium-sized. *Growth* upright, self-branching, bushy. Will make a good bush. Colours best in the sun. Seedling of 'Winston Churchill'.

'Frau Hilde Rademacher'
RADEMACHER 1901
Double
Tube scarlet, short and thick. *Sepals* scarlet, broad, reflexing. *Corolla* lilac-blue, very full, with cerise splashes on the petals. Medium-sized blooms. *Foliage* medium green with red veins. Medium to large-sized leaves. *Growth* upright, rather lax, self-branching and free-flowering. Bush (if staked) or half-basket.

'Fred's First'
WOOLLEY 1978
AFS Registration No 1488
Double
Tube carmine rose, medium length and thickness. *Sepals* carmine rose, fully reflexing and curling. *Corolla* violet, tinged pink at the base of the petals. *Stamens* carmine rose. *Pistil* bright pink. *Foliage* medium green. *Growth* bushy, self-branching, upright. Bush or pyramid. Colours best if grown in shade.

'Freedom'
MARTIN 1961
AFS Registration No 462
Double
Tube bright red, medium length, thick. *Sepals* bright red, broad and completely reflexed. *Corolla* dark blue with red and white marbling on the petals, very frilly. *Foliage* medium to dark green, medium-sized leaves. *Growth* trailer, self-branching, bushy, free-flowering. Bush or basket.

'Freestyle'
GADSBY 1975
AFS Registration No 1313
Single
Tube rose bengal RHS 61D, long and thick. *Sepals* rose bengal RHS 61D, long and held well out. *Corolla* imperial purple RHS 78A, lighter shade at the base of the petals, large bell-shaped, similar to 'Lady Isobel Barnett', but larger. *Foliage* deep green, medium to large size. *Growth* upright, tall growing, vigorous, bushy. Bush or standard. *Parentage* 'Lady Isobel Barnett' × 'Bishop's Bells'.

'Frenchi'
WALTZ 1953
AFS Registration No 166

Double
Tube white with pale pink flush, medium length and thickness. *Sepals* salmon pink, long and broad, recurving to the tube. *Corolla* silvery blue and pale mauve, splashed pink. A very attractive bloom. *Foliage* medium green, medium-sized leaves. *Growth* upright, bushy, self-branching, free-flowering. Bush.

'Frolic'
ERICKSON 1962
AFS Registration No 540
Single
Tube flesh pink, medium length and thickness. *Sepals* flesh pink on top, light pink on the undersides, with green tips, long and wide. *Corolla* soft mallow pink, open and spreading. *Foliage* medium green, medium-sized leaves. *Growth* trailer, bushy, vigorous free-flowering. Basket.

'Frosted Amethyst'
STUBBS 1975
AFS Registration No 1258
Double
Tube bright red, medium length and thickness. *Sepals* bright red, long and broad. *Corolla* amethyst purple with streaks of red, pink and pale amethyst. Petals serrated. Outer petals flare over the long centre of the corolla. *Foliage* medium green, medium-sized. *Growth* semi-trailer which will make a good basket with weights. Very large bloom.

'Frosted Flame'
HANDLEY 1975
Single
Tube white, medium length and thickness. *Sepals* white with pale pink flush on the underside, long and narrow and held well out. *Corolla* bright flame RHS 43C with deeper edge RHS 46A, and pale pink near to the tube. Barrel shaped with overlapping petals. *Stamens and pistil* rose pink. *Foliage* bright green medium to large. *Growth* natural trailer, self-branching and very free-flowering. Flowers early. Makes a good basket. Prefers shade for best colour.

'Frostiana'
ERICKSON/SAYERS 1979
Double
Tube white, medium length. *Sepals* white on top, flushed pink fading to deep pink. The undersides white, flushed pink. Sepals longish, reflexing. *Corolla* lilac with pink splashing on petals, petaloids lilac splashed pink. *Foliage* dark green, leaves round and short. *Growth* semi-trailer which will make a good basket. Prefers heat for best results. Attractive and showy blooms.

'Frost's Midas Touch'
FROST 1979
AFS Registration No 1508
Single
Sport of 'Display'
Self-colour, same as 'Display', but smaller. *Tube* longer and sepals do not recurve. *Corolla* small. *Foliage* variegated green and gold. *Growth* upright and bushy, self-branching. Introduced in Zimbabwe in 1973.

'Frosty'
NIEDERHOLZER 1947
Single
Tube crimson red, medium length and thickness. *Sepals* dark crimson, long and broad, upturned. *Corolla* pure white, long and compact. *Foliage* medium green, medium to large leaves. *Growth* natural trailer, bushy, self-branching, free-flowering. Basket.

'Frosty Bell'
GADSBY 1970
AFS Registration No 977
Single
Tube pink, short and of medium thickness. *Sepals* pink, long and completely reflexed against the tube. *Corolla* white with pink veining, opening almost bell-shaped. *Foliage* darkish green, medium-sized, very long leaves, serrated. *Growth*

upright, bushy, vigorous and free-flowering. Bush. *Parentage* 'Upward Look' × 'Ting-a-Ling'.

'Fuchsia King'
PENNISI 1969
AFS Registration No 817
Double
Tube fuchsia pink, short and of medium thickness. *Sepals* fuchsia pink, medium length. *Corolla* fuchsia pink ageing to deep rose pink with pink marbling. *Foliage* medium green, small leaves. *Growth* natural trailer, self-branching, bushy and free-flowering. Basket.

'Fuchsia Mike'
CONLEY 1953
AFS Registration No 149
Semi-double
Tube bright red, short and medium thickness. *Sepals* bright red, long and upturned. *Corolla* purple shading to carmine red, medium-sized blooms. *Foliage* medium to dark green, with darker veins, long and pointed leaves. *Growth* vigorous, upright, bushy, self-branching, free-flowering. Bush or basket.

'Fuksie Foetsie'
VAN DER GRIJP (Netherlands) 1979
Single, breviflora type
Tube ivory white, shading to flesh pink, small, thick. *Sepals* of the same colour, very small. *Corolla* white, turning pink as the bloom ages. *Foliage* green, small, serrated. *Growth* upright, bushy, vigorous, free-flowering. *Parentage F. microphylla* ×.

'Fuksie Vort'
VAN DER GRIJP 1973
Breviflora type
Tube light pink ageing to rose red. *Sepals* greenish white, ageing red. *Corolla* white, turning to rose on maturity. *Foliage* small, light green, serrated. *Growth* bushy, upright, free-flowering. Bush.

'Gaity'
SCHNABEL 1953
AFS Registration No 111
Double
Tube bright crimson, medium length and thickness. *Sepals* bright crimson, long and upturning. *Corolla* rose bengal, full, medium-sized blooms. *Foliage* medium green, medium-sized leaves. *Growth* upright, low growing, bushy, free-flowering. Bush.

'Gala'
GEO MARTIN
AFS Registration No 673
Double
Tube pale pink, short and thick. *Sepals* pink with green tips, broad and reflexing. *Corolla* centre petals blue, outer petals pink and shades of salmon pink and lavender. Very loose petalled, but attractive colouring, medium-sized blooms. *Foliage* medium green, small to medium-sized leaves. *Growth* bushy, though tending to be rather lax, self-branching and free-flowering. Bush.

'Galathea'
NEIDERHOLZER 1946
Single
Tube pale pink, medium length and thickness. *Sepals* pale pink, longish and upturned. *Corolla* deep pink, fairly large blooms. *Foliage* medium green, medium to large-sized leaves. *Growth* upright, bushy, quite vigorous, free-flowering. Bush.

'Gambit'
HANDLEY 1971
AFS Registration No 985
Single
Tube crimson RHS 52A, short and thin. *Sepals* crimson, narrow and reflexing to the tube. *Corolla* white with pale pink veining on the overlapped petals. Small blooms. *Foliage* medium green, small leaves. *Growth* upright, self-branching, free-flowering. Bush.

'Gardena'
FAIRCLO 1946
Double
Tube red, medium length and thickness.

Sepals red, long, broad and slightly upturned. *Corolla* white, very full and fluffy, large blooms. *Foliage* medium green, medium to large-sized leaves. *Growth* natural trailer, vigorous, free-flowering. Basket.

'Garden Beauty'
GADSBY 1978
AFS Registration No 1481
Double
Tube rose red, thick, medium length. *Sepals* waxy rose red, broad. *Corolla* violet blue, flushed carmine and neyron rose. Large, with 14 petals. *Stamens* red. *Growth* vigorous, upright and bushy, very heavy bloomer. Bush or summer bedder. Believed seedling of 'Lena'.

'Garden Grove'
GORMAN 1970
AFS Registration No 919
Double
Tube pinkish green, medium length and thickness. *Sepals* greeny cream on top, light pink flush on the undersides, and with green tips. *Corolla* different shades of pink on the several layers of petals. Medium-sized blooms. *Foliage* medium green, medium-sized leaves. *Growth* upright, bushy, free-flowering. Bush.

'Garden News'
HANDLEY 1978
AFS Registration No 1453
Double
Tube pink, RHS 52D, short and thick. *Sepals* pink RHS 52D, on top, frosty rose pink RHS 52C on the underside, broad and short, arching from the base of the corolla. *Corolla* shades of magenta-rose, RHS 57B, and 61C, base of the petals rose pink RHS 52C. *Petals* 10 to 12 short, ruffled and curled. *Stamens and pistil* rose pink. *Foliage* mid-green, slightly serrated. *Growth* self-branching, tall growing, vigorous upright. Early flowering, bush.

'Garnet'
NEIDERHOLZER 1946
Single
Tube red, medium length and thickness. *Sepals* red, longish and upturned. *Corolla* deep red, medium-sized blooms. *Foliage* medium green, medium-sized leaves. *Growth* upright, vigorous, bushy and free-flowering. Bush or standard.

'Gartenmeister Bonstedt' (16)
BONSTEDT 1905
Triphylla
Tube long, thin, brick-red, slightly bulging. *Sepals* brick red, small. *Corolla* brick red, short. *Foliage* dark bronzy reddish-green on the upper surface, reddish purple on the undersides, medium to large-sized leaves. *Growth* upright, vigorous but not self-branching, very free-flowering. Bush.

'Gay Anne'
GADSBY 1974
AFS Registration No 1221
Single to semi-double
Tube claret rose RHS 50A, medium length, rather thick. *Sepals* claret rose RHS 50A, on top, crimson RHS 52A on the undersides, medium length, broad and reflexing. *Corolla* mallow pink RHS 72D, petals edged magenta rose RHS 64C and veined rose, with pink shading at the base. *Foliage* medium green, medium-sized leaves, serrated. *Growth* upright, self-branching, vigorous, bushy and very free-flowering, very easy to grow and train to shape. Named in honour of HRH Princess Anne. Bush. Seedling from 'Leonora'.

'Gay Damosel'
RYLE 1977
AFS Registration No 1434
Double
Tube pink, medium length and thickness. *Sepals* neyron rose RHS 55B, long and thin. *Corolla* ruby red RHS 61A at the lower end of the petals, fading to white at the base. Medium-sized bloom. *Stamens and pistil* rhodonite red. *Foliage* forest green RHS 138A, medium-sized leaves. *Growth* upright, self-branching, bushy

and free-flowering. *Parentage* 'Viva Ireland' × 'Joe Kusber'. Bush or standard.

'Gay Darr'
SOO YUN FIELD 1965
AFS Registration No 643
Double
Tube white with pinkish flush, medium length and thickness. *Sepals* reddish white, long and narrow with a fine reddish line around the edges. *Corolla* orchid, medium size, *Foliage* natural trailer, free-flowering, good-sized blooms. Basket.

'Gay Fandango'
NELSON 1951
AFS Registration No 176
Double
Tube carmine pink, medium length and thickness. *Sepals* carmine pink on top, slightly deeper colouring on the undersides, long and arching upwards. *Corolla* rosy claret, lighter at the base of the petals, medium to large-sized bloom. *Foliage* medium green, medium to large-sized leaves, finely serrated. *Growth* lax upright, very vigorous, free-flowering. Bush or standard.

'Gay Future'
GADSBY 1975
AFS Registration No 1314
Single
Tube white, slightly flushed neyron rose, short and thin. *Sepals* white, lightly flushed neyron rose RHS 55A, with green tips, slight recurve at the tips, colour is deeper when grown in the sun. *Corolla* violet RHS 87A, shading to white, bell-shaped. *Foliage* deep green, serrated, medium-sized. *Growth* natural trailer, self-branching, bushy and free-flowering. Basket but can be trained to bush.

'Gay Garland'
REID 1975
AFS Registration No 1305
Double
Tube mimosa yellow RHS 8D medium length and thickness. *Sepals* white flushed neyron rose on top, neyron rose RHS 55A, on the underside. Long standing straight out on opening, turning up slightly on maturity. *Corolla* central petals ruby red RHS 61A with tinges of purple and shaded from pale rose to white at the base of the petals. The smaller outer petals are blotched neyron rose. At the start and finish of the season it will throw single flowers. Occasional petaloids. *Corolla* long and flaring. *Foliage* deep green, medium-sized. *Growth* bushy, quite lax, very floriferous. Bush. *Parentage* 'Monstera' × 'Moon Mist'.

'Gay Lynne'
MARTIN 1960
AFS Registration No 443
Semi-double
Tube white, thin, medium length. *Sepals* white on top, pink on the underside, long and arching. *Corolla* smoky blue fading to orchid, medium-sized blooms, full. *Foliage* light green, small leaves. *Growth* natural trailer, vigorous, bushy, free-flowering. Basket.

'Gay Parasol'
STUBBS 1979
AFS Registration No 1501
Double
Tube ivory green, short and thick. *Sepals* ivory with faint magenta streaks down the edges, fading to ivory overlaid magenta. Not recurving, but lifting above the corolla like a parasol. *Corolla* dark reddish purple fading to bright burgundy red, fairly short, opening flat as it matures. *Foliage* medium to dark green with red veining, slightly serrated. *Growth* medium, self-branching upright which will make a good bush plant. Light-coloured buds contrast well with the dark open blooms.

'Gay Time'
NEIDERHOLZER-WALTZ 1949
Double
Tube pale pink, medium length and thickness. *Sepals* fuchsia pink medium length, upturned. *Corolla* deep blue with splashes

of pink on the petals, which are also edged pink, medium-sized blooms. *Foliage* medium green, medium-sized leaves. *Growth* upright, vigorous, self-branching, bushy and free-flowering. Bush.

'Gazebo'

TIRET 1969
AFS Registration No 830
Semi-double
Tube neyron rose, medium length and thickness. *Sepals* neyron rose, longish. *Corolla* salmon red, full, large blooms. *Foliage* medium green, medium to large-sized leaves. *Growth* natural trailer, bushy, vigorous, free-flowering. Basket.

'Geisha'

NEIDERHOLZER 1947
Single
Tube dark red, medium length and thickness. *Sepals* dark red, long, upturned. *Corolla* pale purple, loose petalled, medium-sized blooms. *Foliage* medium green, medium-sized leaves. *Growth* upright, vigorous, bushy, free-flowering. Bush.

'Geisha Girl'

PUGH 1974
AFS Registration No 1160
Double
Tube red RHS 52A, medium length and thickness. *Sepals* red, recurving completely to the tube. *Corolla* red-purple RHS 67D, medium-sized bloom, very full (22 petals) no petaloids. *Foliage* medium green RHS 137A, medium-sized leaves. *Growth* upright, vigorous, bushy, self-branching, free-flowering and very easy to grow. Bush or standard.

'General Ike'

WALKER AND JONES 1950
Double
Tube crimson, long and thin. *Sepals* crimson, long, narrow and curling. *Corolla* deep aster violet with splashes of white and crimson at the base of the petals, very full, medium-sized blooms. *Foliage* medium green, medium-sized leaves. *Growth* upright, vigorous, long branches, free-flowering. Bush, basket or espalier.

'General Monk' (156)

Raiser and date unknown
Double
Tube cerise, short, and of medium thickness. *Sepals* cerise, short, broad and completely reflexed. *Corolla* bluish-purple, maturing to reddish purple, veined pink, and with white shading at the base of the petals. Small to medium-sized bloom, frilly and full. *Foliage* medium green, small to medium-sized leaves, serrated. *Growth* upright, bushy, vigorous, self-branching and free-flowering. An easy cultivar to grow. Bush.

'General Wavell'

W.W. WHITEMAN 1942
Double
Tube pink, thick, medium length. *Sepals* deep salmon pink with green tips, broad and upturned. *Corolla* cerise with pink marbling to the petals, very full and fluffy, medium-sized blooms. *Foliage* medium to dark green, medium-sized leaves, finely serrated. *Growth* upright, bushy, self-branching, free-flowering. Bush.

'Genevieve Gibson'

FOSTER 1974
AFS Registration No 1171
Double
Tube dull white with pink veins, medium length, thin. *Sepals* rhodamine pink, curling upwards to the tube. *Corolla* amethyst violet flushed rhodamine pink, slightly flared. *Foliage* mistletoe green, small to medium-sized leaves. *Growth* upright, bushy, vigorous and very free-flowering. Bush.

'Genii' (19)

REITER 1951
Single
Tube cerise, thin, medium length. *Sepals*

cerise, small and narrow, curving upwards. *Corolla* very dark purple on opening, maturing to a reddish purple, compact, small blooms. *Foliage* pale to medium yellowish green when grown out of doors in full sun, but tends to turn green in the greenhouse or shaded position. Smallish leaves, finely serrated. *Growth* upright, bushy, vigorous, self-branching and very free-flowering. Bush or garden hardy.

'Genni'
FUCHSIA-LA 1968
AFS Registration No 801
Single to semi-double
Tube red, long and thin. *Sepals* red, long. *Corolla* white, longish, loose petalled. *Foliage* medium green, medium-sized leaves. *Growth* upright, but tending to be rather lax, bushy, free-flowering. Bush or half-basket. (Not to be confused with 'Genii'.)

'Georgana'
H. TIRET 1955
AFS Registration No 237
Double
Tube pink, medium length and thickness. *Sepals* pink on top with green tips, slightly darker shade on the undersides, long, broad and reflexed over the tube. *Corolla* lavender blue, veined pink, and marbled white and pink. *Foliage* medium green, medium to large leaves, finely serrated. *Growth* upright, bushy, vigorous and free-flowering. Bush.

'George Barr'
HAZARD 1930
Single
Tube white, flushed pale pink, thin, medium length. *Sepals* white with green tips, long, narrow and completely recurved to the tube. *Corolla* violet purple, fading with age, and slightly paler colouring at the base of the petals. Small flowers. *Foliage* medium green, small, serrated. *Growth* upright, vigorous, very free-flowering. Bush or standard.

'George Johnson'
DOYLES 1977
AFS Registration No 1429
Single
Tube rose pink, long, medium thickness. *Sepals* rose pink, slightly recurving. *Corolla* rose vermilion, tubular, medium-sized. *Stamens* red. *Pistil* pink, and long. *Foliage* medium green with red petiole, medium-sized leaves. *Growth* upright, bushy and vigorous, free-flowering. Bush.

'George Roe'
GADSBY 1972
AFS Registration No 1065
Double
Tube crimson, medium length and thickness. *Sepals* crimson with green tips, broad and waxy, held low over the corolla. *Corolla* white, with crimson petaloids, very full and compact. Medium-sized flowers. *Foliage* medium green with red veins, medium-sized leaves, very finely serrated. *Growth* upright, bushy, vigorous, self-branching and very free-flowering. Bush. *Parentage* 'Swingtime' × 'Tom Pacey'.

'George Travis'
TRAVIS 1956
Double
Tube white, short and thick. *Sepals* white on top, pale pink shading on the undersides, and with green tips. Long, broad, and curling up over the tube. *Corolla* lilac blue with a silvery case, paler at the base of the petals, globular shape, full and compact. *Foliage* medium green, small to medium-sized leaves, serrated. *Growth* upright, free-flowering, bushy and vigorous. A nice colour combination, but rather prone to red spider mite attacks. Bush.

'Georgia Peach'
CASTRO 1973
AFS Registration No 1104
Semi-double
Tube white, medium length and thickness. *Sepals* white, medium length,

curling up towards the tube. *Corolla* bright peach pink with white marbling on the petals which are ruffled. *Foliage* medium green, medium-sized leaves. *Growth* very lax, bushy, free-flowering. Basket.

'Gift Wrap'

KENNETT 1969

AFS Registration No 865

Double

Tube white, medium length and thickness. *Sepals* white with green tips, medium length, upturned. *Corolla* dianthus purple in the centre with white marbling on the petals which flare out and turn to bright red as the flower matures. White petaloids. Large blooms. *Foliage* medium green, medium to large leaves. *Growth* natural trailer, vigorous, free-flowering. Basket.

'Gilda'

HANDLEY 1971

AFS Registration No 986

Double

Tube pale pink, thick, medium length. *Sepals* pale flesh pink on top, salmon pink on the undersides, short and slightly upturned. *Corolla* coral pink, deeper on the edges of the petals, small to medium-sized blooms. *Foliage* yellowish green, changing to green, very large leaves serrated. *Growth* upright, vigorous, bushy but tending to be rather lax. Bush.

'Ginia'

WATCHORN/BEHRENDS 1970

Registered 1974

AFS Registration No 1159

Single

Tube bright rose pink, medium length and thickness. *Sepals* bright rose pink, horizontal on opening and curling up as they mature. *Corolla* bright violet purple, rose at the base of the petals, opening tight and maturing to form rolled tubes. *Foliage* light green, small to medium-sized leaves. *Growth* upright, vigorous, self-branching, bushy and free-flowering. Bush or garden hardy. *Parentage F. m. macrostema* ×.

'Giselle'

BLACKWELL

Semi-double

Tube white, medium length and thickness. *Sepals* white on top, pink flush on the undersides, green tips short, broad and held well up towards the tube. *Corolla* lilac blue with pink veins, ageing to pale lilac, bell-shaped with numerous petaloids. *Foliage* medium green, medium-sized, serrated leaves. *Growth* upright, bushy, free-flowering. Bush.

'Gladiator'

LEMOINE 1889

Double

Tube pale carmine, short and thick. *Sepals* pale carmine, short and broad, curling completely over the tube. *Corolla* white, veined and splashed carmine red, opening rather loosely. *Foliage* medium green, small to medium-sized leaves, slightly serrated. *Growth* upright, free-flowering, bushy. Bush.

'Glad Rags'

FUCHSIA FOREST-CASTRO 1962

AFS Registration No 514

Double

Tube white with pink flush, medium length and thickness. *Sepals* white on top, pink on the undersides, longish and broad. *Corolla* very pale pink and orchid in the centre, overlaid pink, very compact and full, medium-sized blooms. *Foliage* medium green, medium-sized leaves. *Growth* natural trailer, long branches, quite vigorous and free-flowering. Basket.

'Gladys'

NIEDERHOLZER 1946

Single

Tube rose pink, small, medium thickness. *Sepals* pink, small. *Corolla* campanula violet, compact, small blooms. *Foliage* medium green, small to medium-sized leaves. *Growth* upright, vigorous, bushy, self-branching and free-flowering. Bush.

'Glenby'

BRAZIER 1975
AFS Registration No 1266
Double
Tube rose madder, short and medium thickness. *Sepals* rose madder streaked with pale pink, bending back to the tube and then curling downwards. *Corolla* amethyst violet fading to petunia purple. Petaloids of the same shade. *Foliage* medium green, lanceolate with red petioles. *Growth* self-branching, short-jointed, bushy upright which is very free-flowering and makes an excellent exhibition plant. Bush.

'Glendale'

EVANS AND REEVES 1936
Single
Tube coral pink, small and medium thickness. *Sepals* coral pink, small. *Corolla* coral pink, compact and bell-shaped. *Foliage* medium green, small to medium-sized leaves. *Growth* upright, very vigorous, bushy and free-flowering. Bush. *Parentage F. lycioides* × 'Fireflush'.

'Glitters'

ERICKSON 1963
AFS Registration No 579
Single
Tube salmon pink, long and of medium thickness. *Sepals* salmon pink with green tips, short and held over the corolla. *Corolla* orange salmon, very bright, small and compact blooms. *Foliage* medium green, small to medium-sized, serrated leaves. *Growth* very vigorous, upright, bushy and free-flowering. Bush or summer bedder.

'Glorious'

NIEDERHOLZER 1948
Single
Tube white, medium length and thickness. *Sepals* white on top, rose pink on the undersides. *Corolla* rose bengal, large, loose petalled. *Foliage* medium green, medium-sized, serrated leaves. *Growth* natural trailer, free-flowering, arching branches. Half-basket.

'Glororum'

RYLE 1975
AFS Registration No 1244
Single
Tube neyron rose RHS 55D, thin and of medium length. *Sepals* neyron rose RHS 55D on top, RHS 55B on the undersides, narrow and flared with the tips turned up. *Corolla* amethyst violet RHS 84A, flushed pale pink at the base of the petals. Fades to cyclamen purple RHS 74B with age. Bell-shaped, with wavy edge to the petals. *Anthers* ruby red. *Foliage* medium green with reddish stems. *Growth* upright, self-branching, and free-flowering. Bush or standard. *Parentage* 'Pink Profusion' × 'Lena Dalton'.

'Glory of Bath'

COLVILLE 1965
Double
Tube pink, medium length and thickness. *Sepals* reddish pink, long, wide and curling upwards over the tube. *Corolla* rosy purple with carmine veining, and tinged rose pink at the base of the petals, large, quite loose-petalled blooms. *Foliage* pale green, large, serrated leaves. *Growth* upright, but rather lax, free-flowering, makes an untidy plant. Bush if staked and well pinched.

'Glow'

WOOD 1940
Single
Tube cerise, short and thick. *Sepals* cerise, small. *Corolla* wine purple, suffused scarlet at the base. Small blooms. *Foliage* medium green, smallish leaves. *Growth* upright, bushy, free-flowering. Bush or garden hardy. *Parentage* Seedling × 'Mrs Rundle'.

'Goblin'

GAGNON 1962
AFS Registration No 509

Double
Tube pale pink, short, medium thickness. *Sepals* pale pink, crepe effect on the undersides. *Corolla* blush pink, very full, small blooms. *Foliage* medium green, small to medium-sized leaves. *Growth* semi-trailer, free-flowering, vigorous. Half-basket.

'Goldcrest'
THORNE 1968
Single
Tube pale pink, thin, medium length. *Sepals* pale pink with green tips, long, narrow and completely reflexed. *Corolla* lavender with pink veins, very long and compact. *Foliage* golden yellow ageing to green, medium-sized, long, serrated leaves. *Growth* upright, bushy, self-branching, and free-flowering. Bush.

'Golden Anniversary'
STUBBS 1980
AFS Registration No 1532
Double
Tube greenish white, short and thick. *Sepals* white, broad and sharply pointed. *Corolla* deep blackish purple, fading to royal purple, flaring, the petals fade from dark to pale pink at the base of the tube. *Foliage* new growth is very light green/greenish-gold, fading to light green. *Growth* natural trailer, self-branching and very soft, will make a good basket.

'Golden Dawn'
W.R. HAAG 1951
Single
Tube pale salmon pink, medium length and thickness. *Sepals* pale salmon pink, long, narrow and upturned. *Corolla* light orange, compact, medium-sized blooms. *Foliage* pale to medium green, medium-sized, finely serrated leaves. *Growth* upright, bushy, vigorous, not self-branching, free-flowering, a very attractive flower. Bush or standard.

'Golden Glory'
GORMAN 1970
AFS Registration No 930
Double
Tube pale orange, medium length and thickness. *Sepals* pale orange, upturned. *Corolla* orange, full and of medium size. *Foliage* golden yellow with tinges of red on the petiole. *Growth* natural trailer, vigorous, free-flowering. Basket.

'Golden Marinka'
WEBER 1955
AFS Registration No 401 (1959)
Single
Tube dark red, long, medium thickness. *Sepals* deep red, short and broad, held right over the corolla. *Corolla* slightly deeper red, compact, medium-sized blooms. *Foliage* variegated green and yellow with red veins, medium-sized leaves. *Growth* basket type, trailing growth. Vigorous, easy to train and very free-flowering. Requires the maximum sunlight for the foliage to be at its best colour, and is rather prone to *Botrytis* if overwatered. Excellent exhibition plant for basket or half-basket.

'Golden Treasure'
CARTER 1860
Single
Tube scarlet, medium length and thickness. *Sepals* scarlet, curling upwards towards the tube. *Corolla* magenta purple, compact, medium-sized. *Foliage* variegated yellow and green with red veining. *Growth* upright, bushy, not very free-flowering. Rather late to come into bloom. Bush or summer bedder.

'Golden Violet'
PRENTICE 1966
AFS Registration No 665
Double
Tube white, short and thick. *Sepals* white, short, and horizontal. *Corolla* deep violet purple, medium-sized blooms. *Foliage* yellow and pale green with red veins and stems. *Growth* natural trailer, vigorous, bushy and free-flowering. Basket or half-basket.

'Goldilocks'
HAAG 1950
Semi-double
Tube bright red, medium length and thickness. *Sepals* bright red, medium length, upturned. *Corolla* white, striped rose, rather open and loose. *Foliage* golden yellow, medium-sized leaves. *Growth* upright, bushy, free-flowering. Bush.

'Gold Leaf'
GADSBY 1974
AFS Registration No 1222
Single
Tube china rose RHS 58D, short, medium thickness. *Sepals* china rose with green tips, longish and held well up over the tube. Deeper pink on the undersides. *Corolla* clear creamy white, medium-sized. *Foliage* citron green RHS 151B on the young growth, ageing to medium green. *Growth* lax upright, bushy, self-branching and free-flowering.

'Goldsworth Beauty'
SLOCOCK 1952
Single
Tube pale cerise red, thick, medium length. *Sepals* pale cerise, short and broad, slightly reflexed. *Corolla* reddish purple, fairly compact, small to medium-sized. *Foliage* medium green, medium-sized, broad leaves, serrated. *Growth* vigorous, bushy, upright, self-branching and very free-flowering. Bush or garden hardy.

'Golondrina' (93)
NIEDERHOLZER 1941
Single
Tube pale reddish pink, long, medium thickness *Sepals* bright red, long, narrow and twisting slightly. *Corolla* dark magenta with scarlet veins and crimson blotches paler at the base of the petals. Medium-sized blooms. *Foliage* medium green, medium-sized leaves, serrated. *Growth* vigorous, free-flowering hanger, more upright when grown out of doors. Basket or bush as summer bedder.

'Good News'
FUCHSIA LA 1967
AFS Registration No 697
Double
Tube pink, medium length and thickness. *Sepals* pink, longish, upturned. *Corolla* deep rose pink, medium to large bloom, fairly compact. *Foliage* darkish green, medium to large leaves. *Growth* lax upright, bushy and free-flowering. Bush or half-basket.

'Goody Goody'
CASTRO 1969
AFS Registration No 838
Single
Tube white, medium length and thickness. *Sepals* white, medium length. *Corolla* deep purple, fading to orchid purple, medium-sized bloom. *Foliage* medium green, medium-sized leaves. *Growth* upright, bushy, self-branching and free-flowering. Bush.

'Gordon B. Lloyd'
FAIRCLO 1947
Single
Tube red, medium length and thickness. *Sepals* red, longish and reflexing slightly. *Corolla* pink, medium-sized blooms. *Foliage* medium green, medium-sized leaves, serrated. *Growth* upright, bushy, vigorous and free-flowering. Bush.

'Gordon's China Rose'
GORDON 1953
Single to semi-double
Tube white, medium length and thickness. *Sepals* white with pink flush, pale pink on the undersides, green tipped, broad and slightly curved at the tips. *Corolla* lavender pink, pale pink at the base of the petals and darker on the edges, medium-sized blooms. *Foliage* medium green, medium-sized, serrated leaves. *Growth* upright, but tending to be rather lax, bushy, free-flowering. Bush.

'Gov. "Pat" Brown'
MACHADO 1962
AFS Registration No 497

Double
Tube white with pink flush, medium length and thickness. *Sepals* white, flushed pale pink, green tips. Broad and curling upwards to the tube. *Corolla* violet purple, splashed pink at the base of the petals, very full and fluffy, medium-sized blooms. *Foliage* yellowish green, medium-sized leaves. *Growth* natural trailer, bushy and free-flowering. Basket.

'Grace'
R. HOLMES 1974
AFS Registration No 1203
Single
Tube crimson RHS 52A, medium length and thickness. *Sepals* crimson with green tips, longish and curling upwards. *Corolla* cyclamen purple RHS 74B with scarlet veins, paler at the base of the petals. Medium-sized blooms. *Foliage* medium green with red veins and stems, small leaves, serrated. *Growth* vigorous, upright, bushy, tending to be rather lax when grown indoors. Bush or basket. *Parentage* 'Percy Holmes' × 'Jack Acland'.

'Grace Darling'
GADSBY 1972
AFS Registration No 1066
Single
Tube pale pink, short and thick. *Sepals* pale pink, short and broad, curving back towards the tube. *Corolla* white, open bell-shaped, medium-sized blooms. *Stamens* red. *Foliage* medium green, small, serrated. *Growth* upright, bushy, vigorous, self-branching and very free-flowering. Bush. *Parentage* 'Sleigh Bells' ×.

'Grace Eybel'
PANCHARIAN 1975
AFS Registration No 1297
Semi-double
Tube green with shades of pink, short and thin. *Sepals* white, shaded rose, with green tips, long, narrow and curled. *Corolla* light blue shaded rose, medium size. *Pistil* light pink, bone-coloured stigma. *Foliage* medium green, round to oval shape, serrated. *Growth* semi-trailer which will make a good basket or bush.

'Gracious Lady'
PENNISI 1970
AFS Registration No 887
Double
Tube rose pink, medium length and thickness. *Sepals* deep rose pink, long and narrow, upturned. *Corolla* maroon with salmon pink markings on the petals, large blooms. *Foliage* medium green, medium to large-sized leaves, serrated. *Growth* natural trailer, vigorous, free-flowering. Basket.

'Graf Witte'
LEMOINE 1899
Single
Tube carmine, short, medium thickness. *Sepals* carmine, medium length, held up close to the tube. *Corolla* purple with cerise veining, small to medium size, bell-shaped. *Foliage* yellowish green with crimson veining, small to medium-sized, serrated leaves. *Growth* upright, bushy, free-flowering. Bush or garden hardy. Hybrid of *F. coccinea*.

'Granada'
SCHNABEL 1957
AFS Registration No 290
Double
Tube deep carmine, short and of medium thickness. *Sepals* deep carmine, short and broad, held well up against the tube, paler on the undersides, and with green tips. *Corolla* deep purple with carmine markings on the outer petals, large blooms, very striking colouration. *Foliage* dark green with crimson veining, medium to large leaves slightly serrated. *Growth* upright, bushy, self-branching and, for its size, very free-flowering. Bush.

'Grand Prix'
FUCHSIA LA 1972
AFS Registration No 1020

Double
Tube white, medium length and thickness. *Sepals* porcelain white on top, rose pink on the undersides. *Corolla* delft rose at the base of the petals and on the tips, shading to pansy violet in the centre, medium-sized blooms. *Foliage* medium green, large leaves. *Growth* upright, vigorous, self-branching and free-flowering. Bush.

'Grand Slam'
KENNETT-CASTRO 1973
AFS Registration No 1106
Double
Tube white, medium length and thickness. *Sepals* white on top, pale crepe pink on the undersides, curling back towards the tube. *Corolla* pale lavender purple maturing to fuchsia-magenta with pink marbling on the petals, large blooms. *Foliage* dark green, large-sized leaves. *Growth* natural trailer, long, arching branches, free-flowering. Needs careful pinching in its early stages. Basket.

'Grasmere' (66)
S. TRAVIS 1973
AFS Registration No 1151
Single
Tube coral red, long and thin, triphylla type. *Sepals* coral red with green tips, longish and spreading. *Corolla* deep coral-pink, compact. *Foliage* deep green, large-sized leaves. Young leaves have a pink base. *Growth* natural trailer, self-branching, bushy and very free-flowering in clusters, very vigorous. Bush, standard or basket. *Parentage F. cordifolia* × *F. lycioides.*

'Gray Dawn'
SOO YUN FIELD 1965
AFS Registration No 645
Double
Tube white with reddish flush, medium length and thickness. *Sepals* reddish white. *Corolla* blue grey, fading to grey, medium-sized blooms, compact. *Foliage* bright green, medium-sized leaves with red stems. *Growth* trailer, bushy, vigorous, free-flowering. Basket or half-basket.

'Gray Lady'
REITER 1952
AFS Registration No 129
Double
Tube greenish white with pink flush, medium length and thickness. *Sepals* pinkish white, held upright. *Corolla* pale campanula violet with a greyish-blue cast, fading to lavender blue. *Foliage* medium green, medium to large-sized leaves, serrated. *Growth* upright, vigorous, bushy, free-flowering, very attractive colouring. Bush or standard.

'Grayrigg'
THORNLEY 1978
AFS Registration No 1468
Single
Tube white, flushed green, short and thin. *Sepals* flush pink with green tips, deeper pink on the underside. *Corolla* soft pink (RHS 69D) compact, medium-sized blooms. *Foliage* pale green, small. *Growth* vigorous, self-branching and bushy upright. Bush. *Parentage* 'Silverdale' × 'Silverdale' seedling.

'Great Scott'
TIRET 1960
AFS Registration No 433
Double
Tube rose red, medium, length and thickness. *Sepals* rose red, longish and broad. *Corolla* jasper red, very large and full petalled. *Foliage* medium to darkish green, large leaves. *Growth* upright, very vigorous, bushy and self-branching. Bush.

'Greenfinger'
TOLLEY 1974
AFS Registration No 1230
Single
Tube baby pink, short and of medium thickness. *Sepals* baby pink with a green stripe along the centre of each one,

medium size. *Corolla* creamy white, bell-shaped, medium-sized blooms. *Foliage* medium green, medium-sized leaves. *Growth* upright, bushy, vigorous, self-branching and short-jointed. Free-flowering. The combination of creamy white and green makes this an unusual coloured cultivar. Good exhibition variety. Bush.

'Greenrigg Bell'
RYLE 1977
AFS Registration No 1435
Single
Tube pink, medium thickness, short. *Sepals* neyron rose RHS 55B, on top, underside deeper rose RHS 55A. *Corolla* roseine purple RHS 68A, shading to pink RHS 68B at the base. *Foliage* new leaves are citron green RHS 151A, fading to lettuce green RHS 144A. *Growth* upright, self-branching, small and bushy. Bush or standard.

'Grinnell Bay'
ADKINS 1980
Introduced 1964, registered 1980
AFS Registration No 1553
Single
Tube rose pink, thin and of medium length. *Sepals* rose pink tipped green, recurving against the tube on maturity. *Corolla* red purple, small to medium size. Edge of petals open dark purple, fading to medium purple, then rose. *Foliage* dark green, small to medium size, cordate, serrated margins. *Growth* natural trailer, will make a good basket.

'Groovy'
CASTRO 1969
AFS Registration No 839
Single
Tube pink, thick and of medium length. *Sepals* coral pink, long, narrow and curling upwards towards the tube. Green tipped. *Corolla* magenta with pink veining, fuchsia pink at the base of the petals, medium to large, close bell-shaped blooms. *Foliage* medium green, small to medium-sized, serrated leaves. *Growth* upright, bushy, free-flowering. Tends to be rather lax when grown in heat. Bush or half-basket.

'Gruss aus dem Bodethal' (163)
TEUPEL 1904
Single
Tube crimson, short and thick. *Sepals* crimson, short, horizontal. *Corolla* darkest purple, almost black on opening, small to medium-sized blooms. *Foliage* medium green, small to medium-sized leaves, finely serrated. *Growth* upright, bushy, self-branching, free-flowering and very easy to grow. Bush or summer bedder.

'Gualala Blue'
SOO YUN FIELD 1966
AFS Registration No 681
Double
Tube rose pink, medium length and thickness. *Sepals* rose pink, medium size, upturned. *Corolla* blue to orchid, serrated edges to the petals, large blooms. *Foliage* medium green, large leaves. *Growth* vigorous, lax, bushy, free-flowering. Bush or basket.

'Guinevere'
DALE 1952
Single
Tube white, medium length and thickness. *Sepals* white with green tips, long, narrow and curling upwards. *Corolla* orchid blue, changing to pale purple blue as the bloom ages, long and compact. Medium-sized blooms. *Foliage* medium green, medium-sized leaves, finely serrated. *Growth* bushy, vigorous, spreading habit. Difficult to grow to shape if not pinched in its early stages. Bush.

'Gulliver'
REITER 1948
Single
Tube white, medium length and thickness. *Sepals* waxy white, medium length, upturned. *Corolla* dark tyrian rose, medium to large blooms. *Foliage* medium green, small to medium-sized leaves.

Growth dwarf upright, bushy, self-branching, free-flowering. Bush.

'Gus Niederholzer'
NIEDERHOLZER/WALTZ 1949
Tube carmine red, medium length and thickness. *Sepals* carmine, long. *Corolla* veronica blue, large blooms. *Foliage* medium green, medium to large-sized leaves. *Growth* upright, vigorous, self-branching and free-flowering. Bush.

'Gustave Dore'
LEMOINE 1880
Semi-double to double 4 in (10 cm)
Tube pale pink, long and thin. *Sepals* pale pink, long, narrow, recurving. *Corolla* white, with pinkish veins, full and well-shaped. *Foliage* light green, small to medium size, serrated. *Growth* vigorous but tends to be lax, free-flowering, self-branching, and bushy. Bush or standard.

'Gypsy Baron'
MUNKNER 1952
Double
Tube cardinal red, medium length and thickness. *Sepals* cardinal red. *Corolla* dusky bluish-violet, very full, medium-sized blooms. *Foliage* medium to darkish green, medium-sized leaves. *Growth* upright, vigorous, bushy, free-flowering. Bush or standard.

'Gypsy Prince'
ERVIN 1952
AFS Registration No 146
Semi-double
Tube bright red, medium length and thickness. *Sepals* bright red, upturned. *Corolla* deep rose, in four sections, medium to large blooms. *Foliage* medium green, medium-sized leaves. *Growth* upright, vigorous, bushy, free-flowering, self-branching. Bush. Sport of 'Gypsy Queen'.

'Gypsy Queen'
BULL 1865
Double
Tube red, medium length and thickness. *Sepals* red, arching upwards to the tube. *Corolla* deep purple, full and of medium size. *Foliage* medium green, medium-sized leaves. *Growth* upright, bushy, vigorous and free-flowering. Bush.

'Half and Half'
SOULES AND BROWN 1952
AFS Registration No 134
Semi-double
Tube red, small and thick. *Sepals* rose pink on top, deeper on the undersides, medium length. *Corolla* pale creamy white with red veins, medium-sized blooms. *Foliage* medium green, medium-sized, serrated leaves. *Growth* upright, bushy, vigorous and free-flowering. Bush.

'Hanora's Sister'
JAMES TRAVIS 1973
AFS Registration No 1141
Single
Tube ivory white flushed rose pink, long and of medium thickness. *Sepals* ivory white, flushed rose pink on top, glowing pink on the undersides, long and narrow. *Corolla* vivid pink, square shape, medium-sized bloom. *Foliage* deep green, medium-sized ovate leaves. *Growth* upright, self-branching, bushy and vigorous. Free-flowering. Bush or standard. *Parentage* 'Mrs Rundle' × 'Evening Light'.

'Hap Hazard'
HAZARD 1930
Double
Tube red, medium length and thickness. *Sepals* red, long and broad. *Corolla* deep violet purple with white edges to the petals. *Foliage* medium to dark green, medium-sized leaves. *Growth* upright, bushy, self-branching and free-flowering. Bush.

'Happy Birthday'
Introduced by SCHNEIDER 1980
AFS Registration No 1588
Raiser unknown
Single

Tube rose, pink, short. *Sepals* rose pink with green tips, long and thin. *Corolla* blue, changing to rose at the base, long. *Foliage* dark green, serrated, small and thin. *Growth* upright, bushy. Bush.

'Happy Day'
SOO YUN 1978
AFS Registration No 1450
Double
Tube spinel red, short, medium width. *Sepals* crimson, 1 in (25 mm) long, curving upwards. *Corolla* white with neyron rose stripe in the centre, and marbled at the base. 1 in (25 mm) long and $1\frac{5}{8}$ in (41 mm) wide. *Stamens* crimson with brown tips. *Pistil* crimson with brown tips. *Foliage* medium green, scalloped edges, $1\frac{7}{8}$ in (48 mm) wide and $3\frac{5}{8}$ in (92 mm) long. *Growth* natural trailer, bushy and vigorous. Very free-flowering. Will make a good basket, or bush if pinched early.

'Happy Fellow' (189)
WALTZ 1966
AFS Registration No 655
Single
Tube pale salmon pink, medium length and thickness. *Sepals* pale salmon on top, deeper on the underside, green tips. Broad and reflexed over the tube. *Corolla* dark orange, paler at the base, very compact, medium-sized blooms. *Foliage* pale yellowish green, small to medium-sized leaves, serrated. *Growth* upright, bushy, vigorous, self-branching and free-flowering. Bush or standard.

'Happy Talk'
FUCHSIA FOREST 1964
AFS Registration No 606
Double
Tube white, medium length, thickish. *Sepals* white on top, pink on the undersides, green tips, slightly upturned. *Corolla* magenta with pink petaloids, rather loose, medium-sized. *Foliage* medium green, medium-sized leaves, serrated. *Growth* natural trailer, bushy, free-flowering. Basket or half-basket.

'Hapsburgh'
ROZAIN-BOUCHARLAT 1911
Single
Tube white with a pink flush, short, medium thickness. *Sepals* white, flushed pink, short and broad, waxy appearance. *Corolla* deep violet blue, medium-sized. *Foliage* medium green, medium-sized leaves. *Growth* upright, bushy, self-branching, free-flowering. Bush or summer bedder.

'Harbour Bridge'
LOCKERBIE 1971
AFS Registration No 1001
Double
Tube pale rose pink, short, medium thickness. *Sepals* pink, short and reflexed, with green tips. *Corolla* lavender blue with phlox pink blotches at the base of the petals, large and flared. *Foliage* medium green, medium to large-sized leaves. *Growth* upright, vigorous, bushy, free-flowering. Heat-resistant. Named after the famous Sydney Harbour Bridge in Australia. Bush or standard.

'Hardy Fred'
WOOLLEY 1980
AFS Registration No 1567
Single
Tube bright red, short and thin. *Sepals* bright red, long and pointed. *Corolla* deep magenta fading to cerise, compact and medium size. *Stamens* bright red, pistil red. *Foliage* dark green with purple splashes, medium-sized. *Growth* upright, bushy. Bush or standard.

'Harmony'
NIEDERHOLZER 1946
Single
Tube pale geranium lake, medium length and thickness. *Sepals* pale geranium lake, medium length, upturned. *Corolla* rose pink, medium-sized blooms. *Foliage* medium green. *Growth* trailer, bushy, free-flowering. Half-basket.

'Harriett'
SOO YUN 1971
AFS Registration No 947

Double
Tube white with a pink flush, short, medium thickness. *Sepals* white on top, flushed pink on the undersides, green tips, rather broad and held upwards towards the tube. *Corolla* blue, slightly darker on the petal edges, and shaded to white at the base. Very full and fluffy, medium-sized blooms. *Foliage* darkish green, small to medium-sized leaves, finely serrated. *Growth* natural trailer, bushy, free-flowering. Basket or half-basket.

'Harry Dunnett'
BAKER/DUNNET 1974
AFS Registration No 1198
Single
Tube spinel red, RHS 54B, triphylla type, medium length and thickness, slightly bent. *Sepals* neyron rose RHS 55C, spinel red at the base, small and tapered. *Corolla* shrimp red RHS 33C, very small and compact. *Foliage* darkish green RHS 137B, with a velvety sheen and amber veining. Medium-sized leaves. *Growth* upright, self-branching, bushy and free-flowering. Bush.

'Harry Hotspur'
RYLE 1975
AFS Registration No 1245
Single
Tube pink, short and thick. *Sepals* white flushed pink RHS 69A, on the outside where the sepals join at the junction of the tube there are four small spur-like projections, hence the name. *Corolla* violet, RHS 82A, overlapping petals, medium size. *Anthers* spinel red RHS 54A. *Foliage* medium green with red petioles. *Growth* bushy, upright, vigorous. Bush.

'Hathersage'
GADSBY 1975
AFS Registration No 1282
Double
Tube pale pink, long and of medium thickness. *Sepals* neyron rose RHS 58C, wide, well carried out from the corolla. *Corolla* roseine purple RHS 68C with red veins, shading to amaranth rose RHS 56A, medium size and well formed. *Foliage* medium green. *Growth* vigorous, self-branching, bushy, upright, free-flowering. *Parentage* 'Joan Pacey' × 'Prosperity'.

'Haverthwaite'
THORNLEY 1966
Registered 1972
AFS Registration No 1061
Double
Tube eau de nil RHS 155A, long and thin. *Sepals* white on top, pale pink on the underside with green tips, longish and curling upwards to the tube. *Corolla* deep lavender pink, base of the petals rose, small and compact RHS 87A to 87D. *Foliage* medium green, small to medium-sized leaves, finely serrated. *Growth* upright, bushy, vigorous, self-branching and free-flowering. Bush or standard. *Parentage* 'Hawkshead' × 'Kings Ransom'.

'Hawkshead'
TRAVIS 1973
AFS Registration No 1142
Single
Tube white, short and of medium thickness, slight greenish tinge. *Sepals* white, flushed green, broad and pointed. *Corolla* pure white, barrel shaped. *Foliage* deep green, small, serrated leaves. *Growth* upright, vigorous, self-branching and bushy. Bush or standard. *Parentage F. magellanica* var. *molinae* × 'Venus Victrix'.

'Hayward'
BRAND 1951
AFS Registration No 90
Double
Tube deep red, short and of medium thickness. *Sepals* deep red, short and broad. *Corolla* deep violet purple, medium-sized blooms. *Foliage* medium to darkish green, medium-sized leaves. *Growth* upright, bushy and free-flowering. Bush.

'Hazel Marsh'
SCHNABEL-PASKESEN 1959
AFS Registration No 378
Double
Tube pale rose pink, short and thick. *Sepals* white on top, splashed pale pink on the undersides, green tips. Broad and upturned. *Corolla* pale orchid purple, large and open. *Foliage* medium green, large, finely serrated leaves. *Growth* natural trailer, compact growing, free-flowering. Basket. Sport of 'His Excellency'.

'Healdsburg'
SOO YUN 1969
AFS Registration No 849
Double
Tube light red, medium length and thickness. *Sepals* light red on top, dark red on the undersides, light green tips. *Corolla* light purple, full, large-sized bloom. *Foliage* medium green, medium-sized leaves. *Growth* lax bush, spreading, free-flowering. Bush or half-basket.

'Heart Throb'
HODGES 1963
AFS Registration No 567
Double
Tube pale pink, short and thick. *Sepals* white on top with green tips, pale pink on the undersides, broad and pointed, held straight upwards to cover the tube. *Corolla* lavender blue, ageing to pink, with shades of white in the centre and at the base of the petals. A very open corolla, large-sized blooms. *Foliage* medium green, medium-sized, broad leaves, serrated. *Growth* upright, bushy, vigorous, free-flowering. Bush.

'Heather Hobbs'
R. HOLMES 1978
AFS Registration No 1460
Single
Tube crimson (RHS 52A), short, medium width. *Sepals* crimson (RHS 52A) on outside, slightly paler inside, yellow tips. Long and thin, unswept, occasionally reflexing and twisting. *Corolla* white, veined neyron rose (RHS 55A) with a pink cast (RHS 55C), bell-shaped. *Stamens and pistil* crimson. *Foliage* yellow green, small, ovate and slightly serrated. Petiole, young stems and part of centre vein are red. *Growth* upright, self-branching, vigorous and free-flowering. *Parentage* 'Hugh Morgan' ×.

'Hebe'
STOKES 1848
Single
Tube white with a pink flush, long and thin. *Sepals* white on top, pink flush on the underside, green tips. Long, narrow and completely turned up to cover the tube. *Corolla* violet purple, maturing to reddish purple, very compact, bloom long. *Foliage* medium green, small to medium-sized leaves, finely serrated. *Growth* lax upright, vigorous, free-flowering. Bush or summer bedder.

'Hecate'
FOSTER 1972
AFS Registration No 1038
Single
Tube dark red, medium length and thickness. *Sepals* dark red, long and broad. *Corolla* very pale pink, deep red veins, long and bell-shaped. *Foliage* pale to medium green with dark red stems, serrated, medium-sized leaves. *Growth* natural trailer, bushy, vigorous and free-flowering. Prefers shade for best results. Basket.

'Heidi Ann' (145)
SMITH 1969
AFS Registration No 818
Double
Tube crimson, short and thick. *Sepals* crimson cerise, short, broad and reflexed. *Corolla* bright lilac purple, veined cerise, paler at the base of the petals and with numerous petaloids. Very full and fluffy. Small to medium-sized bloom. *Foliage* dark green, small leaves, finely serrated. *Growth* upright, bushy, self-branching and vigorous, very free-flowering, excellent exhibition variety. Bush or quarter

standard. *Parentage* 'Tennessee Waltz' × 'General Monk'.

'Heidi Weiss' (126)
TALCONESTON 1973
AFS Registration No 1111
Double
Tube crimson, short and of medium thickness. *Sepals* crimson, short and broad, reflexing. *Corolla* white with scarlet veining, full, medium-sized bloom. *Foliage* darkish green, small to medium-sized leaves, finely serrated. *Growth* upright, self-branching, bushy, free-flowering, good exhibition variety. Sport of 'Heidi Ann'.

'Heinrich Henkel'
See under 'Andenken an Heinrich Henkel'.

'Heirloom'
KENNETT 1968
Double
Tube white with pink flush, medium length and thickness. *Sepals* pale pink on top, darker on the undersides, green tips, upturned. *Corolla* lavender purple heavily marbled pink and white, quite full and open. Medium-sized blooms. *Foliage* medium green, medium-sized, serrated leaves. *Growth* natural trailer, free-flowering. Basket.

'Helen Hummel'
GAGNON 1969
AFS Registration No 845
Double
Tube red, long and thin. *Sepals* red, long and upturned, crepe appearance. *Corolla* deep purple fading to reddish shade at the base of the petals which are serrated. Full and fluffy, medium-sized bloom. *Foliage* dark green, medium-sized leaves. *Growth* natural trailer, free-flowering, vigorous. Basket.

'Helen McGrath'
BROWN-NESSIER 1952
AFS Registration No 118
Double
Tube cerise, medium length and thickness. *Sepals* cerise, upturned. *Corolla* violet purple with phlox-pink marbling on the petals, medium-sized blooms. *Foliage* medium green, medium-sized leaves. *Growth* upright, vigorous, bushy, free-flowering. Bush or standard.

'Hello Dolly'
MRS E. HOLMES 1969
Single
Tube pink, short and thick. *Sepals* pink on top, deeper pink on the undersides, long and broad pointing downwards then turning up at the tips. *Corolla* white, lightly veined pink, rather loose petalled, and of medium size. *Foliage* medium green, large, serrated leaves. *Growth* upright, vigorous, self-branching and very free-flowering. Bush.

'Henriette Ernst'
ERNST 1841
Single
Tube scarlet, very short and thick. *Sepals* scarlet, broad and held horizontally, slightly curled at the tips. *Corolla* magenta purple, fading to red, at the base of the petals, and with reddish veins, loose-petalled and of medium size. *Foliage* medium green, medium-sized, broad and serrated leaves. *Growth* upright, bushy, self-branching and slow-growing. Bush or garden hardy.

'Henri Poincaré'
LEMOINE 1905
Single
Tube red, medium length and thickness. *Sepals* red, broad and longish, recurving over the tube. *Corolla* violet purple with red veins, bell-shaped, quite a long bloom. *Foliage* darkish green, medium-sized leaves. *Growth* lax upright, bushy, and free-flowering. A most attractive coloured cultivar which unfortunately is not self-branching and tends to be rather floppy. If pinched early it can be trained to shape as a medium-sized bush. Bush.

'Herald'
SANKEY 1887
Single
Tube scarlet, medium length, thick and bulbous. *Sepals* scarlet, short and upturned. *Corolla* deep bluish-purple with cerise veining, changing to reddish purple on maturity, medium-sized blooms. *Foliage* medium green with crimson veining, medium-sized, serrated leaves. *Growth* upright, bushy, self-branching and vigorous. An easy to grow cultivar, and good exhibition variety. Bush or garden bedder.

'Herbe de Jaques'
SCHNEIDER 1978
Single
Tube scarlet, medium length and thickness. *Sepals* purple. *Corolla* scarlet, medium-sized blooms. *Foliage* variegated, mottled, and spotted, with red colour predominant. *Growth* natural trailer, will make a good basket or standard. *Foliage* variegation is best when hard pinched. Basket. Sport of 'Corallina'.

'Her Highness'
SOO YUN 1969
AFS Registration No 848
Double
Tube bright red, medium length and thickness. *Sepals* bright red, large, broad and upturned. *Corolla* lilac with red veining, fading to light rose pink as the bloom matures. Large blooms. *Foliage* medium green, large leaves. *Growth* natural trailer, heavy bloomer, vigorous. Basket.

'Heritage'
LEMOINE 1902
Single $4\frac{1}{2}$ in (11 cm)
Tube crimson scarlet. *Sepals* crimson scarlet, short and broad, reflexing. *Corolla* purple, loose petalled, medium-sized blooms. *Foliage* medium green, medium-sized leaves, serrated. *Growth* upright, bushy, free-flowering but not a fast grower. Bush or summer bedder. Similar to 'Heron' but more floriferous.

'Her Ladyship'
WALTZ 1961
AFS Registration No 491
Double
Tube pale pink, medium length and thickness. *Sepals* pale pink on top, deeper pink on the underside, long, broad and upturned. *Corolla* orchid blue, splashed pink at the base of the petals, large bloom. *Foliage* medium green, medium to large leaves. *Growth* lax upright, vigorous, bushy, free-flowering. Bush or half-basket.

'Hermione'
HAZARD
Double
Tube shell pink, medium length and thickness. *Sepals* shell pink, upturned. *Corolla* white with a pink flush on the petals, medium-sized bloom. *Foliage* medium green, medium-sized leaves. *Growth* vigorous, upright, bushy, self-branching and free-flowering. Bush or standard.

'Heron' (159)
LEMOINE 1891
Single
Tube deep cerise, short and of medium thickness. *Sepals* cerise, broad, slightly curled at the edges, and held horizontally over the corolla. *Corolla* violet-magenta, slightly veined cerise in the centre of the petals, open and rather loose petalled. *Foliage* medium green, medium-sized, serrated leaves. *Growth* vigorous, upright, self-branching and very free-flowering. Bush.

'Hesitation'
BRAND 1951
AFS Registration No 89
Double
Tube pale pink, medium length and thickness. *Sepals* pale pink, long, narrow and upturned. *Corolla* centre petals white, and long, outer, shorter petals pink. *Foliage* medium green, medium-sized leaves, serrated. *Growth* spreading, lax,

bushy, free-flowering. Bush or half-basket.

'Heston Blue'
RAWLINS 1966
Semi-double to double
Tube white, long, medium thickness. *Sepals* white flushed pink, green tips, very long, narrow and upswept. *Corolla* smoky blue, changing to mauve as the bloom matures, and with white shading at the base of the petals. *Foliage* medium green, medium-sized, serrated leaves. *Growth* upright, bushy, not self-branching, free-flowering. A very attractive blue shaded cultivar. Bush.

'H.G. Brown'
W.P. WOOD
Single 1949
Tube deep scarlet, short and of medium thickness. *Sepals* deep scarlet, short, pointed. *Corolla* dark lake, medium sized blooms *Foliage* dark green, small to medium sized leaves. *Growth* bushy, spreading, free-flowering. Bush or garden hardy.

'Hidcote Beauty'
WEBB 1949
Single
Tubes creamy white, thick, medium length. *Sepals* creamy, waxy white, short and broad, green tips. *Corolla* pale salmon pink, with a pale flush. *Foliage* pale to medium green, small to medium-sized leaves. *Growth* upright, bushy, vigorous, self-branching and free-flowering. Bush or basket.

'High Noon'
PANCHARIAN 1975
AFS Registration No 1292
Single
Tube red, short and thin. *Sepals* red with darker red stripes, green tips. Darker red on the underside, long and narrow. *Corolla* white, with red veins at the base. White fan shape with red centre and two red petaloids. *Stamens and pistil* red, stigma white. *Foliage* medium green with pronounced veins. *Growth* vigorous, bushy, self-branching upright. Bush.

'High Peak'
BROUGH 1977
Double
Tube white, short, medium thickness. *Sepals* white, short and slightly upturned. *Corolla* white, shade very pale pink at the base of the petals, small to medium-sized blooms. *Foliage* medium green, small to medium-sized leaves. *Growth* lax upright, self-branching, bushy and free-flowering. Bush or half-basket.

'Hi Jinks'
KENNETT 1969
AFS Registration No 776
Double
Tube white, long and of medium thickness. *Sepals* white on top, pink on the undersides, green tipped. Short, broad and held flat over the corolla. *Corolla* rosy purple with white streaks, numerous petaloids of the same colour, very fluffy, medium-sized blooms. *Foliage* medium green, medium to large-sized, serrated leaves. *Growth* natural trailer, bushy, self-branching, free-flowering. Basket.

'Hill Top'
J.A. WRIGHT 1980
AFS Registration No 1601
Double
Tube light red, medium length and width. *Sepals* light red, arching backwards. *Corolla* very light pink mottled with red, and with darker pink veins. Large corolla. *Foliage* medium green. *Growth* upright, vigorous, free-flowering. Best colour develops in the sun. Bush. Seedling of 'Topper'.

'Hindu Belle'
MUNKNER 1959
Single
Tube white, medium length, rather thick. *Sepals* white on top, white with a pink flush on the undersides, green tips, long broad and upturned. *Corolla* burgundy red, paler on maturity, medium-sized

blooms. *Foliage* medium green, medium to large-sized leaves, very finely serrated. *Growth* upright, vigorous and free-flowering. Needs careful pinching in its early stages to train it to shape. Bush or summer bedder.

'His Excellency'
REITER 1952
AFS Registration No 128
Double
Tube white, short and medium thick. *Sepals* white, long and arching upwards. *Corolla* violet purple, changing to orchid purple, and with pinkish white markings at the base of the petals. Medium-sized blooms. *Foliage* medium green, medium-sized leaves. *Growth* upright, vigorous, bushy, free-flowering. Bush.

'His Majesty'
HAAG AND SON 1952
Double
Tube red, medium length and thickness. *Sepals* red, longish, upturned. *Corolla* orange-red, medium to large blooms. *Foliage* medium green, medium-sized leaves. *Growth* trailer, very lax, free-flowering. Half-basket.

'Hispano'
NIEDERHOLZER 1948
Single to semi-double
Tube pale red, medium length and thickness. *Sepals* red, upturned. *Corolla* white with lavender veins and markings, medium-sized blooms. *Foliage* medium green, medium-sized leaves. *Growth* upright, vigorous, self-branching, free-flowering.

'H.O. Barnaby'
HUBBARD 1967
AFS Registration No 704
Double
Tube red, medium length and thickness. *Sepals* red, longish, broad and upturned slightly. *Corolla* bright purple fading to wine red, large blooms. *Foliage* medium green, medium-sized leaves. *Growth* upright, vigorous, stiff-growing, free-flowering. Bush or standard.

'Holiday'
KENNETT/CASTRO 1973
AFS Registration No 1107
Semi-double
Tube pink, medium length and thickness. *Sepals* pale pink with pale green and pink stripes on top, glowing pink on the underside. Very long, curling and twisting back towards the tube. *Corolla* deep purple in the centre, overlaid pink and white. The outer petals and petaloids are white, large, showy blooms. *Foliage* medium green, medium-sized, oblong leaves. *Growth* natural trailer, free-flowering. Basket.

'Hollydale'
FAIRCLO 1946
Double
Sport of 'Winston Churchill' with similar habit of growth and foliage, the only difference being that the corolla is pink.

'Hollydale Sport'
Sport of 'Hollydale' which itself is a sport of 'Winston Churchill'. The growth habit and foliage are again similar to 'Winston Churchill', but the corolla is white.

'Hollywood Park'
FAIRCLO 1953
Semi-double
Tube cerise, medium length and thickness. *Sepals* cerise, longish, upturned. *Corolla* white with a pale pink flush, medium-sized blooms. *Foliage* medium green, medium-sized leaves. *Growth* upright, vigorous, bushy and free-flowering. Bush.

'Honeychile'
CHILES 1953
AFS Registration No 162
Single
Tube rose pink, short and medium thickness. *Sepals* rose pink, long, narrow and reflexed. *Corolla* violet-blue, small blooms. *Foliage* medium green, small leaves. *Growth* natural trailer, self-branching, bushy and very free-flowering. Half-basket.

'Horatio'
GREEN 1977
Single
Tube pink, long and thin. *Sepals* pale pink, longish and narrow. *Corolla* orchid pink, medium-sized blooms. *Foliage* medium green, medium-sized leaves. *Growth* natural trailer, vigorous, free-flowering. Basket.

'Hot Pants'
JIMENEZ 1974
AFS Registration No 1166
Double
Tube red, thick and of medium length. *Sepals* pale red, longish, upturned. *Corolla* white with red veining, very full and fluffy, medium-sized bloom. *Foliage* medium green, medium-sized leaves. *Growth* natural trailer, vigorous, free-flowering. Basket.

'Howlett's Hardy'(158)
HOWLETT 1952
Single
Tube scarlet, thin, medium length. *Sepals* scarlet, long and narrow, reflexed. *Corolla* bright violet purple with scarlet veining, and paler at the base of the petals. *Foliage* medium green, small to medium-sized, longish serrated leaves. *Growth* upright, vigorous, bushy, and free-flowering. Bush or garden hardy.

'Hugh Morgan'
R. HOLMES 1974
AFS Registration No 1204
Semi-double
Tube pinkish cerise, medium length and thickness. *Sepals* pinkish cerise, longish, broad and upturned, completely covering the tube. *Corolla* white with pink veining, long, numerous sepaloids. *Foliage* medium green, medium-sized, slightly serrated leaves. *Growth* upright, vigorous, bushy, and free-flowering. Bush. Seedling of 'Pink Flamingo'.

'Hula Girl'
PASKESEN 1972
AFS Registration No 1023
Double
Tube deep rose pink, medium length and thickness. *Sepals* deep rose pink, broad and reflexing slightly. *Corolla* white, shaded pink at the base of the petals, and with pale pink veins, large and very full. *Foliage* medium green, shaded red on the underside and red veins, medium to large-sized, serrated leaves. *Growth* natural trailer, bushy and very free-flowering. Large flowers. Basket.

'Humboldt Holiday'
HASSETT 1980
AFS Registration No 1533
Double
Tube pinkish white, thin and of medium length. *Sepals* pinkish white on top, frosty pink underneath, curling upwards with a slight twist. *Corolla* violet, splashed pink, fading to white at the base of the petals, loose petalled, large. *Foliage* golden green, veined magenta with magenta red underneath, changing to light green with age, stems magenta red. *Growth* trailer, self-branching. Basket or standard with support. Best colour develops in the shade. *Parentage* 'Mary Ellen' × 'Cosmopolitan'.

'Icarus'
KENNETT-CASTRO 1973
AFS Registration No 1108
Single
Tube white, short and of medium thickness. *Sepals* white with green tips, held horizontally with tips curling up. *Corolla* rosy-purple at the centre with white petaloids between the sepals, medium-sized bloom, very open and untidy. *Foliage* medium green, medium-sized leaves. *Growth* natural trailer, bushy, free-flowering. Basket.

'Iceberg'
MITCHINSON 1980
AFS Registration No 1538
Single
Tube carmine with distinct red stripes, medium length and width. *Sepals* white, slightly marked red on the outside, reflexed. *Corolla* white with rolled petals

holding their shape well, compact. *Foliage* medium to dark green, elliptical in shape, serrated leaf margins, medium to large in size. *Growth* upright, self-branching, bushy. Bush or standard. Colour develops best in the shade. *Parentage* 'Norman Mitchinson' × 'Baby Pink'.

'Icecap'
GADSBY 1968
AFS Registration No 971 (1971)
Semi to semi-double
Tube bright red, short, medium thickness. *Sepals* bright red, short and broad, pointing down over the corolla. *Corolla* white with cerise veining, small to medium-sized bloom. *Foliage* medium to darkish green, small to medium-sized, slightly serrated leaves. *Growth* upright, vigorous, self-branching, bushy and free-flowering. Bush. *Parentage* 'Snowcap' × 'Bon Accorde'. An improvement on 'Snowcap', good exhibition variety.

'Ice Cream Soda'
CASTRO 1972
AFS Registration No 1030
Semi-double
Tube pale greenish white, medium length and thickness. *Sepals* white with pink flush, broad, long and curling backwards to the tube. *Corolla* white with pale pink markings, flaring out, and with many flaring petaloids of the same colouring, very full, medium-sized blooms. *Foliage* darkish green, medium to large, serrated leaves. *Growth* bushy, vigorous, semi-tailer, free-flowering. Bush or basket.

'Iced Champagne'
JENNINGS 1968
Single
Tube pale pink, thin, medium length. *Sepals* pink with green tips, broad and reflexed. *Corolla* pale pink with darker veins, medium-sized bloom with loose petals. *Foliage* medium green with red veins, large, serrated leaves. *Growth* upright, bushy, self-branching and vigorous. Very free-flowering, and a good exhibition variety. Bush.

'Ichiban'
FUCHSIA-LA 1973
AFS Registration No 1074
Double
Tube white with pink flush, short and thick. *Sepals* white, flushed pink, broad and of medium length. *Corolla* cyclamen purple at the edges of the petals, spinel pink at the base, the whole fading to china rose as the bloom ages. Very large flower. *Foliage* dark green, large-sized leaves. *Growth* natural trailer, vigorous, bushy and free-flowering. Prefers shaded conditions. Basket.

'Igloo'
PASKESEN 1965
AFS Registration No 633
Double
Tube white with pale pink flush, medium length and thickness. *Sepals* white with green tips, medium length and reflexed. *Corolla* white, medium-sized bloom. *Foliage* medium green, small to medium-sized leaves. *Growth* vigorous, upright, bushy and free-flowering. Blooms early and in clusters. Bush or standard.

'Igloo Maid'
MRS E. HOLMES 1972
Double
Tube white, long, medium thickness. *Sepals* white with green tips, short, broad and held on top of the corolla, slightly upturned at the tips. *Corolla* white, faintly tinged pink, small to medium-sized bloom. *Foliage* yellowish green, medium-sized leaves, serrated. *Growth* upright, bushy, self-branching, free-flowering. Bush.

'Illusion'
KENNETT 1966
AFS Registration No 676
Semi-double to double
Tube white, medium length and thickness. *Sepals* white on top, pale pink on the undersides, green tips. Broad and held straight upwards towards the tube. *Corolla* pale lavender blue, maturing to a darker blue, with splashes of white and

pink, very full and fluffy, large blooms. *Foliage* medium green, large leaves, serrated. *Growth* upright, vigorous, bushy and free-flowering. A very attractive flower.

'Imperial'
PASKESEN 1969
AFS Registration No 826
Double
Tube pale pink, short and thick. *Sepals* rosy red, broad, upturned slightly. *Corolla* deep violet blue fading to imperial purple, with streaks of rose at the base of the petals. Very full and fluffy, large blooms. *Foliage* medium to darkish green, medium-sized leaves. *Growth* upright, bushy, free-flowering and fairly vigorous. Bush.

'Impudence' (130)
SCHNABEL 1957
AFS Registration No 291
Single
Tube carmine red, short, medium thickness. *Sepals* carmine red, broad, curling upwards to the tube. *Corolla* white with carmine veining, petals spread out horizontally. *Foliage* medium green, serrated medium-sized leaves. *Growth* upright, vigorous, not self-branching, very free-flowering. Very unusual flower but easy to grow. Requires pinching early to train it to shape. Bush.

'Ina Claire'
HAZARD
Single
Tube pink. *Sepals* pink. *Corolla* pink. *Foliage* medium green, medium-sized leaves. *Growth* upright, vigorous, tall-growing, bushy and free-flowering. Bush or standard.

'Indian Maid'
WALTZ 1962
AFS Registration No 524
Double
Tube scarlet, medium length and thickness. *Sepals* scarlet, very bright, long, narrow and recurving. *Corolla* royal purple, very full, slightly loose petalled, medium blooms. *Foliage* darkish green, medium-sized leaves. *Growth* lax bush, longish branches, free-flowering. Although this is sometimes listed as a trailer, it will make a beautiful bush if pinched hard in its early stages. Bush or half-basket.

'Indian Prince'
SOO YUN 1971
AFS Registration No 944
Double
Tube white, short, medium thickness. *Sepals* white on top, pale pink on the undersides, short and turning upwards. *Corolla* lavender, full, medium-sized bloom. *Foliage* medium green, serrated, longish medium-sized leaves. *Growth* upright, bushy, free-flowering. Bush.

'Ingleside'
BROWN AND SOULES 1951
AFS Registration No 73
Double
Tube white, short and thick. *Sepals* pale pink, short and upturned. *Corolla* very dark blue with white and pink marbling, medium-sized bloom. *Foliage* medium to dark green, medium-sized leaves. *Growth* natural trailer, bushy, free-flowering. Half-basket or basket.

'Innocence'
REITER 1952
AFS Registration No 130
Double
Tube crimson red, short and medium thick. *Sepals* pale rose pink, darker towards the tube, short and upturned. *Corolla* pure white, spreading and loose-petalled. *Foliage* medium green, small leaves. *Growth* upright, bushy, self-branching, free-flowering. Bush.

'Inspiration'
NELSON 1952
Double
Tube pink, medium length and thickness. *Sepals* pink, broad, slightly upturned. *Corolla* darker pink, full, medium-sized

blooms. *Foliage* mid-green, medium-sized leaves. *Growth* lax bush, self-branching, free-flowering. Half-basket or bush if staked and pinched early.

'Intellectual'
PENNISI 1971
AFS Registration No 1016
Double
Tube white, small with green stripes. *Sepals* pink, tipped green, short and broad. *Corolla* imperial purple, paler in the centre, medium-sized, boxed-shaped bloom. *Foliage* medium green, small leaves. *Growth* trailer, bushy, free-flowering. Basket or half-basket.

'Interlude'
KENNETT 1960
AFS Registration No 429
Double
Tube waxy white, flushed pink, long and thin. *Sepals* waxy white, flushed pink. *Corolla* centre petals violet-purple, outer petals pale orchid pink, medium-sized bloom. *Foliage* medium green, medium-sized leaves. *Growth* natural trailer, bushy, very attractive, free-flowering, and self-branching. Basket or half-basket.

'Intrepid'
SOO YUN 1970
AFS Registration No 913
Double
Tube white, pink flush, medium length and thickness. *Sepals* white, edged pink, and with green tips. *Corolla* pure white, medium-sized bloom. *Foliage* deep green, medium-sized leaves with red stems. *Growth* trailer, vigorous, free-flowering. Basket.

'Invasion'
ANTONELLI 1971
AFS Registration No 1004
Double
Tube pale pink, medium length and thickness. *Sepals* pale reddish-pink, broad, upturned. *Corolla* rich purple, ageing to orchid, very full and fluffy, large bloom. *Foliage* medium to darkish green, medium-sized leaves. *Growth* trailer, bushy, vigorous, free-flowering. Basket.

'Iona'
TRAVIS 1958
AFS Registration No 1143 (1973)
Single
Tube waxy cream, long, medium thickness. *Sepals* pale rose pink on top, clear pink on the undersides, long, medium thickness. *Corolla* clear pink suffused lilac rose at the base of the petals, deepening to lilac blue at the edges, medium to large blooms. *Foliage* deep green, medium-sized leaves. *Growth* upright, self-branching, vigorous, bushy, free-flowering. Bush or standard *Parentage* 'Opalescent' × 'Formosissima'.

'Irene Ryle'
RYLE 1975
AFS Registration No 1246
Single
Tube neyron rose RHS 58C, medium length and width. *Sepals* neyron rose RHS 58C, tips turned up, medium-sized. *Corolla* aster violet RHS 87C with slight veining at the base. Petals folded in. *Foliage* lettuce green, medium size. *Growth* upright, vigorous, bushy, free-flowering. Bush/standard. *Parentage* 'Bobby Shaftoe' × 'Goldcrest'.

'Iris Amer'
AMER 1967
Double
Tube very pale pink, thick, medium length. *Sepals* white on top, pale pink on the undersides, tipped green, broad and upturned, flushed pink. *Corolla* reddish pink, shaded carmine and with red-orange marbling on the outer petals. Medium-sized blooms. *Foliage* deep green, medium to large-sized, serrated leaves. *Growth* upright, vigorous, short-jointed, sturdy stems, free-flowering. Bush.

'Irish Rose'
REITER 1948
Double

Tube pale chartreuse, medium length and thickness. *Sepals* pale chartreuse, upturned. *Corolla* pale rose pink, medium-sized bloom. *Foliage* medium green. *Growth* upright, bushy, self-branching, free-flowering. Bush.

'Isis'
LEMOINE 1880
Single
Tube crimson, very small. *Sepals* crimson, short and pointed. *Corolla* crimson, compact, very small bloom. *Foliage* bluish-green, small leaves. *Growth* upright, bushy, very free-flowering. Bush.

Do not confuse with the following.

'Isis'
ROZAIN-BOUCHARLAT 1890
Semi-double
Tube cerise, very small. *Sepals* cerise, short, narrow. *Corolla* white with cerise veining, very small bloom. *Foliage* medium green, small leaves. *Growth* upright, bushy, free-flowering. Bush.

'Isle of Mull' (63)
TOLLEY/FUCHSIAVALE 1978
AFS Registration No 1455
Single
Tube light magenta with dark veins, short, medium thickness. *Sepals* baby pink, veined flesh pink, medium-sized, broad, pointed, and slightly upturned. *Corolla* rose magenta, splashed metallic pink, short and flared. *Foliage* medium green, ovate and slightly serrated. *Growth* self-branching, bushy, upright, very free-flowering, medium-sized bloom. Short-jointed. *Parentage* 'Barbara' ×.

'Italiano'
FUCHSIA FOREST 1966
AFS Registration No 668
Double
Tube pale pink, medium length and thickness. *Sepals* pale salmon pink. *Corolla* deep purple, fading to burgundy, very full, medium-sized bloom. *Foliage* medium green, medium-sized leaves. *Growth* natural trailer, bushy and vigorous, free-flowering. Basket.

'Ivan Gadsby'
GADSBY 1970
AFS Registration No 875
Double
Tube greenish white, large and thick. *Sepals* waxy white, longish. *Corolla* magenta rose, medium to large blooms. *Foliage* medium green, long, pointed leaves, serrated edges. *Growth* upright, vigorous, self-branching, free-flowering. Prefers shade. Bush or standard. *Parentage* 'Pepi' × 'Bridesmaid'.

'IXL'
WALKER AND JONES 1950
Semi-double
Tube pale pink, medium length and thickness. *Sepals* very pale pink, reflexing. *Corolla* pure white, loose petalled. *Foliage* medium green, medium-sized leaves. *Growth* upright, tending to be rather lax, bushy, free-flowering. Bush or half-basket.

'Jack Acland'
HAAG AND SON 1952
Semi-double
Tube bright pink, longish, medium thickness. *Sepals* bright pink, slightly upturned. *Corolla* dark rose, red on opening, fading to rich rose-red. Medium to large blooms. *Foliage* medium green, medium to large leaves. *Growth* upright, bushy, self-branching and very free-flowering. Often confused with 'Jack Shahan', but more upright than that cultivar. Bush or standard.

'Jack King'
R. HOLMES 1978
AFS Registration No 1461
Double
Sport from 'General Monk'/Identical to 'Heidi Ann'. *Tube* crimson (RHS 52A), short, medium thickness. *Sepals* crimson (RHS 52A) outside, rose red (RHS 58C) at the base, fading to rose purple (RHS 75B). Some petals overlaid pale pink,

centre petals fluted. *Foliage* small, mid-green, serrated, centre vein starts red, stems red. *Growth* self-branching, bushy, upright, very free-flowering, very vigorous.

'Jack of Hearts'
FUCHSIA FOREST 1967
AFS Registration No 724
Double
Tube pink, medium length, rather thick. *Sepals* pink with green tips, broad and turned up slightly. *Corolla* white, very full and fluffy, with numerous petaloids which are splashed and veined pink. Medium to large blooms. *Foliage* medium green, medium to large leaves, serrated. *Growth* natural trailer, free-flowering. Basket.

'Jackpot'
FUCHSIA FOREST 1966
AFS Registration No 669
Double
Tube pink, long and rather thin. *Sepals* pink, long and broad, held horizontal with the tips turning upwards. *Corolla* blue when it first opens, with pink marbling on the petals, ageing to lavender, large ruffled blooms. *Foliage* medium green, narrow, medium-sized, serrated leaves. *Growth* trailer, tends to send out very long branches so that a lot of pinching is needed to train it to shape. Very free-flowering, and an attractive flowered variety. Basket.

'Jack Shahan' (65)
TIRET 1949
Single
Tube pale rose bengal, long and of medium thickness. *Sepals* rose bengal with green tips, medium length, slightly curled upwards. *Corolla* rose pink, very compact, medium-sized blooms. *Foliage* medium green, leaves longish, medium-sized and serrated. *Growth* natural trailer, self-branching, vigorous, bushy, and very free-flowering. Tends to flower on the ends of the branches, but is a superb exhibition basket plant. Basket or half-basket.

'Jamboree'
REITER 1955
AFS Registration No 231
Double
Tube pinkish white, thick, medium length. *Sepals* salmon pink on top, deeper pink on the undersides. *Corolla* shades of carmine and salmon pink, medium-sized, rather compact bloom. *Foliage* darkish green, medium-sized, serrated leaves. *Growth* upright, bushy, free-flowering. Bush or summer bedder.

'James Lye'
LYE 1869
Semi-double to double
Tube cerise, medium length and thickness. *Sepals* cerise, short, broad. *Corolla* bluish purple, paler at the base of the petals, medium-sized bloom. *Foliage* medium green, medium-sized leaves. *Growth* upright, bushy, self-branching, free-flowering. Bush.

'James Travis'
THORNE 1960
AFS Registration No 456
Double
Tube red, medium length and thickness. *Sepals* red. *Corolla* clear blue, medium to large-sized flower. *Foliage* medium green, medium-sized leaves. *Growth* upright, bushy, vigorous, free-flowering. Bush or garden hardy.

'James Travis'
S. TRAVIS 1972
Breviflora type
Single
Tube vivid coral pink, thick and of medium length. *Sepals* coral pink, spreading and slightly reflexing, $\frac{1}{5}$ to $\frac{1}{3}$ in (5 to 7 mm) long. *Corolla* salmon pink, fading to dusky pink, petals, $\frac{1}{10}$ to $\frac{1}{4}$ in (3 mm to 6 mm) in length. *Stamens* rose pink. *Pistil* rose pink. *Foliage* Lincoln green on top, paler underneath, glossy, small. *Growth* bushy, self-branching, vigorous, free-flowering. Bush or standard.

'Jandel'
FUCHSIA LA 1975
AFS Registration No 1264
Double
Tube white, medium length and width. *Sepals* white, tipped pink, and reflexed. *Corolla* orchid, medium size, round and flaring. *Foliage* medium green, small to medium size. *Growth* semi-trailer. Bush or basket with weights.

'Jane Lye'
LYE 1870
Single
Tube pale pink, long and thin. *Sepals* pale pink, long, narrow, arching slightly upwards. *Corolla* mauvish pink, slightly paler at the base of the petals, very compact, medium-sized bloom. *Foliage* pale to medium green, medium-sized, serrated leaves. *Growth* bushy, rather lax, upright, free-flowering.

'Japana'
EASTWOOD/YANCEY 1980
AFS Registration No 1569
Double
Tube white RHS 155A, short and thin. *Sepals* azalea pink RHS 38A, medium length, slightly reflexed, with green tips. *Corolla* azalea pink RHS 41C at the base extending well up into the petal—main colour rose bengal RHS 57B, edges beetroot purple RHS 72B, ruffled and pleated. *Pistil* pink. *Stamens* same as corolla. *Foliage* medium green RHS 137A, 2 in (5 cm) long, serrated edges. Centre vein and stems red. *Growth* natural trailer — will make a good basket. Prefers shaded conditions.

'Jaunty'
WEIR 1973
AFS Registration No 1081
Double
Tube carmine red, thick medium length. *Sepals* carmine, short and broad. *Corolla* orchid pink, square shaded, large bloom. *Foliage* medium green, medium to large leaves. *Growth* upright, vigorous, tall and bushy, free-flowering. Bush.

'Jean'
REITER 1953
Single
Tube white, pale pink flush, medium length and thickness. *Sepals* white, flushed pink, medium length, broad, upturned. *Corolla* deep Tyrian rose, flaring, medium-sized blooms. *Foliage* medium green, medium sized leaves, serrated. *Growth* trailing habit, free-flowering, vigorous. Basket.

'Jean Burton'
GADSBY 1968
Registered 1971
AFS Registration No 979
Tube pale pink, medium length and thickness. *Sepals* rhodamine pink, reflexing. *Corolla* pure white, bell-shaped, medium-sized bloom. *Foliage* medium green, medium-sized leaves. *Growth* upright, bushy, self-branching, free-flowering. Bush. *Parentage* 'Sleigh Bells' × 'Citation'.

'Jeanette Broadhurst'
BROADHURST 1974
AFS Registration No 1195
Single
Tube rose-madder, medium length and thickness. *Sepals* rose madder, short and broad. *Corolla* marbled rose madder and mauve, short petals, medium-sized bloom. *Foliage* light green, medium-sized leaves. *Growth* natural trailer, very free-flowering. Basket.

'Jean Ewart'
GEORGE ROE 1981
Single
Tube china rose (RHS 58D), short, medium thickness. *Sepals* china rose, short, pointed, curling back. *Corolla* amaranth rose (RHS 65A), very compact, small to medium-sized bloom. *Foliage* medium green, small to medium-sized leaves. *Growth* vigorous, upright, bushy, self-branching, and very free-flowering. *Parentage* 'Mipam' × 'Carol Roe'. Named after the Assistant

Secretary of the British Fuchsia Society. Bush or quarter standard.

'Jeanne Rose'
PRENTICE/VEE JAY 1978
AFS Registration No 1486
Double
Tube rose pink of medium length and thickness. *Sepals* dark rose, creped underside. *Corolla* mauve, outer petals have rose markings at base. *Foliage* medium green, red stems. *Growth* a natural, free-flowering trailer, makes a good basket.

'Jennie Rachel'
CHEETHAM 1979
AFS Registration No 1526
Double
Tube white, medium length, thick. *Sepals* white with green tips, turn pink in full sun. *Corolla* rose red RHS 58C veined rose bengal RHS 57B. Petals sometimes show white patches. Petaloids of the same colour as the corolla. *Stamens* white. *Pistil* white. *Foliage* dark green, long leaves up to 5 in (12.5 cm) in length. *Growth* tall growing upright which will make a good bush with judicial pinching. Blooms very large, but not very free-flowering.

'Jerry Copley'
COPLEY 1966
AFS Registration No 694
Semi-double
Tube bright red, medium length and thickness. *Sepals* bright red, longish, upturned. *Corolla* white with reddish veining, bell-shaped, medium size. *Foliage* medium green, medium-sized leaves. *Growth* natural trailer, bushy, vigorous, free-flowering. Basket.

'Jessie Ryle'
RYLE 1975
AFS Registration No 1247
Single
Tube whitish rose RHS 56D, short and thick. *Sepals* neyron rose RHS 56A on the underside, whitish rose. RHS 56D on top, long and narrow, slightly twisted. *Corolla* deep mallow purple RHS 72B, shading to phlox pink RHS 62B at the base, fading to beetroot purple RHS 71C as the bloom ages. *Anthers* rose red RHS 56B. *Foliage* green RHS 138B, with red centre veins. *Growth* upright, bushy, free-flowering. Bush or standard.

'Jess Walker'
COPLEY GARDENS 1967
AFS Registration No 744
Tube red, short and medium thick. *Sepals* red, long and narrow, held horizontally. *Corolla* white, flaring to saucer shape, very full with numerous white petaloids. *Foliage* medium green, medium-sized leaves. *Growth* trailer, free-flowering. Basket.

'Jezebel'
WALKER/FUCHSIARAMA
AFS Registration No 1511
Semi-double
Tube cherry red, short. *Sepals* cherry red with green tips. *Corolla* peony pink with cherry red streaks, full and tightly rolled. Tips of the sepals tend to cling together while opening, showing the corolla like a lantern. *Foliage* medium green. *Growth* medium upright which will make a good bush. The best colour develops if the plant is grown in the shade.

'Jim Fairclo'
HEDLUND 1951
Double
Tube dark crimson, medium length and thickness. *Sepals* crimson, longish, broad, upturned. *Corolla* dark burgundy, darker at the base of the petals, wide petals, medium to large-sized blooms. *Foliage* medium green, large, crinkled leaves. *Growth* vigorous, upright, bushy and free-flowering. Bush or standard.

'Jinx'
SCHNABEL/PASKESEN 1960
AFS Registration No 419
Single
Tube waxy white, small, medium thickness. *Sepals* waxy white on top, slightly

tinged carmine on the undersides, longish, broad. *Corolla* deep carmine, medium-sized bloom. *Foliage* dark green, medium-sized, leathery leaves. *Growth* lax upright, free-flowering, bushy. Bush or half-basket.

'Joan Cooper'
WOOD 1953
Single
Tube pale rose pink, long, thin. *Sepals* pale rose pink, narrow, green tips. Pointing slightly downwards, reflexing with maturity. *Corolla* cherry red, compact, small blooms. *Foliage* light green, longish medium-sized, serrated leaves. *Growth* upright, bushy, self-branching, free-flowering. Bush or excellent garden hardy.

'Joan Helm'
TIRET 1972
AFS Registration No 1071
Double
Tube white, tinged pink, medium length and thickness. *Sepals* white, longish, broad, upturned. *Corolla* deep lilac with pink streaks on the petals, full, medium-sized bloom. *Foliage* medium green, medium-sized leaves. *Growth* natural trailer, bushy, free-flowering. Basket.

'Joan Hurd' (51)
BOWYERS (date not known)
Semi-double to double
Tube white, flushed pink, short, medium thickness. *Sepals* white, flushed pink on top, deeper pink on the undersides, green tips. *Corolla* pale pink, full, medium-sized blooms. *Foliage* medium to darkish green, small to medium-sized leaves. *Growth* upright, bushy, self-branching, free-flowering. A very pretty flower, but one which has the unfortunate habit of 'balling'—rotting before, or shortly after, opening. Bush. 'Flirtation Waltz' seedling.

'Joan Leslie'
Raiser unknown, imported into America by Reiter 1953
Double
Tube deep red, medium length and thickness. *Sepals* deep red, medium length, broad and upturned. *Corolla* rich royal purple, medium-sized bloom. *Foliage* medium to darkish green, medium-sized leaves. *Growth* upright, bushy, free-flowering. Bush.

'Joanne'
PUGH 1978
AFS Registration No 1458
Single
Tube orient pink RHS 36A, short and thin. *Sepals* rose bengal RHS 61D, green tips on the upper side. *Corolla* red purple RHS 773A 1 in (2.5 cm) long. *Stamens and pistils* crimson RHS 52A. *Foliage* medium green RHS 137C, 2½ in (6 cm) long, 1½ in (4 cm) wide. *Growth* bushy, self-branching, natural trailer. Will make a good basket but can also be trained to a small bush.

'Joanne Bakker'
RYLE 1978
AFS Registration No 1475
Single
Tube with pink stripes, thick and of medium length. *Sepals* spinel red (RHS 54B), thick and waxy, shading to white at the tips, held horizontally and with the tips slightly upturned. *Stamens and pistil* pink. *Corolla* white, veined red, bell-shaped and slightly flaring at the bottom. *Foliage* medium green. *Growth* upright and bushy. Bush or standard. *Parentage* 'Leonora' × 'Ting-a-Ling'.

'Joanne Lynn'
ADKINS 1980
(introduced 1970)
AFS Registration No 1554
Semi-double
Tube white with a pinkish cast. *Sepals* white with a pink cast on top, undersides darker crepe pink, broad. *Corolla* fuchsia purple, medium size. *Foliage* medium green, ovate, with serrate margins, medium size. *Growth* upright, vigorous, bushy. Bush or standard.

'Joan of Arc'
REITER 1947
Double
Tube white, medium length and thickness. *Sepals* white, green tips, longish. *Corolla* white, faintly tinged pink, medium-sized bloom. *Foliage* medium green, medium-sized, serrated leaves. *Growth* bushy, upright, spreading, free-flowering. Bush or half-basket.

'Joan Pacey'
GADSBY 1972
AFS Registration No 1067
Single
Tube white, tinged pink, long, medium thickness. *Sepals* pink on top, darker pink on the undersides, green tips, long, narrow and twisting upwards slightly. *Corolla* phlox pink, long, fairly compact, medium-sized bloom. *Foliage* light to medium green, medium-sized, serrated leaves. Excellent exhibition plant. Bush or standard. *Parentage* 'Rosabel' × 'Sleigh Bells'.

'Joan's Delight'
GADSBY 1977
AFS Registration No 1428
Single
Tube crimson, short and medium thickness. *Sepals* crimson, small and short. *Corolla* violet blue, small. *Foliage* medium green, small. *Growth* dwarf, self-branching, upright. Good small pot plant, but difficult to train. Good for small pot culture. *Parentage* 'Wee Lass' × 'Cloverdale'.

'Joan Smith'
THORNE 1958
Single
Tube flesh pink, long and thin. *Sepals* flesh pink, long and narrow, reflexing completely up and over the tube. *Corolla* soft pink, shaded cerise, small and compact. *Foliage* medium green, medium-sized, heavily serrated leaves. *Growth* upright, bushy, extremely vigorous and difficult to control, free-flowering. Bush.

'Joe Kusber' (60)
PENNISI 1968
Double
Tube white, short and medium thick. *Sepals* white, long, with pink tips. *Corolla* blue-purple with pink variegations on the petals. Very full and fluffy, large, attractive blooms. *Foliage* medium green, medium to large leaves. *Growth* upright, bushy, free-flowering. Bush.

'John E. Davis'
NIEDERHOLZER 1946
Single
Tube white, medium length and thickness. *Sepals* geranium lake. *Corolla* magenta, medium-sized, loose-petalled. *Foliage* medium green, medium-sized, serrated leaves. *Growth* trailer, free-flowering. Basket.

'John Forbes'
FORBES 1888
Double
Tube scarlet-cerise, short and thick. *Sepals* scarlet-cerise, slightly upturned. *Corolla* purple, tinged scarlet at the base of the petals, medium-sized bloom. *Foliage* medium green, small to medium-sized, serrated leaves with red veining. *Growth* upright, bushy, free-flowering. Bush.

'John Fraser'
R. HOLMES 1977
AFS Registration No 1419
Single
Tube rose red RHS 58C, veined RHS 58B, medium length and width. *Sepals* rose red RHS 58C, on top, rose red RHS 58B on the undersides, green tips, semi-reflexed. *Corolla* imperial purple RHS 78A, rose red RHS 58B at the base, veined rose red, fading to cyclamen purple RHS 78B. *Stamens* rose red, anthers carmine, style pink with yellow stigma. *Foliage* medium green, small to medium, lanceolate, slightly serrated, petiole and part of the centre vein red. *Growth* semi-trailer, self-branching, bushy. Basket or bush.

'John Lockyer'
MRS E. HOLMES 1969
Single
Tube pink, thick, medium length. *Sepals* dark pink, green tips, broad and turning up towards the tube. *Corolla* magenta-purple, pale pinkish shade at the base of the petals and darker, reddish-purple edges, medium-sized blooms. *Foliage* medium green, medium to large leaves, slightly serrated. *Growth* upright, self-branching, vigorous, free-flowering. Easy to grow. Bush.

'John Marsh'
SCHNABEL 1963
AFS Registration No 584
Sport of 'Shalimar'
Tube white, thick, medium length. *Sepals* white with green tips, broad and curling upwards. *Corolla* pale orchid pink with pink veining, very full and fluffy, medium to large blooms. *Foliage* medium green, medium-sized, finely serrated leaves. *Growth* natural trailer, free-flowering in the right conditions, but a difficult one to grow. Basket.

'Johnny'
BROWN AND SOULES 1952
AFS Registration No 136
Semi-double
Tube red, short, medium length. *Sepals* rose pink, broad, upturned. *Corolla* white and pink petals, red veining, and overlaid blue. Medium-sized bloom. *Foliage* medium green. *Growth* bushy, upright, self-branching and free-flowering. Bush.

'Johnny Marine'
YORK 1952
AFS Registration No 138
Semi-double
Tube bright red, medium length and thickness. *Sepals* bright red, longish, slightly reflexed. *Corolla* pure white, spreading, loose-petalled. Medium-sized blooms. *Foliage* medium green, medium-sized leaves. *Growth* upright, bushy, self-branching, free-flowering. Bush.

'John Prentice'
GAGNON 1965
AFS Registration No 619
Tube rose pink, medium length and thickness. *Sepals* deep rose pink, longish, crepe effect. *Corolla* lavender blue with a pink stripe on the outer petals, and fading to fuchsia pink as the bloom ages. Full and compact. *Foliage* medium green, medium-sized leaves. *Growth* trailer, bushy, vigorous, free-flowering. Basket.

'John's Prize'
PRENTICE 1967
AFS Registration No 719
Double
Tube dark rose pink, medium length and thickness. *Sepals* deep rose pink, long, upturned. *Corolla* deep blue with some pink marbling on the petals, medium-sized blooms. *Foliage* dark green with red veins, small leaves. *Growth* bushy, self-branching, free-flowering trailer. Half-basket.

'John Suckley'
SUCKLEY 1966
Single to semi-double
Tube white with a pink flush, long, medium thickness. *Sepals* pink on top, deeper pink on the undersides, green tips, broad, curling upwards towards the tube. *Corolla* lavender blue veined rose pink, pale pink at the base of the petals. Medium-shaped blooms. *Foliage* medium green, small to medium, serrated leaves. *Growth* natural trailer, self-branching, bushy, free-flowering. Basket.

'Joker'
DE GRAAF 1976
Semi-double
Tube rose pink, short, medium thickness. *Sepals* rose pink, paler towards the tips which are green. *Corolla* multiple shades of red and blue, numerous petaloids, medium sized bloom, rather open. *Stamens and style* rose pink. *Foliage* medium green with red stems and centre vein. *Growth* trailer, but can also be grown as an upright, good sized, long lasting

blooms, self-branching, free-flowering. Bush or basket. *Parentage* 'Lena' ×.

'Joseph Holmes'
R. HOLMES 1980
AFS Registration No 1556
Single
Tube dawn pink with darker veins, medium length and thickness, green tip. *Sepals* dawn pink on top with darker edges and green tips. Undersides creped dawn pink—medium length, recurving slightly at the tips, but held slightly below the horizontal. *Corolla* neyron rose RHS 55A, bell-shaped and slightly flaring, with mandarin red RHS 40B at the base and edges of the petals, dawn pink RHS 49A veins at the base. *Foliage* medium green RHS 137C with lighter veins, serrated, ovate. Leaf stalk and part of the central vein are pink. *Growth* natural trailer, self-branching, lax, free-flowering. Will make a good basket.

'Josie'
PENNISI 1970
AFS Registration No 892
Double
Tube rose pink, short and thick. *Sepals* rose pink, medium length, upturned. *Corolla* rose pink with pink variegations, box type, medium-sized blooms. *Foliage* medium green, medium-sized leaves. *Growth* trailer, self-branching, bushy, free-flowering. Basket.

'Joyce'
BRAND 1949
Semi-double
Tube pale pink, medium length and thickness. *Sepals* rose pink, long and upturned. *Corolla* pink, medium-sized bloom, loose-petalled. *Foliage* medium green, medium to large leaves. *Growth* trailer, vigorous, bushy, free-flowering. Basket.

'Joy Patmore' (46)
TURNER 1961
Single
Tube white, short and thick. *Sepals* white with green tips, narrow and curling upwards. *Corolla* pinkish cerise, white at the base of the petals and rather darker at the edges, opening to a nice bell shape. *Foliage* medium green, medium-sized leaves. *Growth* upright, bushy, self-branching and free-flowering. A very good exhibition variety, easy to grow and train. Bush.

'Jubie-Lin'
COPLEY GARDENS 1964
AFS Registration No 616
Double
Tube red, long and medium thickness. *Sepals* red, long, spreading. *Corolla* very deep purple, full, fluffy, very large blooms. *Foliage* bright green, medium to large-sized leaves. *Growth* trailer, vigorous, self-branching, and free-flowering. Basket.

'Jubilee'
REITER 1953
AFS Registration No 193
Double
Tube white, medium length and thickness. *Sepals* white, long and spreading. *Corolla* bright red fading to a paler shade at the base, with edges of dark Tyrian rose, medium to large blooms. *Foliage* medium green, medium-sized leaves. *Growth* vigorous, bushy, upright, free-flowering and self-branching. Bush.

'Judy'
WEAVER/FUCHSIARAMA 1977
AFS Registration No 1431
Single
Tube dark pink to rose, medium length and thickness. *Sepals* rose pink. *Corolla* deep orchid rose, medium size. *Foliage* variegated, shades of green, white and yellow. *Growth* natural trailer, basket plant. Sport of 'Amapola'.

'Jules Daloges'
LEMOINE 1907
Double $4\frac{1}{2}$ in (11 cm)
Tube scarlet, short, medium thickness. *Sepals* scarlet, completely recurving. *Corolla* bluish violet-mauve with pink

edged petals. *Foliage* dark green, medium-sized leaves. *Growth* vigorous, upright. Self-branching, free-flowering. Bush.

'Julia'
GORMAN 1970
AFS Registration No 929
Double
Tube red, medium length and thickness. *Sepals* red, long, narrow and curling upwards to the tube. *Corolla* very dark purple, full, medium-sized bloom. *Foliage* medium to darkish green, medium-sized leaves. *Growth* lax bush, vigorous, self-branching and free-flowering. Bush or basket.

'Julie Horton' (73)
GAGNON 1962
AFS Registration No 511
Semi-double
Tube pale pink, long, medium thickness. *Sepals* pale pink with green tips, long, narrow. *Corolla* pink, medium-sized bloom with overlapping petals. *Foliage* dark green, leathery, medium-sized leaves. *Growth* trailer, free-flowering, vigorous and long-lasting. Basket.

'June Revell'
HANDLEY 1975
AFS Registration No 1274
Single
Tube pink RHS 52C, thin and short. *Sepals* deep rose RHS 55A, long and narrow. *Corolla* mauve RHS 74C, pink at the base and veined crimson. The petals have picotee edges of purple RHS 71A, and are overlapping. *Foliage* yellow green RHS 144B. *Growth* upright, bushy and free-flowering. Will take full sun—foliage develops its best colour in the sun. Bush.

'Junior Miss'
HODGES 1949
Double
Tube red, medium length and thickness. *Sepals* deep red, medium length, upturned. *Corolla* bluish-mauve with splashes of pink, very attractive, medium-sized bloom. *Foliage* medium green, medium-sized serrated leaves. *Growth* upright, bushy, vigorous, self-branching and free-flowering. Bush.

'Juno'
KENNETT 1966
AFS Registration No 677
Single
Tube white with greenish tinge, long and thin. *Sepals* white with green tips, long and completely upturned over the tube. *Corolla* dark red, fading to cerise, long and compact. *Foliage* medium to large-sized, pale green serrated leaves, very broad. *Growth* very vigorous, self-branching, free-flowering trailer. Half-basket or can be trained to fan, espalier, etc.

'Jupiter 70'
R. HOLMES 1970
AFS Registration No 1209 (1974)
Single
Tube pale pink RHS 37B, medium length, slightly thick. *Sepals* scarlet RHS 43D, with green tips, narrow, medium length, and upswept. *Corolla* crimson RHS 52A, mandarin red RHS 40C at the base of the petals, small, bell-shaped blooms. *Foliage* pale to medium green, large, heavily serrated leaves with veins and stem of a paler green shade. *Growth* upright, bushy, self-branching, free-flowering Bush or summer bedder. *Parentage* 'Percy Holmes' × 'San Francisco'.

'Kaleidoscope'
GEORGE MARTIN 1966
AFS Registration No 674
Double
Tube red, medium length and thickness. *Sepals* red. *Corolla* shades of purple through to pale lavender, with streaks of pink and red over the petals, giving the bloom a multicoloured appearance which changes as the season progresses, hence the name 'Kaleidoscope'. Very large, fluffy blooms. *Foliage* medium green, medium to large leaves. *Growth*

upright, bushy, vigorous and free-flowering. Needs staking if required as a bush plant. Bush.

'Karan'
Raiser GADSBY 1968
Registered 1971
AFS Registration No 966
Single
Tube rose red, medium length and thickness. *Sepals* rose red, short. *Corolla* blue bird blue, medium-sized bloom. *Foliage* medium green. *Growth* upright, bushy, free-flowering. Flowers held well out from the foliage. Bush. *Parentage* 'Upward Look' seedling ×.

'Kathleen'
PUGH 1974
AFS Registration No 1163
Double
Tube orient pink (RHS 36A) short, medium thickness. *Sepals* neyron rose RHS 55C, flaring. *Corolla* RHS 159D, (orange-white group) very full and medium-sized bloom. *Foliage* medium green, medium to large-sized leaves. *Growth* upright, bushy, vigorous, free-flowering, preferring shade conditions for the best colour. Bush or standard.

'Kathy Gorringe'
GAGNON 1962
AFS Registration No 510
Semi-double
Tube pink, medium length and thickness. *Sepals* pink, long and narrow. *Corolla* greyish blue shading to soft orchid pink, medium size. *Growth* medium green, medium-sized leaves. *Growth* trailer, vigorous, free-flowering. Half-basket.

'Kathy Louise'
ANTONELLI 1963
AFS Registration No 558
Double
Tube carmine red, medium length and thickness. *Sepals* carmine, crepe effect on the undersides, long, broad and curling upwards over the tube. *Corolla* rosy lilac with rose pink veins, full, rather loose, medium-sized bloom. *Foliage* dark green, medium-sized, serrated leaves. *Growth* trailer, very vigorous but not self-branching, a very attractive bloom. Basket.

'Kay Louise'
GAGNON 1963
AFS Registration No 555
Double
Tube pale pink, medium length and thickness. *Sepals* pale pink. *Corolla* pure white, very full and frilly, medium-sized bloom. *Foliage* darkish green, small leaves. *Growth* lax upright, vigorous, free-flowering. Bush if staked, or basket.

'Keepsake'
KENNETT 1961
AFS Registration No 477
Double
Tube pink, short and thick. *Sepals* white on top, pale pink flush on the undersides, broad and upturned. *Corolla* cerise-purple, centre petals rolled, outer petals of the same colour, paler towards the base, very full and fluffy, medium-sized bloom. *Foliage* medium green, small to medium-sized, serrated leaves. *Growth* upright, bushy, self-branching and free-flowering. Bush.

'Kegworth Beauty'
SMITH 1974
AFS Registration No 1226
Single
Tube white, long, medium thickness. *Sepals* white, short and waxy, held over the corolla. *Corolla* amaranth rose RHS 65A, paler at the base of the petals, small bloom. *Foliage* medium green, medium-sized serrated leaves. *Growth* bushy, upright, close-jointed, free-flowering. Bush.

'Kegworth Carnival'
SMITH 1979
Double
Tube white, medium length and thickness. *Sepals* white, longish and narrow. *Corolla* tyrian purple passing to rose-bengal

small to medium-sized blooms. *Foliage* medium green, medium-sized leaves. *Growth* lax upright, free-flowering, vigorous. Bush if staked, or basket.

'Kegworth Supreme'
SMITH 1979
Single
Tube empire rose RHS 48C, medium length and thickness. *Sepals* empire rose on top, darker shade on the undersides. *Corolla* fuchsia purple, medium-sized bloom. *Foliage* dark green, medium-sized leaves. *Growth* upright, bushy, short-jointed, free-flowering. Bush.

'Ken Lewis'
GAGNON 1969
AFS Registration No 844
Single
Tube white with pink veining, medium length and thickness. *Sepals* pure white. *Corolla* bright rose-pink, bell-shaped, medium-sized bloom. *Foliage* medium green, medium-sized leaves. *Growth* natural trailer, self-branching, bushy and free-flowering. Half-basket.

'Kentish Maid'
R. HOLMES 1976
AFS Registration No 1339
Single
Tube jasper red RHS 39B, thick and of medium length. *Sepals* carmine rose RHS 52D, on top, rose bengal RHS 61D on the undersides, green tips. Long, medium width, upswept. *Corolla* beetroot purple RHS 71C, fading to fuchsia purple at the base of the petals, Indian lake RHS 60A at the edges. Small to medium-sized bloom. *Foliage* medium green, small to medium-sized, serrated leaves. *Growth* bushy, upright, self-branching, free-flowering and very easy to grow. Bush.

'Kents Bank'
THORNLEY 1978
AFS Registration No 1467
Single
Named after Kent's Bank Station on the edge of Morecambe Bay. *Tube* creamy white, thin and of medium length. *Sepals* creamy white flushed pink, narrow and slightly downswept. *Stamens and pistil* soft pink. *Corolla* cyclamen purple RHS 74A. *Foliage* medium green, narrow. *Growth* natural trailer which will make a good basket. Will withstand full sun. *Parentage* 'Falling Stars' × 'Hawkshead'.

'Keystone'
HAAG 1945
Single
Tube pink, thin, medium length. *Sepals* pale pink on top, darker undersides, green tips. Curling round towards the tube. *Corolla* very pale pink, compact, small to medium-sized bloom. *Foliage* medium green, medium-sized, narrow and finely serrated leaves. *Growth* upright, bushy, self-branching, free-flowering, a nice exhibition variety. Bush.

'Khada'
G. ROE 1973
Single
Tube rose red. *Sepals* rose red. *Corolla* white with rose veining. *Flowers* small, very prolific. Flowers held erect. *Growth* upright, bushy, compact. Makes a good $3\frac{1}{2}$ in (9 cm) pot plant for exhibition purposes. *Parentage* 'Snowcap' × 'Margaret Roe'.

'Kimberly'
MUNCKNER 1963
AFS Registration No 565
Semi-double
Tube white, medium length, thick. *Sepals* white with green tips, long, broad and curling up towards the tube. Sepals shaded pink on the underside. *Corolla* deep violet blue, marbled phlox pink, and paler pink at the base of the serrated petals. Medium-sized bloom. *Foliage* medium green, medium to large-sized leaves, finely serrated. *Growth* trailer, free-flowering and very attractive. Basket.

'King George'
HOWLETT 1911
Single
Tube pink, thick and of medium length. *Sepals* pinkish-cerise, long, medium width, held straightened out and upturned at the tips. *Corolla* bluish-mauve, with rose-pink veining. Lighter colour at the base of the petals, medium-sized bloom. *Foliage* light to medium green, medium to large-sized. Serrated leaves with reddish veins. *Growth* upright, bushy, self-branching and free-flowering. Bush. Presented by the raiser to HM King George V in 1912 with its sister plant, 'Queen Mary'. Seedling from 'Mrs Marshall'.

'King of Bath'
COLVILLE
Double
Tube pinkish-red, long, medium thickness. *Sepals* carmine red, broad and slightly upturned towards the tube. *Corolla* deep plum purple, flushed pale rose, medium-sized bloom and very compact. *Foliage* darkish green, medium to large, finely serrated leaves. *Growth* rather lax, bushy, upright, free-flowering. Bush, if staked, or half-basket.

'King of Hearts'
FUCHSIA FOREST 1965
AFS Registration No 627
Double
Sport of 'Queen of Hearts'.
Tube red, thin, medium length. *Sepals* red, broad, turned up towards the tube. *Corolla* pale lavender, splashed red, pink and white on the outer petals, numerous petaloids, open, loose-petalled blooms. *Foliage* medium green, medium-sized, serrated leaves. *Growth* trailer, bushy, free-flowering. Basket.

'King of Siam'
COLVILLE 1965
Single
Tube light red, longish and medium thick. *Sepals* scarlet, long and narrow, held well down over the corolla. *Corolla* reddish purple, paler at the base of the petals. Compact and of medium size. *Foliage* light to medium green, large-sized, serrated leaves. *Growth* lax bush, self-branching, vigorous and free-flowering. Very easy to grow. Bush or half-basket.

'King's Ransom' (56)
SCHNABEL 1954
AFS Registration No 195
Double
Tube white, medium length and thickness. *Sepals* medium length, white, turning up over the tube. *Corolla* bright violet purple, medium-sized bloom. *Foliage* medium green, medium-sized, longish and finely serrated leaves. *Growth* upright, bushy, vigorous, and free-flowering. Bush or standard.

'Kiwi'
TIRET 1966
AFS Registration No 687
Double
Tube greenish white, short and thick. *Sepals* white with green tips, medium length, broad and held on top of the corolla, then turning up on maturity. *Corolla* reddish purple, paler at the base of the petals, very full and fluffy, medium-sized bloom. *Foliage* medium green, medium-sized, serrated leaves. *Growth* natural trailer, vigorous, free-flowering. Bush or basket.

'Kolding Pearl'
Raiser and date unknown. Believed to have originated in Denmark.
Single
Tube waxy white, medium length and thickness. *Sepals* white with green tips, held low over the corolla. *Corolla* bright pink with overlay of salmon-orange, small to medium-sized bloom. *Foliage* pale to medium green, medium-sized, broad and serrated leaves. *Growth* upright, vigorous, bushy, self-branching and very free-flowering. Easy to grow, and a very attractive coloured cultivar. Bush.

'Komeet'

DE GROOT 1970

Single

Tube red, short and medium thick. *Sepals* red, very long and narrow. *Corolla* reddish purple fading to reddish lilac, medium-sized blooms. *Foliage* medium to dark green, medium-sized leaves. *Growth* upright, bushy, vigorous and free-flowering. Bush. *Parentage F. regia typica* × 'Beacon'.

'Komeet van Halley' ('Halley's Comet')

VAN WIERINGEN 1970

Single

Tube white, flushed rose, long and thin. *Sepals* white with rose pink flush, long, narrow and upturned at the tips, which are green. *Corolla* deep lilac red, paler shade at the base of the petals. Medium to large-sized blooms. *Foliage* darkish green with red veins, medium-sized leaves. *Growth* lax bush, free-flowering and vigorous. Bush (if staked) or basket.

'Kon-Tiki'

TIRET 1965

AFS Registration No 652

Double

Tube white, medium length and thickness. *Sepals* white, with pale pink flush, medium length. *Corolla* pinkish violet, full, medium-sized blooms. *Foliage* medium green, medium-sized leaves. *Growth* lax bush, quite vigorous, free-flowering. Bush or basket.

'Koralle' (13)

BONSTEDT 1905

Triphylla type

Tube long, medium thickness, salmon-orange. *Sepals* short, salmon-orange. Corolla of the same colour, small. Total length of the bloom is about $2\frac{1}{4}$ in (6 cm). *Foliage* deep sage green with veins of a paler shade, and an overall velvety sheen. Medium to large leaves. *Growth* upright, vigorous, very free-flowering. Bush. *Parentage F. triphylla* ×. Sometimes incorrectly called 'Coralle'.

'Kwintet' (94)

VAN WIERINGEN 1970

Single

Tube dark rose pink, long and of medium thickness. *Sepals* short, dark rose, medium length and held horizontal. *Corolla* rose red, medium-sized and slightly bell-shaped. *Foliage* medium green, small to medium-sized leaves, very slight serrations. *Growth* upright, bushy, self-branching, very vigorous and free-flowering. Early-blooming and very easy to grow. Bush.

'La Bergere'

DE GRAAF 1976

Single

Tube white, faintly tinged rose, quite short and thick. *Sepals* white, small and upturned. *Corolla* creamy-white, small to medium-sized bloom. *Foliage* medium green, small to medium-sized leaves. *Growth* lax, bushy, free-flowering. Basket or half-basket. *Parentage* 'La Campanella' ×.

'La Bianca'

TIRET 1950

AFS Registration No 64

Single

Tube greenish white, short, medium thickness. *Sepals* white with a faint green stripe, and green tips, broad, medium length and curling upwards. *Corolla* white, long and loose-petalled, medium-sized bloom. *Foliage* medium green, medium to large, serrated leaves. *Growth* very lax, bushy, free-flowering, preferring to be grown in the shade. Bush or half-basket.

'La Campanella' (50)

BLACKWELL 1968

Semi-double

Tube white, faintly tinged pink, short and thick. *Sepals* white on top, slightly flushed pink on the underside, shortish and broad, held level with slight upturning at the tips to start with, then reflexing. *Corolla* imperial purple with some cerise veining, ageing to lavender. Small to medium-sized blooms. *Foliage* medium green, smallish leaves. *Growth* lax, bushy, very vigorous, and exceptionally free-flowering. Basket or half-basket.

'Lace Petticoats' (33)
TIRET 1952
AFS Registration No 145
Double
Tube white short, medium thickness. *Sepals* white with green tips, short and broad, upturning to cover the tube. *Corolla* pure white, very full and fluffy, medium-sized bloom. *Foliage* medium to darkish green, medium-sized, ovate, serrated leaves. *Growth* upright, rather lax, bushy and free-flowering. Bush.

'Laddie'
J.A. WRIGHT 1980
AFS Registration No 1602
Double
Tube light carmine, medium length and width. *Sepals* light carmine with white stripes down the centre, arching back. *Corolla* light purple, large. *Foliage* medium green, large. *Growth* upright, free-flowering, bushy. Bush. 'Peppermint Stick' seedling.

'Lady Ann'
TIRET 1953
AFS Registration No 155
Double
Tube white, short and medium thick. *Sepals* white on top, faint tinge of pink on the underside, green tips, long, broad and spreading. *Corolla* purplish blue with phlox pink marbling, petals curled and spreading, medium-sized bloom. *Foliage* medium green, medium-sized leaves. *Growth* upright, bushy, vigorous, free-flowering. Bush.

'Lady Beth'
MARTIN 1958
AFS Registration No 364
Double
Tube pink, short, medium thickness. *Sepals* pink on top, deeper shade of pink on the undersides, broad and recurving over the tube. *Corolla* violet-blue, paler with age. Petals splashed rose-pink. Medium to large, fluffy bloom. *Foliage* light to medium green, medium to large-sized, serrated leaves. *Growth* upright, lax, free-flowering. Best grown as a trailer. Basket.

'Lady Boothby'
RAFFILL 1938
Single
Tube crimson red, short and thin. *Sepals* crimson, short and broad, held almost horizontal. *Corolla* very dark purple, almost black on opening, pink at the base of the petals and with cerise veining. Small, very compact bloom. *Foliage* darkish green, small to medium-sized, finely serrated leaves. *Growth* extremely vigorous, upright, very long branches with long internodes. Requires a great deal of pinching if it is to be kept in check. *Parentage F. alpestris* × 'Royal Purple'. Name in July 1939 after the then President of the BFS during the Society's visit to Kew.

'Ladybower'
GADSBY 1970
Registered 1971
AFS Registration No 964
Double
Tube cardinal red, medium length and thickness. *Sepals* cardinal red. *Corolla* creamy white, very full, with petaloids flushed crimson. Medium-sized bloom. *Foliage* medium green, medium-sized leaves. *Growth* upright, vigorous, free-flowering. Bush or basket. *Parentage* 'Swingtime' × 'Tom Pacey'.

'Lady Isobel Barnett' (148)
GADSBY 1968
Registered 1971
AFS Registration No 978
Single
Tube rose red, thickish, medium length. *Sepals* rose red, held straight out. *Corolla*

rose purple with imperial purple edges to the petals. *Foliage* light to medium green, medium-sized leaves, serrated. *Growth* very vigorous, upright, bushy and exceptionally free-flowering. Blooms held well out from the foliage. If this plant has a fault it is that the exceptional amount of pollen tends to cover the leaves, making it rather unsightly. Bush.

'Lady Kathleen Spence'
RYLE 1974
Registered 1975
AFS Registration No 1248
Single
Tube medium length, whitish to pale pink. *Sepals* whitish rose on top, amaranth rose RHS 65A underneath. Long, thin and standing out well. *Corolla* delicate lavender shade RHS 85A, fading to RHS 76A. *Anthers* beetroot purple RHS 71A. *Foliage* large, medium green. *Growth* bushy, medium upright but can be trained as a basket plant if weighted. Does best in the shade to keep its colour. It is not self-branching, and requires pinching to get it into shape. Cuttings are susceptible to *Botrytis*, and mature plants tend to suffer die-back in winter. Seems to be very attractive to greenfly. *Parentage* 'Bobby Shaftoe' × 'Schneewitchen'. Awarded the BFS Gold Certificate of Merit 1976.

'Lady La Tasha'
SOO YUN 1979
AFS Registration No 1492
Double
Tube crimson, thick and of medium length. *Sepals* crimson, 2 in (5 cm) long, smooth on top and with a crepe effect on the undersides. Curling up towards the stem. *Corolla* violet fading to rose bengal at the base of the petals. *Petals* up to 3 in (7.5 cm) wide, scalloped at the tips, and opening flared, with many petaloids streaked crimson. *Foliage* light to medium green, 2½ in (6.3 cm) long with green veins and red stems. *Growth* self-branching, bushy upright, which requires pinching and will make a good bush or standard. Heavy bloomer. Will make a basket if grown with weights.

'Lady Lillian Cash'
PENNISI 1971
AFS Registration No 1017
Double
Tube white, medium length and thickness. *Sepals* white with pinkish flush, long and narrow, upturned. *Corolla* roseine purple, centres of the petals white, serrated edges. Large flower. *Foliage* medium green, medium to large leaves. *Growth* natural trailer, vigorous, free-flowering. Basket.

'Lady Magenta'
SOO YUN 1977
AFS Registration No 1406
Double
Tube off-white, long, medium thickness. *Sepals* white on top, underside white heavily shaded roseine purple, curling up to the tube. *Corolla* magenta, full double skirt with top skirt petals brushed pale solferino purple. Large and full. Petals have serrated edges. *Stamens* pale magenta. *Pistil* pale magenta. *Foliage* pale lime to lemon as it matures, magenta veins, serrated, and of medium size. *Growth* natural trailer. Will make a very good basket.

'Lady Ransome'
GORMAN 1970
AFS Registration No 925
Semi-double
Tube white, medium length and thickness. *Sepals* white, upturned. *Corolla* white, slight touch of pink at the base of the petals, medium-sized bloom. *Foliage* medium green, medium-sized, serrated leaves. *Growth* upright, bushy, free-flowering. Bush.

'Lady Thumb' (123)
ROE 1967
Semi-double
Sport of 'Tom Thumb'
Tube carmine, short and thin. *Sepals* carmine pink, short, narrow, held below the

horizontal. *Corolla* white with pink veins, small and compact bloom. *Foliage* medium green, small, slightly serrated. *Growth* upright, bushy, self-branching, exceptionally free-flowering. Excellent exhibition plant. Bush or quarter standard.

'La Fiesta'
KENNETT 1962
AFS Registration No 535
Double
Tube white, short and thick. *Sepals* white with green tips, broad, horizontal and turning up at the tips. *Corolla* reddish purple with white petaloids splashed cerise, medium-sized bloom with flaring petaloids. *Foliage* medium green, broad, ovate, medium-sized leaves. *Growth* trailer, self-branching, vigorous, free-flowering. Half-basket.

'La France'
LEMOINE 1885
Double
Tube scarlet, short and thick. *Sepals* scarlet, short, broad and recurving over the tube. *Corolla* violet-purple with scarlet veins, becoming paler on maturity, and paler at the base of the petals. Medium to large-sized, rather loose-petalled blooms. *Foliage* medium green, medium-sized, serrated leaves. *Growth* upright, bushy, self-branching and vigorous. Bush.

'Laga'
FELIX 1978
Single
Tube scarlet, small, thick. *Sepals* scarlet, small, broad. *Corolla* white, small, blooms held erect. *Foliage* medium green, small to medium-sized leaves. *Growth* upright, bushy, free-flowering. Bush.

'La Honda'
CHILES 1953
AFS Registration No 164
Semi-double
Tube pink, medium length and thickness. *Sepals* dark pink, recurving multi-sepalled. *Corolla* rosy purple, medium-sized bloom. *Foliage* medium green, medium to large leaves. *Growth* very vigorous, upright, free-flowering. Bush or standard.

'Lakeside'
THORNLEY 1967
AFS Registration No 1062 (1972)
Single to semi-double
Tube bright pink, short and thin. *Sepals* bright pink to neyron rose RHS 55A, short with green tips, recurving but not completely. *Corolla* bluish-violet RHS 88C, fading to lilac-blue and with pinkish veins. Compact, small bloom. *Foliage* medium green, small finely serrated leaves. *Growth* trailer, very vigorous, bushy, self-branching and very free-flowering. Tends to bud very early before leaf growth is well underway, so early buds should be removed. Excellent exhibition variety. Basket or half-basket.

'La Neige'
LEMOINE 1873
Double
Tube purplish red, short and thick. *Sepals* reddish violet, long and broad, pointed tips, reflexing. *Corolla* white with very little veining, full, petals short and folded. *Foliage* medium green, medium-sized leaves. *Growth* upright, vigorous, free-flowering, described by Porcher as one of the finest red and whites. Bush.

'La Neige'
TIRET 1965
AFS Registration No 650
Double
Tube white with faint pink flush, medium length and thickness. *Sepals* white on top, pale pink flush on the undersides, green tips. Short and broad, curling up to the tube. *Corolla* white, very full but inclined to be rather loose, medium-sized bloom. *Foliage* medium green, longish, medium-sized, serrated leaves. *Growth* upright, rather lax, self-branching, free-flowering. Bush or basket.

'La Petite'
PASKESEN 1966
AFS Registration No 662
Semi-double
Tube pink, short and thick. *Sepals* pink with green tips, recurving. *Corolla* phlox pink, medium-sized bloom. *Foliage* medium green, medium-sized, serrated leaves. *Growth* lax upright, self-branching, free-flowering. Bush or basket.

'La Quinta'
TIRET 1970
AFS Registration No 899
Double
Tube white, short, medium thickness. *Sepals* white, longish and upturned. *Corolla* deep purple, very full, medium-sized. *Foliage* medium green, medium-sized, serrated leaves. *Growth* natural trailer, free-flowering. Basket.

'L'Arlesienne' (85)
COLVILLE 1968
Semi-double
Tube pale pink, medium length and thickness. *Sepals* pale pink with green tips, long, narrow and curling upwards to the tube. *Corolla* white, veined palest pink, opening well out as it matures, medium-sized bloom. *Foliage* light to medium green, medium-sized, serrated leaves. *Growth* upright, bushy, vigorous, self-branching and free-flowering. A very attractive flower.

'Lassie'
S. TRAVIS 1959
Registered 1973
AFS Registration No 1152
Double
Tube bright crimson, medium length, medium thickness. *Sepals* bright crimson, broad, held horizontally over the top of the corolla, glossy appearance on top, and crepe underneath. *Corolla* pure white with slight carmine veining, very full and compact, medium-sized bloom. *Foliage* dark green, glossy, medium-sized, serrated leaves. *Growth* lax upright, self-branching, vigorous, free-flowering. Basket. *Parentage* 'Swingtime' ×.

'Laura'
NIEDERHOLZER 1946
Single
Tube white, medium length and thickness. *Sepals* neyron rose, long and upturned. *Corolla* fuchsia pink, long, medium-sized blooms. *Foliage* medium green. *Growth* upright, bushy, free-flowering. Bush or standard.

'Laura'
MARTIN 1968
AFS Registration No 774
Double
Tube red, medium length and thickness. *Sepals* red, long, broad, upturned. *Corolla* sky blue, ageing to lavender blue, large blooms. *Foliage* medium green, medium to large leaves. *Growth* bushy but lax, vigorous, free-flowering. Bush or half-basket.

'Laura Sutter'
NESSIER 1956
AFS Registration No 122
Single
Tube pale rose pink, medium length and thickness. *Sepals* pale rose pink, medium length, upturned. *Corolla* pale silver-blue, bell shaped, medium-sized bloom. *Foliage* medium green. *Growth* lax upright, bushy, free-flowering. Bush or half-basket.

'Laurie'
ANTONELLI 1963
AFS Registration No 557
Double
Tube pale pink, medium length and thickness. *Sepals* pale pink, long, narrow with green tips. *Corolla* rhodamine pink with four large petals in the centre and numerous smaller outside petals. Very full, large blooms. *Foliage* darkish green, medium to large-sized leaves. *Growth* trailer, vigorous, bushy, free-flowering. Basket.

'Lavender and Old Lace'
HAZARD
Single
Tube pink, medium length and thickness. *Sepals* pink, upturned. *Corolla* pale lavender, medium-sized blooms. *Foliage* medium green, serrated leaves. *Growth* upright, bushy, self-branching and free-flowering. Bush.

'Lavender Basket'
HAZARD
Double
Tube red, medium length and thickness. *Sepals* long and broad, upturned, red. *Corolla* rosy-mauve, medium-sized bloom. *Foliage* medium to darkish green, medium-sized leaves. *Growth* natural trailer, free-flowering. Basket.

'Lavender Kate'
MRS HOLMES 1970
Double
Tube pale pink, medium length and thickness. *Sepals* pink, long and broad. *Corolla* lavender-blue, medium to large blooms. *Foliage* medium green, medium-sized leaves. *Growth* upright, bushy, free-flowering. Bush.

'Lavender Lace'
FRANCESCA 1977
AFS Registration No 1421
Single
Tube white, short. *Sepals* pink, turning flat between the petals. *Corolla* light lavender, darkening with age, petals notched, very small. *Pistil and stamens* white. *Foliage* medium green, small and serrated. *Growth* natural trailer, self-branching and bushy, dwarf. Miniature plant. Basket, miniature standard.

'Lavender Lady'
PUGH 1974
AFS Registration No 1164
Single
Tube red (RHS 36A) short, and of medium thickness. *Sepals* red RHS 55Cx on top, frosted red on the undersides, medium length and width, completely recurving to the tube. *Corolla* purple violet RHS 82C with red-purple markings. Medium-sized bloom. *Foliage* medium green with red veins, medium-sized leaves. *Growth* lax upright, bushy, free-flowering. Bush.

'Lazy Lady'
MARTIN 1960
AFS Registration No 444
Semi-double
Tube pale red, medium length and thickness. *Sepals* light red, long, narrow and curling. *Corolla* medium blue, shading to lighter blue at the base of the petals. Medium-sized blooms. *Foliage* medium green, medium-sized, serrated blooms. *Growth* natural trailer, bushy, free-flowering. Basket.

'Le Berger' (30)
DE GRAAF 1977
Semi-double
Tube creamy white, short, medium thickness. *Sepals* white, short, pointed. *Corolla* white, very faint pink tinge to the petals, small to medium-sized bloom. *Foliage* medium green, small to medium-sized leaves. *Growth* trailer, lax, bushy, free flowering. Keeps its colour best if grown in the shade or semi-shade conditions. Basket. *Parentage* 'La Campanella' seedling.

'Lena'
BUNNEY 1862
Semi-double to single
Tube pale flesh pink, short, medium thickness. *Sepals* pale flesh pink on top, darker on the undersides, green tips. Broad and upturned. *Corolla* purple, paler at the base of the petals, medium-sized bloom. *Foliage* light to medium green, medium-sized, serrated leaves. *Growth* lax bush, vigorous, self-branching, very free-flowering and bushy. Can be trained to most shapes. Bush (if hard pinched) or basket. Often confused with 'Eva Boerg' (q.v.).

'Lena Dalton' (108)
REIMERS 1953
Double
Tube pale pink, short, medium thickness. *Sepals* pale pink, broad and reflexed. *Corolla* lavender blue maturing to a rosy-mauve shade, very compact, small to medium-sized bloom. *Foliage* darkish green, small to medium-sized, serrated leaves with red veining. *Growth* upright, bushy, self-branching and free-flowering. A very good exhibition variety. Bush or quarter standard.

'L'Enfant Prodigue'
LEMOINE 1887
Semi-double
See under 'Enfant Prodigue'.

'Leonora' (74)
TIRET 1960
AFS Registration No 434
Single
Tube pink, medium length and thickness. *Sepals* pink, long and narrow, recurving. Green tips. *Corolla* pink, bell shaped, medium-sized bloom. *Foliage* medium green, small to medium-sized, serrated leaves. *Growth* upright, bushy, self-branching and free-flowering. An excellent exhibition plant. Bush or standard.

'Leonora Rose'
STILWELL 1974
Single
Tube pale pink, medium length and thickness. *Sepals* pale pink with green tips, recurving. *Corolla* blush-pink, with a white flush, medium-sized bloom. *Foliage* medium green, small to medium-sized, serrated leaves. *Growth* upright, bushy, free-flowering. Bush. Sport of 'Leonora'.

'Libra'
CASTRO 1971
AFS Registration No 952
Semi-double to double
Tube white, medium length and thickness. *Sepals* white on top, pale pink on the undersides, longish and broad. *Corolla* pale blue, shading to lavender with splashes of pink on the outer petals, medium to large, compact bloom. *Foliage* medium green, medium to large leaves. *Growth* natural trailer, free-flowering, bushy. Basket.

'Liebestraume'
BLACKWELL 1966
Double
Tube white with pale pink flush, short, medium thickness. *Sepals* greenish white on top with green tips, flushed pink on the undersides, short, broad and completely reflexed over the tube. *Corolla* pale lavender with deeper markings on the petals, white at the base of the petals and pink veining and splashes. Small to medium-sized blooms, fairly compact. *Foliage* medium to darkish green, medium-sized, slightly serrated leaves. *Growth* upright, bushy, free-flowering. Bush.

'Liebriez' (134)
KOHNE 1874
Single
Tube pale cerise-pink, medium length and thickness. *Sepals* cerise pink, recurving. *Corolla* pink with deeper pink veining, small and fairly compact bloom. *Foliage* medium green, small, serrated leaves. *Growth* upright, bushy, self-branching and very free-flowering. A very good exhibition plant for small pot classes. Bush or quarter standard.

'Lightning'
TIRET 1970
AFS Registration No 934
Double
Tube ivory white, long and thin. *Sepals* ivory white, long, with green tips and upturned. *Corolla* orange-red, long and compact, medium-sized bloom. *Foliage* dark green, medium-sized leaves. *Growth* lax bush, vigorous, bushy, free-flowering. Bush or basket.

'Lilac'
HAAG AND SON 1952
Single

Tube pale pink, longish, medium thickness. *Sepals* pale pink, long, narrow, pointing downwards clear of the corolla, pale green tipped. *Corolla* lilac, compact, medium to large-sized bloom. *Foliage* medium green, medium-sized, serrated leaves. *Growth* lax, spreading bush, free-flowering, rather too stiff branched to make a basket. Bush.

'Lilac Lustre' (149)
MUNKNER 1961
AFS Registration No 480
Double
Tube rose red, short, medium thickness. *Sepals* rose red, broad, upturned. *Corolla* powder blue to lilac, very compact, broad pleated petals. Medium-sized bloom. *Foliage* bright green, medium-sized leaves. *Growth* upright, bushy, vigorous, self-branching and free-flowering. Very beautiful cultivar. Bush or summer bedder.

'Lilac 'n' Rose'
WALTZ 1958
AFS Registration No 353
Double
Tube white, flushed pale pink, medium length and thickness. *Sepals* white, flushed pink, long and pointed, upturning. *Corolla* lilac, maturing to rose-pink, medium-sized, compact bloom. *Foliage* medium green, medium-sized leaves. *Growth* trailer, bushy, free-flowering. Basket.

'Lilac Princess'
HANDLEY 1979
AFS Registration No 1502
Single
Tube greenish white, short and thick. *Sepals* short, greenish white on the outside and pale pink on the underside, held well out from the corolla. *Corolla* deep lilac RHA 79B, shading to pink RHS 55C at the base of the petals. *Stamens and pistil* pink with deep rose RHS 55A tips. *Foliage* dark green. *Growth* self-branching upright which will make a good bush. Prefers full sun for best colour.

'Lilac Time'
PENNISI 1967
AFS Registration No 714
Double
Tube white, short and of medium thickness. *Sepals* white with green tips, upturned. *Corolla* pale lilac, full and compact, large. *Foliage* medium green, medium to large size. *Growth* trailer, bushy, vigorous, free-flowering. Basket. Very attractive blooms.

'Lilani'
NIEDERHOLZER 1947
Double
Tube dark red, medium length and thickness. *Sepals* dark red, slightly reflexed. *Corolla* rhodamine purple, edges of the petals scalloped. Large blooms. *Foliage* medium to dark green, medium-sized leaves. *Growth* upright, vigorous, bushy, free-flowering. Bush or standard.

'Lilian Alderson'
TRAVIS 1975
AFS Registration No 1319
Single
Tube spinel red RHS 54B, medium length and thickness. *Sepals* neyron rose RHS 55B, tipped scheeles green, long and slender, recurving as the flower ages. *Corolla* ruby red RHS 61A, neyron rose RHS 55B at the base of the petals, short and compact, but flaring as the bloom matures. *Foliage* medium green, very large (up to 5 in, 12.5 cm, in length), heavily serrated and veined. *Growth* vigorous, tall upright and bushy. Bush, standard, pyramid or cordon, and can be trained to basket with weight. Colours best in shaded conditions.

'Lilla Wright'
W. HOBSON 1977
Double
Tube pink, short and thick. *Sepals* pink with green tips, broad and upturned to the tube. *Corolla* lilac-blue with pinkish markings on the outer petals, medium-sized, rather open bloom. *Foliage* medium green, small to medium-sized leaves.

Growth upright, bushy, vigorous, self-branching and free-flowering. Bush or standard.

'Lillibet'
HODGES 1954
Double
Tube white with a pink flush, long, medium thickness. *Sepals* white on top, flushed pink on the undersides, long, narrow and completely reflexed. *Corolla* rose pink, long and compact. *Foliage* medium green, medium-sized leaves, serrated. *Growth* trailer, vigorous, free-flowering. Basket.

'Lime Sherbert'
ANNS GARDENS/GAGNON 1966
AFS Registration No 660
Double
Tube greenish white, short and thick. *Sepals* white with green tips, long, narrow and completely recurving to the tube. *Corolla* white, faintly tinged pink, long, medium-sized bloom. *Foliage* medium green, medium-sized, broad, serrated leaves. *Growth* upright, vigorous, bushy. Bush.

'Linda Copley'
COPLEY 1966
AFS Registration No 691
Double
Tube pale pink, thin, medium length. *Sepals* pale pink on top, darker shade of pink on the underside, green tips. Very broad sepals held over the corolla and pointing downwards. *Corolla* pink, full and compact, medium-sized bloom. *Foliage* medium green, medium-sized, serrated leaves. *Growth* very lax upright which requires a lot of pinching and staking if it is to be made into any shape at all. Bush.

'Lindisfarne'
RYLE 1972
AFS Registration No 1168
Semi-double
Tube very pale shell pink RHS 37D, short and of medium thickness. *Sepals* pale pink, tinged with crimson at the base, crepe underside, and with green tips, short and broad. *Corolla* dark violet RHS 87A, with a deeper purple shade at the edges of the petals, flushed crimson at the base. Small to medium-sized bloom. *Foliage* medium green (RHS 137B), medium-sized leaves. *Growth* vigorous, bushy, self-branching and very free-flowering upright. A very good exhibition variety. Bush or quarter standard.

'Lindy'
ANTONELLI 1965
AFS Registration No 634
Double
Tube pale pink, medium length and thickness. *Sepals* pale pink, long and broad, upturned. *Corolla* white with pale pink veins and some pink splashes on the petals, very full and compact, medium to large blooms. *Foliage* medium green, medium-sized leaves. *Growth* trailer, bushy, free-flowering, vigorous. Basket.

'Linhope Sprite'
RYLE 1975
AFS Registration No 1249
Single
Tube rose bengal RHS 57B, long and thin. *Sepals* phlox pink RHS 62B, hanging downwards with a slight curve. *Corolla* rich violet purple RHS 77A, medium size, very compact. *Anthers* ruby red RHS 59A. *Foliage* medium green, serrated, with light red stems. *Growth* natural trailer. Basket. *Parentage* 'Coxeen' × 'Mrs Lawrence Lyon'.

'Lisa'
ANTONELLI 1965
AFS Registration No 637
Double
Tube bright rose pink, medium length and thickness. *Sepals* rose pink, long and broad, upturned. *Corolla* rich lavender, fading to orchid, very full, large blooms. *Foliage* medium green, medium to large leaves serrated. *Growth* trailer, vigorous, bushy, free-flowering. Basket.

'Little Bit'
SOO YUN 1975
AFS Registration No 1267
Double
Tube light crimson, thin, 2 in (5 cm) long. *Sepals* light crimson, some white on top and with light green tips. On the underside sepals are crimson. Sepals curve back to the tube. *Corolla* royal blue fading to light purple. Petals have a light grey edge and there is some crimson variegation at the base of the petals with crimson veining. One petaloid. *Stamens* dark pink. *Anthers* rust coloured, and pistil light pink. *Foliage* medium green, up to 3 in (7.5 cm) long, with red branches and stems. *Growth* semi-trailer which will make a basket with weights. Self-branching, vigorous and free-flowering. Basket.

'Little Catbells'
TRAVIS 1980
AFS Registration No 1582
Single
Tube white, short. *Sepals* rose, very small, reflexed. *Corolla* white, changing to rose, very small. Total length of the flower ¼ in (6 mm). *Foliage* medium to light green, ovate. *Growth* upright, vigorous, free-flowering. Berries jet black. *Parentage* Encliandra ×. Develops its best colour in the shade.

'Little Fellow'
SOO YUN 1973
AFS Registration No 1095
Single
Tube red, short and of medium thickness. *Sepals* red, narrow and curling outwards. *Corolla* red, small, compact, small blooms. *Foliage* dark green, small to medium-sized, serrated leaves. *Growth* lax bush, vigorous, self-branching, bushy and free-flowering. Bush or basket.

'Little Frosty'
FIELD 1980
AFS Registration No 1562
Double
Tube white, ½ in (13 mm) long. *Sepals* white on top, light pink underneath, long, with green tips. *Corolla* bright rose pink changing to pale orchid, with white spots at the base. Four petaloids of pale orchid with white spots, much smaller than the petals. *Stamens* deep pink. *Pistil* white, with yellow stigma. *Foliage* light green, red stems, medium to large. *Growth* lax bush, can be grown either as a basket, with weights, or as an upright. Prefers heat for best results.

'Little Jewel'
SOO YUN 1975
AFS Registration No 1268
Single
Tube shiny dark carmine, medium length and thickness. *Sepals* shiny dark carmine on top, dark flat carmine on the undersides, star-shaped, and standing out well clear of the corolla. *Corolla* light purple, variegated carmine at the base of the petals, medium-sized. *Stamens* red. *Filaments* red and white. *Pistil* red, stigma white. *Foliage* medium green, 4 in (10 cm) × 2 in (5 cm), green stems. *Growth* upright, self-branching, bushy and vigorous. Bush or standard. Prefers partial shade.

'Little Pewee'
PENNISI 1970
AFS Registration No 894
Double
Tube rose pink, small, medium thickness. *Sepals* rose pink, short, with green tips. *Corolla* deep purple shade, with rose pink variegations, box type, small blooms. *Foliage* medium green, small leaves. Too small for a basket. Half-basket.

'Little Pinkey'
SOO YUN 1979
AFS Registration No 1493
Single
Tube pink, medium length, thick. *Sepals* light pink with green tips, darker pink underneath, tips curling up. *Corolla* lilac purple fading to deep pink, with red veins, opens bell-shaped. *Stamens* red, *pistil* pink with white tip. *Foliage* light green,

serrated, 2 in (5 cm) long with light pink stems. *Growth* self-branching, small upright which will make a good bush or standard, but can be made to trail if weights are used. Very heavy bloomer.

'Little Rascal'
SOO YUN 1974
AFS Registration No 1182
Single
Tube bright red, short and thin. *Sepals* bright red, longish and narrow. *Corolla* purple, with red shade at the base of the petals, small to medium-sized bloom. *Foliage* light green and dark green dappled effect with the new growth light red. Stems and branches also red, leaves medium size. *Growth* bushy, vigorous, tending to be rather lax, very free-flowering. Bush.

'Little Ronnie'
DE COLA 1975
AFS Registration No 1310
Semi-double
Tube light rose, short and of medium thickness. *Sepals* rosy crimson, short, broad and upturned. *Corolla* dark blue, ageing to mauvish blue, remains compact and rosette-like. *Foliage* bright green, small. *Growth* upright, bushy, vigorous, self-branching and free-flowering. Requires little pinching to make a good plant. Bush or small standard.

'Liver Bird'
THORNLEY 1978
AFS Registration No 1469
Single
Tube short, soft pink RHS 39B. *Sepals* soft pink RHS 39B with green tips, paler on undersides. *Corolla* claret rose RHS 50A. *Foliage* medium green, medium size. *Growth* upright, bushy, will make a good bush but requires pinching. *Parentage* 'Chang' ×.

'Liz'
RON HOLMES
Double
Tube greenish-white, medium length and thickness. *Sepals* pale pink on top, deeper shade of pink on the undersides, green tips, broad and reflexed over the tube. *Corolla* very pale pink, with veins and splashes of darker pink, very fluffy, open bloom of medium size. *Foliage* medium green with crimson veining, medium-sized, serrated leaves. *Growth* upright, vigorous, bushy and free-flowering. Bush or summer bedder.

'Loeky' (137)
DE GRAAF (Netherlands) 1979
Single
Tube rose red, medium length and thickness. *Sepals* rose-red, short, broad and reflexed to the tube. *Corolla* rosy-lilac with reddish veining, and pale red at the base of the petals. The bloom opens almost flat. *Foliage* medium green with red centre veins and stems. Medium-sized, longish, serrated leaves. *Growth* upright, bushy, very free-flowering. Bush. 'Joy Patmore' seedling.

'Lolita'
TIRET 1963
AFS Registration No 574
Double
Tube white with faint pink tinge, thin, medium length. *Sepals* white, tinged rose pink, deeper pink on the undersides, green tips, curling upwards to the tube. *Corolla* porcelain blue, maturing to lilac blue, slightly paler at the base of the petals and lightly veined. Medium-sized blooms. *Foliage* medium green, rather large serrated leaves. *Growth* natural trailer with thin stems, very free-flowering. Half-basket.

'Lollypop'
WALKER AND JONES 1950
Single
Tube pink, medium length and thickness. *Sepals* spinel pink, long and upturned. *Corolla* bright plum purple shading to peony purple, large petals, medium to large, compact bloom. *Foliage* medium

green, medium-sized leaves. *Growth* trailer, bushy, free-flowering. Half-basket.

'Lonely Ballerina'
BLACKWELL 1962
Double
Tube deep carmine red, thin, medium length. *Sepals* deep carmine, short and broad, reflexing. *Corolla* white with carmine veining and carmine splashes on the petals. Medium-sized blooms. *Foliage* medium green with red veining, medium-sized, serrated leaves. *Growth* trailer, vigorous, self-branching and free-flowering.

'Lonesome George'
PENNISI 1970
AFS Registration No 886
Double
Tube white, medium length and thickness. *Sepals* white on top, pale pink on the undersides, green tips. *Corolla* maroon with pale salmon pink variegations, medium-sized, compact blooms. *Foliage* medium green, medium-sized, serrated leaves. *Growth* trailer, bushy, vigorous, free-flowering. Basket.

'Loraine'
MUNKNER 1952
Double
Tube deep red, medium length and thickness. *Sepals* deep red, broad and upturned. *Corolla* pink, veined rose pink, medium-sized, compact bloom. *Foliage* medium green, serrated, medium-sized leaves. *Growth* upright, vigorous, bushy, free-flowering. Bush or standard.

'Lord Byron'
LEMOINE
Single 3 in (7.5 cm)
Tube deep cerise, short and thin. *Sepals* deep scarlet-cerise, recurving slightly. *Corolla* very dark purple, with red veining, and a paler shade at the base of the petals, open saucer-shaped, small to medium-sized bloom. *Foliage* medium green, medium-sized serrated leaves. *Growth* upright, self-branching, free-flowering. Bush.

'Lord Lonsdale'
Raiser and date not known
Single
Tube pale apricot pink, thick, longish. *Sepals* apricot pink with green tips, broad and drooping over the corolla. *Corolla* orange-salmon, medium-sized blooms. *Foliage* lightish green, serrated and crinkled, medium-sized leaves. *Growth* upright, vigorous, free-flowering. Bush. Often confused with 'Aurora Superba' which is a smaller flower and less vigorous.

'Lord Roberts'
LEMOINE 1909
Single 5 in (12.5 cm)
Tube scarlet cerise, short and thick. *Sepals* scarlet cerise, held horizontal. *Corolla* dark purple with scarlet veining, and pink shading at the base of the petals. Medium to large, compact blooms. *Foliage* medium green with red veins, medium-sized, serrated leaves. *Growth* vigorous, upright, bushy, free-flowering. Bush, standard.

'Lothario'
KENNETT 1971
AFS Registration No 954
Semi-double
Tube pink, medium length and thickness. *Sepals* pink, long, narrow and upturned. *Corolla* fuchsia purple, very full, large bloom. *Foliage* medium green, medium to large leaves. *Growth* trailer, bushy, free-flowering. Basket.

'Lotty Hobby'
EDWARD 1939
Single
Tube dark scarlet red, thin, short. *Sepals* dark red, small and pointed. *Corolla* scarlet, very small blooms ('Breviflora' ×). *Foliage* medium to dark green, very small and heavily serrated. *Growth* upright, bushy, vigorous and very free, if late,

flowering. Difficult to train into shape, but will make a nice bush or quarter standard; alternatively does well as a garden hardy.

'Louise Emershaw'

TIRET 1972
AFS Registration No 1072
Double
Tube white, long, medium thickness. *Sepals* white on top with green tips, pale pink on the undersides, long, narrow and flaring outwards and upwards. *Corolla* jasper red RHS 39A, ageing to pale cerise red with tinges of pink at the base of the petals. Fairly compact, medium to large bloom. *Foliage* medium green, large serrated leaves. *Growth* natural trailer, vigorous, free-flowering. Half-basket.

'Lovable'

ERICKSON 1963
AFS Registration No 580
Double
Tube deep red, short, medium thickness. *Sepals* deep red, short and broad, arching upwards and over the top of the corolla. *Corolla* orchid pink with darker veining, very full and fluffy, medium to large bloom. *Foliage* medium green, small to medium-sized leaves. *Growth* trailer, vigorous, long-branching but not self-branching. So it requires pinching early to attain a good shape. Bush or half-basket.

'Love in Bloom'

STUBBS 1977
AFS Registration No 1412
Double
Tube flesh-coloured, medium length and thickness. *Sepals* white to pale flesh, long, broad and tapering, turning up and reflexing slightly as they mature. *Corolla* luminous magenta to brilliant coral, opening very full, some serrated petals, flaring. *Foliage* dark green, medium-sized, red stemmed new growth. *Growth* a natural trailer which will make a good basket.

'Love Knot'

WALKER/FUCHSIA LA 1979
AFS Registration No 1512
Double
Tube rose madder, medium length and thickness. *Sepals* rose madder, stiff, wide and turning up at the tips. *Corolla* cobalt violet streaked with rose madder, edges amethyst violet. Large and ruffled with the outer petals adhering to the sepals Bloom opens square-shaped. *Foliage* spinach green, new growth bright lime green. *Growth* medium upright, branches tend to arch down with the weight of the blooms. Will make a good bush, and can be trained as a basket. Develops the best colour if grown in the shade.

'Loveliness'

LYE 1869
Single
Tube waxy white, thick, medium length. *Sepals* waxy white, medium length, recurved. *Corolla* rosy cerise, compact, medium-sized, bloom. *Foliage* light to medium green, medium-sized, serrated leaves. *Growth* upright, bushy, self-branching, free-flowering. Bush or standard.

'Lovely Blue'

SOO YUN 1977
AFS Registration No 1407
Double
Tube off white, veined light roseine purple, medium length and width. *Sepals* white, brushed pale roseine purple at the base, medium size, curling towards the tube. *Corolla* large and full, roseine purple at the base darkening to violet purple at the tips of the petals. *Stamens and pistil* roseine purple. *Foliage* medium green, wide, red veined, slightly serrated. *Growth* semi-trailer, bushy. Basket or bush.

'Lovely Lady'

PASKESEN 1967
AFS Registration No 700
Double
Tube pale pink, medium length and

thickness. *Sepals* white, tinged pale pink, upturned. *Corolla* carmine rose, with the outer petals splashed pale pink, medium to large, compact blooms. *Foliage* medium green, medium to large leaves. *Growth* upright, vigorous, bushy and free-flowering. Bush or standard.

'Lucky Strike'
NIEDERHOLZER 1943
Semi-double
Tube pink, medium length and thickness. *Sepals* pink on top with green tips, darker shade on the underside, longish and completely reflexed. *Corolla* purple, splashed pink, medium-sized blooms. *Foliage* medium green, medium-sized, finely serrated leaves. *Growth* upright, bushy, vigorous, and free-flowering. Bush.

'Luella'
GAGNON 1969
AFS Registration No 842
Semi-double
Tube white, flushed pale pink, medium length and thickness. *Sepals* white, flushed pale pink on top, deeper pink on the undersides, long and pointed. *Corolla* white, four slim petals in the centre, four scalloped petals at the base and a further two white, spoon-shaped petals under each scalloped petal, giving the bloom a very lacy appearance. Medium-sized blooms. *Foliage* medium green, medium-sized leaves. *Growth* lax bush, free-flowering and very attractive. Half-basket or bush if staked early.

'Lula Bell'
HAAG AND SON 1953
Semi-double
Tube red, small and medium thick. *Sepals* red, short, pointed. *Corolla* white, small to medium-sized bloom. *Foliage* medium green, small to medium leaves. *Growth* upright, bushy, dwarf, free-flowering. Bush.

'Lullaby'
REITER 1953
AFS Registration No 191
Double
Tube white, medium length and thickness. *Sepals* white, longish, recurved. *Corolla* warm rose pink, very full, medium-sized bloom. *Foliage* medium green, medium-sized leaves. *Growth* trailer, bushy, free-flowering. Basket.

'Lunar Light'
ANTONELLI 1971
AFS Registration No 1005
Double
Tube pale salmon-pink, medium length and thickness. *Sepals* pale salmon, longish, upturned. *Corolla* light orange-red, compact, medium-sized bloom. *Foliage* medium green, medium-sized leaves. *Growth* lax upright, bushy, vigorous, free-flowering. Bush or basket.

'Luscious'
MARTIN 1960
AFS Registration No 445
Double
Tube pale cerise, long and thin. *Sepals* cerise with green tips, long, broad and upturned to the tube. *Corolla* dark wine purple with red, orange and pinkish marbling on the petals. Inner petals long with numerous petaloids. Medium-sized blooms. *Foliage* darkish green, medium-sized, serrated leaves. *Growth* very lax, best grown as a trailer, free-flowering. Half-basket.

'Lustre'
BULL 1868
Single
Tube creamy white, short and thick. *Sepals* creamy white, broad and short, reflexing. *Corolla* salmon pink, white at the base of the petals, small compact bloom. *Foliage* dull green, small to medium-sized, serrated leaves. *Growth* free-flowering, bushy, upright and self-branching. Bush.

'Lustre Improved'
CARTER PAGE 1870
Single
Tube creamy white, thick, medium

length. *Sepals* creamy white, tinged with pink and with green tips, short and narrow, held slightly above the horizontal. *Corolla* salmon-red, small to medium-sized, compact bloom. *Foliage* medium green, small, serrated leaves. *Growth* upright, bushy, free-flowering. Not an easy cultivar to grow well. Bush.

'Luther King'
PENNISI 1970
AFS Registration No 893
Double
Tube red, long and thin. *Sepals* red, box shaped, tips turning inwards. *Corolla* deep purple, very open and loose-petalled, medium to large bloom. *Foliage* medium green, medium to large leaves. *Growth* trailer, bushy, vigorous, free-flowering. Basket.

'Luv'
KENNETT 1969
AFS Registration No 866
Single
Tube pink, medium length and thickness. *Sepals* pink, long, curving. *Corolla* blue, fading to lavender blue, bell-shaped, medium-sized bloom. *Foliage* mid-green, medium-sized leaves. *Growth* trailer, bushy, free-flowering. Basket.

'Lye's Excelsior'
JAMES LYE 1887
Single
Tube waxy white, short, thick. *Sepals* waxy white, on top, pinkish tinge on the undersides, short and quite broad. *Corolla* bright scarlet-cerise, medium blooms. *Foliage* light to mid-green, medium-sized leaves. *Growth* upright, bushy, self-branching, free-flowering. A very attractive cultivar. Bush or summer bedder.

'Lye's Favourite'
JAMES LYE 1886
Single
Tube flesh pink, short, thickish. *Sepals* flesh pink, held well out from the corolla. *Corolla* orange-cerise, compact, well-formed, small to medium-sized bloom. *Foliage* light to mid-green, medium-sized serrated leaves. *Growth* upright, bushy, free-flowering. Bush. *Parentage* 'Arabella' improved × 'James Lye'.

'Lye's Unique' (47)
JAMES LYE 1886
Single
Tube waxy white, long, medium thickness. *Sepals* waxy white, narrow, held well out. *Corolla* salmon-orange, compact, medium-sized bloom. *Foliage* dull green, medium-sized leaves. *Growth* upright, vigorous, self-branching and free-flowering. One of Lye's most popular introductions. Good exhibition variety. Bush or standard.

'Lynda'
TIRET 1970
AFS Registration No 900
Double
Tube pale pink, medium length and thickness. *Sepals* pale pink, very long, narrow and upturned. *Corolla* violet purple with considerable marbling on the petals, flaring, medium to large bloom. *Foliage* medium green, medium to large-sized leaves. *Growth* trailer, bushy, vigorous, free-flowering. Basket.

'Lynn Ellen'
ERICKSON 1962
AFS Registration No 541
Double
Tube rose pink, short and thick. *Sepals* rose pink, broad and upturned to the tube. *Corolla* rose-purple maturing to bright rose, outer petals with salmon pink marbling. Medium-sized, loose-petalled bloom. *Foliage* medium size, longish serrated leaves, medium green. *Growth* upright, bushy, vigorous, free-flowering. Bush.

'Lyric'
KENNETT 1964
AFS Registration No 612
Double
Tube white, faintly tinged pink, medium

length and thickness. *Sepals* white, flushed pale pink, long, broad and upturned. *Corolla* orchid rose, fading to various shades of pink, long and thin, with numerous petaloids. Large blooms. *Foliage* medium green, medium to large-sized leaves. *Growth* trailer, vigorous, bushy, free-flowering. Basket.

'Ma Cat'
PALKO/SOO YUN 1978
AFS Registration No 1445
Double
Tube white with a pink stripe, thick, medium length. *Sepals* phlox pink on top, phlox pink to orchid pink inside, long recurved. *Corolla* cyclamen purple, fading to mallow purple at the sepals, and cup-shaped, tight 1 in (25 mm) long, stamens rhodamine pink, brown tips. *Foliage* Georgian green, $3\frac{1}{2}$ in (89 mm) long and $2\frac{3}{8}$ in 60 mm) wide, green stems. *Growth* natural trailer, heavy bloomer. Makes a very good basket.

'Macchu Picchu' (180)
DE GRAAF 1977
Single
Tube pale orange-salmon, fairly long. *Sepals* pale orange-salmon with green tips, short, pointed. *Corolla* salmon; orange, small to medium-sized bloom. *Stamens and style* light salmon-orange. *Foliage* medium green with red centre veins, medium-sized leaves. *Growth* rather lax grower, will withstand sun and warmth, free-flowering, not self-branching and needs careful pinching to grow to any recognised shape. Bush or basket. *Parentage F. speciosa seedling* ×.

'Machell'
PALKO/SOO YUN 1979
AFS Registration No 1497
Double
Tube rose bengal HCC 25. *Sepals* rose bengal HCC 25, short and thin. *Corolla* spectrum violet HCC 735/2 with magenta HCC 27 at the base of the petals. Petaloids spectrum violet. *Foliage* light green, scalloped edges, $1\frac{3}{4}$ in (45 mm) long. *Growth* upright, self-branching and bushy. Will make a good bush or standard, will trail with weights.

'Madame Chang'
HAZARD
Single
Tube orange-red, short, medium thickness. *Sepals* orange red, small, pointed. *Corolla* pink, small-sized bloom. *Foliage* medium to darkish green, small. *Growth* upright, vigorous, needs careful pinching, free-flowering. Bush or standard.

'Madame Cornelissen'
CORNELISSEN 1860
Single to semi-double
Tube crimson, short, medium thickness. *Sepals* crimson, held almost horizontal. *Corolla* white with cerise veins, fairly compact, smallish bloom. *Foliage* dark green, small, longish leaves, serrated. *Growth* upright, bushy, vigorous, self-branching, and free-flowering. Bush or garden hardy.

'Madame Danjoux'
SALTER 1843
Double
Tube carmine cerise, short, medium thickness. *Sepals* carmine cerise, long, broad, reflexing. *Foliage* medium green. *Corolla* very pale violet-purple. *Growth* upright, vigorous, bushy, free-flowering. Bush.

'Madame Lantelme'
LEMOINE 1912
Double
Tube cerise, medium length and thickness. *Sepals* cerise, long, broad and reflexing slightly. *Corolla* white, very full, slightly veined pink, large bloom. *Foliage* light green, medium-sized leaves. *Growth* upright, but tending to spread and becomes rather straggly. Needs careful and early pinching to make a good plant. Bush or quarter standard.

'Madame van der Strasse'
HAZARD
Double

Tube crimson, medium length and thickness. *Sepals* crimson, reflexing. *Corolla* white with crimson veins and flushing, open, loose-petalled small to medium-sized bloom. *Foliage* dark green with dark veining, medium-sized, finely serrated leaves. *Growth* upright, bushy, self-branching and free-flowering. Bush or summer bedder.

'Magenta Flush'
GADSBY 1970
AFS Registration No 878
Double
Tube spinel red, medium length and thickness. *Sepals* spinel red with green tips, held well back. *Corolla* magenta rose with rose-red flush to the petals, medium to large-sized bloom. *Foliage* dark green, medium-sized, serrated leaves. *Growth* upright, self-branching, vigorous, bushy and free-flowering. Bush or standard.

'Magenta Magic'
CROCKETT 1969
AFS Registration No 825
Double
Tube ivory, medium length and thickness. *Sepals* neyron-rose RHS 55B on top, camellia-rose on the undersides with green tips. *Corolla* magenta rose RHS 64C, flushed and edge camellia rose, large bloom. *Foliage* medium green, medium-sized, longish leaves. *Growth* bushy, self-branching, vigorous, willowy branches, free-flowering. Bush.

'Maggie Little'
RYLE 1975
AFS Registration No 1250
Single
Tube crimson RHS 52A with paler pink streaks, short and of medium thickness. *Sepals* crimson RHS 52A, shiny on top, short and broad, reflexed. *Corolla* imperial purple RHS 78A, ageing to dark mallow purple RHS 72B small and compact. *Anthers* rhodonite red RHS 51A. *Foliage* medium green, serrated edges. *Growth* upright, vigorous, bushy and free-flowering. Bush or standard. *Parentage* 'Ruthie' × 'Schneewitchen'.

'Magic'
GORMAN 1970
AFS Registration No 923
Double
Tube white, medium length and thickness. *Sepals* white with green tips. *Corolla* dark magenta with marbling on the petals, medium-sized blooms. *Foliage* bright green, large-sized leaves. *Growth* upright, bushy, vigorous, free-flowering. Bush or standard.

'Magic Flute'
HANDLEY 1975
AFS Registration No 1275
Single
Tube waxy white, $1\frac{1}{2}$ in (4 cm) in length, and very thick. *Sepals* white, tipped chartreuse, narrow, and held at right angles to the tube. *Corolla* clear coral-rose RHS 43C/D, white at the base, corolla is funnel-shaped and petals overpale. *Stamens and pistil* pale pink. *Foliage* bright green, medium size. *Growth* natural trailer, self-branching and vigorous. Free-flowering. Basket, or can be trained as upright.

'Magic Lantern'
HANDLEY 1976
AFS Registration No 1369
Single
Tube salmon pink, long and thin. *Sepals* salmon pink on top, orange-salmon on the undersides, held well out from the tube. *Corolla* orange at the base of the petals, to flame in the centre, darker edges. *Foliage* dark green, medium-sized. Fast-growing, free-blooming, two blooms per leaf axil. Orange flowers set off well against the dark green foliage. Bush or shrub.

'Maharaja'
CASTRO 1971
AFS Registration No 950
Double

Tube pink, medium length and thickness. *Sepals* pink with green tips on top, salmon pink on the undersides, broad and reflexed. *Corolla* dark purple with salmon pink and orange splashes, very full, medium to large-sized bloom. *Foliage* light green with red veining, medium-sized, serrated leaves. *Growth* upright, tending to be rather lax, vigorous and free-flowering. Bush or basket.

'Major Heaphy'
Raiser unknown
Single
Tube reddish orange, thin, medium length. *Sepals* reddish orange with green tips, short, narrow and held well out from the corolla. *Corolla* deep brick red, small, compact bloom. *Foliage* medium green, small to medium-sized, serrated leaves. *Growth* upright, bushy, self-branching, free-flowering. Dislikes dry conditions. Bush or quarter standard.

'Malibu'
EVANS 1953
AFS Registration No 183
Single
Tube coral-pink, medium length and thickness. *Sepals* coral-pink, longish and upturned. *Corolla* rose-madder, medium-sized, bell-shaped bloom. *Foliage* medium green, medium to large leaves. *Growth* bushy, upright, vigorous, free-flowering. Bush.

'Mandarin'
SCHNABEL 1963
AFS Registration No 582
Semi-double
Tube pale salmon pink, with stripes of a deeper shade, thick, medium length. *Sepals* salmon pink on top with green tips, deeper shade on the undersides, long, broad and reflexed slightly. *Corolla* bright orange-carmine, longish, medium-sized bloom. *Foliage* dark green, medium-sized serrated leaves. *Growth* lax upright, vigorous and free-flowering. Not an easy cultivar to train to shape. Bush.

'Mantilla'
REITER 1948
AFS Registration No 1
Single, triphylla type
Tube deep carmine, very long and slender. *Sepals* deep carmine, short and pointed. *Corolla* deep carmine, compact and small. *Foliage* bronzy green, medium sized leaves. *Growth* trailer, bushy, free flowering. Very attractive long ($3\frac{1}{2}$ in, 9 cm) blooms in clusters. Basket or half-basket.

'Maori Maid'
TIRET 1966
AFS Registration No 690
Double
Tube red, medium length and thickness. *Sepals* red, broad, slightly upturned. *Corolla* purple, very full, medium-sized bloom. *Foliage* medium to darkish green, medium-sized leaves. *Growth* trailer, bushy, free-flowering. Half-basket or basket.

'Maranda'
FAIRCLO
Semi-double
Tube crimson, medium length and thickness. *Sepals* crimson, longish, broad and upturning. *Corolla* rosy purple, medium-sized, loose-petalled bloom. *Foliage* medium green, medium-sized leaves. *Growth* trailer, bushy, vigorous, free-flowering. Half-basket.

'Mardi Gras'
REEDSTROM 1958
AFS Registration No 358
Double
Tube red, medium length and thickness. *Sepals* red, long and broad, reflexed. *Corolla* very dark purple, with pink mottling on the petals, large blooms. *Foliage* medium green, medium to large leaves, serrated. *Growth* upright, vigorous, free-flowering and bushy. Bush or basket with weights.

'Margaret' (157)
W.P. WOOD 1939
Double

Tube carmine red, medium length, and thickness. *Sepals* carmine red, completely reflexing over the tube. *Corolla* violet-purple, veined cerise, pink at the base of the petals, very full, small double bloom. *Foliage* medium green, small to medium-sized slightly serrated leaves. *Growth* upright, very vigorous, self-branching, bushy and free-flowering. Not one which is happy in a pot, but excellent as a garden hardy where, within two years, it will make a huge bush. Bush or garden hardy. *Parentage F. magellanica* var. *molinae* × 'Heritage'.

'Margaret B. Herron'
FAIRCLO 1947
Double
Tube crimson, medium length and thickness. *Sepals* crimson, longish, recurving. *Corolla* purple, full but with a very ragged appearance. Spreading, medium-sized blooms. *Foliage* medium green, medium-sized leaves. *Growth* trailer, bushy, very free-flowering. Half-basket.

'Margaret Brown' (80)
W.P. WOOD 1949
Single
Tube rose pink, short, medium thickness. *Sepals* rose pink, short, held slightly below the horizontal. *Corolla* pale rose pink with deeper veining, small bloom. *Foliage* light green, small, serrated leaves. *Growth* upright, bushy, self-branching, free-flowering. Bush or summer bedder.

'Margaret Roe' (176)
GADSBY 1968
Registered 1971
AFS Registration No 975
Single
Tube pale rose pink, short and thick. *Sepals* rose red with green tips, broad, horizontal. *Corolla* pale violet-purple veined pink, paler at the base of the petals, small to medium-sized blooms. *Foliage* medium green, medium-sized serrated leaves. *Growth* upright, bushy self-branching and very free-flowering. Blooms are held out from the foliage and upright. Although an excellent exhibition variety, blooms become very pale when grown in shaded conditions, richer colouring coming from plants grown outdoors. Bush, standard or summer bedder.

'Margaret Rose'
N.D. HOBBS 1976
AFS Registration No 1380
Single
Tube neyron rose, short and thick. *Sepals* neyron rose with green tips, opening horizontal. *Corolla* neyron rose with picotee edge to the petals of spinel red. *Foliage* medium green, medium to large leaves. *Growth* upright, vigorous, bushy and free flowering. Bush or standard. Named after HRH the Princess Margaret.

'Margaret Susan'
R. HOLMES 1974
AFS Registration No 1205
Single
Tube pale red, medium length and thickness. *Sepals* carmine RHS 52A on the top, RHS 52B on the underside, green tips, long, quite narrow, reflexing at right angles to the tube and corolla. *Corolla* fuchsia purple RHS 67B, carmine rose at the base of the petals, edges and veined cardinal red RHS 53C, very compact, medium-sized bloom. *Foliage* mid-green with red stems, medium to large-sized, serrated leaves. *Growth* upright, bushy, self-branching, free-flowering. Bush. *Parentage* 'Hugh Morgan' × 'Melody'.

'Margaret Swales'
SWALES 1974
AFS Registration No 1177
Semi-double
Tube ivory white, pink at the base, short and thick. *Sepals* ivory RHS 157D with green tips, longish, broad and waxy. *Corolla* carmine rose shading to white at the base of the petals. Large petaloids striped carmine rose to white, medium-sized bloom. *Foliage* dark green, medium-

sized leaves. *Growth* natural trailer, free-flowering. Half-basket. Sport of 'La Fiesta'.

'Margaret Thatcher'
GADSBY 1978
AFS Registration No 1482
Single
Tube pale pink, short and medium thickness. *Sepals* white with greenish flush, recurving to the tube. *Corolla* bluebird blue passing to spectrum violet, few petaloids. *Foliage* medium green. *Growth* vigorous, self-branching, bushy upright. Blooms early. Bush plant. *Parentage* 'Christine Clements' × 'Forward Look'.

'Margery Blake'
W.P. WOOD 1950
Single
Tube scarlet, thin, short. *Sepals* scarlet, short and broad, not reflexed. *Corolla* reddish-purple, very compact, small bloom. *Foliage* medium green, small, serrated leaves. *Growth* upright, bushy, self-branching and very free-flowering. Bush or garden hardy.

'Margharita'
MILLER 1970
Double
Tube soft pink, medium length and thickness. *Sepals* soft pink. *Corolla* white, compact, medium-sized bloom. *Foliage* upright, bushy, vigorous and very free-flowering. Does best as a second year plant. Bush.

'Margie'
REIMERS 1953
AFS Registration No 170
Double
Tube white with pink flush, medium length and thickness. *Sepals* pinkish, medium length, upturned. *Corolla* lavender-orchid, very attractive bloom with ruffled petals, which have serrated edges. *Foliage* medium green, medium-sized, serrated leaves. *Growth* upright, bushy, long-branching, free flowering. Bush.

'Marginata'
NIEDERHOLZER 1946
Single
Tube vermilion, medium length and thickness. *Sepals* vermilion, long and broad. *Corolla* rose bengal, edged with a darker shade. Large blooms. *Foliage* medium green, medium to large leaves. *Growth* trailer, bushy, vigorous, free-flowering. Half-basket.

'Marilyn'
MARTIN 1961
AFS Registration No 463
Double
Tube pink, long, medium thickness. *Sepals* pink, long and broad, curling. *Corolla* white, medium-sized, very compact bloom with several petaloids. *Foliage* medium green, medium-sized leaves. *Growth* lax bush, vigorous, bushy, free-flowering. Bush or half-basket.

'Marin Belle'
REEDSTROM 1959
AFS Registration No 388
Single
Tube salmon pink, medium length and thickness. *Sepals* salmon pink, long and reflexing over the tube. *Corolla* bright pansy violet with pink veins, medium-sized, bell-shaped bloom. *Foliage* medium green, medium-sized, slightly serrated leaves *Growth* upright, bushy, self-branching, free-flowering and very vigorous. A very pretty variety. Bush.

'Marin Glow' (61)
REEDSTROM 1954
AFS Registration No 204
Single
Tube white, short, medium thickness. *Sepals* white with green tips, short, broad and slightly upturned. *Corolla* bright imperial purple, pink tinge at the base of the petals, maturing to magenta violet. Compact, medium-sized bloom. *Foliage* medium green, small to medium-sized, serrated leaves. *Growth* upright, bushy, vigorous, self-branching, very

free-flowering. A superb exhibition variety of outstanding colouring. Bush.

'Marinka' (116)
ROZAIN-BOUCHARLAT 1902
Single
Tube red, long, medium thickness. *Sepals* red, short and broad, held over and around the corolla to start, then opening to just below horizontal. *Corolla* dark red, medium-sized, compact bloom. *Foliage* medium to darkish green, medium-sized leaves with reddish veining. *Growth* excellent basket plant, bushy, vigorous, very free-flowering and one of the easiest to grow. Excellent exhibition variety for basket use, although the foliage does mark badly if exposed to sudden draughts or cold temperatures. Basket.

'Marionette'
REITER 1946
Double
Tube white with pink flush, medium length and thickness. *Sepals* white flushed pink on top, deeper pink on the undersides. *Corolla* white, compact, medium-sized bloom. *Foliage* mid-green, medium-sized, serrated leaves. *Growth* upright, bushy, vigorous, free-flowering. Bush.

'Marion Young'
YOUNG 1980
AFS Registration No 1572
Double
Tube red RHS 61B, short and of medium thickness. *Sepals* red RHS 61B, broad, reflexing up to cover the tube and ovary. *Corolla* pink RHS 74D, shaded lilac RHS 75A, medium to large. Petaloids are the same size and colour as the petals. *Foliage* yellow green RHS 144A, medium size. *Growth* upright, vigorous and bushy. Will make a good bush or standard. Sport of 'La France'.

'Marjory'
HAZARD
Single
Tube pale pink, medium length and thickness. *Sepals* pink, longish and broad, upturned. *Corolla* bluish-purple, loose-petalled, medium-sized bloom. *Foliage* medium green, medium-sized leaves. *Growth* trailer, bushy, free-flowering. Bush.

'Mars'
HANDLEY 1977
AFS Registration No 1414
Semi-double
Tube rose pink, short and thick. *Sepals* pink (RHS 49A) on top, rose (RHS 52B) on the underside. *Corolla* cardinal red (RHS 53C) with the edges and base of petals lighter red (RHS 50A). *Foliage* mid-green, narrow. *Growth* natural trailer, self-branching, bushy and early flowering. Basket.

'Martina'
HANDLEY 1971
AFS Registration No 987
Single
Tube white, slightly flushed pink, short, medium thickness. *Sepals* white on top, flushed pink on the undersides. *Corolla* lilac (RHS 72D), white at the base of the petals, medium-sized blooms. *Foliage* medium green, medium-sized leaves. *Growth* upright, vigorous, bushy, free-flowering. Bush.

'Martin's Magic'
MARTIN 1962
AFS Registration No 518
Double
Tube pink, medium length and thickness. *Sepals* reddish pink, medium length, broad, upturned. *Corolla* bright magenta red, compact, medium-sized bloom. *Foliage* medium to darkish green, medium-sized, serrated leaves. *Growth* lax bush, vigorous, bushy, self-branching and free-flowering. Bush.

'Martin Smedley'
GADSBY 1968
Registered 1971
AFS Registration No 974
Single
Tube pale neyron rose, short, medium

thickness. *Sepals* neyron rose with green tips, short and broad, upturned. *Corolla* wisteria blue, white at the base of the petals and in the centre, nice bell-shaped, medium-sized bloom. *Foliage* medium green, medium to large, finely serrated leaves. *Growth* upright, bushy, vigorous and free flowering. Bush.

'Martin's Midnight'
MARTIN 1959
AFS Registration No 370
Double
Tube bright red, medium length and thickness. *Sepals* bright red, broad, slightly upturned. *Corolla* deep blue, medium-sized, compact blooms. *Foliage* medium green, medium-sized, serrated leaves. *Growth* upright, bushy, self-branching and free-flowering. Bush.

'Marty'
TIRET 1962
AFS Registration No 527
Double
Tube pink, medium length and thickness. *Sepals* pink, broad, upturned. *Corolla* orchid-pink, compact, medium-sized bloom. *Foliage* medium green, medium-sized, serrated leaves. *Growth* lax bush, vigorous, free-flowering. Half-basket or bush.

'Mary' (14)
BONSTEDT 1894
Single
Triphylla type
Tube brilliant scarlet red, long, slender. *Sepals* brilliant scarlet, short. *Corolla* brilliant scarlet, short petalled. Long blooms. *Foliage* dark green with reddish-purple veins and purple shading on the undersides. Medium-sized, narrow leaves. *Growth* upright, free-flowering. Needs careful watering. Bush. *Parentage F. triphylla × F. corymbiflora.*

'Mary Clare'
SCHULTE 1951
AFS Registration No 93
Semi-double
Tube creamy white, short, medium thickness. *Sepals* white at the base, creamy pink to the tips, reflexed. *Corolla* shading from pink to rosy-claret, white at the base of the petals, medium-sized bloom. *Foliage* medium green, medium-sized leaves. *Growth* upright, fairly vigorous, free-flowering. Bush. Sport of 'Blue Moon'.

'Mary di Barnardo'
PENNISI 1969
AFS Registration No 816
Double
Tube white, short and of medium thickness. *Sepals* white, broad. *Corolla* pale pink with variegated edges, and a blue spot on the tips of the petals, large, compact blooms. *Foliage* dark green, medium to large leaves. *Growth* upright, bushy, free-flowering. Bush.

'Mary Ellen'
ANTONELLI 1971
AFS Registration No 1006
Double
Tube pale pink, medium length and thickness. *Sepals* pale pink, longish and broad. *Corolla* lavender blue on opening, fading as the bloom ages. Medium-sized, fairly compact bloom. *Foliage* mid-green, medium-sized leaves. *Growth* trailer, bushy, free-flowering. Basket.

'Mary Kipling'
ATKINSON 1980
AFS Registration No 1548
Single
Tube white, suffused neyron rose, medium length and thickness. *Sepals* white, suffused neyron rose on top, creped neyron rose on the underside, short. Green tipped. *Corolla* methyl violet with prominent rose veins which turn to rose on maturity. Bell-shaped. *Foliage* dark green, with red veins, small. *Growth* vigorous, self-branching upright. Free-flowering and bushy. Will make a good bush or standard.

'Mary Lockyer'
COLVILLE 1967
Double

Tube carmine red, medium length and thickness. *Sepals* carmine with green tips, broad and curling up over the tube. *Corolla* pale lilac with carmine and pink marbling on the outer smaller petals, very open, loose-petalled, medium to large bloom. *Foliage* medium green, medium to large, finely serrated leaves. *Growth* vigorous, upright, bushy, and free-flowering. Bush or summer bedder.

'Mary Miloni'
PENNISI 1969
AFS Registration No 813
Double
Tube white with pale pink flush, medium length and thickness. *Sepals* white on top with pinkish stripes, pink on the undersides. *Corolla* deep purple, marbled pink. Medium-sized, compact bloom. *Foliage* medium green, small leaves. *Growth* upright, bushy, free-flowering. Bush.

'Mary Pennisi'
PENNISI 1971
AFS Registration No 1014
Double
Tube white, short, thick. *Sepals* white, medium length, green tips. *Corolla* purple, shaded light rose pink at the base of the petals, medium-sized blooms. *Foliage* medium green, small, broad leaves. *Growth* trailer, bushy, vigorous, free-flowering. Basket.

'Mary Poppins' (183)
NEED 1967
Double
Tube pale apricot. Medium length and thickness. *Sepals* pale apricot with pinkish tips. *Corolla* orange vermilion, medium size, compact. *Foliage* mid-green, medium-sized, serrated leaves. *Growth* upright, bushy, free-flowering. Bush.

'Mary Thorne'
THORNE 1953
Single
Tube scarlet, short and thick. *Sepals* scarlet, longish, slightly upturned. *Corolla* reddish violet, shaded scarlet at the base of the petals, small to medium-sized bloom, fairly compact. *Foliage* dark green, medium-sized, broad, serrated leaves. *Growth* upright, bushy, self-branching and free-flowering. Bush or garden hardy.

'Mary Wright'
J.A. WRIGHT 1980
AFS Registration No 1603
Double
Tube bright pink, medium length and width. *Sepals* bright pink, arching back. *Corolla* bright pink, large. *Foliage* medium green, large. *Growth* vigorous and bushy upright. Standard or bush. 'Lace Petticoats' seedling.

'Masquerade'
KENNETT 1963
AFS Registration No 590
Double
Tube greenish-white, medium length, quite thick. *Sepals* pale flesh pink on top, deeper shade of pink on the underside, long, broad and upturned around the tube. Green tips. *Corolla* dark purple with pink marbling, and maturing to deep red-purple, very open, loose-petalled, medium-sized bloom. *Foliage* darkish green, medium-sized leaves. *Growth* trailer, vigorous, free-flowering. Basket.

'Maureen Munro'
GEORGE ROE 1980
Single
Tube neyron rose, short and of medium thickness. *Sepals* neyron rose (RHS 55B) short, held out horizontally. *Corolla* amethyst-violet (RHS 81C), small, compact bloom. *Foliage* medium green, small leaves. *Growth* upright, bushy, self-branching, very free-flowering and vigorous. Very good exhibition variety. Bush, quarter standard or summer bedder. *Parentage* 'Alison Ewart' × 'Carol Peet'.

'Mauve Beauty'
BANKS 1869
Double
Tube cerise, short, medium thickness.

sepals cerise, curling and reflexing towards the tube. *Corolla* mauvish-lilac, ageing to pale purple, with cerise veins, medium-sized, loose-petalled bloom. *Foliage* medium green, new growth reddish near the petiole, small to medium-sized, broad, serrated leaves. *Growth* upright, bushy, self-branching and free-flowering. Bush or summer bedder.

'Maxine Elizabeth'
TIRET 1950
AFS Registration No 65
Single
Tube waxy pink, thick, short. *Sepals* white with a pink flush on top, salmon-pink on the undersides, long and broad. *Corolla* rose-red with the edges of the petals flushed orange. Medium-sized bloom. *Foliage* medium green, medium-sized leaves. *Growth* upright, vigorous, bushy, free-flowering. Bush.

'May-Dalene'
GAGNON 1964
AFS Registration No 603
Tube bright red, crepe effect, medium length and thickness. *Sepals* bright red, crepe, longish, upturned. *Corolla* bright pink with rose-pink veining, large blooms. *Foliage* medium green, medium to large-sized leaves, serrated. *Growth* vigorous, bushy, upright, free-flowering. Bush or standard.

'May Prentice'
PRENTICE 1966
AFS Registration No 667
Double
Tube pink, longish, medium thickness. *Sepals* pink, long, broad and upturned. *Corolla* white, shaded pink at the base of the petals, and with pink veins. Medium to large blooms. *Foliage* medium green, medium-sized, serrated leaves. *Growth* upright, vigorous, bushy, free-flowering. Easy to grow. Bush.

'May Queen'
MARTIN 1962
AFS Registration No 519
Double
Tube white with slight pink flush, medium length and thickness. *Sepals* white, flushed pink, upturned. *Corolla* pale blue in the centre, outer petals edged pink, medium-sized compact bloom. *Foliage* dark green, medium-sized leaves. *Growth* lax bush, free-flowering. Needs staking if grown as an upright. Bush or half-basket.

'Maytime'
TIRET 1965
AFS Registration No 649
Double
Tube pink, medium length and thickness. *Sepals* rosy-pink, medium length, broad, reflexed. *Corolla* lilac, full and compact, medium-sized bloom. *Foliage* medium green, medium-sized leaves. *Growth* trailer, bushy, free-flowering. Basket.

'Mazda'
REITER 1947
Single
Tube orangy pink, short and very thick. *Sepals* orange-pink, medium length, narrow and reflexed. *Corolla* carmine-orange, slightly paler at the base of the petals, longish, bell-shaped bloom. *Foliage* medium to darkish green, medium-sized, serrated leaves. *Growth* upright, vigorous, bushy, free-flowering. Bush or standard.

'Meadowlark'
KENNETT 1971
AFS Registration No 956
Semi-double
Tube white, long, thin. *Sepals* white with green tips, broad, overhanging the corolla. *Corolla* bright purple and rose pink with white streaks. Centre petals longish and surrounded by shorter frilled petals, medium-sized bloom. *Foliage* medium green, medium to large, finely serrated leaves. *Growth* natural trailer, free-flowering. Basket.

'Meditation'
BLACKWELL
Double

Tube bright scarlet, short, medium thickness. *Sepals* scarlet, small, broad and upturned slightly. *Corolla* creamy white with carmine veining, small, fluffy, bloom. *Foliage* medium green, small, broad, serrated leaves. *Growth* upright, bushy, free-flowering. Bush or summer bedder.

'Medusa'
DE GRAAF 1976
Semi-double
Tube red, longish, medium thickness. *Sepals* red, long curling. *Corolla* white with rose-pink veining on the petals, very large blooms with red and white petaloids standing out from the corolla. *Foliage* medium green, medium to large leaves. *Growth* trailer or hanger, very vigorous, free-flowering. Basket or standard. *Parentage* 'Centrepiece' ×.

'Mei Ling'
NIEDERHOLZER 1947
Semi-double
Tube pink, medium length and thickness. *Sepals* pale pink, medium length, reflexing. *Corolla* very pale purple, medium-sized, loose-petalled blooms. *Foliage* mid-green, medium-sized leaves. *Growth* trailer, bushy, vigorous, fairly free-flowering. Half-basket.

'Mel Newfield'
SCHNABEL 1952
AFS Registration No 109
Double
Tube red, short and thin. *Sepals* turkey red, long, narrow and reflexed. *Corolla* amethyst violet RHS 81C, marbled carmine red, and maturing to cyclamen purple RHS 74A, medium-sized blooms. *Foliage* medium to darkish green, medium-sized leaves. *Growth* upright, vigorous, bushy, very free-flowering. Bush or standard.

'Melody'
REITER SNR 1942
Single
Tube pale rose pink, long and thin. *Sepals* pale rose pink, long, narrow and reflexed. *Corolla* pale cyclamen purple, very compact medium-sized bloom. *Foliage* bright green, medium-sized, serrated leaves. *Growth* upright, bushy, easy to shape, very free-flowering. A very nice variety in pleasant pastel shades. Bush, standard or summer bedder.

'Melody Ann'
GAGNON 1966
AFS Registration No 657
Double
Tube white, short and thick. *Sepals* pale pink with green tips on top, darker shade of pink on the undersides, long and broad, curling slightly. *Foliage* dark green with crimson veins, medium to large, serrated leaves. *Growth* upright, lax, free-flowering. Bush (if staked) or basket.

'Mel Riha'
SOO YUN 1975
AFS Registration No 1269
Semi-double
Tube light pink, thin and of medium length. *Sepals* pink on top with darker pink veins. Dark pink on the underside. Green tips. Sepals extend outwards and downwards, twisting on maturity. *Corolla* blue, variegated pink at the base of the petals, flaring out as the flower matures, and the blue fading to lavender. Six petaloids. *Foliage* dark green, $4 \times 2\frac{1}{2}$ in (10×6 cm) with red stems and branches. *Growth* semi-trailer, free-flowering. Basket.

'Mendocini Mini'
FRANCESCA 1975
AFS Registration No 1290
Single
Tube white, thin and short. *Sepals* white on the back, pink on the front, very small. *Corolla* light purple turning to dark pink, very small. *Stamens* deep red, pistil white. *Foliage* medium green, very small and serrated. *Growth* natural trailer, self-branching and free-flowering. Basket (miniature), or small upright if trained.

'Mephisto' (113)
REITER 1941
Single
Tube scarlet, thin, medium length. *Sepals* scarlet, small, upturned. *Corolla* crimson red, very compact small blooms. *Foliage* medium green, medium-sized serrated leaves. *Growth* extremely vigorous, upright and bushy. Very free-flowering, flowers in clusters. Bush outdoors.

'Mercurius'
DE GROOT 1971
Single
Tube red, short, medium thickness. *Sepals* red, long, broad and upturned. *Corolla* purple, fading to reddish-purple, medium-sized blooms. *Stamens and style* red. *Foliage* medium green with red centre veins and a metallic sheen to the medium-sized leaves. *Growth* upright with somewhat horizontal growing branches, vigorous, bushy and fairly free-flowering. Bush. *Parentage F. regia typica* × 'Beacon'.

'Merle Hodges'
HODGES 1950
AFS Registration No 70
Double
Tube rose-pink, medium length and thickness. *Sepals* rosy-red, long and broad, upturned. *Corolla* a very delicate shade of powder blue, with light fuchsia pink veining. A most attractive, medium-sized bloom. *Foliage* medium green, medium-sized leaves. *Growth* bushy, tending to be rather lax, free-flowering. Bush or basket.

'Merry England'
GADSBY 1968
Registered 1971
AFS Registration No 980
Double
Tube rose pink, thin, medium length. *Sepals* white on top, pinkish flush on the undersides, broad and reflexed over the tube. *Corolla* violet purple, splashes of rose-pink at the base of the petals. Very compact, medium-sized bloom. *Foliage* medium green, large, finely serrated leaves. *Growth* upright, vigorous, bushy and free-flowering. Bush.

'Merry-Go-Round'
MUNKNER 1952
Double
Tube red, longish, medium thickness. *Sepals* red, long and reflexed. *Corolla* deep petunia purple, outer petals splashed and overlaid with shades of salmon, medium to large blooms. *Foliage* medium green, medium-sized, serrated leaves. *Growth* bushy, rather lax, free-flowering. Needs support if grown as a bush. Bush or basket.

'Merry Mary'
FUCHSIA FOREST 1965
AFS Registration No 624
Double
Tube pink, long and thin. *Sepals* pink on top, deeper pink on the undersides, long, broad and upturned. *Corolla* white with pink veins and splashed pink on the outer petals, fairly compact, medium-sized bloom. *Foliage* medium green, medium-sized, longish leaves. *Growth* natural trailer, vigorous, self-branching and bushy. Very free-flowering. Basket.

'Merry Widow'
MUNKNER 1952
Double
Tube bright red, medium length and thickness. *Sepals* bright red, broad, upturned. *Corolla* pink and white with rose-pink veining from the base. Medium-sized, compact blooms. *Foliage* medium green, medium-sized leaves. *Growth* trailer, bushy, vigorous, free-flowering. Basket.

'Merseyside'
PENNISI 1970
AFS Registration No 906
Semi-double
Tube tangerine, long, medium thickness. *Sepals* tangerine, long, narrow. *Corolla* tangering with rose-pink variegations. Medium-sized bloom. *Foliage* medium green, medium-sized, loose-petalled

blooms. *Growth* trailer, bushy, fairly free-flowering. Basket.

'Mexicali Rose'
FUCHSIA FOREST/CASTRO 1962
AFS Registration No 515
Double
Tube dark red, medium length and thickness. *Sepals* dark red, long and broad, upturned. *Corolla* deep magenta with orange-red marbling on the petals. Very full, large blooms. *Foliage* light yellow-green, medium-sized leaves. *Growth* upright, vigorous, bushy, free-flowering. A very attractive contrast between flower and foliage. Bush.

'Mia van der Zee'
DE GRAAF 1978
Single
Tube rose-red, medium length and thickness. *Sepals* rose-red, medium length, broad, slightly upturned. *Corolla* reddish-purple, paler at the base of the petals, medium-sized blooms. *Foliage* medium green, small to medium-sized leaves. *Growth* lax bush, vigorous, self-branching, very free-flowering. Bush or half-basket. *Parentage* 'La Campanella' ×.

'Michelle'
HANDLEY 1972
AFS Registration No 1055
Single
Tube dark pink, short, medium thickness. *Sepals* blush-pink, RHS 56C, reflexing completely over the tube. *Corolla* clear blush-pink RHS 56C, medium to large blooms. *Foliage* dark green, medium-sized, serrated leaves. *Growth* upright, bushy, very free-flowering. Bush.

'Micky Goult'
GEORGE ROE 1981
Single
Tube lightly flushed pink, short, medium thickness. *Sepals* pinkish, turning to deeper pink shade, held horizontal. *Foliage* medium green, small to medium-sized leaves. *Corolla* mallow purple RHS 73D, small, compact blooms. *Growth* upright, vigorous, self-branching and very free-flowering. It will make a good exhibition plant, and is also eminently suitable as a summer bedder. Bush. *Parentage* 'Bobby Shaftoe' × 'Santa Barbara'.

'Midge'
J.W. FARRINGTON/WALTZ 1961
AFS Registration No 490
Double
Tube pink, short, thin. *Sepals* pink on top, deeper pink on the undersides, short, broad and recurving. *Corolla* clear silver-blue, very small and compact blooms. *Foliage* dark green, small leaves. *Growth* dwarf, bushy, self-branching; a beautiful little plant. Bush.

'Midnight Cowboy'
FOSTER 1973
AFS Registration No 1092
Single
Tube dark red, short, medium thickness. *Sepals* dark red, short and broad, flaring at right angles to the corolla. *Corolla* deep rich purple, small and compact, flaring slightly on maturity. *Foliage* light to medium green, red stems, small to medium-sized serrated leaves. *Growth* upright, bushy, free-flowering. Bush or standard.

'Midnight Sun'
WALTZ 1960
AFS Registration No 440
Double
Tube pink, long and thin. *Sepals* pink on top, carmine red on the undersides, short, broad and reflexing slightly. *Corolla* very dark burgundy purple, outer petals splashed red and pink, very full, medium to large blooms. *Foliage* medium green, medium to large, finely serrated leaves. *Growth* upright, bushy, very vigorous, self-branching and free-flowering. Bush or standard.

'Mieke Meursing' (139)
HOPGOOD 1969
Single

Tube carmine red, short, medium thickness. *Sepals* carmine red, longish, narrow and reflexing. *Corolla* rose-pink with deeper veining, compact when first open, then becoming rather loose. Small to medium-sized bloom. *Foliage* medium green, small to medium-sized, serrated leaves. *Growth* upright, bushy, vigorous, self-branching, and very free-flowering. Excellent exhibition plant, but has the tendency to show extra petals and sepals. Leaves mark badly when grown in the cold or in a draughty spot. Bush or standard.

'Milky Way'
PASKESEN 1967
AFS Registration No 702
Double
Tube white with pale pink flush, medium length and thickness. *Sepals* pale pink. *Corolla* white, very full and compact, medium-sized bloom. *Foliage* mid-green, medium-sized leaves. *Growth* trailer, bushy, very free-flowering, prefers to be grown in the shade to preserve its white colour. Basket.

'Mindrum Gold'
RYLE 1975
AFS Registration No 1251
Double
Tube rose bengal RHS 58C, medium length and thickness. *Sepals* rose red RHS 56B on top, neyron rose 58C on the undersides, curving slightly upwards. *Corolla* violet RHS 82B, fading to violet purple RHS 77B, small. *Foliage* the young leaves are absinthe yellow RHS 145B, fading to RHS 146B. *Growth* dwarf, bushy, self-branching, upright. Bush—good for small pot culture.

'Ming'
JENNINGS 1968
Single
Tube short and thick, orange-red. *Sepals* orange-red on top, darker on the undersides, green tips. Short, broad and reflexing slightly. *Corolla* cherry red, small, compact blooms. *Foliage* light to medium green, small, broad, serrated leaves. *Growth* upright, bushy, vigorous, free-flowering. Bush or summer bedder.

'Mini'
CASTRO 1969
AFS Registration No 840
Tube white, small, thin. *Sepals* white, flushed pink, and with green tips. *Corolla* pinkish lavender to magenta rose, very small blooms. *Foliage* medium green, small leaves. *Growth* upright, bushy, free-flowering. Bush.

'Mirage'
G. MARTIN 1966
AFS Registration No 675
Double
Tube white, thick, medium length. *Sepals* white, broad, reflexing. *Corolla* opening medium blue and fading to a pale orchid shade, large fluffy blooms. *Foliage* lightish green, medium-sized, serrated leaves. *Growth* trailer, bushy, fairly free-flowering. Basket.

'Miramar'
NEIDERHOLZER 1946
Single
Tube ivory white, medium length and thickness. *Sepals* neyron rose, longish, upturned. *Corolla* solferino purple, open and loose-petalled, medium-sized bloom. *Foliage* medium green, medium-sized leaves. *Growth* upright, bushy, vigorous, free-flowering. Bush.

'Mirandy'
FAIRCLO 1947
Semi-double
Tube pink, medium length and thickness. *Sepals* dark pink, long, narrow and recurved. *Corolla* water melon pink, medium-sized, loose-petalled blooms. *Foliage* medium green, large, serrated leaves. *Growth* trailer, bushy, vigorous, fairly free-flowering. Basket.

'Miss America'
HAAG
Double

Tube red, medium length and thickness. *Sepals* red, long and broad. *Corolla* pure white, opening very wide, loose-petalled, large blooms. *Foliage* medium green, medium to large leaves. *Growth* upright, vigorous, bushy, free-flowering. Bush.

'Miss California' (83)
HODGES 1952
AFS Registration No 71
Semi-double
Tube pink, long, medium thickness. *Sepals* pink on top, darker shade of pink on the undersides, long and narrow, fully reflexing. *Corolla* white with pink veins, very compact, medium-sized bloom. *Foliage* medium green, medium-sized, narrow, serrated leaves. *Growth* upright, bushy, self-branching and very free-flowering. A very attractive, easy to grow cultivar. Bush or standard.

'Miss Great Britain'
GADSBY 1968
Registered 1971
AFS Registration No 981
Single
Tube dark pink to rose red, medium length and thickness. *Sepals* creamy white with green tips, long and twisting. *Corolla* wisteria blue fading to imperial purple, medium to large blooms. *Foliage* medium green, medium to large leaves. *Growth* upright, vigorous, bushy, self-branching, free-flowering, but tends to be rather late. Bush.

'Miss Harney County'
GAGNON 1967
AFS Registration No 706
Tube red, medium length and thickness. *Sepals* red, long, broad, upturned. *Corolla* medium shade of dark blue, paler at the base of the petals, medium-sized blooms. *Foliage* medium to darkish green, medium-sized, serrated leaves. *Growth* trailer, bushy, vigorous, fairly free-flowering. Basket.

'Mission Bells'
WALKER AND JONES 1948
Single
Tube scarlet, short, medium thickness. *Sepals* scarlet, medium length, broad and reflexing. *Corolla* vivid purple, splashed cerise at the base of the petals, medium-sized, bell-shaped blooms. *Foliage* medium green, medium-sized, serrated leaves. *Growth* bushy, upright, vigorous, self-branching and free-flowering. A beautiful cultivar when well grown. Bush or standard. Good summer bedder.

'Miss Leucadia'
STUBBS 1971
AFS Registration No 999
Double
Tube pale pink, medium length and thickness. *Sepals* pink, green tips, recurving slightly. *Corolla* pale pink with picoteed edges, medium-sized bloom with flaring petals. *Foliage* mid-green, medium-sized leaves. *Growth* natural trailer, bushy, free-flowering, almost a self pink. Basket.

'Miss Louise'
TIRET 1964
AFS Registration No 594
Double
Tube pink, medium length and thickness. *Sepals* pink, long, broad and reflexed. *Corolla* clear pink, very full and fluffy, medium-sized bloom. *Foliage* medium green. *Growth* trailer, bushy, vigorous and free-flowering. Basket.

'Miss New York'
STREET 1961
AFS Registration No 457
Double
Tube bright red, medium length and thickness. *Sepals* bright red, longish, upturned slightly. *Corolla* pink, very full, medium to large bloom. *Foliage* medium to dark green, medium-sized leaves. *Growth* upright, bushy, very free-flowering. Bush or standard. Sport of 'Swingtime'.

'Miss Norwalk'
GORMAN 1970
AFS Registration No 922
Double

Tube coral pink, medium length and thickness. *Sepals* coral pink, broad, reflexed slightly. *Corolla* dark purple, paler at the base of the petals, fading to dark rose-pink. Medium-sized blooms. *Foliage* medium green, medium-sized, serrated leaves. *Growth* trailer, bushy, free-flowering. Basket.

'Miss Vallejo'
TIRET 1958
Double
Tube pale pink, medium length and thickness. *Sepals* pale pink with green tips, longish and broad. *Corolla* deep pink with wide streaks of rose pink on the petals, medium-sized, compact bloom. *Foliage* medium green, medium-sized leaves. *Growth* upright, bushy, vigorous and free-flowering. A very beautiful cultivar. Bush (requires support).

'Miss Washington'
MOUNCER 1961
AFS Registration No 458
Double
Tube light red, medium length and thickness. *Sepals* light red, broad and upturned. *Corolla* white, with light red veining, medium to large blooms. *Foliage* medium green, medium to large, serrated leaves. *Growth* trailer, bushy, vigorous, free-flowering. Basket. Sport of 'Fort Bragg'.

'Missy Wiltshire'
PENNISI 1971
AFS Registration No 1011
Double
Tube dark pink, short, medium thickness. *Sepals* dark pink, long, broad, upturned. *Corolla* lilac, compact, medium to large blooms. *Foliage* mid-green, medium-sized leaves. *Growth* natural trailer, bushy, free-flowering. Basket.

'Mitford Queen'
RYLE 1977
AFS Registration No 1436
Double
Tube white, medium length and thickness. *Sepals* white on top, white with pink tinge and green tips on the underside. Downswept. *Corolla* creamy white (RHS 155A), with minimum of shading at the base. *Foliage* mid-green, RHS 146A. *Growth* upright, self-branching, tall and bushy. Bush or standard.

'Molesworth'
LEMOINE 1903
Double
Tube cerise, medium length and thickness. *Sepals* cerise, broad and upturned. *Corolla* creamy white with cerise veining, very full and fluffy, medium-sized blooms. *Foliage* medium green, small to medium-sized, serrated leaves. *Growth* bushy, lax, trailing type, self-branching and very free-flowering. Bush (if staked) or half-basket.

'Mona Liza'
NEIDERHOLZER 1947
Single
Tube pale pink, small, thin. *Sepals* pale pink, short, narrow, horizontal. *Corolla* pure white, small and compact. *Foliage* medium green, small to medium-sized leaves. *Growth* upright, bushy, self-branching, and free-flowering. Dwarf bush.

'Money Spinner'
J. LOCKYER 1974
Single
Tube neyron rose, rather thick, medium length. *Sepals* neyron rose on top, deeper on the undersides, long, narrow and curling upwards to hide the tube. *Corolla* imperial purple ageing to magenta, large blooms, fairly compact. *Foliage* medium green, medium-sized, heavily serrated, leaves. *Growth* upright, but rather lax, free-flowering. Basket or standard.

'Monsieur Joule'
LEMOINE 1890
Single
Tube crimson, short, medium thickness. *Sepals* crimson, shortish, recurving completely to the tube. *Corolla* pale violet-purple, fading slightly at the base of the

petals, compact, small blooms. *Foliage* medium green, small to medium-sized leaves. *Growth* upright, vigorous, self-branching and free-flowering. Strongly resembles 'Abbé Farges'. Approx. 2 in (5 cm) long. Bush or quarter standard.

'Monsieur Thibaut' (174)
LEMOINE 1898
Single
Tube cerise-red, thick, medium length. *Sepals* cerise-red, broad, recurving slightly. *Corolla* magenta with cerise veining, paler shade at the base of the petals. Compact, medium-sized blooms. *Foliage* darkish green, medium-sized, broad, finely serrated leaves. *Growth* upright, bushy, self-branching and very free-flowering. Bush or standard.

'Monsoon'
LOCKERBIE 1971
AFS Registration No 1002
Double
Tube very pale pink, medium length and thickness. *Sepals* pale pink, broad. *Corolla* sky blue, very full, petals flaring. Medium to large bloom. *Foliage* medium green, medium-sized leaves, serrated. *Growth* upright, bushy, free-flowering. Will withstand heat. Bush.

'Monte Rosa'
COLVILLE 1966
Double
Tube pink, medium length and thickness. *Sepals* pink with green tips, long, narrow and completely reflexed. *Corolla* white with pink veins, rather loose, medium-sized bloom. *Foliage* light to medium green, medium-sized, serrated leaves. *Growth* upright, bushy, self-branching and free-flowering. Easy to grow. Bush.

'Montezuma'
FUCHSIA LA 1967
AFS Registration No 698
Double
Tube carmine rose, medium length and thickness. *Sepals* carmine rose with green tips, long and broad. *Corolla* tyrian rose, edges of the petals have a smoky tinge, and the base of the petals shaded carmine rose. Large, fluffy blooms. *Foliage* medium green, medium to large leaves. *Growth* trailer, bushy, vigorous and free-flowering. Basket.

'Moonlight'
WALTZ 1953
AFS Registration No 167
Semi-double
Tube greenish-white, short and of medium thickness. *Sepals* greenish-white with pale green tips and frosted effect. Long and narrow. *Corolla* very pale flesh pink, veined pale rose. Overlapping petals, medium-sized bloom. *Foliage* mid-green, medium-sized, serrated leaves. *Growth* upright, vigorous, self-branching, free-flowering. Bush or can be trained to basket with weights.

'Moonlight Sonata'
BLACKWELL
Single
Tube pink, long, medium thickness. *Sepals* pink, long, broad and upturned. *Corolla* pale purple with pink veining, and shaded pink at the base of the petals, compact, medium-sized bloom. *Foliage* medium green, broad, medium-sized, serrated leaves. *Growth* lax upright, vigorous, bushy, free-flowering. Bush, standard or basket.

'Moorland Beauty'
PUGH 1975
AFS Registration No 1237
Semi-double
Tube red RHS 48A, medium length and thickness. *Sepals* neyron rose RHS 55B on top, frosted neyron rose RHS 55A on the undersides, tips white. Recurving $1\frac{1}{5}$ in (30 mm) long, $\frac{1}{2}$ in (12 mm) wide. *Corolla* violet RHS 87A, shading to red purple RHS 73B at the base. *Stamens and pistil* neyron rose. *Growth* bushy, self-branching, upright and free-flowering. *Foliage* green RHS 137A, medium size. Bush or standard.

'More Beauty'
GORMAN 1970
AFS Registration No 940
Double
Tube white, with pale pinkish flush, medium length and thickness. *Sepals* white, flushed pale pink. *Corolla* pale lavender, veined rose-pink, large, full blooms. *Foliage* medium green, medium-sized, serrated leaves. *Growth* lax bush, vigorous, free-flowering. Bush or basket.

'Morning Glory'
NEIDERHOLZER/WALTZ 1951
AFS Registration No 92
Single
Tube creamy white, medium length and thickness. *Sepals* creamy white with pale pink flush, longish, upturned. *Corolla* clear orchid pink, medium-sized, compact bloom. *Foliage* medium green, medium-sized leaves. *Growth* upright, bushy, self-branching and free-flowering. Bush.

'Morning Glow'
GADSBY 1975
AFS Registration No 1302
Double
Tube neyron rose, medium length and thickness. *Sepals* neyron rose RHS 55B, held well back towards the tube. *Corolla* pale wisteria blue RHS 92C, shading to gentian blue RHS 94D. *Foliage* light green, medium size. *Growth* upright, self-branching, bushy and very free-flowering. Develops the best colour in shaded conditions. Bush. *Parentage* 'Rosedale' × 'Albion'.

'Morning Light'
WALTZ 1960
AFS Registration No 441
Double
Tube coral-pink, thick, medium length. *Sepals* white with green tips, pale pink on the undersides and on the edges, very broad and reflexed to the tube. *Corolla* lavender blue with splashes of pink, medium-sized bloom. *Foliage* yellowish green with red veins, medium-size serrated leaves. *Growth* lax upright, bushy, free-flowering. Like most fuchsias with pale foliage it is prone to *Botrytis*. Bush.

'Morrells'
L. HOBBS 1978
AFS Registration No 1463
Double
Tube crimson RHS 52A, medium length and thickness. *Sepals* rose red (RHS 58B) outside, neyron rose (RHS 58C) inside, boat-shaped and held horizontally. *Corolla* lavender violet RHS 80B, lightly veined neyron rose. Medium-sized, squarish, flaring when mature. *Foliage* dark green (RHS 137A) with cardinal red mid-rib. *Growth* bushy, tall, very vigorous upright which requires pinching to shape.

'Mosedale Hall'
THORNLEY 1974
AFS Registration No 1216
Single
Tube cream with pale green flush, short, medium thickness. *Sepals* cream on top, pink flush on the undersides. *Corolla* violet (RHS 86 c), barrel-shaped, small blooms. *Foliage* dark green, small ovate leaves. *Growth* upright, bushy, self-branching, free-flowering. Bush. *Parentage* 'Silverdale' × 'Silverdale'.

'Moth Blue'
TIRET 1949
Double
Tube red, short, medium thickness. *Sepals* red, long, narrow and upturning. *Corolla* deep lilac blue, very full, large bloom. *Foliage* medium to darkish green, medium-sized leaves. *Growth* trailer, bushy, vigorous, very attractive free-flowering plant. Basket.

'Moulin Rouge'
TIRET 1960
AFS Registration No 435
Double
Tube pink, medium length and thickness. *Sepals* pink, longish and upturned. *Corolla* pale blue with pink markings, large,

compact blooms. *Foliage* medium green, medium-sized, serrated leaves. *Growth* lax bush, vigorous, free-flowering. Bush or basket.

'Mountain Haze'
HAAG 1950
Double
Tube pale pink, short and of medium thickness. *Sepals* pale pink short, narrow, recurving slightly. *Corolla* pale smoky-blue, medium-sized, compact bloom. *Foliage* mid-green, medium-sized leaves. *Growth* upright, bushy, vigorous, free-flowering. Bush.

'Mountain Mist' (52)
CROCKETT 1971
AFS Registration No 960
Double
Tube greenish white, short and thick. *Sepals* white with pink flush on top. deeper pink on the undersides, green tips, broad, upturned slightly. *Corolla* pale greyish-mauve, pink shading at the base of the petals. Full and fluffy, medium-sized bloom. *Foliage* medium green, small to medium-sized, serrated leaves. *Growth* upright, bushy, free-flowering. Needs careful pinching. Bush.

'Moz'
J.A. WRIGHT 1980
AFS Registration No 1604
Double
Tube scarlet, medium length and thickness. *Sepals* scarlet, arching back. *Corolla* bishops blue and bright red, large. *Foliage* medium green, large. *Growth* vigorous, free-flowering, self-branching, upright and bushy. Bush or standard. 'Swingtime' seedling.

'Mr A. Huggett' (166)
Raiser not known
Single
Tube scarlet, short and thick. *Sepals* scarlet, short, broad and slightly upturned. *Corolla* pinkish purple, deeper at the edges of the petals and pink at the base, small, very compact blooms. *Foliage* medium green, medium to large leaves, finely serrated. *Growth* upright, bushy, self-branching and vigorous. Free-flowering. Very good exhibition variety. Bush.

'Mr Big'
PENNISI 1970
AFS Registration No 886
Double
Tube pink, medium length and thickness. *Sepals* pink on top, magenta on the underside, longish. *Corolla* main petals purple, with magenta variegations on the lower petals which drop below the rest of the bloom. Large, rather untidy blooms. *Foliage* medium green, medium to large leaves. *Growth* natural trailer, bushy, vigorous, free-flowering. Basket.

'Mrs Anthony Lipp'
CHILES 1953
AFS Registration No 161
Double
Tube pale pink, medium length and thickness. *Sepals* neyron rose, long, broad and with crepe effect. *Corolla* violet and smoky-blue on alternate petals, medium to large blooms. *Foliage* mid-green, medium-sized, serrated leaves. *Growth* upright, vigorous, bushy and free-flowering. Bush.

'Mrs C.B. Hallmark'
GAGNON 1963
AFS Registration No 553
Double
Tube white, medium length and thickness. *Sepals* white, flushed coral-pink, longish, pointed and recurving. *Corolla* creamy white, very full, medium-sized bloom. *Foliage* light green, medium-sized leaves. *Growth* lax bush, vigorous, bushy, free-flowering. Basket or bush if staked.

'Mrs Chas Soules'
BROWN AND SOULES 1951
AFS Registration No 74
Double
Tube white, short, medium thickness. *Sepals* pale pink, short, horizontal. *Corolla*

blue with pink and white marbling on the petals, medium-sized, compact bloom. *Foliage* medium green, medium-sized, serrated leaves. *Growth* trailer, bushy, vigorous, free-flowering. Basket.

'Mrs Churchill'

GARSON

Single to semi-double

Tube red, thin, medium length. *Sepals* red, broad, curling upwards over the tube. *Corolla* pinkish-white, marbled deep pink and veined crimson. Medium-sized, bell-shaped bloom. *Foliage* medium green with red veins, longish, medium-sized serrated leaves. *Growth* upright, bushy, free-flowering, but rather straggly. Bush.

'Mrs Hellier'

GORMAN 1970

AFS Registration No 933

Double

Tube red, medium length, and thickness. *Sepals* red, broad, recurving slightly. *Corolla* purple, paler at the base of the petals. Fairly full and compact, medium-sized bloom. *Foliage* darkish green, medium-sized serrated leaves. *Growth* upright, bushy, free-flowering. Bush.

'Mrs John D. Fredericks'

EVANS AND REEVES 1936

Single

Tube pale salmon pink, short, thin. *Sepals* salmon pink, short, pointed. *Corolla* slightly darker pink, small and compact. *Foliage* darkish green, small, serrated leaves. *Growth* upright, bushy, vigorous, self-branching and very free-flowering. Makes an excellent exhibition plant. Bush or quarter standard. *Parentage* *F. lycoides* × 'Fireflush'.

'Mrs Lawrence Lyon'

REITER 1952

Semi-double

Tube ivory pink, medium length and thickness. *Sepals* ivory pink. *Corolla* pale fuchsia purple, compact, medium-sized bloom. *Foliage* medium green, medium-sized leaves. *Growth* upright, bushy, free-flowering. Bush. Sport of 'Nonpareil'.

'Mrs Lovell Swisher' (77)

EVANS AND REEVES 1942

Single

Tube pink, long, thin. *Sepals* pinkish white on top, deeper shade on the undersides, pale green tips, short, narrow and held horizontal. *Corolla* pale carmine red, paler shades at the base of the petals, small, very compact bloom. *Foliage* medium green, medium-sized, serrated leaves. *Growth* upright, vigorous, self-branching and very free-flowering. Although self-branching, it will benefit from careful pinching as it tends to make long growths between branches otherwise. Bush or standard.

'Mrs Mabel Gorman'

GORMAN 1970

AFS Registration No 920

Double

Tube pale bright red, medium length and thickness. *Sepals* bright red on top, crepe effect on the underside. *Corolla* deep violet-purple with bluish centre. Petaloids pink and white, rather ragged appearance. Medium-sized bloom. *Foliage* mid-green, medium-sized leaves. *Growth* upright, vigorous, bushy, free-flowering. Bush or standard.

'Mrs Marshall'

JONES

Single

Tube creamy white, thick, medium length. *Sepals* creamy white, held well out from the corolla. *Corolla* rosy-cerise, compact, medium-sized bloom. *Foliage* medium green, small to medium-sized serrated leaves. *Growth* upright, bushy, vigorous, self-branching, free-flowering and very easy to grow. Needs careful watering otherwise leaves can quickly turn yellow and drop. Bush.

'Mrs Phyllis Reid'

REID 1977

AFS Registration No 1438

Double
Tube carmine (RHS 52B) short, medium thickness. *Sepals* rose red (RHS 58B), smooth on top, creped undersides, short to medium length, broad, reflexing to the tube. *Corolla* neyron rose (56D) blotched rose red (RHS 58B) and magenta (RHS 66B) at the base of the petals, veined magenta. Very large, two-tiered blooms. *Pistil and stamens* rose red (RHS 58C). *Foliage* dark green, medium-sized. *Growth* upright, self-branching, bushy. Very free-flowering. Bush, standard.

'Mrs Popple' (155)
ELLIOTT 1899
Single 2–2½ in (5–6 cm)
Tube scarlet, short and thin. *Sepals* scarlet, short and broad. *Corolla* violet-purple, paler at the base of the petals and lightly veined cerise. *Foliage* dark green, small, narrow, serrated leaves. *Growth* upright, vigorous, bushy, free-flowering. Bush, standard or garden hardy.

'Mrs (W.) Rundle' (182)
RUNDLE 1883
Single 3 in (7.5 cm)
Tube waxy pale rose, long and thin. *Sepals* flesh pink with green tips, long, narrow and slightly reflexing. *Corolla* orange crimson, compact, small. *Foliage* light green, medium-sized, broad, serrated leaves. *Growth* vigorous, but straggly, free-flowering. Bush or summer bedder.

'Mrs Susan Pugh'
PUGH 1978
AFS Registration No 1459
Single
Tube striped orient pink RHS 36C and azalea pink RHS 38A, medium length and thickness. *Sepals* pink RHS 38A, with green RHS 191C, tips, shiny on top, matt below, outward curving. *Corolla* red purple RHS 58B, very faint veining. *Stamens* red RHS 52D. *Foliage* green RHS 137C. *Growth* very vigorous, self-branching, and free-flowering, upright. Bush, standard, pyramid. *Parentage* 'Chang' ×.

'Mrs W.P. Wood'
WOOD 1949
Single
Tube pale pink, short and thin. *Sepals* pale pink, long, narrow and upturned. *Corolla* white, longish, compact, small blooms. *Foliage* light green, small, serrated leaves. *Growth* upright, bushy, vigorous, free-flowering. Bush or garden hardy.

'Mr W. Rundle'
RUNDLE 1896
Single 4½ in (11.5 cm)
Tube rose pink, long and thin. *Sepals* rose pink, short, downswept. *Corolla* orange vermilion, very compact, smallish blooms. *Foliage* medium green, small, serrated leaves. *Growth* vigorous but straggly, bushy, free and early-flowering. Bush or standard.

'Mumtaz'
HAZARD
Double
Tube carmine red, medium length and thickness. *Sepals* carmine red, short, broad, held well out. *Corolla* creamy white, rather pointed, full and compact, medium-sized bloom. *Foliage* yellowish green, medium-sized leaves with touches of pink in the young, early growth. *Growth* upright, bushy, vigorous, free-flowering. Bush.

'Muriel'
Raiser unknown
Single 5 in (12.5 cm)
Tube scarlet, long and thin. *Sepals* scarlet with green tips, long and reflexed. *Corolla* bluish magenta, veined cerise, and lighter at the base of the petals, very loose-petalled, medium bloom. *Foliage* medium green, medium-sized, serrated leaves. *Growth* vigorous, lax, free-flowering. Basket or weeping standard.

'My Baby'
PALKO/SOO YUN 1978
AFS Registration No 1446
Semi-double
Tube rhodamine pink, long and medium

thickness. *Sepals* pale rhodamine pink with light green tips, $\frac{1}{2}$ in (13 mm) wide, $\frac{7}{8}$ in (22 mm) long, curving upwards. *Corolla* magenta rose fading to spiraea red at the sepals, medium length, loose. *Foliage* light green with scalloped edges. 2 in (50 mm) wide and $3\frac{3}{4}$ in (95 mm) long. *Growth* very free-flowering, vigorous, trailing growth. Basket or bush.

'My Darling'
SOO YUN 1970
AFS Registration No 910
Double
Tube light red, medium length and thickness. *Sepals* light red, longish and broad. *Corolla* red and white variegated at the base, with the centre petals reddish white with red veining, large, fluffy blooms. *Foliage* mid-green, medium to large leaves, serrated. *Growth* trailer, vigorous, bushy, free-flowering. Basket.

'My Dream'
SOO YUN 1977
AFS Registration No 1408
Double
Tube crimson, short, medium thickness. *Sepals* crimson, $1\frac{1}{2}$ in (4 cm) long, curling up to the tube. *Corolla* orchid pink, blending to light pink, $1\frac{1}{2}$ in (4 cm) long, large, flared and ruffled. *Stamens and pistil* crimson with brown tips. *Foliage* medium green, long, wide and red veined. *Growth* semi-trailer. Basket or bush.

'My Fair Lady'
COLVILLE 1966
Double
Tube rose pink, medium length and thickness. *Sepals* deep pink with green tips, long, broad and curling upwards. *Corolla* lavender, maturing to pinkish purple, pink shading at the base of the petals, large, loose-petalled bloom. *Foliage* medium green, medium to large-sized, serrated leaves. *Growth* upright, vigorous, busy, free-flowering. Bush or standard.

'My Love'
SOO YUN FIELD 1966
AFS Registration No 683
Double
Tube rose pink, medium length and thickness. *Sepals* deep rose pink, short, narrow. *Corolla* light orchid, small, compact bloom. *Foliage* mid-green, medium-sized, serrated leaves. *Growth* semi-trailer, bushy, free-flowering. Needs early pinching to shape. Half-basket.

'My Sport'
GORMAN 1970
AFS Registration No 924
Single
Tube pale red, small to medium thick. *Sepals* red, short, held well out. *Corolla* deep purple, paler at the base of the petals, small compact bloom. *Foliage* dark green with red stems, small to medium, curling leaves. *Growth* trailer, fairly vigorous, bushy, free-flowering. Half-basket.

'My Valentine'
MARTIN 1964
AFS Registration No 608
Double
Tube dark pink, medium length and thickness. *Sepals* dark pink, longish, broad and upturned. *Corolla* light pink, very full and compact. *Foliage* dark green, medium-sized, serrated leaves. *Growth* bushy, lax, vigorous, free-flowering. Bush or half-basket.

'Nancy'
NEIDERHOLZER 1948
Single
Tube carmine, medium length and thickness. *Sepals* carmine, narrow and reflexing. *Corolla* phlox pink, medium-sized flaring bloom. *Foliage* medium green, medium-sized, serrated leaves. *Growth* upright, bushy, self-branching and short-jointed, free-flowering. Bush.

'Nancy Lou'
STUBBS 1971
AFS Registration No 998
Double
Tube pale pink, thickish, medium length.

Sepals pink on top, deeper on the undersides, green tips. Long, broad and reflexed to the tube. *Corolla* pure white, very full and fluffy, large blooms. *Foliage* medium green, large, serrated leaves. *Growth* upright, vigorous, bushy, free-flowering. A superb greenhouse plant, not difficult to grow and most rewarding. Bush or standard.

'Narcissus'
NEIDERHOLZER 1946
Single
Tube ivory white, medium length and thickness. *Sepals* ivory, reflexing. *Corolla* orchid purple, medium-sized, loose-petalled bloom. *Foliage* medium green, medium-sized, serrated leaves. *Growth* upright, vigorous, bushy, free-flowering. Bush.

'Native Dancer'
TIRET 1965
AFS Registration No 648
Double
Tube bright red, medium length and thickness. *Sepals* bright red, longish, curling. *Corolla* deep purple, reddish at the base of the petals, full, medium-sized bloom. *Foliage* medium to darkish green, medium-sized leaves. *Growth* lax, bushy, vigorous, very free-flowering. A very attractive, easy to grow variety. Half-basket or bush if staked and pinched early.

'Nautilus'
LEMOINE 1902
Double
Tube cerise, thin, medium length. *Sepals* cerise, long, narrow, recurving. *Corolla* white with cerise veins, compact, medium-sized bloom. *Foliage* medium to darkish green, medium-sized serrated leaves. *Growth* upright, bushy, self-branching and free-flowering. Bush.

'Neil Clyne'
CLYNE 1975
AFS Registration No 1285
Single
Tube neyron rose, short and thick. *Sepals* neyron rose RHS 55A crepe effect on the undersides, and reflexing. *Corolla* violet fading to cyclamen RHS 74B. *Foliage* spinach green, narrow, medium-sized. *Growth* upright, self-branching, bushy and very free-flowering. Bush or standard. *Parentage* 'La Campanella' × 'Winston Churchill'.

'Nellie Eastwood'
EASTWOOD/YANCEY 1980
AFS Registration No 1570
Double
Tube light pink RHS 56C, short, medium thickness. *Sepals* rhodamine pink RHS 62A with lighter pink tips, and light pink RHS 56C at the base, narrow, $1\frac{1}{2}$ in (4 cm) long, slightly curling. *Corolla* cyclamen purple RHS 74B with light pink to white markings on the outer petals, slightly ruffled and compact. Medium size. *Stamens* cyclamen purple and white. *Foliage* medium green RHS 137A with red veins and stems, medium size. *Growth* natural trailer. Self-branching, vigorous and bushy. Basket.

'Nellie's Lantern'
TOLLEY 1973
AFS Registration No 1157
Double
Tube pale cerise, veined white, medium length and thickness. *Sepals* flesh pink, suffused a darker shade of pink, medium length sitting well over the corolla. *Corolla* geranium pink with numerous petals in shades of geranium pink, very full and compact bloom. *Foliage* mid-green, medium-sized leaves. *Growth* upright, willowy, self-branching and free-flowering. Needs early pinching and staking to make a good plant. Bush.

'Neon'
SCHNABEL 1949
Single
Tube ivory white with palest pink flush, short, thin. *Sepals* ivory white, flushed rose on top, deeper rose on the underside. *Corolla* rhodamine purple with edges of

geranium lake, small compact blooms. *Foliage* mid-green, small to medium-sized leaves. *Growth* upright, vigorous, bushy, free-flowering. Bush or standard.

'Nettala'
FRANCESCA 1973
AFS Registration No 1090
Single
Tube dark red, short and thick. *Sepals* dark red, short and stubby. *Corolla* violet red, medium-sized bloom. *Foliage* medium green, small to medium-sized. *Growth* vigorous, upright, bushy and free-flowering. Will grow well in full sun. Bush or standard. Sport of 'Chang'.

'Neue Welt'
MAHNKE 1912
Single
Tube crimson, short, medium thickness. *Sepals* crimson, small, slightly upturned. *Corolla* violet purple with carmine veins, paler at the base of the petals and fading somewhat with maturity. Small, very compact bloom. *Foliage* medium green, small, finely serrated. *Growth* upright, bushy, self-branching and very free-flowering. Bush.

'New Fascination'
NEIDERHOLZER 1940
Single
Tube bright reddish pink, medium length and thickness. *Sepals* carmine red on top, brighter on the undersides, reflexed. *Corolla* rose pink, heavily marked with carmine splashes and with red veins. Very open, medium-sized bloom. *Foliage* medium green, medium-sized, serrated leaves. *Growth* upright, bushy, vigorous, free-flowering and easy to grow. Bush or standard.

'New Hope'
DAVIS 1970
AFS Registration No 903
Double
Tube white, medium length and thickness. *Sepals* white, medium-sized, broad. *Corolla* white, very full and fluffy, medium-sized bloom. *Foliage* mid-green, medium-sized leaves. *Growth* trailer, bushy, short-jointed, free-flowering. Basket.

'New Horizon'
REITER JR 1950
AFS Registration No 59
Double
Tube pale rose pink, short, medium thickness. *Sepals* pale pink, short, broad. *Corolla* darkish lobelia blue, medium-sized, compact bloom. *Foliage* mid-green, medium-sized leaves. *Growth* upright, vigorous, self-branching and free-flowering. Bush.

'Niagara'
SCHNABEL-PASKESEN 1961
AFS Registration No 459
Double
Tube white, medium length and thickness. *Sepals* white with pale pink edges, broad, crepe effect. *Corolla* clear white with rose pink veins, medium-sized, flaring blooms. *Foliage* mid-green, medium-sized leaves. *Growth* trailer, bushy, vigorous, arching, free-flowering. If grown in the shade, blooms will be almost pure white. Basket.

'Nicola'
DALGLIESH 1964
Single
Tube cerise short, medium thickness. *Sepals* cerise, long, broad and reflexing completely over the tube. *Corolla* violet-purple with cerise veins, lighter at the base of the petals. Open saucer-shaped blooms. *Foliage* medium green, longish, medium-sized, serrated leaves. *Growth* upright, bushy, free-flowering. Bush. *Parentage* 'Citation' × 'Swanley Gem'.

'Nicola Jane' (138)
DAWSON 1959
Double
Tube pinkish cerise, thick, medium length. *Sepals* cerise with green tips, broad and reflexing. *Corolla* pale pink

with darker veining, flushed red. Medium-sized, loose-petalled bloom. *Foliage* medium green, small to medium-sized, serrated leaves. *Growth* upright, bushy, self-branching, free-flowering. Bush or garden hardy.

'Nicolette'
HANDLEY 1973
AFS Registration No 1135
Single
Tube white with pink flush, short and thick. *Sepals* pink on top, deeper pink on the undersides, green tips, broad and slightly recurving. *Corolla* fuchsia purple, deeper at the edges and pink at the base of the petals, compact, medium-sized bloom. *Foliage* medium green, medium-sized, broad, serrated leaves. *Growth* upright, bushy, self-branching and very free-flowering. Bush.

'Nicolina'
GADSBY 1973
AFS Registration No 1123
Single
Tube rose-red, medium length and thickness. *Sepals* rose bengal on top, rose bengal on the undersides, recurving to the tube. *Corolla* white, with an unusual picotee edging of cyclamen purple, medium to large-sized, open bell-shaped bloom. *Foliage* rich green, medium-sized leaves. *Growth* upright, bushy, rather wiry stems, free-flowering. Needs early pinching to form a reasonable shape. *Parentage* 'Bishop's Bells' × 'White Bride'.

'Nightingale'
WALTZ 1960
AFS Registration No 442
Double
Tube white, short and of medium thickness. *Sepals* white, flushed pink, short, broad. *Corolla* deep purple in the centre, fading on maturity to bright magenta. Outer petals shades of pink, white and coral pink, large, frilly bloom. *Foliage* dark green, medium-sized leaves. *Growth* natural trailer, very free-flowering, most attractive bloom. Basket.

'Nina'
YORK 1953
AFS Registration No 189
Double
Tube pale pink, medium length and thickness. *Sepals* pale pink, long, broad and reflexing. *Corolla* white, flaring and with picotee edges to the petals, medium-sized bloom. *Foliage* mid-green, medium-sized, serrated leaves. *Growth* trailer, vigorous, bushy, longish branches and free-flowering. Basket.

'Nina Wills' (75)
WILLS 1961
Registered 1973
AFS Registration No 1129
Single
Tube pink, thin, medium length. *Sepals* pink, long, narrow and upturned. *Corolla* baby pink, small and compact. *Foliage* light to medium green, small, serrated leaves. *Growth* upright, self-branching, bushy and very free-flowering. Bush or standard or summer bedder. Sport from 'Forget-me-not'.

'Nino'
PENNISI 1971
AFS Registration No 1018
Double
Tube white, long and thin. *Sepals* white, long, narrow, recurving. *Corolla* ruby red, very full and compact, medium-sized bloom. *Foliage* medium green, small leaves. *Growth* natural trailer, bushy, vigorous, free-flowering. Basket.

'Niobe'
REITER JR 1950
AFS Registration No 61
Semi-double
Tube pale pink, medium length and thickness. *Sepals* pale pink, longish and broad. *Corolla* tyrian rose, rather open, medium to large bloom. *Foliage* mid-green, medium-sized leaves. *Growth* natural

trailer, bushy, self-branching and free-flowering. Basket.

'Nobility'
MARTIN 1961
AFS Registration No 464
Double
Tube dark red, medium length and thickness. *Sepals* dark red, longish, broad, upturned. *Corolla* light blue shading to orchid pink, compact, medium-sized bloom. *Foliage* medium green, medium-sized leaves. *Growth* lax bush, vigorous, free-flowering. Very attractive flower. Bush or basket.

'Nola'
HAZARD
Single
Tube pinkish, short, medium thickness. *Sepals* white with pink flush, longish, held well out. *Corolla* pink with shades of lavender, paler at the base of the petals, medium-sized bloom. *Foliage* mid-green, vigorous, bushy and free-flowering. Bush or standard.

'Norma'
HAZARD
Double
Tube red, medium length, and thickness. *Sepals* red, short, pointed, slightly reflexed. *Corolla* deep lavender, paler shade at the base of the petals, medium-sized bloom. *Foliage* mid-green, small to medium-sized, serrated leaves. *Growth* dwarf upright, bushy, free-flowering. Bush.

'Normandy Bell'
MARTIN 1961
AFS Registration No 465
Single
Tube pale pink, short and thick. *Sepals* pale pink, with green tips, long, broad and slightly upturned. *Corolla* pale mauve-purple with pink veining. Paler shade at the base of the petals. Bell-shaped, medium-sized bloom. *Foliage* medium green, medium-sized, longish, serrated leaves. *Growth* lax, bushy, free-flowering. Basket.

'Norman Mitchinson'
RYLE 1978
AFS Registration No 1477
Single
Tube pinkish white, short and thick. *Sepals* white with green tips, slightly pink on the undersides, waxy polished look. *Corolla* rich purple RHS 80A with pink and white flecks. *Foliage* green RHS 137A. *Anthers* rose pink, stigma chrome yellow RHS 158A. *Growth* medium self-branching upright, which will make a good bush or standard.

'Northern Light'
GORMAN 1970
AFS Registration No 931
Double
Tube pure white. *Sepals* pure white. *Corolla* dark purple. *Foliage* very light green. *Growth* upright, self-branching and bushy. Will make a good bush or a standard, and can be trained as a basket with weights.

'Northern Pride'
RYLE 1979
AFS Registration No 1528
Double
Tube pink, medium length and thickness. *Sepals* rhodamine pink RHS 62A inside, and phlox pink RHS 62B on the underside. Small. *Corolla* outer petals beetroot purple RHS 71A, inside petals which are larger are fuchsia purple RHS 67B. *Stigma* white, anthers chrysanthemum pink RHS 185A. *Foliage* medium green. *Growth* strong, self-branching upright, which will make a good bush or standard. Develops the best colour in the shade. Named to commemorate the 21st Anniversary of the British Fuchsia Society's Northern Show.

'Northern Queen'
DE FRANCISCO/SOO YUN FUCHSIA GARDENS 1980
AFS Registration No 1558
Double
Tube rhodonite red, medium length and thickness. *Sepals* rhodonite red 2 in

(5 cm) long. *Corolla* spectrum violet with scarlet at the base of the petals. Six petaloids of the same colour and length as the petals. *Filaments* pink. *Anthers* brown. *Stigma* brown. *Foliage* light green, 2 in (5 cm) in length by 1¼ in (3 cm) wide. Will make a good bush or standard. *Growth* upright, free-flowering, bushy.

'Northumbrian Belle'
RYLE 1970
Registered 1973
AFS Registration No 1115
Single
Tube neyron rose RHS 55A, short and of medium thickness. *Sepals* bright neyron rose, long and narrow. *Corolla* aster blue RHS 88B, fading to petunia purple. RHS 78A with bengal rose veining RHS 57C, bell-shaped. *Foliage* medium green RHS 137B. *Growth* free flowering, self-branching upright which will make a good bush or standard. Develops the best colour in the shade.

'Northway'
GOLICS 1976
Single
Tube pale pink, short and thick. *Sepals* pale pink, short, broad and reflexing. *Corolla* cherry red, small, compact bloom. *Foliage* light to medium green, small leaves. *Growth* upright, bushy, self-branching and free-flowering. Requires careful attention to feeding otherwise the foliage becomes very pale and the whole plant insipid. Heavy nitrogen early will produce the required result. Bush or basket. *Parentage* 'La Campanella' × 'Howlett's Hardy'.

'Norvell Gillespie'
PENNISI 1969
AFS Registration No 832
Double
Tube white, medium length and thickness. *Sepals* white on top, pale pink on the undersides, long and narrow. *Corolla* dark orchid, very compact, large bloom. *Foliage* medium green, medium-sized leaves. *Growth* natural trailer, bushy, free-flowering, attractive flower. Basket.

'Not So Big'
MACHADO 1962
AFS Registration No 500
Double
Tube white, medium length, and thickness. *Sepals* pale pink, held well out. *Corolla* bluish, paler at the base of the petals, medium to large bloom. *Foliage* medium green, medium-sized, serrated leaves. *Growth* upright, bushy, vigorous, free-flowering. Flowers held well out above the foliage on stiff stems. Bush or standard.

'Novato'
SOO YUN 1972
AFS Registration No 1042
Single
Tube white, faintly tinged green, long and thin. *Sepals* white on top with light green tips, undersides white with pale pink tinge, longish. *Corolla* pale scarlet shading to salmon, medium size, compact blooms. *Foliage* medium green, medium-sized leaves with serrated edges. Branches red. *Growth* semi-trailer, bushy, free-flowering. Bush or basket with weights.

'Novella'
TIRET 1967
Semi-double
Tube flesh pink, long and thin. *Sepals* rosy pink, long and upturning slightly. *Corolla* salmon-orange, fairly compact, medium-sized blooms. *Foliage* medium green, medium-sized, serrated leaves. *Growth* trailer, lax, bushy, free-flowering. Bush, if staked, or basket.

'Nutshell'
DE GRAAF 1977
Single
Tube rose pink, short and bulbous. *Sepals* rose pink on top, salmon pink on the underside, spreading over the corolla. *Corolla* orange-red, petals loosely folded, compact, medium-sized bloom. *Stamens*

light red. *Style* pink. *Foliage* medium green, small to medium-sized leaves. *Growth* trailer, slow growing, self-branching, free-flowering. Basket. *Parentage* 'La Campanella' ×.

'Oberon'
J. TRAVIS 1958
Registered 1973
AFS Registration No 1144
Not to be confused with 'Oberon' (BANKS 1864). *Tube* mauve pink, long and waxy, of medium thickness. *Sepals* mauve pink, waxy and small, pointed and reflexed. *Corolla* mauve pink if grown in the shade, coral if grown in the sun, petals very small and pointed. *Foliage* small, breviflora type. *Growth* bushy, self-branching, upright. Can be trained to most shapes, very suitable for bonsai growth. Flowers minute. *Parentage* 'Breviflora' ×.

'Ocean Beach' (181)
KROGH 1975
AFS Registration No 1298
Single
Tube light salmon, of medium length and width. *Sepals* light salmon with green tips on top, salmon on the underside. *Corolla* salmon orange, mottled with salmon-rose, small. *Sepals* medium length, stiff and flat. *Foliage* dark green, tinted dark red around the growing tips. *Growth* bushy, upright. Bush or small standard. Needs careful pinching.

'Ocean Mist'
FRANCESCA 1977
AFS Registration No 1422
Single
Tube white, medium length, thin. *Sepals* white, smallish. *Corolla* white, very small. *Stamens* white. *Pistil* flaring open. *Foliage* dark green, fern like. *Growth* natural trailer, self-branching, bushy. Basket, can be trained to bush or quarter standard.

'Odd Ball'
PRENTICE 1966
AFS Registration No 666
Tube pale pink, very long, medium thickness. *Sepals* pale pink, opening flat. *Corolla* pale blue, irregular and crumpled look to the petals, fading to light orchid. *Foliage* small, medium green. *Growth* upright, bushy and free-flowering. Can be made to trail as the growth is somewhat lax. Bush.

'Odd Beauty'
SOO YUN 1973
AFS Registration No 1096
Double
Tube light red, short and thick. *Sepals* light red, tipped green, broad, opening out and curling upwards. *Corolla* blue, variegated pink mainly at the base of the petals, and with pink streaks to the tips. Medium to large blooms. *Foliage* medium green, large leaves, serrated. *Growth* semi-trailer, bushy, self-branching, very free-flowering. Can be pinched to make either bush or basket.

'Oh Boy'
HAZARD
Double
Tube bright red, medium length and thickness. *Sepals* bright red, long, upswept. *Corolla* white, veined red, large, loose-petalled bloom. *Foliage* mid-green, medium-sized leaves, serrated. *Growth* upright, vigorous, free-flowering. Bush.

'Old Del Monte'
HAZARD
Single
Tube carmine-red, medium length and thickness. *Sepals* carmine red, longish, reflexing. *Corolla* purple with red shading at the base of the petals Medium-sized bloom, fairly compact. *Growth* natural trailer, bushy, free-flowering. Basket. *Foliage* medium green, medium-sized leaves.

'Old Lace'
BROWN AND SOULES 1953
Single
Tube pale pink, medium length and thickness. *Sepals* pale rose-pink, with orchid

shades at the base of the petals. Long, open-petalled bloom with scalloped petals. *Foliage* medium green, medium-sized, serrated leaves. *Growth* upright, vigorous, free-flowering. Needs pinching early. Bush or standard.

'Old Smoky'
SCHMIDT 1952
AFS Registration No 112
Double
Tube flesh pink, medium length and thickness. *Sepals* flesh pink on top, pink on the undersides, long and spreading. *Corolla* old rose, with a decided smoky cast on the petals. *Foliage* mid-green, medium-sized leaves. *Growth* bushy, lax upright, free flowering. Bush or basket with weights.

'Olive Jackson'
HANDLEY 1974
AFS Registration No 1193
Semi-double
Tube rose pink, short, medium thickness. *Sepals* rose pink on top with green tips, darker pink on the undersides, reflexing to the tube. *Corolla* hyacinth-blue, ageing to lilac purple, white at the base of the petals, compact, medium-sized bloom. *Foliage* medium green, very broad, medium-sized, finely serrated leaves. *Growth* upright, bushy, vigorous, free-flowering. Bush.

'Olympiad'
FOSTER 1973
AFS Registration No 1087
Double
Tube red, medium length and thickness. *Sepals* red, long, narrow and curling. *Corolla* white with red veins, tips slightly serrated, large bloom. *Foliage* light to medium green with dark red stems, serrated medium-sized leaves. *Growth* natural trailer, vigorous, bushy, free-flowering. Shade is required for the best colouring. Basket.

'Olympic Lass'
SUTHERLAND 1967
AFS Registration No 745
Double
Tube white, thin, medium length. *Sepals* white with a pale pink flush, green tips, long, narrow and recurving. *Corolla* pinkish purple with deep purple edge to the petals. Longish, medium-sized, compact bloom. *Foliage* medium green, small to medium serrated leaves. *Growth* natural trailer, bushy, not too free-flowering. Basket.

'Omeomy'
KENNETT 1963
AFS Registration No 591
Semi-double
Tube pale pink, short, medium thickness. *Sepals* pale pink, long, narrow and upturning. *Corolla* dianthus purple with overlay and marbling of coral pink. Large, compact bloom. *Foliage* medium green, medium-sized leaves. *Growth* natural trailer, bushy, vigorous, free-flowering. Basket.

'100%'
GAGNON 1964
AFS Registration No 602
Semi-double
Tube white, medium length and thickness. *Sepals* white with green tips, medium length, upturned. *Corolla* lavender blue on opening, changing to a bright rose shade, medium-sized, loose-petalled bloom. *Foliage* dark green, small leaves. *Growth* natural trailer, bushy, vigorous and very free-flowering. A very attractive flower. Half-basket.

'Oos'
VAN DER GRIJP 1973
Breviflora type
Tube, sepals and corolla red. Very small flowers. *Foliage* mid-green, small and serrated. Bush *Parentage F. parviflora* × *F. microphylla.*

'Oosje'
VAN DER GRIJP 1973
Breviflora type
Tube and sepals red, ageing to dark red. *Corolla* whitish red, ageing to dark red.

Very small flowers. *Foliage* medium green, small and serrated. *Growth* upright bushy. Bush. *Parentage F. parviflora* × *F. microphylla.*

'Opalescent'
FUCHSIA LA 1951
Double
Tube china-rose, medium length and thickness. *Sepals* china-rose, broad. *Corolla* pale violet, shaded rose pink and opal, medium to large blooms. *Foliage* medium green, medium to large leaves. *Growth* upright, longish branches, free-flowering. Needs pinching. Bush.

'Orange Cocktail'
HANDLEY 1972
AFS Registration No 1056
Single
Tube pale salmon pink, long, slender. *Sepals* pale salmon pink, green tips, short, broad and upturned. *Corolla* clear orange in the centre of the petals and at the base, deeper orange at the edges, medium-sized, compact bloom. *Foliage* light to medium green, medium to large, serrated leaves. *Growth* bushy, tending to be rather lax, free-flowering. Half-basket or bush if staked.

'Orange Crush' (185)
HANDLEY 1972
AFS Registration No 1057
Single
Tube orange-salmon RHS 41C, waxy, of medium length and thickness. *Sepals* orange-salmon RHS 41C, thick and spiky. *Corolla* bright orange RHS 33A, paler at the base of the petals which overlap. *Foliage* medium green, small to medium size. *Growth* upright, bushy, short-jointed, free and early flowering. Bush.

'Orange Crystal'
HANDLEY 1980
AFS Registration No 1541
Single
Tube orange RHS 33C, medium length and thickness. *Sepals* orange (RHS 40D), 1 in (2.5 cm) long, tipped green, and held horizontally. *Stamens and pistil* orange (RHS 40D). *Foliage* mid-green, close-jointed, small and serrated. *Growth* upright, self-branching, bushy and vigorous. Flowers of medium size, colouring similar to 'Lord Lonsdale'. Bush.

'Orange Drops'
MARTIN 1963
AFS Registration No 572
Single
Tube light orange, long and of medium thickness. *Sepals* light orange, broad and pointed. *Corolla* orange, smoky effect on the edges of the petals. The flowers tend to hang in clusters. *Foliage* medium green, largish. *Growth* bushy, upright, free-flowering. Bush. One of the best orange fuchsias.

'Orange Flare'
HANDLEY 1972
AFS Registration No 1058
Single
Tube orange-salmon, RHS 40D, short and thick. *Sepals* orange-salmon RHS 40D, short and broad. *Corolla* light orange RHS 33B at the base of the petals, shading to deep orange RHS 40A on the outer edges of the petals, flaring. *Foliage* medium green. *Growth* upright, self-branching, bushy and free-flowering. Flowers early. Develops its best colour if grown in the sun. Bush.

'Orange King'
J.A. WRIGHT 1975
AFS Registration No 1306
Semi-double
Tube white, medium length and thickness. *Sepals* pale pink on top, rich frosty pink on the undersides arching back. *Corolla* opens orange and matures to a rich smoky pink, mottled rich orange at the base of the petals. *Foliage* medium green, serrated. *Growth* upright, bushy, free-flowering, tends to be rather stiff. Bush.

'Orange Mirage'
TIRET 1970
AFS Registration No 896
Single
Tube pale salmon pink, thick, medium length. *Sepals* salmon pink with green tips. Long, broad and curling slightly. *Corolla* dull orange salmon, medium-sized, fairly compact bloom. *Foliage* light green, medium-sized serrated leaves. *Growth* trailer, vigorous, free-flowering. Basket.

'Orangy'
REEDSTROM 1962
AFS Registration No 547
Single to semi-double
Tube pale salmon, long and thin. *Sepals* pale salmon with green tips, long and upturned. *Corolla* pale orange, compact, medium-sized bloom. *Foliage* pale yellowish green, medium to large serrated leaves. *Growth* natural trailer, vigorous, bushy and free-flowering. Half-basket.

'Oregon'
BACHER 1947
Tube flesh-pink, long and thin. *Sepals* flesh pink, long and narrow, with white stripes. *Corolla* crimson red, large, compact bloom. *Foliage* medium green, medium to large leaves. *Growth* natural trailer, bushy, free-flowering. Basket. Sport of 'America'.

'Oregon Trail'
HODGES 1949
Single
Tube crimson, medium length and thickness. *Sepals* crimson, longish, upturned. *Corolla* light purple, medium-sized, open saucer-shaped blooms. *Foliage* mid-green, medium-sized leaves. *Growth* lax, spreading, bushy, free-flowering. Bush.

'Organza'
NESSIER 1953
Double
Tube rose pink, medium length and thickness. *Sepals* pink, broad, spreading. *Corolla* heliotrope blue, very full and fluffy, medium-sized bloom. *Foliage* medium green, medium-sized leaves. *Growth* upright, vigorous, self-branching and free-flowering. Bush or standard.

'Oriental Lace'
FRANCESCA 1975
AFS Registration No 1291
Single
Tube soft light red, short. *Sepals* soft light red, tipped chartreuse. *Corolla* deep purple, very small. *Stamens* pinkish red. *Pistil* pinkish red. *Foliage* dark green, small and slender, lacy effect. *Growth* upright, bushy, vigorous, very free-flowering and showy. Bush, standard, etc.

'Oriental Lantern'
SOO YUN 1970
AFS Registration No 912
Double
Tube white, faintly tinged pink, medium length and thickness. *Sepals* white on top, faintly tinged pink on the undersides. *Corolla* cerise, opens lantern shape, medium-sized bloom. *Foliage* bright green, medium-sized leaves. *Growth* natural trailer, bushy, free-flowering. Half-basket.

'Oriental Princess'
MACHADO 1963
AFS Registration No 560
Semi-double
Tube pale pink, small, medium thickness. *Sepals* pale pink, opening to a pagoda shape and upturning. *Corolla* white, bell-shaped. *Foliage* pale green, small. Branches wiry. *Growth* natural trailer, self-branching, free-flowering. Basket.

'Oriental Sunrise'
SOO YUN 1975
AFS Registration No 1270
Single
Tube light orange, short and thin. *Sepals* light orange with light green tips, on top, darker orange on the undersides, star-shaped and standing straight out. *Corolla* dark orange, flaring. Medium-sized. *Stamens* dark orange with white tips. *Pistil*

dark orange with white tips. *Foliage* medium green, medium size, stems red. *Growth* semi-trailer, vigorous, bushy, free-flowering. Basket (with weights) or upright.

'Ortenburger Festival'
TOPPERWEIN/FUCHSIARAMA 1977
AFS Registration No 1432
Single
Tube red, short and thick. *Sepals* deep red, broad and outspread. *Corolla* blue violet, turing reddish on maturity, flaring and bell-shaped. *Foliage* deep green. *Growth* self-branching, bushy, upright. Small, early flowering. Bush, quarter standard. Introduced in Germany 1973.

'Other Fellow'
HAZARD 1946
Single
Tube white, medium length, medium thickness. *Sepals* white with green tips, short, narrow and held horizontal. *Corolla* pink with white shading at the base of the petals, small and compact. *Foliage* medium green, small, finely serrated leaves. *Growth* upright, bushy, self-branching and free-flowering, a very attractive, small bloom. Makes a good exhibition plant, but it requires careful watering. Bush or summer bedder.

'Pacific Grove'
NEIDERHOLZER 1947
Double
Tube crimson, medium length and thickness. *Sepals* dark crimson, long, broad and curling upwards to cover the tube. *Corolla* light Bishop's violet in the centre, outer petals pale crimson, numerous petaloids, medium-sized, loose-petalled bloom. *Foliage* medium green, medium to large-sized, serrated leaves. *Growth* upright, very vigorous, self-branching and bushy. Free-flowering. Bush.

'Pacific Queen'
WALTZ 1963
AFS Registration No 587
Double
Tube pinkish white, short and thick. *Sepals* pink with white tips. Short, broad, and held flat over the top of the corolla. *Corolla* dark rose-pink, fading to bright rose. Very full and fluffy, medium-sized bloom. *Foliage* dark green, medium-sized, very finely serrated leaves. *Growth* upright, vigorous, bushy and free-flowering. A most attractive flower, easy to grow. Bush.

'Pacquesa' (120)
CLYNE 1975
AFS Registration No 1286
Single
Tube deep red, short and of medium thickness. *Sepals* deep red with crepe undersides, reflexing. *Corolla* white with deep red veining. *Foliage* parsley green, almond-shaped. *Growth* upright, vigorous, bushy, short-jointed, very free-flowering. Excellent exhibition plant as a bush, but tends to throw semi-double flowers. *Parentage* 'Pacific Queen' × 'Sheryl Ann'.

'Pageant'
KENNETT 1960
AFS Registration No 430
Double
Tube white, shaded pale pink, short, medium thickness. *Sepals* white on top, flushed pink on the underside, broad, upturned. *Corolla* violet purple with deep coral pink marbling. Medium-sized, slightly flaring bloom. *Foliage* mid-green, medium sized leaves. *Growth* lax upright, bushy, vigorous, free-flowering. Bush or basket.

'Painted Desert'
PASKESEN 1966
AFS Registration No 664
Double
Tube white, medium length and thickness. *Sepals* white with green tips. *Corolla* bluish-purple with pink and white splashes on the petals, maturing to bright carmine. *Foliage* mid-green, medium-sized leaves. *Growth* trailer, bushy, vigorous, free-flowering. Basket. *NB* A

cultivar with the same name was introduced by Fuchsia La in 1954 but is an upright growing double with red sepals and smoky blue corolla with reddish marbling.

'Pale Beauty'
LOCKERBIE 1971
AFS Registration No 1000
Double
Tube pale pink, short, medium thickness. *Sepals* pale pink, short, fully reflexed. *Corolla* white, very full, open, large bloom. Will show tinges of pink on the corolla unless grown in the shade. *Foliage* medium green, medium to large-sized leaves. *Growth* lax, upright, vigorous, heat resistant and very free-flowering, considering the size of the blooms. Bush or basket.

'Pale Flame'
STUBBS 1978
AFS Registration No 1441
Double
Tube pale carmine, short, medium thickness. *Sepals* pale carmine rose, long, twisting and curling. *Corolla* opens claret rose to carmine rose at the base of the petals, fading to delft rose to azalea pink. Long and tightly rolled, but slightly flaring as it matures. *Foliage* dark green with red veins. New growths have red stems. *Growth* tends to be lax and trailing and with weights will basket well. Basket.

'Pallas Athene'
TRAVIS 1980
AFS Registration No 1583
Single
Tube light green (*eau de nil*), short and thick. *Sepals* light green, small. *Corolla* light green (*eau de nil*) when first open, changing to red (RHS 55A), as do the tube and sepals. Total length of the flower is from 12 mm to 15 mm. *Foliage* light green, small, ovate. Will make a good bush or pyramid. *Growth* upright, self-branching. Colours best in shaded conditions. *Parentage* Encliandra ×.

'Pamela Hutchinson'
GADSBY 1978
AFS Registration No 1483
Single
Tube pale pink, medium length and width. *Sepals* cyclamen rose with green tips. *Corolla* light hyacinth blue, medium size. *Foliage* dark green, medium to large. *Growth* vigorous, short-jointed, upright. Will make a good bush but requires regular pinching.

'Pantaloons'
FUCHSIA FOREST 1966
AFS Registration No 670
Semi-double
Tube pink, longish and bulbous, medium thickness. *Sepals* light red, long, broad and held out well. *Corolla* plum purple with petaloids hanging down below the main petals. These are of the same colour. *Foliage* medium green, medium-sized, narrow leaves. *Growth* trailer, bushy, free-flowering. Needs early pinching to form the basic shape. Easy to grow and a most unusual, attractive bloom. Bush (if well pinched).

'Papa Bleuss' (105)
TIRET 1956
Double
Tube greenish white, short and of medium thickness. *Sepals* crepe white with green tips on top, pink flush on the undersides. Short, broad and slightly upturned. *Corolla* deep violet blue, maturing to reddish purple, shaded pink at the base of the petals, very full, medium-sized bloom. *Foliage* medium green with reddish veining, medium to large-sized finely serrated leaves. *Growth* upright, though tending to be rather lax, bushy, and free-flowering. Bush, if staked, or basket.

'Papoose'
REEDSTROM 1960
AFS Registration No 423
Single
Tube scarlet, thin, medium length. *Sepals* scarlet, short, pointed and held well out.

1 *F. arborescens*

2 *F. boliviana*

3 *F. cordifolia*

4 *F. boliviana* var. *luxurians*

5 *F. boliviana* var. *luxurians* 'Alba'

6 *F. fulgens* 'Rubra Grandiflora'

7 *F. hemsleyana*

8 *F. splendens* × *F. fulgens*

9 *F. magellanica* var. *macrostema* 'Variegata'

10 *F. procumbens*

11 *F. denticulata* (*F. serratifolia*)

12 'Billy Green'

13 'Koralle'

14 'Mary'

15 'Thalia'

16 'Gartenmeister Bonstedt'

17 'Traudchen Bonstedt'

18 'Andenken an Heinrich Henkel'

19 'Genii'

20 'Rosecroft Beauty'

21 'Cloth of Gold'

22 'Autumnale' ('Burning Bush')

23 'Tricolor' (*see* 'Natural Variants')

24 'Sunray'

25 'White King'

26 'Evensong'

27 'Ting-a-Ling'

28 'Sleigh Bells'

29 'Alaska'

30 'Le Berger'

31 'Annabel'

32 'Shy Lady'

33 'Lace Petticoats'

34 'Cotton Candy'

35 'Crinoline'

36 'Trewince Twilight'

37 'Put's Folly'

38 'Sea Shell'

39 'Flirtation Waltz'

40 'Collingwood'

41 'Aintree'

42 'President Margaret Slater'

43 'Sweetheart'

44 'Celia Smedley'

45 'Bow Bells'

46 'Joy Patmore'

47 'Lye's Unique'

48 'Cascade'

49 'Buttercup'

50 'La Campanella'

51 'Joan Hurd'

52 'Mountain Mist'

53 'Blush of Dawn'

54 'Bon Accorde'

55 'Violet Bassett-Burr'

56 'King's Ransom'

57 'Auntie Jinks'

58 'Fiona'

59 'Estelle Marie'

60 'Joe Kusber'

61 'Marin Glow'

62 'Preston Guild'

63 'Isle of Mull'

64 'Rose Churchill'

65 'Jack Shahan'

66 'Grasmere'

67 'Pink Bon Accorde'

68 'Pink Quartette'

69 'Angela Leslie'

70 'Pink Fairy'

71 'Southgate'

72 'Powder Puff'

73 'Julie Horton'

74 'Leonora'

75 'Nina Wills'

76 'Pink Cloud'

77 'Mrs Lovell Swisher'

78 'Susan Travis'

79 'Pink Jade'

80 'Margaret Brown'

81 'Eleanor Leytham'

82 'Pink Marshmallow'

83 'Miss California'

84 'Bountiful'

85 'L'Arlesienne'

86 'Reverend Doctor Brown'

87 'Sophisticated Lady'

88 'White Spider'

89 'First Kiss'

90 'Ron Holmes'

91 'Curtain Call'

92 'Prince Syray'

93 'Golondrina'

94 'Kwintet'

95 'String of Pearls'

96 'Andromeda'

97 'Border Queen'

98 'Coquet Dale'

99 'Pink Darling'

100 'Alison Ewart'

101 'Coquet Bell'

102 'Alice Ashton'

103 'Symphony'

104 'Cliff's Unique'

105 'Papa Bleuss'

106 'The Tarns'

107 'Chillerton Beauty'

108 'Lena Dalton'

109 'Paula Jane'

110 'Red Spider'

111 'Trail Blazer'

112 'Empress of Prussia'

113 'Mephisto'

114 'Santa Cruz'

115 'Rufus'

116 'Marinka'

117 'Falling Stars'

118 'Andrew Ryle'

119 'Red Rum'

120 'Pacquesa'

121 'Tolling Bell'

122 'Yuletide'

123 'Lady Thumb'

124 'White Pixie'

125 'Alice Hoffman'

126 'Heidi Weiss'

127 'Snowcap'

128 'Alwin'

129 'Citation'

130 'Impudence'

131 'Bouffant'

132 'Texas Longhorn'

133 'David Alston'

134 'Liebriez'

135 'R.A.F.'

136 'Display'

137 'Loeky'

138 'Nicola Jane'

139 'Mieke Meursing'

140 'Beacon'

141 'Bland's New Striped'

142 'Queen of Derby'

143 'Dutch Mill'

144 'Blue Waves'

145 'Heidi Ann'

146 'Tristesse'

147 'Pixie'

148 'Lady Isobel Barnett'

149 'Lilac Lustre'

150 'Ridestar'

151 'Court Jester'

152 'Abbé Farges'

153 'Royal Purple'

154 'Alice Travis'

155 'Mrs Popple'

156 'General Monk'

157 'Margaret'

158 'Howlett's Hardy'

159 'Heron'

160 'Baby Blue Eyes'

161 'Brutus'

162 'David Perry'

163 'Gruss aus dem Bodethal'

164 'Tom Thumb'

165 'Tennessee Waltz'

166 'Mr A. Huggett'

167 'Cloverdale Pearl'

168 'Upward Look'

169 'Derby Imp'

170 'Swanley Gem'

171 'Peppermint Stick'

172 'Dollar Princess'

173 'Achievement'

174 'Monsieur Thibaut'

175 'Tuonela'

176 'Margaret Roe'

177 'Aurora Superba'

178 'Swanley Yellow'

179 'Bittersweet'

180 'Macchu Picchu'

181 'Ocean Beach'

182 'Mrs Rundle'

183 'Mary Poppins'

184 'Daisy Bell'

185 'Orange Crush'

186 'Tour Eiffel'

187 'Stardust'

188 'Clair de Lune'

189 'Happy Fellow'

190 'Coachman'

191 'Chang'

192 'The Doctor'

Corolla very dark purple, lighter at the base of the petals. Small compact bloom. *Foliage* medium green, small, narrow, finely serrated leaves. *Growth* bushy, self-branching, tending to be rather lax, but very free flowering and easily trained to most recognised shapes. Easy to grow. Bush, quarter standard.

'Parisienne'
FUCHSIA FOREST/CASTRO 1963
AFS Registration No 568
Double
Tube deep pink, medium length and thickness. *Sepals* deep pink, longish, broad, upturned. *Corolla* violet-blue, rosette shaped. Outer petals ruffled and overlaid pink. Medium-sized, open bloom. *Foliage* mid-green, medium-sized leaves. *Growth* lax, bushy, vigorous, free-flowering. Bush or basket.

'Parkside'
SCHNABEL 1949
Single
Tube light crimson, medium length and thickness. *Sepals* light crimson, long, broad, upturned. *Corolla* purple, bell-shaped, fading to deep rose pink. Medium to large-sized blooms. *Foliage* medium green, medium-sized leaves. *Growth* trailer, bushy, free-flowering. Basket.

'Partner'
PALKO/SOO YUN 1979
AFS Registration No 1498
Single
Tube white, thick, medium length. *Sepals* pale pink, green tips $1\frac{3}{4}$ in (4.5 cm) long. *Corolla* bishop's violet HCC 34, fading to fuchsia purple HCC 28. Petaloids attached to petals. *Stamens* pink. *Pistil* white. *Foliage* light green, 4 in (10 cm) long, with red veins, and red stems. *Growth* self-branching, bushy, natural trailer. Basket or bush. Best colour in the shade.

'Party Frock'
WALTZ 1953
Semi-double
Tube rose pink, medium length and thickness. *Sepals* rose pink, green tips, long and curling upwards to the tube. *Corolla* pastel blue, splashed rose and with slight rose veining. Medium-sized, loose-petalled bloom. *Foliage* mid-green, with reddish veins, medium-sized, serrated leaves. *Growth* upright, vigorous and free-flowering. Bush or standard.

'Party Gown'
REIMERS 1953
AFS Registration No 171
Double
Tube pink, thin, medium length. *Sepals* pink, long and recurved. *Corolla* pale blue, fading slightly as the bloom matures. Medium-sized bloom. *Foliage* medium green, medium-sized, serrated leaves. *Growth* trailer, bushy, free-flowering. Basket.

'Passing Cloud'
JONES 1959
Single
Tube pale pink, medium length and thickness. *Sepals* rose madder, long, narrow, held slightly lower than the horizontal. *Corolla* pale violet, purple, pink shades at the base of the petals, and some marbling. Very compact, medium-sized bloom. *Foliage* medium green, small to medium, heavily serrated leaves. *Growth* upright, vigorous, bushy and free-flowering. An easy cultivar to grow. Bush or summer bedder.

'Pat'
SOO YUN FIELD 1966
AFS Registration No 684
Double
Tube rose pink, short, medium thickness. *Sepals* pink, short, pointed. *Corolla* light purple, compact, small to medium-sized bloom. *Foliage* bright green, medium-sized leaves. *Growth* trailer, bushy, self-branching, free-flowering. Half-basket.

'Pathetique'
BLACKWELL 1960
Double

Tube dark red, medium length and thickness. *Sepals* dark red, short, broad and slightly reflexed. *Corolla* white with red veining, medium-sized, loose-petalled bloom. *Foliage* darkish green with red veining, medium-sized leaves. *Growth* upright, vigorous, bushy and free-flowering. Bush.

'Pat Meara'
V. MILLER 1963
Single
Tube pink, thickish, medium length. *Sepals* pink, long, broad and turned up completely against the tube. *Corolla* veronica-blue, shaded white at the base of the petals, very open, bell-shaped, long bloom. *Foliage* medium green, medium-sized, longish, finely serrated leaves. *Growth* upright, bushy, free-flowering. Not easy to grow. Bush. *Parentage* 'Citation' × 'Uncle Charlie'.

'Patricia'
WOOD 1940
Single
Tube pale salmon pink, short, thin. *Sepals* waxy salmon pink, short, pointed. *Corolla* rosy-cerise, small, compact bloom. *Foliage* medium green, small to medium-sized leaves. *Growth* upright, bushy, free-flowering. Bush or garden hardy.

'Patricia'
NEIDERHOLZER 1946
Single
Tube geranium lake, medium length and thickness. *Sepals* geranium lake, long, broad, upturned. *Corolla* magenta, large bloom. *Foliage* medium green, medium to large leaves. *Growth* upright, vigorous, bushy and free-flowering. Bush or standard.

'Patricia Ewart'
ROE 1980
Single
Tube crimson (RHS 52A), medium length and thickness. *Sepals* crimson, long, narrow and upswept, well clear of the corolla. *Corolla* rhodamine pink (RHS 63A), heavily veined crimson. Opens very tight and slender. *Foliage* medium green, medium-sized, narrow leaves, serrated. *Growth* upright, vigorous, self-branching, bushy and free-flowering. Good exhibition cultivar. Bush or quarter standard, or can be used as a summer bedder. *Parentage* 'Mipam' × 'Mieke Meursing'.

'Pattie Anderson'
HUBBARD 1967
AFS Registration No 705
Single
Tube red, medium length and thickness. *Sepals* red, long, narrow and upturned. *Corolla* royal purple, medium-sized bloom. *Foliage* medium to darkish green, medium-sized leaves. *Growth* upright, vigorous, bushy and free-flowering. Bush or standard.

'Patty Evans'
EVANS AND REEVES 1936
Double
Tube white with pale pink flush, long, medium thickness. *Sepals* waxy white with a rose-pink flush, long and narrow, curving upwards. *Corolla* white with pale pink flush and veins, medium-sized, fluffy bloom. *Foliage* mid-green with crimson veining, medium-sized, serrated leaves. *Growth* upright, bushy and free-flowering. Bush.

'Paula Jane' (109)
TITE 1975
AFS Registration No 1263
Semi-double
Tube venetian pink RHS 49C, short and of medium thickness. *Sepals* carmine rose, arching upwards, covering the tube. *Corolla* beetroot purple RHS 71A, changing to ruby red RHS 61A as the flower develops, with a pale pink flush near the sepals, opens small and compact then flares. *Foliage* medium green, slightly serrated with reddish stems. *Growth* upright, bushy, vigorous, very free-flowering. Bush. Makes a very good exhibition plant.

'Paul Cambon'
LEMOINE 1909
Double
Tube scarlet, short, thick. *Sepals* scarlet, short and broad, reflexing slightly. *Corolla* violet-purple, very full and fluffy, multi-petalled, medium-sized bloom. *Foliage* medium green with reddish veining, medium to large, serrated leaves. *Growth* upright, bushy, free-flowering, not an easy one to grow, but worth trying. Bush.

'Pauline Rawlins'
BRIDGER 1959
Double
Tube pale pink, medium length and thickness. *Sepals* pink with green tips, short, broad and curling upwards. *Corolla* bright pink, very full and fluffy, rather loose-petalled, medium-sized bloom. *Foliage* darkish green, medium-sized, finely serrated leaves. *Growth* upright, vigorous, bushy, self-branching and free-flowering. Bush or summer bedder.

'Paul Roe'
GEORGE ROE 1981
Double
Tube crimson (RHS 52A), short, medium thickness. *Sepals* crimson, narrow, slightly upturned. *Corolla* violet (RHS 83B) with crimson veins, medium-sized blooms. *Foliage* light green, medium-sized leaves. *Growth* upright, bushy, vigorous, and free-flowering. Good as an exhibition plant or summer bedder. Bush. *Parentage* 'Glyn Jones' × 'Brutus'.

'Peace'
THORNE 1968
Double
Tube white long, medium thickness. *Sepals* white with green tips, long, broad and completely turned up covering the tube. *Corolla* white, with a pale pink line on each of the petals, rather loose, medium-sized blooms. *Foliage* medium green, medium-sized, broad leaves. *Growth* upright, free-flowering. Bush. *Parentage* 'The Bride' × 'Brentwood'.

'Peachy Keen'
TIRET 1967
AFS Registration No 734
Double
Tube white, long and slender. *Sepals* white, flushed rose pink on top, deeper shade of rose on the undersides, reflexing slightly. *Corolla* salmon-orange, shaded white at the base of the petals. Longish, medium-sized bloom. *Foliage* medium green, medium-sized leaves. *Growth* natural trailer, vigorous, long-branching, free-flowering. Basket.

'Pebble Beach'
NEIDERHOLZER 1947
Single
Tube white, medium length and thickness. *Sepals* pale rose pink, long, narrow and curling upwards. *Corolla* dark solferino purple (RHS 65B) shaded white at the base of the petals, long, compact, medium-sized bloom. *Foliage* medium green, medium-sized, broad, finely serrated leaves. *Growth* natural trailer, vigorous, bushy, free-flowering. Basket.

'Pee Wee Rose'
NEIDERHOLZER 1939
Single
Tube rosy red, thin, medium length. *Sepals* rosy-red, longish, held downwards over the corolla. *Corolla* rosy red, small and very compact. *Foliage* medium green, small, serrated leaves. *Growth* lax, very vigorous, longish branches, free-flowering. Basket or summer bedder.

'Peggy Ann'
SOO YUN 1974
AFS Registration No 1183
Double
Tube light red, veined slightly darker red, short and thin. *Sepals* light red, long and narrow, curling back to the tube. *Corolla* lilac-purple fading to magenta, large, compact bloom. *Foliage* medium green, long, medium-sized leaves. Young leaves are light green with red tinge. Stems and branches turning red. *Growth* trailer, bushy, free-flowering. Basket.

'Peggy King'
WOOD 1954
Single
Tube rosy red, short, medium thickness. *Sepals* rose-red, short, broad and pointed. *Corolla* peony purple, small, compact blooms. *Foliage* medium green, small to medium-sized, serrated leaves. *Growth* upright, bushy, self-branching and free-flowering. Bush or garden hardy.

'Pelleas et Melisande'
BLACKWELL 1968
Single
Tube scarlet, short and thick. *Sepals* scarlet, short, broad and slightly upturned. *Corolla* pale pink with scarlet veining, loose-petalled, medium-sized bloom. *Foliage* medium green, medium-sized leaves. *Growth* upright, vigorous, bushy and free-flowering. Bush.

'Peloria'
MARTIN 1961
AFS Registration No 466
Double
Tube dark red, long and slender. *Sepals* dark red, short, broad and slightly upturned at the tips. *Corolla* centre petals purple, with red petals on the outside, very full, medium-sized bloom. *Foliage* medium green, long, narrow, finely serrated leaves. *Growth* upright, vigorous, bushy and free-flowering. Bush.

'Penrith Beacon'
THORNLEY 1974
AFS Registration No 1217
Single
Tube white, thin, medium length. *Sepals* white on top with green tips. Underside flushed pink, narrow slightly recurved. *Corolla* beetroot purple RHS 71A, fading to spiraea red RHS 63A, short, medium-sized, compact bloom. *Foliage* medium green, medium-sized leaves. *Growth* upright, bushy, self-branching and free-flowering. Bush. *Parentage* 'Chang' ×.

'Peper Harow'
R. HOLMES 1974
AFS Registration No 1206
Single
Tube neyron rose, medium length and thickness. *Sepals* neyron rose RHS 55A, with green tips, slightly upswept towards the tube. *Corolla* mallow purple RHS 72B, veined rose-red, and shaded rose-bengal at the base of the petals. Medium-sized, compact bloom. *Foliage* mid-green, on top, lighter green on the undersides, medium-sized, serrated leaves. *Growth* lax bush, self-branching, vigorous, free-flowering. Makes an excellent basket. Basket or bush if well pinched. *Parentage* 'Percy Holmes' × 'Lakeside'.

'Pepi'
TIRET 1963
AFS Registration No 578
Double
Tube greenish-white, medium length, rather thick. *Sepals* white, heavily flushed rosy-red, short, broad, and held over the top of the corolla. *Corolla* orange-red, with marbling of a paler shade at the base of the petals. Very compact, medium-sized bloom. *Foliage* darkish green, medium-sized, serrated leaves. *Growth* upright, vigorous, bushy, fairly free-flowering. Bush.

'Peppermint Stick' (171)
GARSON 1951
Double
Tube carmine rose, short, medium thickness. *Sepals* carmine, paler shade at the tips, broad and curling up towards the tube. *Corolla* centre petals royal purple, outer petals splashed pink, very full, medium-sized bloom. *Foliage* medium to darkish green, medium-sized, finely serrated leaves. *Growth* upright, bushy, self-branching, very free-flowering and an easy cultivar to grow. Bush.

'Percy Holmes'
R. HOLMES 1974
AFS Registration No 1207
Single
Tube azalea pink RHS 38B, thin, medium length. *Sepals* azalea pink on top with

green tips, deeper shade on the undersides, short, held well out from the tube. *Corolla* rhodonite red RHS 51A, nasturtium red at the base of the petals, compact, small to medium-sized bloom. *Foliage* mid-green, stems, veins and underside lighter green, large, serrated leaves. *Growth* lax upright, bushy, self-branching, and very free-flowering. Bush or basket. *Parentage* 'Coachman' × 'Sunset'.

'Periwinkle'
HODGES 1951
AFS Registration No 86
Single
Tube pink, medium length and thickness. *Sepals* pink, long, narrow and recurving. *Corolla* lavender blue, medium-sized, compact bloom. *Foliage* medium green, medium-sized leaves. *Growth* lax, bushy, willowy branches. Needs early pinching to shape. Bush or basket.

'Perky Pink'
ERICKSON-LEWIS 1959
Double
Tube pale pink, medium length and thickness. *Sepals* pink with green tips, short, broad and upturned. *Corolla* white, flushed pale pink and with pink veining. Very loose, medium-sized bloom. *Foliage* medium green, small to medium-sized, long and narrow, serrated leaves. *Growth* upright, self-branching, bushy, vigorous and free-flowering. An easy cultivar to grow and train. Bush.

'Perry Park'
HANDLEY 1977
AFS Registration No 1415
Single
Tube pale pink, short and thick. *Sepals* pale pink outside, deeper pink RHS 52A, inside, thick and reflexed. *Corolla* bright rose RHS 52A, shaded RHS 53D, and paler at the base, petals overlapping. *Stamens and pistil* rose pink. *Foliage* mid-green, short-jointed, strong stems. *Growth* upright, self-branching, bushy. Flowers medium-sized. Very free-flowering. Bush. Good outdoor bedder.

'Personality'
FUCHSIA-LA 1967
AFS Registration No 699
Double
Tube rose, short and thick. *Sepals* rose red, long, broad, held well out. *Corolla* bright magenta purple, fading to spiraea red, petals slightly marbled rose-pink. Large bloom. *Foliage* medium green, medium-sized, serrated leaves. *Growth* upright, free-flowering. Bush or basket.

'Petaluma'
PENNISI 1967
AFS Registration No 716
Double
Tube white, short, medium thickness. *Sepals* white on top, flushed pale pink on the undersides, broad and reflexing. *Corolla* white, very full, fluffy, medium to large blooms. *Foliage* medium green, medium to large leaves. *Growth* natural trailer, bushy, free-flowering. Basket.

'Peter Pan'
ERICKSON 1960
AFS Registration No 450
Single
Tube pink, medium length and thickness. *Sepals* pink, long, broad and upturned. *Corolla* orchid and lilac shades, medium-sized bloom. *Foliage* bright green, medium-sized leaves. *Growth* trailer, bushy, free-flowering and vigorous. Basket.

'Petite'
WALTZ 1953
AFS Registration No 168
Double
Tube white, flushed rose pink, short and thick. *Sepals* pale rose pink, deeper shade on the underside, short, broad and upturned the tube. *Corolla* lilac-blue with pale rose markings, small, rather open bloom. *Foliage* medium to darkish green, medium-sized, finely serrated leaves.

Growth upright, vigorous, bushy and free-flowering. Bush.

'Petit Point'
DE GRAAF 1976
Single
Tube rose-red, short, medium thickness *Sepals* rose red with green tips. Deeper shade on the undersides. Sepals pointed and held well out. *Corolla* deep reddish-purple, light red at the base of the petals. *Stamens* light red. *Style* rose pink. Very small bloom. *Foliage* medium green, small to medium-sized leaves. *Growth* upright, vigorous, bushy, free-flowering. Bush. *Parentage* 'Alice Hoffman' ×.

'Pharaoh'
NEED 1965
Single
Tube rose bengal, medium length and thickness. *Sepals* white with green tips and rose edges. *Corolla* plum purple, ageing to ruby-red, medium-sized, compact bloom. *Foliage* medium green, medium-sized, serrated leaves. *Growth* upright, bushy and free flowering. Bush.

'Phenomenal'
LEMOINE 1869
Double $4\frac{1}{2}$ in (11 cm)
Tube scarlet, short and thin. *Sepals* scarlet, short and broad, slightly upturned. *Corolla* indigo blue, slightly veined, carmine at base, large and full. *Foliage* medium green, medium-sized, finely serrated leaves. *Growth* vigorous, upright, bushy and free-flowering. Tall bush.

'Phoebe Travis'
TRAVIS 1956
Double
Tube rose pink, medium length and thickness. *Sepals* rose pink, broad and waxy. *Corolla* rosette parma violet, suffused rose pink short, incurved petals. Very full, medium-sized bloom. *Growth* upright, vigorous, bushy and free-flowering. An unusual coloured and very attractive flower. Bush.

'Phyllis'
BROWN 1938
Single to semi-double
Tube rosy-red, short and thick. *Sepals* rosy-red, short, broad, drooping over the corolla. *Corolla* slightly deeper shade of rose-red, compact, small to medium-sized bloom. *Foliage* medium green, small to medium-sized, serrated leaves. *Growth* upright, very vigorous, bushy and free-flowering. One of the easiest fuchsias to grow, but one which is difficult to train to a bushy shape. It will make a standard easily in one season and is certainly one for the beginner.

'Phyrne'
LEMOINE 1905
Double
Tube cerise, medium length and thickness. *Sepals* cerise, short, broad and slightly upturned. *Corolla* white with cerise veining in the centre. Outer petals heavily marked cerise and much shorter. Fluffy, open, medium-sized bloom. *Foliage* medium green, medium to large, serrated leaves with reddish veins. *Growth* upright, vigorous and bushy, but tending to send our many horizontal branches. Free-flowering and very attractive. Bush.

'Picottee'
SCHNABEL 1951
AFS Registration No 78
Semi-double
Tube phlox pink, medium length and thickness. *Sepals* phlox pink, slightly upturned. *Corolla* bishop's violet, shaded pink at the base of the petals which are deeply serrated. Medium-sized bloom. *Foliage* mid-green, medium-sized leaves. *Growth* upright, vigorous, bushy and free-flowering. Bush or standard.

'Pinafore'
KENNETT 1966
AFS Registration No 678
Double
Tube white, fainly tinged green, thin, medium length. *Sepals* white with green

tips, long, slender and turning upright to the tube. *Corolla* raspberry pink, marbled paler shades of pink, and with a paler shade at the base of the petals. Medium-sized, very loose-petalled bloom. *Foliage* medium green, small to medium-sized, longish, finely serrated leaves. *Growth* upright, lax, bushy, fairly free-flowering. Not an easy cultivar to grow, but an attractive bloom well worth trying. Bush.

'Pinch Me'
TIRET 1969
AFS Registration No 831
Double
Tube white, short, thick. *Sepals* white with green tips, long, narrow, held above the horizontal, curling slightly. *Corolla* bishop's purple, shading pink at the base of the petals, very full, but rather loose bloom. *Foliage* medium green, long, narrow, serrated leaves. *Growth* trailer, self branching, bushy, very free-flowering. A very beautiful near-blue fuchsia and one which does equally as well as a summer bedder as it does as a basket.

'Pink Ballet'
SOO YUN 1972
AFS Registration No 1043
Single
Tube pale green, short and thin. *Sepals* white with green tips. Pink flush on top and a deeper pink on the undersides. Longish, curling back over the tube. *Corolla* very pale pink with darker pink variegations on the petals. Pink veining, and green shading at the base. Petals flaring, and with numerous petaloids. Medium-sized blooms. *Foliage* darkish green, medium-sized, serrated leaves. *Growth* vigorous, bushy, very free-flowering. Bush or basket, with weights.

'Pink Ballet Girl'
Raiser and date unknown
Double
Tube cerise, medium length and thickness. *Sepals* cerise, broad, upturned. *Corolla* pink, suffused with pale blue, medium to large, compact bloom. *Foliage* medium green, medium-sized, serrated leaves. *Growth* vigorous, free-flowering, upright and bushy. Bush, standard, pyramid.

'Pink Balloon'
NEIDERHOLZER 1940
Single
Tube dark red, medium length and thickness. *Sepals* dark red, long, broad, upturned. *Corolla* white with pink veining, large, loose-petalled, bloom. *Foliage* medium green, medium to large serrated leaves. *Growth* upright, very vigorous, bushy and free-flowering. Bush or standard.

'Pink Bon Accorde' (67)
THORNE 1959
Single
Tube pale pink, short, medium thickness. *Sepals* pale pink on top, slightly darker on the undersides, green tips, reflexing slightly. *Corolla* pale rose pink, slightly paler shade at the base of the petals, small to medium-sized bloom. *Foliage* medium green, small to medium-sized, slightly serrated leaves. *Growth* upright, bushy, self-branching and free-flowering. The flowers, although held out from the foliage, are not so erect as those of the cultivar 'Bon Accorde'. A good exhibition cultivar. Bush.

'Pink Bow'
HAAG 1948
Single
Tube rose pink, short, medium thickness. *Sepals* deep rose pink, recurving, slightly. *Corolla* soft pink, short, medium-sized bloom. *Foliage* medium green, medium-sized leaves. *Growth* upright, bushy, free-flowering. Bush.

'Pink Chiffon'
WALTZ 1966
AFS Registration No 656
Double
Tube white with pale pinkish flush. *Sepals* white, flushed pale pink, green tips, recurving slightly. *Corolla* pale pink, very

full, deeper shade of pink at the base of the finely scalloped petals. *Foliage* darkish green, medium-sized, slightly serrated leaves. *Growth* natural trailer, bushy, free-flowering. A very attractive cultivar. Basket.

'Pink Cloud' (76)
WALTZ 1955
Single
Tube pink, short and thick. *Sepals* pale pink on top, deeper shade of pink on the undersides and with green tips. Long, medium width, curling upwards to the tube. *Corolla* pale pink with darker veining, rather open, medium to large bloom. *Foliage* medium green, medium-sized, serrated leaves. *Growth* upright, bushy, free-flowering. Bush.

'Pink Darling' (99)
MACHADO 1966
Single
Tube dark pink, short, medium thickness. *Sepals* pale pink on top, deeper pink on the undersides, short and broad, held horizontally. *Corolla* pinkish-lilac, lighter at the base of the petals, small, compact bloom. *Foliage* medium green, small serrated leaves. *Growth* upright, vigorous, and very free-flowering. One that needs careful pinching in its early stages to form a good plant. Bush or quarter standard.

'Pink Delight'
BROWN AND SOULES 1951
AFS Registration No 76
Double
Tube red, short and thin. *Sepals* red, short and pointed. *Corolla* soft pink with red veining, compact, medium-sized bloom. *Foliage* medium green, medium-sized leaves. *Growth* upright, bushy, free-flowering. Bush.

'Pink Delight'
WALTZ 1961
AFS Registration No 492
Double
Tube white, medium length and thickness. *Sepals* white, flushed pale pink, long and curved upwards. *Corolla* clear pink with lavender shading, overlapping petals which fade to a deeper shade as the bloom ages. Medium-sized blooms. *Foliage* dark green, small leaves. *Growth* trailer, willowy branches, vigorous and free-flowering. Basket. Sport of 'Guinevere'.

'Pink Dessert'
KUECHLER 1963
AFS Registration No 551
Single
Tube white, short and thick. *Sepals* white with a pink flush, deeper pink on the undersides, green tipped, long, narrow and reflexing. *Corolla* pale pink, very compact, medium-sized bloom. *Growth* upright, bushy, self-branching and free-flowering. Bush.

'Pink Doll'
PENNISI 1970
AFS Registration No 890
Double
Tube pale pink, medium length and thickness. *Sepals* pale pink on top, deep shade on the underside, reflexed. *Corolla* deep pink, full, medium-sized, box-shaped bloom. *Foliage* medium green, medium-sized, serrated leaves. *Growth* upright, bushy, self-branching and free-flowering. Bush.

'Pink Elegance'
NEIDERHOLZER/WALTZ 1950
AFS Registration No 54
Single
Tube light pink, medium length and thickness. *Sepals* light pink, short, broad, upturned. *Corolla* bright phlox pink, compact, medium-sized bloom. *Foliage* light green, medium-sized leaves. *Growth* trailer, vigorous, very free-flowering. Basket or half-basket.

'Pink Fairy' (70)
WALTZ 1954
Double

Tube pink, medium length and thickness. *Sepals* pink, short, broad and upturned towards the tube. *Corolla* pink with darker pink veining from the base. Full, small to medium-sized bloom. *Foliage* medium green, medium-sized, very finely serrated leaves. *Growth* upright, bushy, self-branching and very free-flowering. Bush.

'Pink Favourite or Favorite'
TIRET 1960
AFS Registration No 436
Double
Known in the USA as 'Pink Favorite', in England as 'Pink Favourite'. *Tube* pink. *Sepals* pink. *Corolla* pink. Large, all pink, bloom. *Foliage* medium green, medium to large, serrated leaves. *Growth* upright, bushy and, for its size, free-flowering. Bush.

'Pink Flamingo'
CASTRO 1961
AFS Registration No 470
Semi-double
Tube longish, pink, medium thickness. *Sepals* pink, green tips, long, broad and upturned to the tube. *Corolla* pale pink with deeper pink veining. Very loose-petalled, medium to large bloom. *Foliage* dark green with reddish veins, medium to large, serrated leaves. *Growth* lax, free-flowering but rather long-stemmed and so requiring very careful pinching and training to make a good plant. Basket or half-basket.

'Pink Galore'
FUCHSIA LA 1958
Registered 1961
AFS Registration No 469
Double
Tube pink, slender, medium length. *Sepals* pink with green tips, long and upturned. *Corolla* soft rose pink, very full and compact, medium-sized bloom. *Foliage* dark glossy green, medium-sized leaves. The young growths and leaves have reddish stems. *Growth* trailer, not particularly vigorous or free-flowering, but a most beautiful cultivar. Needs a lot of pinching to shape. Basket.

'Pinkie'
NELSON 1953
AFS Registration No 181
Double
Tube dark pink, medium length and thickness. *Sepals* dark pink, long, broad, upturned. *Corolla* shell pink, compact, medium-sized blooms. *Foliage* mid-green, medium-sized, serrated leaves. *Growth* upright, bushy, vigorous, free-flowering. Bush.

'Pink Jade' (79)
PYBEN 1958
Single
Tube pink, medium length and thickness. *Sepals* pink with green tips, reflexing. *Corolla* orchid-pink with a darker picotee edge to the petals. Medium-sized, open blooms. *Foliage* mid-green, medium-sized leaves. *Growth* lax upright, fairly free-flowering. Attractive bloom but not an easy grower. Bush.

'Pink Lady'
RYLE 1970
AFS Registration No 1169
Single
Tube deep crimson RHS 55A, long, medium thickness. *Sepals* cream, heavily flushed pink, yellowish green tips, long and narrow. *Corolla* pink with darker pink veins. Medium-sized bloom. *Foliage* mid-green, medium-sized leaves. *Growth* upright, bushy, self-branching and free-flowering. Bush. *Parentage* 'Lena Dalton' × 'Citation'.

'Pink Lemonade'
FOSTER 1974
AFS Registration No 1172
Single
Tube carmine, medium length and thickness. *Sepals* crimson, shading to carmine, with greenish-white tips, curling upwards towards the tube. *Corolla* white, veined carmine, compact, medium-sized bloom. *Foliage* lemon-yellow with magenta-rose veining, medium-sized

leaves. *Growth* upright, bushy, free-flowering. Bush.

'Pink Marshmallow' (82)
STUBBS 1977
AFS Registration No 996
Double
Tube pale pink, longish, medium thickness. *Sepals* pale pink, broad, reflexing, green tips. *Corolla* white with pink veining and with pink shading on the petals. Very large, open, loose-petalled blooms. *Foliage* light green, medium to large-sized, serrated leaves. *Growth* trailer, bushy, free-flowering. Basket or half-basket.

'Pink Pearl'
BRIGHT 1919
Double
Tube pale pink, medium length and thickness. *Sepals* pale pink, recurving slightly. *Corolla* deep rose pink, very full and compact, medium-sized bloom. *Foliage* medium green, medium-sized leaves. *Growth* upright, bushy, vigorous, and self-branching, very floriferous. Bush, standard. Named 'Pink Pearl' on account of its colour. Bright subsequently renamed it 'Mrs Friedlander' after his employer, who admired it.

'Pink Perfection'
NEIDERHOLZER 1947
Double
Tube pink, medium length and thickness. *Sepals* pink, longish, upturned. *Corolla* pale pink, medium-sized, compact bloom. *Foliage* mid-green, medium-sized, serrated leaves. *Growth* upright, bushy, free-flowering. Bush.

'Pink Phoenix'
TOMLINSON 1979
AFS Registration No 1509
Double
Tube pink, long and medium thick. *Sepals* pale pink, long, curling and twisting upwards. *Corolla* lilac, paler at the base of the petals, very full. *Foliage* medium green, medium-sized, serrated leaves. *Growth* trailer, bushy, free-flowering. Sport of 'The Phoenix'.

'Pink Poodle'
KENNETT 1964
AFS Registration No 613
Tube pale pink, medium length and thickness. *Sepals* pale pink with white tips, upturned. *Corolla* pale pink, full and compact, medium-sized bloom. *Foliage* medium green, medium-sized, serrated leaves. *Growth* lax bush, vigorous and free-flowering. Bush or basket.

'Pink Quartette' (68)
WALKER AND JONES 1949
Double
Tube very dark pink, medium length and thickness. *Sepals* reddish-pink, held well out from the corolla. *Corolla* pink, with four distinct tubes cause by the rolled petals. Medium-sized bloom. *Foliage* mid-green, medium-sized leaves. *Growth* upright, bushy, free-flowering. Bush.

'Pink Rozell'
PRENTICE 1970
AFS Registration No 884
Semi-double
Tube rose-pink, medium length and thickness. *Sepals* rose pink, upturned. *Corolla* white, lacy petals, shaded pink at the base and with pink veins. Opens up flat. Medium-sized bloom. *Foliage* mid-green, medium-sized leaves. *Growth* natural trailer, bushy and free-flowering. Vigorous. Basket.

'Pink Ruffles'
GORMAN 1970
AFS Registration No 927
Double
Tube pale cream, medium length and thickness. *Sepals* pale cream with pale green tips. *Corolla* pink with a slight lavender cast, very large and full. *Foliage* medium green, medium to large. *Growth* upright, bushy, vigorous and free-flowering. Basket or bush.

'Pink Shower'
REITER 1948
Semi-double
Tube, sepals, corolla very pale rose pink.

Foliage medium green, small. *Growth* natural trailer, good small basket cultivar with very small blooms, but free-flowering.

'Pink Slippers'
RYLE 1975
AFS Registration No 1252
Single
Tube white, faintly tinged pink, medium length and thickness. *Sepals* pale pinkish white RHS 62D, slight green tips. Sepals are held horizontally with a slight upward curve. *Corolla* pink RHS 68B, slightly veined at the base of the petals. *Anthers* lilac purple RHS 70B. *Leaves* medium green RHS 137C, medium size. *Growth* natural trailer, self-branching, bushy and free-flowering. Requires shade for best colouring. Basket, or can be trained to upright.

'Pink Temptation'
WILLS 1966
Single
Tube white, flushed pink, longish, medium thickness. *Sepals* pinkish white with green tips, long, narrow and slightly upturned. *Corolla* Tyrian rose, lighter shade at the base of the petals, medium-sized bloom. *Foliage* medium to darkish green, medium-sized, serrated leaves. *Growth* upright, bushy, free-flowering. Bush. Sport of 'Temptation'.

'Piquant'
NEIDERHOLZER 1947
Single
Tube pale rose madder, medium length and thickness. *Sepals* pale rose madder. *Corolla* pale magenta. *Foliage* medium green. *Growth* vigorous, upright, bushy, free-flowering. Bush or standard.

'Pirbright'
GEORGE ROE 1981
Single
Tube Rhodamine pink (RHS 62A), long and slender. *Sepals* rhodamine pink, longish, curling slightly upwards. *Corolla* cyclamen purple (RHS 74A), longish, compact bloom. *Foliage* medium green, medium-sized leaves. *Growth* upright, bushy, self-branching, and free-flowering, will make a very good exhibition plant, and is also useful for summer bedding. Bush, quarter standard, or summer bedder. Named after a village in Surrey. *Parentage* 'Glyn Jones' × 'Santa Barbara'.

'Pixie' (147)
RUSSELL 1960
Single
Tube carmine red, short, medium thickness. *Sepals* carmine, short, medium width, upturned. *Corolla* mauve-purple with carmine veins, slightly paler shade at the base of the petals. Small to medium-sized, compact bloom. *Foliage* yellow-green, reddish veining. Small to medium-sized, finely serrated leaves. *Growth* upright, bushy, self-branching, very free-flowering. Good exhibition cultivar. Bush or garden hardy. Sport of 'Graf Witte'.

'Pizzazz'
CASTRO 1975
AFS Registration No 1301
Single
Tube white, medium length and thickness. *Sepals* salmon to orange, medium length, upturned. *Corolla* orange pink, brighter on the edges of the petals which are overlapping. *Foliage* dark green, medium size. *Growth* semi-trailer, bushy, free-flowering and very showy. Basket or upright.

'Plenty'
GADSBY 1974
AFS Registration No 1223
Single
Tube carmine, medium length and thickness. *Sepals* neyron rose RHS 55A, held well back. *Corolla* violet purple RHS 77A, medium size. *Foliage* dark green, medium-sized, long, serrated leaves. *Growth* upright, bushy, close-jointed, very free-flowering. Blooms held out

horizontally from the plant. Excellent exhibition plant. Bush.

'Pleromet'
NEIDERHOLZER 1946
Single
Tube turkey red, long, medium thickness. *Sepals* turkey red, long, broad, upturned. *Corolla* very dark violet-purple, open, loose-petalled, medium to large bloom. *Foliage* medium green, medium-sized, serrated leaves. *Growth* upright, very vigorous, bushy, free-flowering. Bush or standard.

'Polar Sea'
REITER 1953
AFS Registration No 192
Double
Tube white, short, medium thickness. *Sepals* white, long, broad, upturned. *Corolla* imperial purple, with white marbling at the base of the petals. Very full, medium-sized bloom. *Foliage* mid-green, medium-sized leaves. *Growth* upright, vigorous, bushy, free-flowering. A very attractive bloom on a plant which needs much early pinching. Bush or standard.

'Polynesia'
TIRET 1966
AFS Registration No 686
Double
Tube salmon pink, medium length and thickness. *Sepals* salmon pink, long, upturned. *Corolla* salmon-orange, compact, medium-sized bloom. *Foliage* mid-green, medium-sized, serrated leaves. *Growth* natural trailer, bushy, free-flowering. Basket.

'Port Arthur'
STORY 1869
Double
Tube red, short and thick. *Sepals* red, short, broad and held well up from the corolla. *Corolla* purple, very full, small to medium-sized bloom. *Foliage* medium green, small to medium-sized leaves. *Growth* upright, bushy, self-branching and free-flowering. Good exhibition plant. Bush.

'Portola'
SCHNABEL 1947
Semi-double
Tube pale carmine-red, medium length and thickness. *Sepals* carmine red, held well out from the corolla. *Corolla* tyrian rose, medium-sized, compact bloom. *Foliage* mid-green, medium-sized leaves, serrated. *Growth* upright, vigorous, free-flowering. Bush or standard.

'Poseidon'
TRAVIS 1980
AFS Registration No 1584
Tube light apricot, very thin $\frac{1}{3}$ in (9 mm) in length. *Sepals* light apricot with green tips, short and small. *Corolla* apricot, short and small. *Foliage* light sage green, leaves obovate with acuminate tips. *Growth* upright, vigorous, bushy. Bush. Prefers heat for best results. Best colour develops in the shade. Seedling of *F. fulgens* 'Rubra Grandiflora'.

'Postiljon'
VAN DER POST 1975
Single
Tube white, flushed pink, short and stubby. *Sepals* creamy white, flushed rose pink, short, broad and held well out, arching over the corolla. Green tips. *Corolla* rosy-purple, white at the base of the petals. Fairly compact, small bloom. *Stamens* white. *Style* white. *Foliage* medium green, small, serrated leaves. *Growth* self-branching, bushy, vigorous, very free-flowering trailer. Early bloomer, will flower from May to October. Basket. 'La Campanella' seedling.

'Postman'
J.A. WRIGHT 1980
AFS Registration No 1605
Double
Tube dull pink, short. *Sepals* dull pink, small, and arching back. *Corolla* smoky blue, with red splashes, large. *Foliage*

medium green, large. Growth upright, vigorous, free-flowering. Bush or standard. 'Lilac Lustre' seedling.

'Powder Blue'
NEIDERHOLZER 1947
Semi-double
Tube tyrian rose, medium length and thickness. *Sepals* tyrian rose, broad, upturned. *Corolla* very pale blue, full, medium-sized bloom. *Foliage* mid-green, medium-sized leaves. *Growth* upright, vigorous, bushy, free-flowering, a very attractive pastel shaded bloom. Bush.

'Powder Puff' (72)
HODGES 1953
Double
Tube tyrian rose, medium length and thickness. *Sepals* tyrian rose, deeper shade on the undersides, recurving. *Corolla* apple blossom pink, very compact, medium-sized bloom. *Foliage* mid-green, medium-sized leaves. *Growth* natural trailer, bushy, free-flowering. Basket.

'Preference'
WALKER 1970
AFS Registration No 881
Double
Tube white, medium length and thickness. *Sepals* white, broad, upturned. *Corolla* plum purple, slightly paler shade at the base of the petals very full, medium-sized bloom. *Foliage* bright green, medium-sized leaves, serrated. *Growth* upright, bushy, vigorous and fairly free-flowering. Bush.

'Prelude'
KENNETT AND ROSS 1958
Double
Tube white, medium length and thickness. *Sepals* white, broad and curling upwards. *Corolla* the four centre petals are royal purple, the outer petals splashed pink, white, and purple, medium-sized, very full bloom. *Foliage* medium green, medium to large, serrated leaves. *Growth* trailer, vigorous, free-flowering. Requires a lot of early pinching to shape. Basket or half-basket.

Not to be confused with the following.

'Prelude'
BLACKWELL 1960
Single
Tube red, medium length and thickness. *Sepals* red, reflexing. *Corolla* magenta-purple, compact, medium-sized bloom. *Growth* upright, bushy, vigorous, free-flowering. *Foliage* medium green, medium-sized, serrated leaves. Bush.

'Prentice'
PRENTICE 1974
AFS Registration No 1178
Double
Tube white, short and of medium thickness. *Sepals* white with pink flush, long, narrow and pointed, curling back to cover the tube. *Corolla* bright rose pink, outer petals dusky rose. Medium-sized bloom with serrated petals. *Foliage* dark green, medium-sized leaves, serrated. *Growth* trailer, self-branching, bushy, vigorous and free-flowering. Basket.

'Prentice Encore'
PRENTICE 1969
AFS Registration No 852
Semi-double
Tube pink, medium length and thickness. *Sepals* pink, long, broad, upturned. *Corolla* lavender blue, shaded pink at the base of the petals. The petals overlap and gradually fade to lavender. *Foliage* mid-green, medium-sized leaves. *Growth* trailer, rather untidy and willowy, free-flowering. Basket.

'Prentice Frills'
PRENTICE 1969
AFS Registration No 853
Semi-double
Tube rosy-pink, short, medium thickness. *Sepals* rosy pink, medium length, recurving. *Corolla* shades of pink and blue on the petals, green in the centre and petals ruffled and frilly. *Foliage* medium green,

small leaves. *Growth* trailer, bushy, free-flowering. Quite an attractive frilly bloom. Basket.

'Prentice Orchid'
PRENTICE 1967
AFS Registration No 718
Tube white, medium length and thickness. *Sepals* white, longish, upturned. *Corolla* light blue changing to a pinkish orchid shade. Long petals which resemble an orchid, hence the name. Medium-sized blooms. *Foliage* light green, medium-sized leaves. *Growth* natural trailer, vigorous, bushy and free-flowering. Basket.

'Pres. E.A. Elliot'
THORNE 1962
Single
Tube carmine red, medium length and thickness. *Sepals* carmine, long, upturned. *Corolla* reddish-purple, medium-sized blooms. *Foliage* mid-green, medium-sized, serrated leaves. *Growth* upright, bushy, vigorous, free-flowering. Bush.

'President'
STANDISH 1841
Single
Tube bright red, medium length and thickness. *Sepals* bright red, long, medium width, upturned. *Corolla* rosy-purple, paler at the base of the petals. Medium-sized, fairly loose bloom. *Foliage* medium to darkish green with reddish tinge, medium-sized, serrated leaves. *Growth* upright, bushy, self-branching and vigorous. Free-flowering, easy to grow cultivar. Bush.

'President Margaret Slater' (42)
TAYLOR 1973
AFS Registration No 1119
Single
Tube white, long, slender. *Sepals* white with a distinct pink flush and green tips on top. Deeper shade on the undersides. Long, slender and curling slightly upwards. *Corolla* mauve-pink, overlaid salmon pink and lighter shading at the base of the petals. Longish, medium-sized, compact bloom. *Foliage* light to medium green, small to medium-sized, serrated leaves. *Growth* trailer, very vigorous, free-flowering. Makes a superb exhibition standard basket. Basket.

'President Roosevelt'
GARSON 1942
Double
Tube coral red, medium length and thickness. *Sepals* coral red, reflexing. *Corolla* dark violet blue, small blooms. *Foliage* dark green, medium-sized, serrated leaves. *Growth* upright, very vigorous, bushy, free-flowering. Bush or standard.

'President S. Wilson'
THORNE 1969
Single to semi-double
Tube carmine, long and slender. *Sepals* carmine with green tips. Long, slender and held well down over the corolla, turning up slightly at the tips. *Corolla* rosy carmine, long, compact, medium-sized bloom. *Foliage* medium green, medium-sized, ovate, finely serrate leaves. *Growth* trailer, vigorous, long-stemmed, free-flowering, with early pinching it can be made into an excellent basket plant, and a good show specimen. Basket.

'Preston Guild' (62)
THORNLEY 1971
AFS Registration No 1010
Single
Tube white, longish, slender. *Sepals* white, short, broad and upturned. Pink tinged when grown out of doors. *Corolla* violet blue-grey (RHS 83D), small and compact. *Foliage* medium green, small, finely serrated leaves. *Growth* upright, bushy, very free-flowering. Bush or quarter standard.

'Pretty Baby'
SOO YUN 1978
AFS Registration No 1447
Single

Tube tyrian purple, short and thin. *Sepals* tyrian purple, medium length, curving slightly upwards. *Corolla* spiraea red, RHS 63A fading to spiraea red RHS 63B. *Stamens and pistil* tyrian purple. *Foliage* light green scalloped edges. *Growth* bushy, small, upright, free-flowering. Bush.

'Pretty Grandpa'
CASTRO 1969
AFS Registration No 841
Semi-double
Tube pink, medium length and thickness. *Sepals* pink with green tips, slightly deeper shade on the underside. *Corolla* white, veined pink, medium-sized, loose-petalled, bloom. *Foliage* mid-green, medium-sized leaves. *Growth* natural trailer, bushy, free-flowering. Basket.

'Preview'
PASKESEN 1969
AFS Registration No 827
Double
Tube white, deeply flushed pink, medium length and thickness. *Sepals* white, broad, upturned. *Corolla* campanula violet, outer petals splashed white at the base, and fading to petunia purple. Medium-sized bloom. *Foliage* medium green, medium-sized, serrated leaves. *Growth* upright, bushy, free-flowering. Bush.

'Pride of Downey'
WALKER AND JONES 1949
Double
Tube crimson, medium length and thickness. *Sepals* crimson, long and twisted upwards. *Corolla* violet-purple, splashed crimson, full and compact, medium-sized bloom. *Foliage* bright green, medium-sized leaves. *Growth* upright, bushy, vigorous, free-flowering. Bush.

'Pride of the West'
JAMES LYE 1871
Single
Tube reddish pink, long and slender. *Sepals* reddish pink, long, narrow and curling upwards. *Corolla* plum red, rather open bell-shaped, long bloom. *Foliage* medium green, medium-sized, long and narrow, serrated leaves. *Growth* upright, vigorous, willowy stems. Very free-flowering. One which appeared to have lost favour until recent years and is now frequently seen, mainly in nursery displays, as it is not one which can be made into an exhibition plant. Well worth growing. Bush if well pinched in its early stages.

'Prince of Orange'
BANKS 1872
Single
Tube pale salmon pink, medium length, thick. *Sepals* pale salmon pink, short, broad and slightly upturned. *Corolla* orange-salmon, small and fairly compact. *Foliage* light to medium green, medium-sized, serrated leaves. *Growth* upright, bushy, vigorous, free-flowering. A very attractive orange shade. Bush or summer bedder.

'Prince of Peace'
DAVIS 1970
AFS Registration No 904
Double
Tube pinkish white, medium length and width. *Sepals* frosty rose pink, large and flaring. *Corolla* magenta, fading to rose as the bloom matures. *Foliage* medium green, medium to large, serrated leaves. *Growth* semi-trailer, bushy, vigorous and free-flowering. Basket or bush.

'Princess'
SOO YUN 1972
AFS Registration No 1044
Double
Tube light green, thin, $\frac{3}{4}$ in (2 cm) in length. *Sepals* white with pink flush, green tips, 2 in (5 cm) in length. *Corolla* mauve with white variegation on the outer petals, fading to pale rose pink. A few petaloids. *Foliage* medium green with serrated edges. *Growth* bushy, free-flowering, trailer or upright.

'Princess Alice'
WOAKES 1975
AFS Registration No 1316

Double
Tube crimson, medium length and thickness. *Sepals* crimson RHS 52A on top, with green tips, spinel red RHS 54B on the underside, broad and medium length. *Corolla* violet RHS 77A, marbled purple RHS 75A, and veined neyron rose. *Foliage* deep green, medium-sized. *Growth* upright, self-branching, bushy and free-flowering. Bush, standard.

'Princess Dollar'
See 'Dollar Princess' (the correct name).

'Princessita'
NEIDERHOLZER 1940
Single
Tube white, thin, medium length. *Sepals* white, slight pink flush on the underside, long, narrow and upturned. *Corolla* very dark rose pink, medium-sized, slightly open shaped bloom. *Foliage* medium to darkish green, medium-sized, serrated leaves. *Growth* trailer, bushy, vigorous, free-flowering. A very attractive bloom, one which will do well in a pot or basket. Half-basket. *Parentage* 'Fandango' × 'Mrs Rundle'.

'Princess of Bath'
COLVILLE 1968
Double
Tube carmine, short and thick. *Sepals* carmine, short, broad and curled upwards over the tube. *Corolla* very pale pink with carmine-red veining. Large, fluffy open bloom. *Foliage* darkish green with reddish veining, large, serrated leaves. *Growth* upright, bushy, very free-flowering. Bush or standard. 'Queen of Bath' seedling.

'Princess van Orange'
HAAG 1951
Single
Tube pale salmon pink, thin, medium length. *Sepals* pale salmon, long and narrow. *Corolla* rich orange shade, long, medium-sized bloom. *Foliage* dull green, medium-sized, serrated leaves. *Growth* upright, bushy, self-branching and free-flowering. Bush.

'Prince Syray' (92)
WHITE 1975
Single
Tube dawn pink, medium length and thickness. *Sepals* deeper pink, short, broad. *Corolla* vermilion, with neyron rose shading on the edges. Medium-sized, compact bloom. *Foliage* mid-green, medium-sized, serrated leaves. *Growth* upright, bushy, free-flowering. Bush. *Parentage* 'Bon Accorde' × 'Lord Lonsdale'.

'Prosperity'
GADSBY 1974
AFS Registration No 1224
Double
Tube crimson (RHS 52A) thick, medium length. *Sepals* crimson, waxy appearance, long and held well up over the tube. *Corolla* pale neyron rose RHS 56A, flushed and veined rose-red RHS 58B, small to medium-sized, compact bloom. *Foliage* darkish green, glossy, medium to large-sized, serrated leaves. *Growth* upright, vigorous, very free-flowering. Will do well as a garden hardy in sheltered areas. Bush or standard or garden hardy. *Parentage* 'Bishop's Bells' × 'Strawberry Delight'.

'Psychedelic'
CASTRO 1972
AFS Registration No 1031
Single
Tube white, medium length and thickness. *Sepals* pale pink. *Corolla* bright mertiolate-pink with orange cast in the centre, and lighter pink streaks down the petals. Petals wavy and flaring, with the edges turning darker pink on maturity. *Foliage* medium green, large leaves shiny on the upper surface, dull below. *Growth* upright, bushy, self-branching and free-flowering. Unusual colour combination. Bush.

'Puget Sound'
HODGES 1949
Double
Tube rose red, medium length and thick-

ness. *Sepals* rose red, broad, slightly upturned. *Corolla* milky white, large, full and fluffy centre petals with smaller spreading petals with pink overlay on top. *Foliage* medium green, medium-sized, serrated leaves. *Growth* semi-trailer, longish, spreading branches. Free-flowering. Half-basket.

'Pumila'
YOUNG 1821
Single
Tube crimson red, short, thin. *Sepals* crimson, short, broad, held well out. *Corolla* purple, very small, compact bloom. *Foliage* medium to darkish green, small, serrated leaves. *Growth* upright, bushy, very free-flowering, dwarf. Bush or garden hardy. Suitable for rockery planting.

'Purple Ann'
G. ROE 1977
Double
Tube red, short, medium thickness. *Sepals* red, short, pointed, reflexing. *Corolla* violet-purple, very compact, medium-sized blooms. *Foliage* medium to darkish green, medium-sized, serrated leaves. *Growth* upright, bushy, self-branching, vigorous and free-flowering. Bush. *Parentage* 'Heidi Ann' ×.

'Purple Beauty'
KUECHLER 1963
AFS Registration No 550
Double
Tube bright carmine, short, medium thickness. *Sepals* bright carmine, long and broad. *Corolla* purple, shaded red at the base of the petals. Medium-sized, bell-shaped bloom. *Foliage* bright green, medium-sized leaves. *Growth* natural trailer, bushy, free-flowering, very attractive. Basket.

'Purple Graseing'
J.A. WRIGHT 1980
AFS Registration No 1606
Semi-double
Tube red, splashed violet, longish. *Sepals* medium red with splashes, small, arching. *Corolla* light purple with splashes of pink, small. *Foliage* dark green, vigorous. *Growth* upright, vigorous, bushy. Bush. Raiser gives this as a seedling of 'Purple Gem'.

'Purple Heart'
WALKER AND JONES 1950
Double
Tube crimson, long, medium thickness. *Sepals* crimson, waxy, long, medium width. *Corolla* outer petals rose red, inner petals violet, very full, medium-sized bloom. *Foliage* medium to darkish green, medium-sized leaves. *Growth* trailer, longish, willowy branches, free-flowering. Basket or half-basket.

'Purple Sage'
HODGES 1951
AFS Registration No 87
Single
Tube crimson, medium length and thickness. *Sepals* crimson, long, broad and unswept. *Corolla* deep purple, paler at the base of the petals and with crimson veining. Saucer-shaped, opening flat. Medium-sized bloom. *Foliage* darkish green with crimson veins. Medium-sized leaves, finely serrated. Branches thin, purplish shade. *Growth* upright, lax, bushy, free-flowering. Bush or basket.

'Pussy Cat'
FELIX 1978
Single
Tube pinkish orange, long, thick. *Sepals* pinkish orange with green tips, short, pointed and held well out. *Corolla* pinkish orange, small. *Foliage* mid to darkish green, small to medium-sized, serrated leaves. *Growth* upright, fairly vigorous, free-flowering. Bush. *Parentage* 'Leverkusen' ×.

'Put's Folly' (37)
BAKER 1971
Single
Tube pale pink, long and thin. *Sepals* creamy white on top, flushed pale pink on the undersides, green tipped. Held

slightly below the horizontal, well out from the corolla. *Corolla* lilac-rose pink, pale pink at the base of the petals and a slightly darker edge. *Foliage* medium green, large finely serrated leaves. *Growth* natural trailer, very vigorous, self-branching and free-flowering. Easy to grow. Basket or half-basket.

'Quasar'
WALKER 1974
AFS Registration No 1180
Double
Tube white, medium length and thickness. *Sepals* white. *Corolla* Dauphin's violet, shaded white at the base of the petals, medium to large-sized, compact bloom. *Foliage* light green, medium-sized leaves. *Growth* trailer, bushy, vigorous and free-flowering. Basket.

'Queenie'
HAZARD
Double
Tube crimson, medium length and thickness. *Sepals* crimson, long and twisting. *Corolla* violet, splashed with crimson, medium-sized, compact bloom. *Foliage* mid-green, medium-sized, serrated leaves. *Growth* upright, bushy, free-flowering. Bush.

'Queen Lucie'
GORMAN 1970
AFS Registration No 921
Double
Tube pale rose pink, darker at the base. Medium length and thickness. *Sepals* white, pale green tips, long, reflexing. *Corolla* dark silvery-blue, shaded pink at the base of the petals. Very full, medium-sized, compact bloom. *Foliage* darkish green, medium-sized leaves. *Growth* upright, lax, bushy, free-flowering. Needs staking if required as an upright. Bush or basket.

'Queen of Bath'
COLVILLE 1966
Double
Tube darkish pink, medium length and thickness. *Sepals* darkish pink, broad, reflexing. *Corolla* pink, very full and fluffy, medium to large-sized blooms. *Foliage* medium green, medium to large leaves. *Growth* upright, vigorous, bushy, free-flowering. Bush or standard.

'Queen of Derby' (142)
GADSBY 1975
Double
Tube carmine-rose, medium length and thickness. *Sepals* carmine-rose, green tips, broad, reflexing. *Corolla* pale violet-purple, flushed pink and with pink striping on the petals. Medium-sized, compact bloom. *Foliage* mid-green, medium-sized, serrated leaves. *Growth* upright, bushy, tending to spread horizontally, free-flowering. Bush. *Parentage* 'Rose Bower' × 'Magenta Flush'.

'Queen of Hearts'
KENNETT 1961
AFS Registration No 475
Double
Tube carmine, short, medium thickness. *Sepals* carmine, long, broad, flaring. *Corolla* violet purple in the centre, surrounded by carmine pink petaloids. Very full, medium-sized bloom. *Foliage* medium green, medium-sized, serrated leaves. *Growth* trailer, bushy, very vigorous and free-flowering. Basket.

'Queen of Sheba'
MUNKNER 1962
AFS Registration No 544
Double
Tube pale carmine, medium length and thickness. *Sepals* pale carmine, long, broad and upturned. *Corolla* greyish powder-blue, with shades of flesh pink at the base of the petals. Rather open, medium-sized bloom. *Foliage* mid-green, medium-sized leaves, serrated. *Growth* upright, vigorous, bushy and free-flowering. Bush or standard.

'Queen Mary'
C.J. HOWLETT 1911
Single

Tube pale pink, thick, medium length. *Sepals* pink, white tips, long, narrow upturned. *Corolla* rose pink, maturing to deep mauve. Medium-sized, compact bloom. *Foliage* medium green, medium-sized serrated leaves. *Growth* upright, vigorous, bushy and free-flowering if grown indoors. Large flowers. Very late flowering if grown in the garden. Bush. (See also 'King George'.) Seedling from 'Mrs Marshall'.

'Queen's Corsage'
SOO YUN 1971
AFS Registration No 943
Double
Tube light red, short, medium thickness. *Sepals* light red, paler at the tips, upturned. *Corolla* royal purple, fading to light purple, with pink variegations on the outer petals. Large, compact bloom. *Foliage* medium to darkish green, with red stems. Large, serrated leaves. *Growth* semi-trailer, lax, spreading branches, vigorous, free-flowering. Basket.

'Queen's Park'
THORNE 1960
Double
Tube red, medium length and thickness. *Sepals* red, long, broad, upturned. *Corolla* parma-violet, medium-sized, compact bloom. *Foliage* mid-green, medium-sized, serrated leaves. *Growth* upright, bushy, vigorous, free-flowering. Bush.

'Query'
BASS 1848
Single
Identical to 'Chillerton Beauty' (q.v.).

'Radiance'
REITER 1946
Semi-double
Tube crimson, medium length and thickness. *Sepals* crimson, long, broad, upturned. *Corolla* tyrian rose, shaded crimson at the base of the petals and on the edges. Medium-sized, loose-petalled bloom. *Foliage* mid-green, medium-sized leaves. *Growth* upright, bushy, vigorous and free-flowering. Bush.

'Radio'
GORMAN 1970
AFS Registration No 937
Double
Tube red, medium length and thickness. *Sepals* red, long and broad and upturned. *Corolla* deep purple, shaded pink at the base of the petals. Large, full and compact bloom. *Foliage* medium to darkish green, medium-sized leaves. *Growth* upright, bushy, vigorous, free-flowering. Bush.

'R. A. F.' (135)
GARSON 1942
Double
Tube red, medium length and thickness. *Sepals* red, short, broad and reflexed to the tube. *Corolla* rose pink, veined and splashed cerise, very fluffy, medium-sized bloom. *Foliage* medium green, medium-sized, serrated leaves. *Growth* upright, bushy, rather lax, free-flowering. Bush.

'Raggardy Ann'
BRAND 1952
Double
Tube cerise, medium length and thickness. *Sepals* cerise on top, slightly darker on the undersides, long and reflexing. *Corolla* bluish-purple, fading to magenta in the centre with rose-pink petaloids. Medium-sized, rather open blooms. *Foliage* light green, medium-sized, broad, serrated leaves. *Growth* upright, lax, bushy, vigorous and free-flowering bush if well pinched.

'Raggedy Ann'
GAGNON 1965
AFS Registration No 622
Tube white, medium length and thickness. *Sepals* white, tipped chartreuse, broad, upturned. *Corolla* white, rose pink shading at the base of the petals and at the edges. Full, compact bloom. *Foliage* mid-green, medium-sized leaves. *Growth* trailer, bushy, free-flowering. Basket.

'Raintree Legend'
FOSTER 1975
AFS Registration No 1303
Semi-double
Tube white with pale phlox pink overcast, medium length and thickness. *Sepals* white, faintly tinged pale phlox pink at the base. Tips absinthe. Medium length and width, slightly upturned at the tips. *Corolla* white, compact. Medium size. *Stamens* phlox pink, pistil white. *Foliage* medium to dark green, finely serrated. *Growth* upright, bushy, self-branching. Very free-flowering. Bush or standard. Develops best colour in the shade.

'Rambler'
PLUMMER 1953
Single
Tube red, medium length and thickness. *Sepals* red, long, broad and recurving. *Corolla* rosy lilac, long, rather loose-petalled bloom. *Foliage* medium green, medium-sized, serrated leaves. *Growth* very vigorous, upright, bushy and free-flowering. Will need early and careful pinching to form a decent bush. Bush or standard.

'Rambling Rose'
Tube pale pink, flushed green, medium length and thickness. *Sepals* pink with green tips, deeper shade of pink on the undersides, long broad and curling upwards over the tube. *Corolla* pink, deeper pink petaloids. Loose-petalled, medium-sized bloom. *Foliage* medium green, medium-sized, longish, serrated leaves. *Growth* natural trailer, vigorous, bushy and very free-flowering. Will make a lovely basket with careful pinching. Bush.

'Raspberry'
TIRET 1959
AFS Registration No 386
Double
Tube pinkish white, medium length and thickness. *Sepals* pinkish white, long, narrow and upturned. *Corolla* raspberry-rose, medium to large, compact and full blooms. *Foliage* medium green, medium-sized leaves. *Growth* upright, bushy, free-flowering. Bush.

'Ravensbarrow'
THORNLEY 1972
AFS Registration No 1063
Single
Tube red RHS 53C, short, medium thickness. *Sepals* red RHS 53C. *Corolla* pansy, very dark—almost black on opening but fading slightly as the bloom ages. *Foliage* dark green, small, serrated slightly. *Growth* upright, bushy and vigorous, free-flowering. Bush. Excellent exhibition plant. *Pollen parent* 'Gruss aus dem Bodethal'.

'Ray Gagnon'
ANN'S GARDENS/GAGNON 1966
AFS Registration No 658
Double
Tube bright red, medium length and thickness. *Sepals* bright red, long, narrow, upswept. *Corolla* rosy red, medium-sized, bell-shaped bloom. *Foliage* bright, shiny green. Medium-sized leaves. *Growth* upright, lax, bushy, free-flowering. Bush. Needs careful pinching.

'Razzle Dazzle'
MARTIN 1965
AFS Registration No 630
Double
Tube pale pink, thin, medium length. *Sepals* pink, long, broad, and curled completely to the tube. *Corolla* dark purple, darker still on the edges of the petals. Very full, but rather loose-petalled, medium-sized bloom. *Foliage* medium green, medium-sized leaves. *Growth* very vigorous, self-branching, bushy trailer. Free-flowering. Basket.

'Rebecca'
SINGLETON 1980
AFS Registration No 1580
Single
Tube eau de nil (pale green) short and thick. *Sepals* white, slightly recurving. *Corolla* white, saucer-shaped, large.

Foliage medium to light green. *Growth* upright, bushy and free-flowering. Can be trained to most forms. Seedling of 'Ting-a-Ling', which it resembles.

'Redando'
HAAG 1948
Single
Tube red, longish, medium thickness. *Sepals* red, long, narrow and recurving. *Corolla* rose pink with a darker stripe on each of the petals. Medium-sized, loose blooms. *Foliage* mid-green, medium-sized leaves. *Growth* bushy, tending to be rather lax, free-flowering. Half-basket or bush if staked.

'Red Baron'
CASTRO 1972
AFS Registration No 1032
Semi-double
Tube light green to white when mature, short and thin. *Sepals* white, curling back to the tube. *Corolla* bright red with white marbling, loose petals. Short petaloids of the same colour as the corolla. *Foliage* medium green, small to medium size. *Growth* natural trailer, self-branching, vigorous and free-flowering. Basket or upright.

'Red Buttons'
HODGES 1961
AFS Registration No 481
Single
Tube red, thick, medium length. *Sepals* orange red, long and pointed, held well out from the corolla. *Corolla* orange red, medium-sized bloom. *Foliage* mid-green, medium-sized leaves. *Growth* upright, bushy, vigorous and free-flowering.

'Red Dangles'
PANCHARIAN 1975
AFS Registration No 1293
Single
Tube cardinal red, medium length and thickness. *Sepals* carmine red, narrow. *Corolla* scarlet red at the base with red veins, blending to bluish red. Compact and stiff. *Stamens and pistil* red. *Anthers and stigma* pink. *Foliage* dark green on top, lighter undersides, ovate, slightly serrated. *Growth* vigorous, self-branching, upright, bushy, very free-flowering. Bush or standard.

'Red Devil'
GORMAN 1970
AFS Registration No 938
Double
Tube crimson, medium length and thickness. *Sepals* crimson red, broad, upturned. *Corolla* opens very dark purple and matures to crimson red, very full, compact bloom. *Foliage* medium to darkish green with red stems and veins. Medium-sized serrated leaves. *Growth* upright, bushy, vigorous, free-flowering. Bush or standard.

'Red Flame'
SOO YUN 1967
AFS Registration No 728
Semi-double
Tube reddish-white, medium length and thickness. *Sepals* reddish-white, long, broad, upturned. *Corolla* pale lavender fading to flame-red. Medium to large-sized, rather loose-petalled bloom. *Foliage* dark green, medium-sized, serrated leaves. *Growth* semi-trailer, bushy, vigorous, free-flowering. Bush or half-basket.

'Red Jacket'
WALTZ 1958
Double
Tube bright red, medium length and thickness. *Sepals* bright red, long, upturned. *Corolla* white, large, compact, very full bloom. *Foliage* medium to darkish green, medium-sized leaves. *Growth* trailer, bushy, vigorous, free-flowering. A very attractive flower. Basket.

'Red Knight'
TIRET 1967
AFS Registration No 735
Double
Tube red, medium length and thickness. *Sepals* red, long and broad, upturned.

Corolla red, very full, compact, medium to large-sized bloom. *Foliage* dark green, medium size, serrated leaves. *Growth* trailer, bushy, vigorous, free-flowering. Basket or half-basket.

'Red Petticoat'
SOO YUN 1978
AFS Registration No 1451
Single
Tube rose bengal, long medium thickness. *Sepals* rose bengal, $\frac{7}{8}$ in (22 mm) long, with pale green tips. *Corolla* cyclamen purple RHS 74A, $\frac{5}{8}$ in (16 mm) long, fading to fuchsia purple at the base. *Stamens and pistil* spiraea red with plum purple tips. *Foliage* light green, with scalloped edges, $2\frac{3}{8}$ in (60 mm) long by $1\frac{3}{8}$ in (35 mm) wide. *Growth* vigorous, tall growing upright, bush with early pinching.

'Red Princess'
SOO YUN 1973
AFS Registration No 1097
Double
Tube white, thin, medium length. *Sepals* white slightly flushed pink on top, deeper pink shade on the undersides. *Corolla* pale lavender to orchid, variegated pink at the base of the petals. Large, compact blooms. *Foliage* medium green, medium-sized leaves with red stems and serrated. *Growth* trailer, bushy, self-branching and very free-flowering. Basket.

'Red Ribbons'
MARTIN 1960
Double
Tube red, short, medium thickness. *Sepals* red, long and narrow, curling up towards the tube. *Corolla* white, very compact. Medium-sized bloom. *Foliage* mid-green, medium-sized leaves. *Growth* lax, bushy, fairly vigorous, free-flowering. Needs early pinching if it is to be grown successfully as a bush. Bush or half-basket.

'Red Riding Hood'
HAZARD
Double
Tube red, medium length and thickness. *Sepals* red, long, broad, upturned. *Corolla* red, medium-sized, compact blooms. *Foliage* medium to darkish green, medium-sized blooms. *Growth* upright, bushy, vigorous, free-flowering. Bush.

'Red Rover'
HAZARD
Single
Tube red, medium length and thickness. *Sepals* red, longish, upturned. *Corolla* deep purple, reddish at the base of the petals. Medium-sized bloom. *Foliage* medium green, medium-sized, serrated leaves. *Growth* upright, bushy, free-flowering. Bush.

'Red Rum' (119)
HOBSON 1977
Double
Tube bright red, medium length and thickness. *Sepals* bright red, broad, recurving slightly. *Corolla* white. Medium-sized bloom. *Foliage* dark green with red veins, medium-sized, serrated leaves. *Growth* upright, self-branching, bushy and free-flowering.

'Red Sails'
HODGES 1947
Semi-double
Tube cardinal red, medium length and thickness. *Sepals* cardinal red, long and twisting. *Corolla* pink, medium-sized, loose-petalled blooms. *Foliage* mid-green, medium-sized, serrated leaves. *Growth* upright, very vigorous, bushy and free-flowering. Bush.

'Red Shadows'
WALTZ 1962
AFS Registration No 525
Double
Tube crimson, medium length and thickness. *Sepals* crimson, longish, broad and upturned. *Corolla* deep burgundy purple, ageing to ruby red. Medium to large, fluffy and compact bloom. *Foliage* mid-green, medium-sized leaves. *Growth* trailer, bushy, vigorous and free-flowering. Basket.

'Red Spider' (110)
V. REITER JR 1946
Single
Tube crimson, long and slender. *Sepals* crimson, long, narrow and curling upwards. *Corolla* rose madder, deeper on the edges of the petals. Medium-sized bloom. *Foliage* medium green, small to medium-sized, serrated leaves. *Growth* trailer, vigorous, long-branching, free-flowering. Needs some careful pinching in its early stages to shape. Basket or half-basket.

'Red Star'
CROCKETT 1969
AFS Registration No 855
Double
Tube cherry red, medium length and thickness. *Sepals* cherry red on top, paler on the undersides. Held well out. *Corolla* tyrian purple, veined claret-rose. Medium-sized, star-shaped blooms. *Foliage* medium green with red veins, medium-sized leaves. *Growth* upright, vigorous, bushy and very free-flowering. Bush.

'Red Wing'
TIRET 1949
Single
Tube red, medium length and thickness. *Sepals* red, long, narrow and upturned. *Corolla* plum purple, medium-sized, loose-petalled bloom. *Foliage* mid-green, medium-sized, serrated leaves. *Growth* trailer, bushy, vigorous, free-flowering. Half-basket.

'Regal'
Raiser not known
Single
Tube reddish pink, long, medium thickness. *Sepals* reddish-pink, long and narrow, reflexing. *Corolla* rosy purple, long and compact, medium-sized bloom. *Foliage* dark green with reddish veins, medium-sized leaves. *Growth* upright, very vigorous, free-flowering. Difficult to train to shape and best planted in the ground in the greenhouse where it will soon make a very large plant.

'Regal Robe'
ERICKSON/LEWIS 1959
Double
Tube crimson red, medium length and thickness. *Sepals* crimson, longish and broad, reflexing. *Corolla* dark purplish-violet, shaded reddish at the base of the petals and medium-sized bloom. *Foliage* mid-green with reddish veins, medium-sized, finely serrated leaves. *Growth* upright, bushy, self-branching and very free-flowering. Bush.

'Rene'
RYLE 1975
AFS Registration No 1253
Single
Tube crimson, short and thick. *Sepals* crimson RHS 52A, horizontal with slight upward curve, small. *Corolla* violet RHS 87A, shaded pink at the base with red veins, fading to roseine purple RHS 68A. Neat small petals. *Anthers* ruby red. *Foliage* lettuce green RHS 144A, large, spear shaped, serrate. *Growth* upright, self-branching, bushy and free-flowering. Bush/standard.

'Reverend Doctor Brown' (86)
TAYLOR 1973
AFS Registration No 1118
Double
Tube pale pink, short, medium thickness. *Sepals* pale pink on top with green tips, darker shade of pink on the undersides. Reflexing completely to cover the tube. *Corolla* white with pink veins, rather loose-petalled, medium-sized. Bloom. *Foliage* medium green, medium to large, finely serrated. leaves. *Growth* upright, vigorous, self-branching, and bushy. Very free flowering. Bush. *Parentage* 'Sophisticated Lady' × 'Citation'.

'Reverie'
REITER JR 1951
AFS Registration No 84
Double

Tube pale tyrian rose, medium length and thickness. *Sepals* tyrian rose, longish, broad and recurving. *Corolla* tyrian rose, compact, medium-sized bloom. *Foliage* mid-green, small, serrated leaves. *Growth* upright, bushy, self-branching and free-flowering. Bush.

'Rhapsody'
FUCHSIA FARMS 1958
AFS Registration No 330
Double
Tube bright red, medium length and thickness. *Sepals* bright red, long, broad and upturned. *Corolla* dark purple, outer petals marbled rose pink. Medium to large, very full and compact blooms. *Foliage* mid-green, medium-sized, serrated leaves. *Growth* upright, rather lax, bushy and free-flowering. Bush, if staked, or half-basket.

'Rhapsody'
BLACKWELL 1959
Double
Tube bright red, medium length and thickness. *Sepals* bright red, long, broad, reflexed. *Corolla* white, fairly loose-petalled, medium-sized bloom. *Foliage* medium green, medium-sized, serrated leaves. *Growth* upright, bushy, self-branching and free-flowering. Bush.

'Rhythmic'
PLUMMER 1953
Single
Tube dark red, medium length and thickness. *Sepals* dark red, long, broad, held well out. *Corolla* deep maroon. Fairly loose, medium-sized bloom. *Foliage* medium green, medium-sized leaves. *Growth* upright, very vigorous, bushy, free-flowering. Bush or standard.

'Ricky'
EVANS AND REEVES 1953
Double
Tube flesh pink, medium length and thickness. *Sepals* flesh pink on top, slightly deeper shade on the undersides, broad and upturned. *Corolla* pure white, compact, medium-sized bloom. *Foliage* bright green, medium-sized, serrated leaves. *Growth* upright, bushy, vigorous and free-flowering. Bush.

'Ridestar' (150)
BLACKWELL 1959
Double
Tube scarlet, thin, medium length. *Sepals* scarlet, short and broad, reflexing. *Corolla* deep lavender blue with cerise veining and shaded pink at the base of the petals. Very full, fluffy, medium-sized bloom. *Foliage* medium green with reddish veins, small to medium-sized, serrated leaves. *Growth* upright, bushy, self-branching and very free-flowering. An easy cultivar to grow. Bush.

'Rigoletto'
BLACKWELL 1967
Double
Tube deep red, short, medium thickness. *Sepals* deep red, short, broad and recurved. *Corolla* light purple, paler at the base of the petals. Medium-sized, compact blooms, with frilled edges to the petals. *Foliage* mid-green, medium sized, serrated leaves. *Growth* upright, bushy, vigorous, free-flowering. Bush.

'Ringwood Market'
CLYNE 1976
Semi-double
Tube neyron rose, short and of medium thickness. *Sepals* neyron rose, short and broad, held well out. *Corolla* powder-blue, with pink shading at the base of the petals, fading to lilac as the bloom ages. Medium-sized, compact blooms. *Foliage* mid-green, small to medium-sized leaves. *Growth* upright, bushy, vigorous, free-flowering. Bush. *Parentage* 'Tristesse' × 'Susan Ford'.

'Robert Hall'
GADSBY 1970
AFS Registration No 871
Single
Tube neyron rose, thick, medium length.

Sepals neyron rose, long, broad, held well out from the corolla. *Corolla* magenta rose, flushed neyron rose, and slightly paler at the base of the petals. Medium-sized bloom. *Foliage* mid-green, medium-sized serrated leaves. *Growth* lax upright, bushy, vigorous, free-flowering. Bush or half-basket. *Parentage* 'Pink Galore' × 'Athela'.

'Robin'
KENNETT 1967
AFS Registration No 741
Double
Tube white, medium length and thickness. *Sepals* white, long, broad and upturned. *Corolla* dianthus purple, fading with age to bright red, fairly full and compact, medium to large-sized bloom. *Foliage* mid-green, medium-sized leaves, slightly serrated. *Growth* lax upright, bushy, vigorous and free-flowering. Needs early pinching to form a good bush. Bush or basket.

'Rolla'
LEMOINE 1913
Double
Tube pale pink, short, medium thickness. *Sepals* pale pink, short, broad. *Corolla* pure white, tinged pink at the base of the petals. *Foliage* light green, medium-sized leaves. *Growth* vigorous, habit, upright, bushy and free-flowering. Standard/pyramid, or bush.

'Romance'
PASKESEN 1967
AFS Registration No 701
Double
Tube white, greenish tinged, short and thick. *Sepals* white on top, green tips. Undersides faintly flushed pink. Long and broad, curled upwards to the tube. *Corolla* pale violet blue in the centre, outer petals with pink markings, very full and fluffy, medium-sized bloom. *Foliage* medium green, long and narrow, medium-sized, serrated leaves. *Growth* vigorous, self-branching, bushy, free-flowering. Trailer. Basket.

'Rondo'
HANDLEY 1973
AFS Registration No 1133
Single
Tube pink (RHS 52D), short and thick. *Sepals* pink (RHS 52C), long, narrow, recurving. *Corolla* pink RHS 52A, to cerise RHS 57B, and with red edges to the petals which overlap. Long, bell-shaped bloom. *Foliage* mid-green, medium-sized leaves. *Growth* upright, bushy, free-flowering. Bush or standard.

'Ron Ewart'
GEORGE ROE 1981
Single
Tube white, short and thick. *Sepals* white, short and broad, turning backwards. *Corolla* rose bengal RHS 57C, shaded white at the base of the petals, small, compact bloom. *Foliage* mid-green, small to medium-sized leaves. *Growth* upright, bushy, compact, self-branching and free-flowering. Will make a very good exhibition plant. Bush or summer bedder. *Parentage* 'Bobby Shaftoe' × 'Santa Barbara'.

'Ron Holmes' (90)
R. HOLMES 1978
AFS Registration No 1462
Single
Tube pale pink, medium length and width. *Sepals* pale pink on the outside, carmine rose, RHS 52C inside, medium length and width, held at right angles to the tube with the tips upturned slightly. *Corolla* mandarin red (RHS 40B) overlaid carmine RHS 25B, round, medium size. *Foliage* medium green, cordate and serrated. *Growth* vigorous, self-training, bushy, upright. Standard or bush with early pinching.

'Ron Honour'
VFN 1969
Single
Tube red, medium length and thickness. *Sepals* red, short, broad and upturned. *Corolla* violet-purple with red veins.

Compact, rolled petals. *Foliage* mid-green, with reddish veins, medium-sized, finely serrated leaves. *Growth* upright, vigorous, bushy and free-flowering. Bush or summer bedder.

'Ron's Pet'
R. HOLMES 1973
AFS Registration No 1208
Single
Tube pale salmon pink, long and slender. *Sepals* pale salmon, short, narrow and held well out, green tips. *Corolla* salmon-orange, small and compact. *Foliage* light green, small and serrated. *Growth* upright, bushy and free-flowering. Bush.

'Rosabell'
GADSBY 1968
Registered 1971
AFS Registration No 970
Single
Tube white, long and slender. *Sepals* pale neyron rose, long, narrow and curled back to the tube. *Corolla* imperial purple, shading to phlox pink, paler at the base of the petals. Medium to large bloom. *Foliage* mid-green, medium-sized, serrated leaves. *Growth* lax upright, bushy, free-flowering, needs careful pinching to form a good shape. Bush or half-basket. *Parentage* 'Upward Look' ×.

'Rosaly Rooney'
NEIDERHOLZER
Single
Tube white, long and slender. *Sepals* white, long, narrow and recurving. *Corolla* orange-red, medium-sized, serrated leaves. *Growth* trailer, bushy, vigorous, free-flowering. Half-basket.

'Rosana'
NEIDERHOLZER 1946
Semi-double
Tube pale rose pink, medium length and thickness. *Sepals* rose pink, long, broad and recurving. *Corolla* solferino purple, large, loose-petalled bloom. *Foliage* mid-green, medium-sized, serrated leaves. *Growth* upright, very vigorous, free-flowering, needs careful pinching in its early stages to make a compact plant, otherwise it is very rampant. Bush or standard.

'Rose Aylett'
STRUTT 1897
Tube pale carmine red, medium length and thickness. *Sepals* pale carmine, broad, reflexing slightly. *Corolla* lilac-blue, compact, medium-sized blooms. *Foliage* upright, vigorous, bushy and fairly free-flowering. A nice old cultivar, easy to grow. Bush.

'Rose Bower'
GADSBY 1973
AFS Registration No 1124
Double
Tube crimson, medium length and thickness. *Sepals* carmine with green tips. Broad and waxy, held well out. *Corolla* lilac-purple shading to cyclamen purple and flushed crimson. Medium-sized, compact blooms. *Foliage* mid-green, medium-sized, serrated leaves. *Growth* upright, self-branching, bushy, free-flowering. Bush. *Parentage* 'La Fiesta' ×.

'Rose Bradwardine'
COLVILLE 1958
Double
Tube dark rose pink, short, medium thickness. *Sepals* dark rose pink, short, broad, held well over the corolla and turning up at the tips. *Corolla* lavender with splashes of orchid pink. A very full and fluffy medium-sized bloom. *Foliage* mid-green, medium-sized leaves, finely serrated. *Growth* upright, vigorous, bushy, self-branching and very free-flowering. Easy to grow. Bush or standard.

'Rosecroft Beauty' (20)
EDEN 1969
Semi-double
Tube crimson, short, medium thickness. *Sepals* crimson, short, broad, drooping over the corolla. *Corolla* white, with crimson veining, small, compact bloom.

Foliage pale green, with edges of cerise and cream, small leaves. *Growth* upright, bushy, free-flowering. Not a fast grower, and prone to red spider. Bush.

'Rosedale'
GADSBY 1973
AFS Registration No 1068
Double
Tube carmine red, short and thick. *Sepals* carmine on top with green tips, crimson on the underside, broad. *Corolla* magenta-rose, edged tyrian purple, bell-shaped. *Foliage* medium green. *Growth* upright, bushy, free-flowering. Flowers held horizontal. Bush. Seedling of 'Upward Look'.

'Rose Dawn'
EDWARDS 1948
Single
Tube rose pink, short, medium thickness. *Sepals* rose pink, short, broad, held well out. *Corolla* solferino purple, medium-sized, compact bloom. *Growth* trailer, bushy, vigorous and free-flowering. *Foliage* mid-green, medium-sized, serrated leaves. Half-basket.

'Rose Churchill' (64)
Raiser unknown
Identical to 'Winston Churchill' except for the corolla which is rose-pink. Foliage and growth habit similar. Bush.

'Rose Mauve'
SCHNABEL 1951
AFS Registration No 80
Double
Tube neyron rose, medium length and thickness. *Sepals* neyron rose, short, broad and reflexed. *Corolla* clear rosy mauve, very full, medium-sized bloom. *Foliage* mid-green, medium-sized, serrated leaves. *Growth* upright, bushy, self-branching and free-flowering. Easy to grow. Bush.

'Rose of Castile'
BANKS 1855
Single
Tube white, greenish tinged, short and thick. *Sepals* white, green tipped. Slight pinkish flush on the undersides. Short, pointed and held well out. *Corolla* reddish-purple, shaded white at the base of the petals and with a white streak in the centre of each petals. Small, compact bloom. *Foliage* medium green, small, very finely serrated leaves. *Growth* upright, bushy, self-branching and vigorous, very free-flowering. Excellent exhibition variety. Bush or standard.

'Rose of Castile' (improved)
LANE 1871
Single
Tube pale pink, short, medium thickness. *Sepals* pink on top with green tips, deeper shade of pink on the undersides. Broad, held well out over the corolla. *Corolla* opens reddish-violet, with deep pink veins, ageing to reddish purple. Fairly compact, medium-sized bloom. *Foliage* light to medium green, small to medium-sized, serrated leaves. *Growth* upright, bushy, vigorous and very free-flowering. An easy cultivar to grow. Bush, standard, or summer bedder.

'Rose of Denmark'
BANKS 1864
Single
Tube white, slender, medium length. *Sepals* white on top, faintly flushed pink and with green tips. The undersides are a deeper pink. Short, broad and upturned. *Corolla* rosy-purple, with rose pink veins, and shaded pink at the base of the petals. Medium-sized, rather loose bloom. *Foliage* mid-green, medium-sized, longish leaves, slightly serrated. *Growth* upright, bushy, rather lax, free-flowering. Needs careful pinching to train it to shape. Bush.

'Rose of Encinal'
REIMERS 1953
AFS Registration No 172
Double
Tube dark pink, medium length and

thickness. *Sepals* dark pink, short and broad. *Corolla* mottled shades of rose, lavender and magenta, outer petals shaded deeper colour at the base. Medium to large, compact bloom. *Foliage* medium to darkish green, medium-sized leaves. *Growth* upright, bushy, rather stiff-branched, free-flowering. Bush.

'Rose Phenomenal'
Raiser and date unknown
Double
Tube scarlet, short, medium thickness. *Sepals* scarlet, long, broad and reflexing. *Corolla* mauve, veined cerise, petals open and spreading. Very large flower, circumference up to 8 in (20 cm). *Foliage* light green, medium to large leaves. *Growth* vigorous, and compact, upright, bushy and free-flowering. Pyramid/standard.

'Rose Red'
HAZARD
Single
Tube pink, medium length and thickness. *Sepals* pink, longish, recurving. *Corolla* pink, open, medium-sized bloom. *Foliage* mid-green, medium-sized leaves. *Growth* upright, bushy, free-flowering. Bush.

'Rose Reverie'
CROCKETT 1969
AFS Registration No 856
Double
Tube cream, medium length and thickness. *Sepals* neyron rose RHS 55B on top with green tips, slightly deeper shade of neyron rose on the undersides. Broad, upturned. *Corolla* Solferino purple RHS 65B, flushed and veined slightly darker shades of solferino purple and rose madder, Compact, medium to large bloom. *Foliage* dark green, long and pointed, medium-sized leaves. *Growth* upright, bushy and free-flowering. Bush.

'Rosette'
NEIDERHOLZER 1947
Double
Tube rose madder, medium length and thickness. *Sepals* dark rose madder, recurving. *Corolla* dark rhodamine purple, medium-sized, compact bloom. *Foliage* medium to darkish green, medium-sized leaves. *Growth* upright, bushy, free-flowering. Fairly vigorous. Bush.

'Rosie O'Grady'
HODGES 1960
AFS Registration No 453
Double
Tube white, flushed pink, medium length, rather thick. *Sepals* white, flushed pink, green tips on top, undersides a deeper shade of pink. *Corolla* soft rose-pink, very full and compact, medium-sized bloom. *Foliage* mid-green, medium-sized leaves, serrated. *Growth* trailer, bushy, vigorous, free-flowering. Basket.

'Rosy Frills'
HANDLEY 1979
AFS Registration No 1503
Double
Tube greenish-white, medium length and thickness. *Sepals* short and broad, pale pink RHS 49C, inside, very pale pink outside. Pale yellow green tips. *Corolla* deep rose RHS 55A, and 58C, edged red RHS 46D, outer petals streaked salmon RHS 43D. Very full and compact. *Foliage* dark green with red stems and veins. *Growth* spreading, free-flowering. Good basket cultivar.

'Rothbury Beauty'
RYLE 1978
AFS Registration No 1474
Double
Tube rose, short, medium thickness. *Sepals* claret rose RHS 50A, with deep pink shading towards the tube. Short, and held horizontally. *Corolla* light purple RHS 73B, with deep pink markings giving a flecked appearance. *Stamens* cardinal red RHS 53A. *Foliage* medium green, medium-sized, red stems. *Growth* self-branching, bushy and vigorous, upright growth. Very free-flowering. Bush or standard.

'Rough Silk'
BAKER 1970
Single
Tube pale pink, long, medium thickness. *Sepals* pale pink with green tips. Long, slender and curling upwards. *Corolla* deep wine red, shaded pink at the base of the petals. Long, fairly compact bloom. *Foliage* light to medium green, medium-sized, serrated leaves. *Growth* natural trailer, vigorous, bushy, self-branching and very free-flowering. A very attractive flower, but difficult to keep the plant in check as it is so vigorous. Basket or half-basket.

'Roulette'
REITER 1950
AFS Registration No 60
Double
Tube white, flushed pale rose pink, medium length and thickness. *Sepals* white, flushed rose pink on top, deeper rose on the undersides. *Corolla* rose madder, marbled pale rose pink at the base of the petals. Medium, compact bloom. *Foliage* mid-green, medium-sized leaves, serrated. *Growth* lax, bush, vigorous, free-flowering. Bush or half-basket.

'Roxan Rae'
VEE JAY 1979
AFS Registration No 1489
Single
Tube red, short. *Sepals* red, with a darker line down the middle and tipped reddish purple. *Corolla* very dark purple, almost black, with red at the base of the petals. Small. *Foliage* longish, dark green. *Growth* self-branching, trailing habit, free-flowering. Small blooms and foliage, but will make a good basket.

'Royal Crown'
MARTIN 1960
AFS Registration No 446
Double
Tube white, medium length and thickness. *Sepals* waxy white, long, broad, upturned. *Corolla* deep purple in the centre with the outer edges pinkish white, fairly large, compact bloom. *Foliage* dark green, medium to large, serrated leaves. *Growth* upright, rather lax, vigorous, free-flowering. Bush or basket.

'Royal Flush'
HODGES 1952
Single
Tube deep red, short, medium thickness. *Sepals* deep red, long, broad and upturned. *Corolla* royal purple, heavily veined pink, and with flesh pink shading at the base of the petals. Medium-sized bloom which opens flat. *Foliage* mid-green, medium-sized leaves. *Growth* upright, vigorous, bushy, free-flowering. Bush.

'Royal Jester'
SOO YUN 1969
AFS Registration No 847
Double
Tube crimson red, short, medium thickness. *Sepals* crimson red, short, broad, upturned. *Corolla* variegated crimson and ruby red, a most unusual shade. Medium, compact bloom. *Foliage* bright green, medium to large leaves. *Growth* lax, bushy, free-flowering. Needs early pinching and staking if grown as a bush. Bush or half-basket.

'Royal Orchid'
HODGES 1962
AFS Registration No 543
Single
Tube white, long, medium thickness. *Sepals* white, flushed pale carmine. Long, broad and spreading. *Corolla* shades of orchid and blue, fading to deep wine purple with age and flaring. Medium to large, bell-shaped bloom. *Foliage* mid-green, medium-sized, serrated leaves. *Growth* trailer, bushy, vigorous and very showy. Free-flowering. Basket.

'Royal Pink'
SOO YUN 1974
AFS Registration No 1184
Double
Tube light pink with dark pink veins,

long, medium thickness. *Sepals* light pink on top, darker pink on the undersides, long and broad, flaring straight out and curving at the tips. *Corolla* amaranth pink, very full, compact bloom. *Foliage* dark green, large, rounded leaves with red stems and branches. *Growth* trailer, bushy, vigorous and free-flowering. Basket.

'Royal Purple' (153)
LEMOINE 1896
Single to semi-double
Tube deep cerise, short and thick. *Sepals* cerise, broad, held slightly above the horizontal. *Corolla* purple, veined red, and slightly paler at the base of the petals. Compact, medium-sized bloom. *Foliage* medium green, medium-sized, finely serrated leaves. *Growth* upright, bushy, vigorous and free-flowering. Bush.

'Royal Ruby'
GADSBY 1968
Registered 1971
AFS Registration No 972
Double
Tube claret, medium length and thickness. *Sepals* claret, short, broad and reflexed. *Corolla* ruby red, medium-sized, compact blooms. *Growth* upright, bushy, free-flowering. Blooms August/September. Bush. *Parentage* 'Pepi' × 'Royal Purple'.

'Royal Sovereign'
GADSBY 1970
Registered 1971
AFS Registration No 963
Semi-double
Tube crimson, short, medium thickness. *Sepals* crimson on top, undersides spiraea red, held well out. *Corolla* creamy white, medium, compact bloom. *Foliage* mid-green, medium-sized, serrated leaves. *Growth* upright, bushy, vigorous, free-flowering. Bush.

'Royal Touch'
TIRET 1964
AFS Registration No 597
Double
Tube rose pink, medium length and thickness. *Sepals* rose pink, broad, recurving slightly. *Corolla* royal purple, full, compact bloom. *Foliage* mid to darkish green, medium-sized leaves. *Growth* trailer, bushy, vigorous and free-flowering. Basket.

'Royalty'
PLUMMER 1951
Single
Tube red, short, medium thickness. *Sepals* red, held well out from the corolla. *Corolla* royal purple, opening flat and saucer-shaped, base of the petals lighter shade. *Foliage* mid-green, medium-sized leaves. *Growth* upright, bushy, vigorous and free-flowering. Bush.

'Royal Velvet'
WALTZ 1962
AFS Registration No 526
Double
Tube crimson, medium length and thickness. *Sepals* crimson, short, broad and held out over the corolla. *Corolla* deep purple, outer petals splashed crimson, very full, fluffy, medium-sized bloom. *Foliage* mid-green, medium-sized, finely serrated leaves. *Growth* upright, vigorous, bushy, self-branching and very free-flowering. A beautiful cultivar which makes a first class show plant, and is easy to grow. Bush.

'Roy Walker'
WALKER/FUCHSIA LA 1975
AFS Registration No 1265
Double
Tube white with pale pink flush. *Corolla* white, round and flaring, medium-sized. *Sepals* white to pale pink, reflexed. *Stamens and pistil* pink. *Foliage* medium green, medium size. *Growth* upright, bushy, free-flowering. Bush.

'Rubeo'
TIRET 1947
Semi-double

Tube pale carmine red, long, medium thickness. *Sepals* carmine red, long, broad, recurving. *Corolla* rose bengal with geranium lake marbling, medium to large bloom. *Foliage* reddish tinted, wrinkled, medium-sized leaves. *Growth* upright, bushy, vigorous and free-flowering. A very attractive plant, easy to grow. Bush.

'Ruffled Petticoats'
FOSTER 1974
AFS Registration No 1173
Double
Tube rose pink, medium length and thickness. *Sepals* claret rose, short. *Corolla* white, flushed claret rose, full and flared, giving it a ruffled appearance. *Stamens* neyron rose, pistil white with neyron rose cast. *Foliage* mistletoe green, serrated. *Growth* upright, bushy, vigorous, free-flowering. Bush.

'Ruffles'
ERICKSON 1960
AFS Registration No 451
Double
Tube pink, short and waxy, medium thickness. *Sepals* deep pink with green tips, broad and upturned. *Corolla* deep violet purple in the centre, outer petals marbled pink, ruffled petals, spreading, medium-sized, bloom. *Foliage* mid-green, small to medium-sized leaves. *Growth* trailer, bushy, vigorous, free-flowering. Basket.

'Rufus' (115)
NELSON 1952
AFS Registration No 177
Single
Tube bright red, medium length and thickness. *Sepals* red, long, narrow and recurving. *Corolla* bright red, long, compact. Medium-sized blooms, almost a self colour. *Foliage* medium green, medium to large, slightly serrated leaves. *Growth* upright, bushy, vigorous, very free-flowering and easy to grow. Bush or standard. Often incorrectly called 'Rufus the Red'.

'Runner'
TROLLEY 1978
AFS Registration No 1472
Single
Tube pale pink, medium length and width. *Sepals* pale pink, paler tips, medium to broad, upturned. *Corolla* rose pink, short and straight. *Foliage* medium green, oval, longish. *Growth* upright, short-jointed and very floriferous. Best colour in the shade. *Parentage* 'Barbara' × seedling.

'Ruth'
W.P. WOOD 1949
Single
Tube rosy red, medium length and thickness. *Sepals* rose-red, broad, upturned. *Corolla* reddish-purple, medium-sized, compact bloom. *Foliage* mid-green, medium-sized leaves. *Growth* upright, bushy, free-flowering. Bush or garden hardy.

'Ruthie'
BRAND 1951
Double
Tube white, long and slender. *Sepals* white, long, narrow and completely reflexed over the tube. *Corolla* violet-blue, outer petals are splashed rose pink, very full, compact, medium-sized bloom. *Foliage* medium green, medium-sized, ovate, finely serrated leaves. *Growth* upright, bushy, vigorous and free-flowering. A very easy cultivar to grow and train to shape. Bush.

'Ruth King'
TIRET 1967
AFS Registration No 736
Double
Tube pink, medium length and thickness. *Sepals* pink, recurving. *Corolla* lilac and white, medium to large, compact bloom. *Foliage* mid-green, medium to large serrated leaves. *Growth* trailer, vigorous, bushy, free-flowering. Basket.

'Rydal Water'
TRAVIS 1960
Registered 1973

AFS Registration No 1145
Single
Tube pale rose-opal, long and thin. *Sepals* pale rose-opal on top with green tips. Undersides soft rose pink. Long, narrow and twisted. *Corolla* lilac rose, edged deep lavender, silver at the base of the petals. Petals large and overlapping, twisting to form wide funnels. *Foliage* mid-green, medium-sized leaves. *Growth* natural trailer, self-branching, bushy, free-flowering. Can be grown as a bush if pinched and staked early. Bush or basket. *Parentage* 'Opalescent' × 'Fomosissima'.

'Sabina'
TOLLEY 1973
AFS Registration No 1158
Single
Tube pale pink, thin and of medium length. *Sepals* pale pink with green tips. *Corolla* pale magenta pink, short and semi-flaring. *Foliage* yellowish green, medium-sized leaves. *Growth* semi-trailer, bushy, vigorous, fairly free-flowering. Bush or half-basket.

'Sacramento'
REITER 1946
Single
Tube light carmine, medium length and thickness. *Sepals* light carmine, waxy, medium length, held well out. *Corolla* light carmine, compact bloom. *Foliage* mid-green, medium-sized, serrated leaves. *Growth* upright, vigorous, bushy and free-flowering. Bush.

'Sadie Larson'
ANN'S GARDENS/GAGNON 1966
AFS Registration No 659
Double
Tube pale pink, medium length, and thickness. *Sepals* coral rose with white tips, recurving. *Corolla* white, very full, medium-sized bloom. *Foliage* dark green, medium-sized serrated leaves. *Growth* trailer, vigorous, free-flowering. Keeps its colour best when grown in shaded conditions. Basket.

'Sahara'
KENNETT 1966
AFS Registration No 679
Double
Tube pink, short and thick. *Sepals* pink with green tips, long, broad and upturned. *Corolla* pale dianthus purple in the centre with salmon pink outer petals and petaloids. Medium to large, fluffy bloom. *Foliage* mid-green, long, serrated leaves. *Growth* upright, bushy, free-flowering and easy to grow into a nice plant. Bush.

'Sally'
FUCHSIA FOREST 1967
AFS Registration No 725
Double
Tube white, medium length and thickness. *Sepals* white on top, pale pink on the undersides, recurving. *Corolla* bright pale lavender, paler at the base of the petals. Medium, compact bloom. *Foliage* mid-green, medium-sized leaves. *Growth* trailer, bushy, vigorous and free-flowering. Basket.

'Sally Ann'
PENNISI 1971
AFS Registration No 1012
Double
Tube white, medium length and thickness. *Sepals* white on top with green tips. Undersides pale pink, flaring straight outwards. *Corolla* shades of rose pink, compact, medium-sized bloom. *Foliage* medium green, broad, serrated leaves. *Growth* trailer, bushy, vigorous and free-flowering. Basket.

'Salmon Glow'
HANDLEY 1978
AFS Registration No 1454
Single
Tube pale salmon RHS 37B, $1\frac{1}{2}$ in (4 cm) long, thin. *Sepals* salmon RHS 41D, green tips, held at right angles to the tube. *Corolla* orange salmon RHS 40C, shading to RHS 40D at the base of the petals which are short and overlapping and hold their colour well. *Stamens and pistil* salmon. *Foliage* small to medium light green.

Growth lax, self-branching and bushy. Bush or basket.

'Sambo'
GAGNON 1967
AFS Registration No 710
Double
Tube red, medium length and thickness. *Sepals* red, held well out. *Corolla* very dark reddish blue ageing to wine purple. Compact bloom. *Foliage* medium to darkish green, medium-sized leaves. *Growth* upright, bushy, but rather lax. Bush, if well pinched in its early stages, or half-basket.

'Sampan'
TIRET 1965
AFS Registration No 651
Double
Tube pinkish, short and thick. *Sepals* rose pink, short and broad, held over the top of the corolla. *Corolla* rosy red, paler shades at the base of the petals, very full and fluffy medium-sized bloom. *Foliage* light to medium green, longish serrated leaves. *Growth* trailer, bushy, free-flowering. Basket.

'Sampson's Delight'
FUCHSIA LA 1980/BARRETT
AFS Registration No 1571
Semi-double
Tube carmine pink, medium length and thickness. *Sepals* carmine pink on top, coral pink on the undersides, medium length, reflexing completely over the tube. *Corolla* rose red streaked coral, bell-shaped and slightly flared. *Anthers* deep garnet. *Foliage* spinach green with purple madder veining, large, ovate. *Growth* tall growing, vigorous upright and bushy. Bush.

'Samson'
PETERSON 1957
Double
Tube pink, long and slender. *Sepals* pink with green tips on top, slightly deeper shade of pink on the undersides. Long, fairly broad, and held well out. *Corolla* deep purple with pale pink veins, and shaded pink at the base of the petals. Medium-sized compact bloom. *Foliage* variegated pale green and yellow, medium sized, ovate, finely serrated leaves. *Growth* trailer, bushy, vigorous. Basket or half-basket.

'San Carlos'
NEIDERHOLZER 1946
Single
Tube rose bengal, medium length and thickness. *Sepals* rose bengal, longish, reflexing. *Corolla* amethyst violet, loose-petalled, medium-sized bloom. *Foliage* mid-green, medium-sized, serrated leaves. *Growth* upright, bushy, free-flowering. Bush.

'Sandboy'
HALL 1967
Registered 1973
AFS Registration No 1117
Single
Tube pinkish white, short and thin. *Sepals* very deep pink (RHS 55C), small, narrow and curling back to the tube. *Corolla* very dark mauve RHS 78A, flushed light mauve at the base of the petals fading slightly with age. Small, bell-shaped bloom. *Foliage* mid-green (RHS 137B), medium-sized, ovate, serrated. *Growth* upright, self-branching, bushy, exceptionally free-flowering. This is perhaps one of the best fuchsias raised in the past decade—it will make an outstanding exhibition bush, is one of the few fuchsias which will retain its buds indoors, and can withstand central heating, and will continue to bloom throughout the winter months indoors if given sufficient light. Very easy to propagate but as the cuttings start budding immediately they have rooted, a lot of time can be spent disbudding these until blooms are required. It will do well in a window box, remaining compact and flowering over a long period. *Parentage* ('Ballet Girl' × 'Fascination') × (seedling × ?). Named by the hybridiser, Mrs Margaret Hall, after her father who, she says, was always as 'happy as a sandboy'.

'San Diego'
TIRET 1964
AFS Registration No 598
Double
Tube white, with a pinkish flush, medium length and thickness. *Sepals* pinkish white, medium length, upturned. *Corolla* rosy-red, compact, medium sized bloom. *Growth* trailer, bushy, free flowering. Basket.

'Sandy'
SOO YUN 1974
AFS Registration No 1185
Double
Tube white with pink veins. Medium length and thickness. *Sepals* light pink on top, darker pink undersides, green tips. 2 in (5 cm) long, curving and twisting back to the tube. *Corolla* white, no petaloids. *Foliage* dark green 3 in (1.5 cm) long, light green stems tinged red. *Growth* trailer, heavy bloomer. Basket.

'San Francisco'
REITER 1941
Single
Tube carmine rose, long, medium thickness. *Sepals* carmine rose, short, broad, held well out. *Corolla* geranium lake, short, fairly compact. Long flowers. *Foliage* mid-green, medium-sized, serrated leaves. *Growth* trailer, long, arching branches, vigorous and free-flowering. Basket. *Parentage* 'Robert Blatry' × 'Mrs Victor Reiter'.

'San Jacinto'
EVANS AND REEVES 1951
AFS Registration No 103
Double
Tube shell pink, medium length and thickness. *Sepals* waxy shell pink, broad, slightly reflexed. *Corolla* lilac, fading to lilac pink. Compact medium-sized bloom. *Foliage* medium green, medium-sized, serrated leaves. *Growth* upright, bushy, vigorous, free-flowering. Bush.

'San Leandro'
BRAND 1949
Double
Tube deep carmine red, medium length, fairly thick. *Sepals* deep carmine red, long, narrow and recurving. *Corolla* magenta with vermilion splashes on the outer petals. Full and fluffy compact bloom. *Foliage* darkish green, medium to large leaves, serrated. *Growth* upright, bushy, vigorous and free-flowering. Bush.

'San Luis Obispo'
NELSON 1952
AFS Registration No 178
Double
Tube carmine, medium length and thickness. *Sepals* carmine, broad, held well out from the corolla. *Corolla* light pink with reddish veins. Edges of the petals are slightly serrated. *Foliage* medium green, medium-sized leaves. *Growth* upright, bushy and free-flowering. Bush.

'San Mateo'
NEIDERHOLZER 1946
Double
Tube dark pink, medium length and thickness. *Sepals* dark pink, long, broad, upturned. *Corolla* very dark violet-purple, splashed pink, large blooms. *Foliage* medium green, medium to large leaves, serrated. *Growth* trailer, vigorous, free-flowering. Basket.

'San Pablo'
CRUMLEY 1948
Double
Tube deep rose pink, medium length and thickness. *Sepals* deep rose pink, broad, upturned. *Corolla* lilac pink, very large blooms. *Foliage* medium green, medium large leaves. *Growth* trailer, vigorous, free flowering. Basket. Sport of 'San Mateo'.

'San Pedrian'
FAIRCLO 1947
Single
Tube rose pink, small. *Sepals* rose pink, short, held well out. *Corolla* pink, small and compact. *Foliage* mid-green, small leaves. *Growth* upright, dwarf, bushy, very free-flowering in clusters. Dwarf bush.

'San Rafael'
NEIDERHOLZER 1948
Double
Tube carmine, medium length and thickness. *Sepals* carmine, broad, reflexing. *Corolla* magenta, paler shade of vermilion at the base of the petals. Large, compact bloom. *Foliage* mid-green, medium to large leaves. *Growth* upright, vigorous, bushy and free-flowering. Bush.

'Santa Barbara'
Raiser not known
Single
Tube very pale pink, short, medium thickness. *Sepals* pale pink, short, broad, held well out. *Corolla* rose pink medium-sized bloom. *Foliage* mid-green, medium-sized, slightly serrated leaves. *Growth* upright, bushy, free-flowering. Bush. Much confusion exists concerning this cultivar, and the one grown most commonly under the name 'Santa Barbara' (with white tube and sepals, and salmon-pink corolla) is incorrectly named.

'Santa Claus'
HAZARD
Tube red, short, medium thickness. *Sepals* red, short, held well out. *Corolla* white with red veins, small blooms. *Foliage* mid-green, small leaves. *Growth* upright, bushy, dwarf, free-flowering. Bush.

'Santa Clara'
PENNISI 1969
AFS Registration No 833
Double
Tube white, short, medium thickness. *Sepals* white, flushed rose, held well out. *Corolla* very dark orchid, fading to dark rose pink box type. *Foliage* mid-green, medium-sized leaves. *Growth* trailer, bushy, vigorous, free-flowering, Basket.

'Santa Cruz' (114)
TIRET 1947
Double
Tube crimson, medium length, rather thick. *Sepals* crimson, short, broad and upturned to the tube. *Corolla* very dark crimson, medium-sized bloom. *Foliage* medium green, medium sized, ovate, serrated leaves. *Growth* upright, bushy, vigorous, free-flowering. Bush or standard.

'Santa Lucia'
MUNKNER 1956
Double
Tube deep red, medium length and thickness. *Sepals* deep red, medium length, broad, outspread. *Corolla* orchid pink with deeper pink veining. Medium-sized, compact blooms. *Foliage* mid-green, medium-sized, serrated leaves. *Growth* upright, bushy, free-flowering. Bush.

'Santa Maria'
NELSON 1952
AFS Registration No 179
Double
Tube red, medium length and thickness. *Sepals* red, long, broad and spread out well from the corolla. *Corolla* centre petals white, veined red. Outer petals red with numerous petaloids of the same colour. *Foliage* mid-green, medium-sized, serrated leaves. *Growth* upright, bushy, vigorous and free-flowering. Bush.

'Sara Helen'
COLVILLE 1969
Double
Tube white with faint pink flush, medium length and thickness. *Sepals* white, flushed pink, broad, recurving. *Corolla* opens tyrian purple, lighter at the base of the petals, and fading slightly on maturity. *Foliage* mid-green, medium-sized leaves. *Growth* upright, vigorous, bushy and free-flowering. Bush.

'Sarah Jane'
PUTLEY 1974
Double
Tube rose-pink, short, medium thickness. *Sepals* rose-pink, short, broad. *Corolla* lilac, darker shaded at the base of the petals, small, compact bloom. *Foliage* mid-green, small to medium-sized leaves.

Growth upright, fairly vigorous and bushy, free-flowering. Bush.

'Sarong'
KENNETT 1963
AFS Registration No 593
Double
Tube white, short, thin. *Sepals* white with green tips, and faintly flushed pink. Long, fairly broad, and curling outwards and up to the tube. *Corolla* violet-purple, paler at the base of the petals. Very ragged and untidy medium-sized bloom, flaring on maturity. *Foliage* medium green, large leaves. *Growth* bushy, lax, very vigorous and free-flowering. Half-basket.

'Satellite'
KENNETT 1965
AFS Registration No 642
Single
Tube greenish white, short, rather thick. *Sepals* white with green tips. Medium length, broad and slightly reflexing. *Corolla* dark red, fading to bright red with streaks of pure white down the centre of each petal. A very distinctive bloom. *Foliage* mid-green, medium-sized leaves. *Growth* upright, bushy, free-flowering. A cultivar which is worth growing for the unusual markings on the petals, but one which is very prone to *Botrytis*. Bush.

'Satin's Folly'
MARTIN 1962
AFS Registration No 1125
Single
Tube maroon, long and thin. *Sepals* maroon, long, slender and curving slightly, upwards and out. *Corolla* reddish purple, long, compact. *Foliage* mid-green, medium-sized leaves. *Growth* bushy, lax, vigorous and free-flowering. Half-basket.

'Saturnus'
DE GROOT 1970
Single
Tube red, short, medium thickness. *Sepals* red, very long, held well out. *Corolla* light purple, veined reddish. Paler shade at the base of the petals. Blooms stand well out from the foliage. *Stamens and style* light red. *Foliage* mid-green, medium-sized leaves. *Growth* upright, bushy, small but free-flowering. Bush. *Parentage F. regia typica* × 'Henriette Ernst'.

'Saxondale'
GADSBY 1973
AFS Registration No 1125
Semi-double
Tube crimson RHS 52A, long, medium thickness. *Sepals* crimson, small, broad. *Corolla* amaranth rose RHS 65A, veined rose-red, small bloom. *Foliage* medium green, small leaves. *Growth* upright, dwarf, bushy and free-flowering. Bush, or rockery plant. *Parentage* 'Trase' × 'Lady Thumb'.

'Scarcity'
LYE 1869
Single
Tube deep scarlet, short, thick. *Sepals* deep scarlet, short and upturned. *Corolla* deep purple, shaded scarlet at the base of the petals. *Foliage* medium green, medium-sized, serrated leaves. *Growth* upright, bushy, self-branching and free-flowering. Bush or garden hardy.

'Schnabel'
ANTONELLI 1971
AFS Registration No 1007
Semi-double
Tube salmon orange, medium length and thickness. *Sepals* salmon-orange, broad and reflexing. *Corolla* orange, medium to large blooms. *Foliage* mid-green, large leaves. *Growth* trailer, vigorous, free-flowering. Basket.

'Schneeball'
TWRDY 1874
Semi-double
Tube reddish pink, medium length and thickness. *Sepals* reddish pink, long and curling up over the tube. *Corolla* white with pinkish veining, loose-petalled, medium-sized bloom. *Foliage* pale green, small, finely serrated leaves. *Growth* up-

right, bushy, vigorous and free-flowering. Bush or summer bedder.

'Schneekoppen'
TWRDY 1886
Semi-double
Tube reddish pink, short, rather thick. *Sepals* reddish pink, short, broad and recurved. *Corolla* white, flushed and veined pink. Small to medium-sized, rather open bloom. *Foliage* darkish green, small, narrow and serrated leaves. *Growth* upright, bushy, vigorous and free-flowering. Bush or summer bedder.

'Schneewitchen'
KLEIN 1878
Single
Tube dark pink, short, thick. *Sepals* dark pink, short, broad and slightly upturned at the tips. *Corolla* pinkish-purple, small and very compact. *Foliage* mid-green, small and finely serrated. *Growth* upright, bushy, vigorous and very free-flowering. Bush or garden hardy.

'Schneewitcher'
HOECK 1884
Single
Tube red, short, medium thickness. *Sepals* red, short, broad and slightly upturned. *Corolla* violet-purple with red veins, open bell-shaped. Medium-sized bloom. *Foliage* medium green with reddish veining, small to medium-sized, serrated leaves. *Growth* upright, bushy, self-branching, vigorous and free-flowering. Bush or summer bedder.

'Scotch Heather'
FOSTER 1974
AFS Registration No 1174
Double
Tube white, streaked Venetian pink, medium length and thickness. *Sepals* white flushed Venetian pink on top, tips absinthe. Underside Venetian pink, short and broad flaring outwards and curling at the tips. *Corolla* hyacinth blue to mallow purple, flaring slightly. Full, medium-sized bloom. *Foliage* light green, small to medium-sized leaves, slightly serrated. *Growth* upright, bushy, vigorous, free-flowering. Bush.

'Scottie'
BRAND 1949
Double
Tube dark pink, medium length and thickness. *Sepals* deep pink, long, broad, reflexing. *Corolla* deep violet blue, very full and compact, medium-sized bloom. *Foliage* mid to darkish green, medium-sized leaves. *Growth* natural trailer, vigorous, free-flowering. Basket.

'Sea Foam'
REITER 1948
Semi-double
Tube white, flushed pale pink, short, medium thickness. *Sepals* white, with pink flush, short, recurving. *Corolla* petunia purple with rose pink shading. Paler at the base of the petals. Small compact bloom. *Foliage* medium green, small to medium-sized, serrated leaves. *Growth* upright, bushy, free-flowering. Dwarf bush.

'Seaforth'
NEED 1964
Single
Tube creamy white, waxy, short and thick. *Sepals* creamy white, flushed pale pink, broad, reflexing. *Corolla* lilac pink, paler at the base of the petals and slightly darker at the edges. Medium-sized bloom. *Foliage* medium green, medium-sized, serrated leaves. *Growth* upright, bushy, vigorous and free-flowering. Bush.

'Sealand Prince'
BEES
Single
Tube light red, medium length and thickness. *Sepals* light red, long, narrow and curling upwards. *Corolla* pale violet-purple, maturing to reddish-purple, small to medium bell-shaped bloom. *Foliage* light to medium green, small to

medium, finely serrated leaves. *Growth* upright, bushy and vigorous. Free-flowering. A garden hardy which is most unhappy if grown in a pot.

'Sea Shell' (38)
EVANS 1954
Double
Tube pink, medium length, rather thick. *Sepals* white, flushed pink, broad and recurving completely. *Corolla* pink, heavily veined a deeper shade of pink on the outer petals. Compact, medium-sized bloom. *Foliage* dark green, medium-sized, longish leaves. *Growth* upright, bushy, free-flowering. Bush.

'Sebastopol'
PENNISI 1968
AFS Registration No 755
Double
Tube white, short, medium thickness. *Sepals* white with pink flush, deeper on the undersides, long, broad, and recurving. *Corolla* white splashed pale pink, large, fairly compact bloom. *Foliage* medium green, medium-sized leaves. *Growth* trailer, vigorous, bushy and free-flowering. Basket.

'Sebastopol Belle'
SOO YUN 1967
AFS Registration No 732
Double
Tube white with green tinge, and veined red. Medium length and thickness. *Sepals* white with green tips, long, held well out. *Corolla* light purple, much paler at the base of the petals. Large bloom. *Foliage* mid-green, medium-sized leaves. *Growth* lax, bushy, vigorous, free-flowering. Bush or half-basket.

'Seneca'
LEE 1948
Double
Tube dark turkey red, medium length and thickness. *Sepals* turkey red, long, broad, reflexing. *Corolla* pansy-violet, with splashes of phlox pink, medium-sized bloom. *Foliage* medium to darkish green, medium-sized leaves. *Growth* upright, bushy, vigorous and free-flowering. Bush or standard.

'Sensation'
MUNKNER 1962
AFS Registration No 545
Semi-double
Tube pale pink, short, medium thickness. *Sepals* pink on top, deeper shade on the undersides, long, narrow, and reflexing on the tube. Pale green tips. *Corolla* deep violet-blue, large and long, loose-petalled bloom, with reddish veins and rather paler shade at the base of the petals. *Foliage* mid-green, medium-sized, serrated leaves. *Growth* trailer, very vigorous and free-flowering. Although the bloom tends to look rather untidy, its very size and shape make it a 'Sensation'. Basket.

'September Morn'
HODGES 1953
AFS Registration No 158
Double
Self-coloured rose madder bloom. *Tube* medium length and thickness. *Sepals* broad, long and recurving. *Corolla* very full and compact, medium-sized bloom. *Foliage* medium green, medium-sized leaves. *Growth* trailer, bushy, vigorous, free-flowering. Basket.

'Sequoia'
PAPE 1948
Double
Tube red, medium length and thickness. *Sepals* red, broad, recurving. *Corolla* light lavender with pinkish overlay, medium-sized bloom. *Foliage* mid-green, medium-sized leaves. *Growth* upright, bushy, free-flowering. Bush. Sport of 'Honeymoon'.

'Serenade'
EVANS AND REEVES 1951
AFS Registration No 101
Single
Tube waxy shell pink, medium length and thickness. *Sepals* waxy shell pink, long, broad, recurving. *Corolla* cerise, medium-

sized bloom. *Foliage* mid-green, medium-sized, serrated leaves. *Growth* upright, vigorous, heavy branching, free-flowering. Bush or standard.

'Serendipity'
CASTRO 1973
AFS Registration No 1105
Single
Tube pale pink, medium length and thickness. *Sepals* pink with green tips, folding backwards. *Corolla* lavender pink, merthiolate pink on the edges of the petals maturing to a brighter pink. Numerous petaloids. *Foliage* medium green, cordate, coarse and serrated. *Growth* trailer, bushy, vigorous, free-flowering. Basket.

'Seventeen'
REITER 1947
Double
Tube rose-madder, medium length and thickness. *Sepals* rose madder, broad, recurving. *Corolla* rose madder, medium-sized, compact bloom. *Foliage* mid green, small, leathery leaves. *Growth* bushy, upright, free-flowering. Bush.

'Severn Queen'
TOLLEY/FUCHSIAVALE 1978
AFS Registration No 1456
Single
Tube very pale pink, thin and of medium length. *Sepals* very pale pink, medium size. *Corolla* rose bengal, RHS 57C, semi-flared. *Foliage* Scheoles green, (RHS 143C). *Growth* free-flowering, short-jointed, bushy, tall, upright. Bush, standard or pyramid. *Parentage* 'Barbara' ×.

'Shades of Space'
SOO YUN 1967
AFS Registration No 730
Double
Tube white, faint reddish tinge and red veins. Medium length and thickness. *Sepals* white on top, flushed pink on the undersides, long, broad and recurving. *Corolla* light purple, paler at base, fading to old rose. Large, fairly compact bloom. *Foliage* mid green, medium-sized leaves. *Growth* lax, bushy, vigorous, free-flowering. Needs careful pinching to shape. Basket or bush.

'Shady Blue'
GADSBY 1970
AFS Registration No 880
Single
Tube pinkish carmine, short and bulbous. *Sepals* pinkish carmine, long, broad, and held well out from the corolla. *Corolla* pale violet blue, shaded pink at the base of the petals. Medium sized, compact bloom. *Foliage* mid-green, medium to large serrated leaves. *Growth* upright, very vigorous, bushy and free-flowering. It needs pinching in its early stages to form a good bush. An attractive plant which will do well indoors or out. Bush or standard. *Parentage* 'Upward Look' × 'Caroline'.

'Shangri-La'
MARTIN 1963
AFS Registration No 573
Double
Tube dark pink, medium length and thickness. *Sepals* dark pink to red, long, broad, upturned. *Corolla* pale pinkish white with pink veining, very large, full, fluffy bloom. *Foliage* mid-green, medium-sized leaves. *Growth* trailer, vigorous, free-flowering. Bush.

'Shanley'
AMERICAN 1968
Single
Tube pale salmon orange, long, medium thickness. *Sepals* pale salmon-orange, with green tips. Short, broad and held well out. *Corolla* pale orange, short, compact. *Foliage* medium green, very large, serrated. *Growth* upright, bushy, vigorous and free-flowering. Bush.

'Sharon'
TIRET 1948
Semi-double
Tube pale scarlet, medium length and thickness. *Sepals* pale scarlet, long, broad, recurving. *Corolla* rose bengal with splashes of geranium lake. Medium-sized, fairly compact blooms. *Foliage*

bright green, medium-sized leaves. *Growth* lax, bushy, vigorous, free-flowering. Needs careful early pinching if required as a bush. Bush or half-basket.

'Sharpitor'
NATIONAL TRUST, SHARPITOR
Single
Tube pale pinkish white, small, thin. *Sepals* pale pinkish white, short, broad, held well out. *Corolla* very slightly darker than the sepals, small compact. *Foliage* variegated pale cream and green, small, serrated. *Growth* upright, bushy, self-branching, fairly free, but late flowering. Slow growing, and difficult to propagate. Believed to be a sport of *F. magellanica* var. *molinae*. Plants seem to revert rather easily. Bush.

'Shasta'
KENNETT 1964
AFS Registration No 614
Double
Tube pale pink, short and thick. *Sepals* pale pink with green tips, slightly reflexed, long and broad. *Corolla* white with a few pink petaloids. Medium-sized, compact bloom with slightly frilled petals. *Foliage* medium green, small to medium-sized, serrated leaves. *Growth* upright, vigorous, bushy and free-flowering. Prefers shade conditions for the best colour. Bush.

'Sheila'
FRANCESCA 1973
AFS Registration No 1091
Double
Tube pink, medium length and thickness. *Sepals* shiny pink on top, deep crepe pink on the underside. *Corolla* lavender with pink veining and pink outer petals. Large compact blooms. *Foliage* dark green, medium-sized leaves. *Growth* upright, bushy, vigorous and free-flowering. Bush.

'Sheila Montalbetti'
G. ROE 1980
Single
Tube claret rose RHS 52A, short, medium thickness. *Sepals* crimson, short, broad and held well back. *Corolla* white, with crimson veining. Small blooms. *Foliage* medium green, medium-sized serrated leaves. *Growth* upright, low growing, vigorous and free-flowering. Will make an excellent exhibition plant, and is equally suitable as a summer bedder. Named after a Secretary at the RHS, Wisley. Bush or summer bedder. *Parentage* 'Snowcap' × 'Cloverdale Pearl'.

'Sheila Orr'
G. ROE 1980
Semi-duble
Tube rhodamine pink RHS 63A, medium length and thickness. *Sepals* rhodamine pink, held out horizontally. *Corolla* amethyst violet RHS 84D, medium-sized bloom. *Foliage* pale green, medium-sized leaves. *Growth* upright, vigorous, bushy and free-flowering. Makes a good exhibition plant or summer bedder. Bush or summer bedder. Named after the former Trials Secretary of the RHS, Wisley. *Parentage* 'Susan Ford' × 'Neil Clyne'.

'Shelly Renée'
PRENTICE 1971
AFS Registration No 990
Double
Tube pale pink, short, medium thickness. *Sepals* pale pink, long and narrow, held well out. *Corolla* opening lavender-blue, and turning to dark rose pink. Paler at the base of the petals. Bloom opens flat, medium size. *Foliage* dark green, medium-sized, serrated leaves. *Growth* upright, vigorous, very free-flowering. Bush.

'Sherwood'
GADSBY 1973
AFS Registration No 1126
Single
Dwarf
Tube carmine, short, medium thickness. *Sepals* carmine, short and pointed. *Corolla* neyron rose, veined carmine. Small and compact. *Foliage* medium green, small leaves. *Growth* upright, dwarf, bushy,

early flowering. Bush. *Parentage* 'Trase' × 'Lady Thumb'.

'Shooting Star'
MARTIN 1965
AFS Registration No 631
Semi-double
Tube salmon-red, short, medium thickness. *Sepals* salmon-red, long, narrow, held well out. *Corolla* purple in the centre, with the outer petals and petaloids splashed salmon-red, and pink. Centre opens bell-shaped. *Foliage* mid-green. medium-sized, serrated leaves. *Growth* lax, bushy, vigorous, free-flowering. Bush if well pinched in its early stages, or basket.

'Shot Silk'
THORNLEY 1964
AFS Registration No 1806 (1979)
Double
Tube pink, short. *Sepals* cream with green tips, pink at the base, broad. *Corolla* shot silk effect of pink and blue petals with the colours fusing into one another. *Foliage* medium green. *Growth* upright, vigorous, bushy. Will make a good bush but requires pinching. Prefers heat for best results but will stand low temperatures. *Parentage* 'Pink Galore' × 'Deepdale'.

'Showboat'
WALKER AND JONES 1950
Double
Tube pale rose pink, medium length and thickness. *Sepals* pale rose, broad, recurving. *Corolla* rose pink and hyacinth blue marbling on the petals, medium-sized, compact bloom. *Foliage* bright green, medium-sized leaves. *Growth* trailer, bushy, vigorous and free-flowering. Half-basket.

'Show Girl'
KENNETT 1967
AFS Registration No 742
Double
Tube white, flushed pale pink, medium length and thickness. *Sepals* white, flushed pale pink, medium length, broad and curling upwards over the tube. *Corolla* pale pink, rather loose-petalled, medium-sized bloom. *Foliage* medium green, with reddish veins. Long, medium-sized serrated leaves. *Growth* trailer, bushy, free-flowering. Basket.

'Shuna'
J. TRAVIS 1973
AFS Registration No 1146
Single
Tube warm pink, medium length and thickness. *Sepals* mid-pink, short and broad. *Corolla* warm mid-pink, very compact on opening, but spreading slightly as it matures. *Foliage* mid- to darkish green, small, serrated. *Growth* upright, bushy, self-branching, free-flowering. Will make an excellent exhibition plant. Not the easiest to grow, but worth persevering with. Bush. Sport of 'Countess of Aberdeen'.

'Shuna Lindsay'
TRAVIS 1980
AFS Registration No 1585
Single
Tube red RHS 52A, thick and of medium length. *Sepals* red VHS 51B, at the base, green RHS 138 at the tips, narrow. *Corolla* orange red RHS 32A. *Foliage* dark green. *Growth* upright, self-branching, free-flowering and bushy. Bush. Develops its best colour in the sun. A dwarf *F. denticulata*.

'Shy Lady' (32)
WALTZ 1955
Double
Tube white, short and thick. *Sepals* white with green tips. Long, fairly broad, reflexed. *Corolla* white with the faintest touch of pink on the outer petals. Medium, compact bloom. *Foliage* dark green, small serrated leaves. *Growth* upright, bushy, self-branching and very free-flowering. Bush.

'Shy Look'
GADSBY 1972
AFS Registration No 1069

Single
Tube rose pink, short and thick. *Sepals* crimson, short, broad, held well out. *Corolla* roseine-purple, medium size, open bloom. *Foliage* mid-green, small to medium-sized, serrated leaves. *Growth* upright, bushy, free-flowering, blooms held erect. Bush. *Parentage* 'Upward Look' ×.

'Siboney'
ERICKSON 1963
AFS Registration No 581
Double
Tube soft pink, waxy, medium length and thickness. *Sepals* soft pink, long, broad and recurved. *Corolla* centre petals bluish-violet, outer petals marbled phlox pink. Medium-sized bloom. *Foliage* bright green, medium-sized, serrated leaves. *Growth* natural trailer, vigorous, free-flowering. Basket.

'Sierra Blue'
WALTZ 1957
AFS Registration No 313
Double
Tube white, short and thick. *Sepals* white with green tips, short, broad and slightly upturned. *Corolla* silvery blue with pinkish veining, and shaded white at the base of the petals. Very full, compact, medium-sized bloom. *Foliage* mid-green, medium-sized leaves. *Growth* trailer, bushy, free-flowering. Basket.

'Silverdale'
TRAVIS 1973
AFS Registration No 1147
Single
Tube ivory, short, medium thickness. *Sepals eau de nil*, long, narrow and pointed. *Corolla* pastel lavender shade, compact, barrel-shaped corolla. *Foliage* pale green small. *Growth* upright, self-branching, bushy, free-flowering. Bush. *Parentage F. magellanica* var. *molinae* × 'Venus Victrix'.

'Silver Queen'
HAAG AND SON 1953
Semi-double
Tube deep rose pink, medium length and thickness. *Sepals* deep rose pink, held well out. *Corolla* silver-blue, medium-sized, fairly compact bloom. *Foliage* mid-green, medium-sized leaves. *Growth* upright, low-growing, bushy, very free-flowering. Bush.

'Silver Wings'
FIELD 1980
AFS Registration No 1563
Double
Tube magenta, short and of medium thickness. *Sepals* magenta RHS 66A, $1\frac{1}{4}$ in (3 cm) long. *Corolla* rose purple RHS 75B, with rose purple petaloids. *Foliage* medium green with red centre veins, leaves $2\frac{3}{4}$ in (7 cm) long. *Pistil* pink. *Growth* natural trailer. Basket.

'Silvia'
SCHNABEL 1951
AFS Registration No 79
Double
Tube pale rose pink, medium length and thickness. *Sepals* pale rose pink, broad, held out from the corolla. *Corolla* pure white, full and fluffy, compact bloom. *Foliage* medium green, medium-sized leaves. *Growth* upright, bushy, free-flowering. Bush.

'Simon Side'
RYLE 1977
AFS Registration No 1437
Single
Tube spiraea red RHS 63A, short, medium thickness. *Sepals* white with greenish tips, short, horizontal. *Corolla* ruby red RHS 64A, compact, tube-like. *Foliage* woodpecker green RHS 147A. *Growth* upright, bushy, self-branching, sturdy grower. Bush, small standard. *Parentage* 'Pink Lady' × 'Coxeen'.

'Sincerely'
KENNETT 1961
AFS Registration No 476
Double
Tube white, medium length and thickness. *Sepals* white, broad, recurving

slightly. *Corolla* pure white, faintly tinged pink on the outer petals. Medium-sized, compact bloom. *Foliage* light to medium green, medium-sized leaves. *Growth* trailer, bushy, vigorous and fairly free-flowering. Half-basket or basket.

'Sincerity'
HOLMES 1968
Double
Tube white, flushed pale pink, long and slender. *Sepals* white on top, slightly flushed pink, deeper pink on the undersides. Long, broad and slightly reflexed. *Corolla* white, fairly full, medium-sized bloom. *Foliage* mid-green, medium-sized, serrated leaves. *Growth* upright, bushy, vigorous and free-flowering. Bush.

'Siobhan'
RYLE 1976
AFS Registration No 1403
Semi-double
Tube rose pink, medium length and thickness. *Sepals* white, flushed pink at the base, and deeper pink on the underside, long, broad and held well out from the corolla. *Corolla* white, faintly tinged pink at the base of the petals. *Foliage* mid-green, medium-sized leaves. *Growth* upright, bushy, free-flowering. Bush. *Parentage* 'Joe Kusber' × 'Northumbrian Belle'.

'Siren'
KENNETT/CASTRO 1973
AFS Registration No 1109
Double
Tube white, medium length and thickness. *Sepals* white, green tips, curling up to the tube. *Corolla* pale lavender blue maturing to a darker shade of lavender, purple. Heavily overlaid with white petals and petaloids, opening tight and flaring as the bloom matures. *Foliage* glossy bright green on top, duller on the underside, medium-sized. *Growth* trailer, bushy, free-flowering. Basket.

'Sissy Sue'
FUCHSIA FOREST 1965
AFS Registration No 626
Semi-double
Tube pink, medium length and thickness. *Sepals* pink with green tips on top, deeper shade of pink on the underside. Broad and held well up towards the tube. *Corolla* pale lavender blue, shaded rose-pink, at the base of the sepals and with numerous pink petaloids. Medium-sized bloom. *Foliage* mid-green, longish, medium-sized, serrated leaves. *Growth* trailer, bushy, free-flowering. A very nice, pastel shade cultivar. Basket.

'Sister Esther'
MACHADO 1960
AFS Registration No 449
Double
Tube light pink, medium length and thickness. *Sepals* pale pink, long, broad and recurving. *Corolla* amethyst violet, fading to petunia purple, Paler shade at the base of the petals. Medium to large blooms. *Foliage* medium green, medium-sized leaves. *Growth* trailer, long, willowy, twisting branches, free-flowering. Basket.

'Sister Ginny'
SOO YUN 1974
AFS Registration No 1186
Semi-double
Tube light pink, veined darker pink, long, thin. *Sepals* pale pink on top, deeper shade on the undersides, light green tips, upturned, long and wide. *Corolla* campanula violet to light fuchsia purple at the base of the petals. Medium-sized bloom without petaloids. *Foliage* dark green, medium-sized, pointed leaves, stems and branches brownish red. *Growth* natural trailer, bushy, free-flowering. Basket.

'Skyway'
GADSBY 1970
Registered 1971
AFS Registration No 965
Single
Tube pale pink, medium length and thickness. *Sepals* pale pink on top, deeper shade of pink on the undersides, and with

green tips. Long, fairly broad, and held well out from the corolla. *Foliage* medium green, long, medium-sized, serrated leaves. *Growth* upright, bushy, self-branching and free-flowering. Bush or summer bedder. *Parentage* 'Jean Burton' × 'Rosabell'.

'Sleigh Bells' (28)
SCHNABEL 1954
AFS Registration No 196
Single
Tube white, short, medium thickness. *Sepals* white, long, narrow and recurving, pale green tips. *Corolla* white, medium-sized, bell-shaped. *Foliage* medium green, medium-sized, serrated leaves. *Growth* upright, bushy, vigorous and free-flowering. Bush.

'Slender Lady'
GADSBY 1970
AFS Registration No 879
Single
Tube white, medium length and thickness. *Sepals* white and waxy, flushed pink, long, slender and pointed. *Corolla* violet purple, fading to fuchsia purple, long, fairly compact bloom. *Foliage* bright green, medium-sized, serrated leaves. *Growth* upright, bushy, fairly vigorous, free-flowering. Bush. *Parentage* 'Pepi' × 'Sleigh Bells'.

'Snowball'
REITER 1952
AFS Registration No 127
Double
Tube white, flushed pink, medium length and thickness. *Sepals* white, pink flush at the base, long and reflexed. *Corolla* creamy white, full and fluffy, medium to large bloom. *Foliage* medium green, large, serrated leaves. *Growth* upright, vigorous, bushy, free-flowering. Grows best in shaded conditions. Bush.

'Snowcap' (127)
HENDERSON
Semi-double
Tube scarlet, short and of medium thickness. *Sepals* scarlet, short, broad and held well out. *Corolla* white with reddish veins, small to medium, rather loose-petalled bloom. *Foliage* medium to darkish green, small, serrated leaves. *Growth* upright, vigorous, very free-flowering, but one which needs a lot of pinching early to shape it well. Very easy to grow. Bush, standard, or summer bedder.

'Snowdrift'
KENNETT 1966
AFS Registration No 680
Semi-double
Tube white, short and thick. *Sepals* white with green tips, long, broad and held well out from the corolla with the tips slightly upturned. *Corolla* white with pink veining, loose-petalled, medium-sized bloom. *Foliage* dark green, medium-sized, ovate leaves. *Growth* upright, vigorous, free-flowering. Bush.

'Snowdrift'
COLVILLE 1966
Double
Tube dark rose pink, with light green streaks, long, medium thickness. *Sepals* rose red with green tips, short, broad and held right over the top of the corolla. *Corolla* pure white, but with some reddish veining. Very full, fluffy and compact medium-sized bloom. *Foliage* dark green, medium to large, serrated leaves. *Growth* upright, vigorous, rather lax, free-flowering, requires a lot of pinching to keep it in shape. Basket.

'Snowfire'
STUBBS 1978
AFS Registration No 1442
Double
Tube pink, medium length and thickness. *Sepals* white, wide and tapering, recurving on maturity. *Corolla* bright pink to coral, with white variegations. Bud shows rose pink streaks before opening. *Foliage* dark green, medium-sized. *Growth* free-flowering, upright, and bushy. Bush or standard.

'Snowflake'
WALKER AND JONES 1951
Single
Tube white, medium length and thickness. *Sepals* white, long, recurving straight up to the tube. *Corolla* white, bell-shaped, medium-sized bloom. *Foliage* mid-green, medium-sized leaves. *Growth* trailer, vigorous, bushy, free-flowering. Basket.

'Snow Flurry'
SCHNABEL 1952
AFS Registration No 115
Semi-double
Tube white, pinkish flush at the base, medium length and thickness. *Sepals* white, long, broad, held well out. *Corolla* white, medium-sized, compact bloom. *Foliage* light green, medium-sized leaves. *Growth* lax, bushy with arching growths, fairly vigorous. Will need early pinching to train it to shape. Bush or basket.

'Snow Queen'
HANDLEY 1975
AFS Registration No 1276
Double
Tube white, short and thick. *Sepals* white, short and broad. *Corolla* white, very full, ruffled and of good substance. *Foliage* medium green, leaves crinkled. *Growth* upright, vigorous, free-flowering. Strong stemmed but will require support through weight of blooms. Bush.

'Snowstorm'
HANDLEY 1976
Single to semi-double
Tube greenish-white, thin, medium length. *Sepals* white with pale green tips, completely reflexing. *Corolla* white, medium-sized, compact bloom. *Foliage* mid-green, medium-sized leaves. *Growth* upright, vigorous, free-flowering. Bush.

'Snowtime'
J.A. WRIGHT 1975
AFS Registration No 1307
Double
Tube scarlet, medium length and thickness. *Sepals* scarlet. *Corolla* white. *Foliage* dark green. *Growth* upright, vigorous, free-flowering, needs pinching to make a decent plant. Bush or standard. *Parentage* 'Swingtime' × 'Snowcap'.

'Snowy Summit'
STUBBS 1975
AFS Registration No 1259
Double
Tube white, medium length and thickness. *Sepals* white, long and broad. *Corolla* white, very full. *Stamens* pale pink. *Foliage* medium green with red veins. *Growth* natural trailer, vigorous, bushy, free-flowering. Should be grown in the shade to keep white colouring. Basket.

'So Big'
WALTZ 1955
Double
Tube pale pink, long and slender. *Sepals* pale pink with green tips, slightly deeper on the underside, long and recurving. *Corolla* creamy white with slight pink veining, large, rather loose-petalled bloom. *Foliage* light green, large, serrated leaves. *Growth* natural trailer, vigorous and, for its size, very free-flowering. Basket.

'So Happy'
SOO YUN FIELD 1965
AFS Registration No 647
Double
Tube bright red, medium length and thickness. *Sepals* red, longish, recurved. *Corolla* dark blue, paler at the base of the petals, medium-sized, faintly compact bloom. *Foliage* bright green with reddish stems, medium-sized leaves. *Growth* trailer, vigorous, free-flowering. Basket or half-basket.

'Solana Mar'
HASTINGS 1975
AFS Registration No 1309
Semi-double
Tube peachy pink with pink veining, medium length and thickness. *Sepals*

shades of peach pink, standing straight out. *Corolla* shading from hot pink to lavender pink with darker pink veining. *Foliage* medium green. *Stamens* reddish pink. *Growth* small upright, vigorous, free-flowering. Tends to throw more than four sepals. Bush, small standard.

'Solent Pride'
DEBONO 1980
AFS Registration No 1534
Single
Tube white with slight pink veining, thin, ½ in (13 mm) long. *Sepals* white with pale green tips on top, pale pink on the undersides, flaring back as the bloom matures. *Corolla* red purple RHS 63A, fading to RHS 61B, with RHS 58D, at the base. *Stamens* long, carmine, pistil pink. *Foliage* medium green. *Growth* can be trained as either upright or basket type, free-flowering and self-branching, vigorous, bushy.

'Sonata'
TIRET 1960
AFS Registration No 437
Double
Tube white with a greenish tinge, short, medium thickness. *Sepals* pink with green tips, short, broad and reflexing. *Corolla* white, with pink veining, very fluffy and full with numerous small outer petals. *Foliage* mid-green, medium-sized, longish and serrated leaves. *Growth* upright, bushy and very free-flowering. Bush.

'Sophisticated Lady' (87)
MARTIN 1964
AFS Registration No 609
Double
Tube pale pink, short and of medium thickness. *Sepals* pale pink, very long, broad and held slightly below the horizontal, out from the corolla. *Corolla* white, very full and compact. Short corolla but a medium to large-sized bloom. *Foliage* medium green with reddish veins, small to medium-sized, serrated leaves. *Growth* trailer, bushy, rather long stemmed, free-flowering. A beautiful cultivar. Half-basket.

'So Pretty'
PANCHARIAN 1975
AFS Registration No 1294
Double
Tube red, medium length and thickness. *Sepals* dark red on top, lighter red underneath. *Corolla* lavender blue, blended with white at the base of the petals and with red veining. Numerous petaloids with red base and veins, and white marbling. *Pistil* light red, stigma dark red, anthers pinkish white. *Foliage* dark green on top, lighter on the underside, stems red. *Growth* semi-trailer, bushy, vigorous and free-flowering. Bush or basket.

'South Coast'
DRAPKIN 1979
AFS Registration No 1507
Single
Tube ivory (RHS 4D), medium length and thickness. *Sepals* ivory white with green tips, streaked pink on the underside. *Corolla* opening cerise RHS 64B, fading to deep pink RHS 63A, white at the base of the petals. *Stamens* pink. *Pistil* white, pink at the tip. *Foliage* light green RHS 144A, medium-sized, serrated and with a red vein at the base. *Growth* very vigorous, upright, tall growing and bushy. Heat-tolerant.

'Southgate' (71)
WALKER AND JONES 1952
Double
Tube pale pink, medium length and thickness. *Sepals* pale pink, slightly deeper pink on the undersides, short, broad and upturned. *Corolla* soft pink with deeper pink veining, very compact, fluffy bloom. *Foliage* medium green, medium-sized, long, serrated leaves. *Growth* upright, vigorous, bushy, free-flowering, an easy cultivar to grow. Bush or half-basket.

'South Lakeland'
THORNLEY 1978
AFS Registration No 1466

Single
Tube creamy white, medium length and width. *Sepals* creamy white, flushed pink on top and underside, very firm and held horizontally. *Corolla* turkey red with a blue flush, small white fleck near the base of the petals. Similar colouring to 'Falling Stars' on opening. *Foliage* medium green. *Growth* free-flowering, self-branching, bushy, upright. Will make a good bush, standard or pyramid. Develops its best colour if grown if shade. Named after the South Lakeland Fuchsia Group. *Parentage* 'Falling Stars' × 'Hawkshead'.

'Southlanders'
CASTRO 1971
AFS Registration No 951
Single to semi-double
Tube white, medium length and thickness. *Sepals* white, broad, recurving slightly. *Corolla* lavender purple with white marbling, paler at the base of the petals, and fading to rose pink. Ruffled petals, opening flat. *Foliage* mid-green, medium-sized leaves. *Growth* upright, bushy, vigorous and free-flowering. Bush.

'South Pacific'
HODGES 1951
AFS Registration No 85
Single
Tube crimson, medium length and thickness. *Sepals* crimson; recurving. *Corolla* white, opening saucer-shaped, medium-sized bloom. *Foliage* yellowish green, medium-sized, serrated leaves. *Growth* upright, bushy, vigorous and free-flowering. Bush.

'South Seas'
FUCHSIA FOREST/CASTRO 1963
AFS Registration No 569
Semi-double to double
Tube white, flushed pale pink, medium length and thickness. *Sepals* white, flushed pink, long, broad, recurving. *Corolla* pink, medium sized, compact bloom. *Foliage* mid-green, medium-sized, serrated leaves. *Growth* lax, bushy, vigorous, free-flowering. Will make a good bush if pinched early. Bush or half-basket.

'Sparkles'
JOYCE 1960
Semi-double
Tube red, medium length and thickness. *Sepals* red, recurving slightly. *Corolla* purple, paler at the base of the petals and ageing to paler magenta purple. Medium-sized bloom. *Foliage* mid-green, medium-sized, serrated leaves. *Growth* upright, vigorous, bushy and free-flowering. Bush.

'Sparks'
STUBBS 1980
AFS Registration No 1549
Single
Tube flesh to salmon colouring, medium length and thickness. *Sepals* flesh to salmon, medium length, recurving. *Corolla* orangy-carmine, small and slightly flaring. *Foliage* dark green; 2 in (5 cm) long. *Growth* upright, or trailer, with weights, useful as a bush or basket. Very free-flowering.

'Spectacular'
GAGNON 1969
AFS Registration No 843
Single
Tube pinkish, turning darker pink as it matures, long and slender. *Sepals* white, flushed pink, held well out. *Corolla* white, fairly open, medium-sized bloom. *Foliage* mid-green, medium-sized leaves. *Growth* trailer, fairly vigorous, free-flowering. Half basket.

'Spion Kop'
JONES 1973
AFS Registration No 1128
Double
Tube rose-red, short, medium thickness. *Sepals* rose red, reflexing. *Corolla* white with rose-red veins, flaring slightly. Medium-sized, compact bloom. White petaloids, also veined rose red. *Foliage*

dull green, medium-sized, serrated leaves. *Growth* upright, bushy, self-branching, free-flowering, an excellent exhibition plant. Named after the site of a battle of the Boer War. Bush.

'Splendor Falls'
GAGNON 1962
AFS Registration No 508
Double
Tube tube bright pink, long, medium thickness. *Sepals* bright pink, long, reflexing slightly. *Corolla* dark lavender blue with a pinkish flush at the base of the petals. *Foliage* mid-green, medium-sized, serrated leaves. *Growth* trailer, very vigorous, free-flowering. Basket.

'Spring Bells'
KOOIJMAN 1972
Semi-double
Tube bright red, medium length and thickness. *Sepals* bright red, medium length, broad, held well out. *Corolla* white. *Foliage* medium to darkish green, medium-sized leaves, serrated. *Growth* upright, bushy, vigorous and free-flowering. Bush.

'Spring Shower'
TIRET 1953
AFS Registration No 156
Semi-double
Tube flesh pink, short, medium thickness. *Sepals* flesh pink, upturned to the tube. *Corolla* white, long petals, fairly compact bloom. *Foliage* mid-green, medium-sized leaves, serrated. *Growth* upright, bushy, self-branching, fairly vigorous and free-flowering. Bush.

'Square Dance'
SMALLWOOD 1973
AFS Registration No 1076
Double
Tube pink, medium length and thickness. *Sepals* pink, held well out. *Corolla* light bluish-mauve, fading to carmine, full, square-shaped. *Foliage* mid-green, medium-sized leaves. *Growth* upright, bushy, free-flowering. Bush. *Parentage* 'Pink Quartette' ×.

'Squarehead'
MACHADO 1962
AFS Registration No 498
Tube light red, short, thin. *Sepals* pink on top, light red on the undersides, short, pointed. *Corolla* coral pink, opening up in a square shape. Small bloom. *Foliage* dark green, small leaves. *Growth* trailer, bushy, self-branching. Makes a nice dwarf basket. Basket.

'Stained Glass'
FOSTER 1977
AFS Registration No 1417
Double
Tube china red to rose red, medium length and thickness. *Sepals* china red to rose red, greenish white tips, held well up. *Corolla* amethyst violet, streaked rose red at the base, with two tiers of petals, top set flaring. *Stamens* rose red. *Pistil* greenish-white. *Foliage* medium green. *Growth* semi-trailer. Basket, bush or standard.

'Stanley Cash'
PENNISI 1970
AFS Registration No 905
Double
Tube white, short and thick. *Sepals* white, with green tips, short and broad. *Corolla* deep royal purple, box-shaped. Medium-sized, very full and compact bloom. *Foliage* medium green, medium-sized leaves. *Growth* trailer, bushy, fairly vigorous and free-flowering. Can be grown as a bush if pinched early. A very attractive bloom which does, however, tend to fade badly as it ages. Bush or basket.

'Star Drops'
SOO YUN FIELD 1965
AFS Registration No 646
Double
Tube red, medium length and thickness. *Sepals* red, held well out. *Corolla* creamy white with red veins. Numerous petaloids extend on stems. Fairly open,

medium-sized bloom. *Foliage* mid-green, medium-sized leaves with red stems. *Growth* trailer, bushy, free-flowering. Basket.

'Stardust' (187)

MRS E. HANDLEY 1973
AFS Registration No 1134
Single
Tube salmon pink, thin, medium length. *Sepals* salmon pink on top, salmon-orange on the underside. *Corolla* crimson with scarlet edges and shaded orange at the base of the petals. Small bloom. *Foliage* medium green, medium-sized, narrow leaves. *Growth* upright, bushy, free-flowering. Bush.

'Stargazer'

REITER 1946
Single
Tube pale rose madder, small, medium thickness. *Sepals* pale rose madder. *Corolla* rose madder with imperial purple marbling, small to medium size. *Foliage* medium green. *Growth* bushy, self-branching, upright. Bush, small pot plant.

'Starlet'

KENNETT 1971
AFS Registration No 955
Semi-double
Tube pink, medium length, thickness. *Corolla* lavender pink, maturing to bright pink, flaring. *Sepals* pale pink with green tips, long, broad and held over the corolla. *Foliage* medium green with reddish veins, medium size, serrated. *Growth* upright, bushy, free-flowering, large flower. Bush.

'Starlite'

WALTZ 1961
AFS Registration No 493
Double
Tube dark pink, medium length, slightly bulbous. *Sepals* smoky-rose, with green tips, medium length, broad and held well out over the corolla. *Corolla* deep lilac-blue, with pink marbling. Opens rather flat and star shaped, fairly full, medium-sized bloom. *Foliage* medium green, large, serrated leaves. *Growth* natural trailer, free-flowering. Basket.

'Star of Pink'

SOO YUN 1975
AFS Registration No 1271
Double
Tube pink, short and thin. *Sepals* light pink on top, dark pink underneath, light green tips. flaring straight out with the tips curling upwards. *Corolla* medium pink, flaring out bell-shaped as the bloom matures. *Stamens* dark pink, anthers beige. *Pistil* light pink, stigma white. *Foliage* dark green, small to medium size, with red stems. *Growth* semi-trailer, very free-flowering, bushy and vigorous. Basket.

'Stella Ann'

BAKER/DUNNETT 1974
AFS Registration No 1199
Single
Tube poppy red RHS 40D, thick, medium length, triphylla type. *Sepals* Chinese coral RHS 32D, with green tips, short, wide and opening to display the corolla. *Corolla* Indian orange RHS 32A, rounded. *Foliage* olive green RHS 137B, with strawberry red veining and undersides. *Growth* upright, bushy, vigorous, very free-flowering. Bush or standard.

'Stella Marina'

SCHNABEL 1951
AFS Registration No 81
Double
Tube crimson, medium length and thickness. *Sepals* crimson, long, narrow, recurving. *Corolla* violet-purple with light crimson marbling and faint white patches. Medium-sized, compact bloom. *Foliage* mid-green, medium-sized leaves. *Growth* upright, vigorous, bush and free-flowering. Bush or standard.

'Strawberry Delight'

GADSBY 1970
AFS Registration No 873

Double
Tube crimson, medium length and thickness. *Sepals* crimson, short, broad and reflexed. *Corolla* white with pink veining, and numerous petaloids white flushed pink. Rather ragged, loose-petalled, medium bloom. *Foliage* yellowish green with a bronze sheen, ageing to green. Medium to large, long, serrated leaves. *Growth* upright, lax, bushy, free-flowering. Bush or half basket. *Parentage* 'Trase' × 'Golden Marinka'.

'Strawberry Festival'
HAAG
Double
Tube bright red, medium length and thickness. *Sepals* bright red, long, broad, recurving. *Corolla* pink with deeper veins. Medium to large, fairly compact blooms. *Foliage* mid-green, medium to large, serrated leaves. *Growth* upright, vigorous and free-flowering. Bush.

'Strawberry Fizz'
STUBBS 1971
AFS Registration No 997
Double
Tube pale pink, medium length and thickness. *Sepals* pale pink, long, broad, curling back towards the tube. *Corolla* deep pink with picoteed edges, very full and fluffy, flaring slightly. Medium to large bloom. *Foliage* dark green, medium-sized leaves. *Growth* trailer, vigorous, free-flowering. Basket.

'Strawberry Queen'
HAAG
Single
Tube red, short, medium thickness. *Sepals* red, short, broad, held well out from the corolla. *Corolla* deep strawberry, small, compact bloom. *Foliage* mid-green, small to medium-sized, serrated leaves. *Growth* dwarf upright, bushy, free-flowering. Dwarf bush.

'Strawberry Sundae'
KENNETT AND ROSS 1958
Double
Tube greenish-white, long, medium thickness. *Sepals* white with green tips, broad and held well out. *Corolla* pinkish lilac, very compact, medium-sized bloom. *Foliage* mid-green, medium-sized, finely serrated leaves. *Growth* trailer, bushy, free-flowering. Half-basket.

'Strawberry Supreme'
GADSBY 1970
AFS Registration No 874
Double
Tube waxy crimson, medium length and thickness. *Sepals* waxy crimson, held well out. *Corolla* white with rose-carmine flush. Medium-sized bloom. *Foliage* mid-green, medium sized, serrated leaves. *Growth* upright, bushy, fairly vigorous, free-flowering. Bush. *Parentage* 'Trase' × 'Golden Marinka'.

'Streamliner'
TIRET 1951
AFS Registration No 96
Semi-double
Tube bright crimson, long and thin. *Sepals* bright crimson, long, narrow and twisting. *Corolla* rosy-red, and crimson. Paler at the base of the petals. Long petals, fairly compact bloom. *Foliage* mid-green, medium-sized leaves. *Growth* trailer, long branched, fairly vigorous and free-flowering. Needs pinching early. Basket.

'Striata Perfecta'
BANKS 1868
Single
Tube bright red, medium length and thickness. *Sepals* bright red, long, broad and curling over the tube. *Corolla* deep purple with a pink stripe down the centre of each of the four petals. Long, bell-shaped bloom. *Foliage* darkish green, long and narrow, serrated leaves. *Growth* upright, bushy and vigorous, but needs pinching early to form a good shape. Free-flowering and very attractive. Bush.

'Striding Edge'
THORNLEY 1965
Single
Tube white, slightly flushed rose pink,

medium length and thickness. *Sepals* white with a greenish tinge, long and narrow. *Corolla* soft pink, longish bloom. *Foliage* mid-green, medium-sized, serrated leaves. *Growth* bushy, upright, vigorous. Needs pinching early to make a nice bushy shape. The blooms are unusual in that the sepals spread out, then downwards like a claw over the corolla. Very distinctive. Bush. *Parentage* 'Nightingale' × 'Don Peralta'.

'Striker'
TOLLEY 1974
AFS Registration No 1231
Semi-double
Tube flesh pink, medium length and thickness. *Sepals* white, flesh pink at the base and with green tips, long, pointed and slightly upturned. *Corolla* violet purple, lighter shade at the base of the petals. *Foliage* pale green, medium-sized, ovate, slightly serrated leaves. *Growth* upright, self-branching, bushy, free-flowering. Bush. *Parentage* 'White Spider' ×.

'String of Pearls' (95)
PACEY 1976
Single to semi-double
Tube pale pink, short and thick. *Sepals* pink with green tips, short, medium width, reflexed. *Corolla* pale rosy-purple, small compact bloom. *Foliage* pale green, small, serrated leaves. *Growth* upright, very vigorous, bushy and exceptionally free-flowering. Not an easy one to train into any recognised shape. Bush. *F. lycioides* seedling.

'Stubby'
STUBBS 1975
AFS Registration No 1260
Single
Tube rose to red, short and thick. *Sepals* rose to red, short. *Corolla* purple violet to magenta, petals slightly convex. *Foliage* dark green, small leaves. *Growth* upright, bushy, very free-flowering, short corolla and wide short tube give the flower a 'stubby' look. Bush.

'Suey Ho'
NEIDERHOLZER 1947
Single
Tube pale, phlox pink, medium length and thickness. *Sepals* pale phlox pink. *Corolla* white with red markings, medium-sized, compact bloom. *Foliage* mid-green, medium-sized, serrated leaves. *Growth* upright, vigorous, bushy and free-flowering. Bush or standard.

'Sugar Blues'
MARTIN 1964
AFS Registration No 610
Double
Tube white, tinged pink. *Sepals* white on top, pink tinged undersides, long. *Corolla* dark blue fading to violet blue, with pink shading in the centre, very long and tight. Large bloom. *Foliage* medium green. *Growth* trailer, free-flowering, and bushy. Basket.

'Summer Breeze'
PENNISI 1971
AFS Registration No 1015
Double
Tube white, medium length and thickness. *Sepals* pink, green tipped, short, broad, recurving. *Corolla* campanula violet, paler at the base of the petals, small groups of petaloids in between the petals. Fairly full, fluffy bloom. *Foliage* mid-green, medium-sized leaves. *Growth* trailer, bushy, vigorous and free-flowering. Basket.

'Summer Skies'
NEIDERHOLZER/WALTZ 1949
Single
Tube pale rose pink, medium length and thickness. *Sepals* pale rose, upturned. *Corolla* pale silvery blue, shaded pink at the base of the petals. Medium-sized bloom. *Foliage* medium green, medium-sized, serrated leaves. *Growth* upright, bushy, free-flowering. Bush.

'Summer Snow'
WALTZ 1956
AFS Registration No 272
Semi-double
Tube white, tinged green, long, medium

thickness. *Sepals* white with green tips, long, narrow and reflexed to the tube. *Corolla* creamy white, medium-sized, loose-petalled. *Foliage* mid-green, medium-sized, serrated leaves. *Growth* upright, vigorous, self-branching, and free-flowering. Bush.

'Summer Splendor'
PLUMMER 1953
Double
Tube creamy white, medium length and thickness. *Sepals* creamy white, turning red later in the season, long, broad, and reflexing. *Corolla* rose madder, compact, medium-sized bloom. *Foliage* mid-green, medium-sized, slightly serrated leaves. *Growth* trailer, fairly vigorous, free-flowering. Basket.

'Sunburst'
REITER 1946
Semi-double
Tube pale carmine, medium length and thickness. *Sepals* carmine, long, upturned. *Corolla* crimson, short, fairly compact. *Foliage* mid-green, medium-sized, serrated leaves. *Growth* upright, vigorous, free-flowering. Bush.

'Sundance'
HANDLEY 1974
AFS Registration No 1194
Single
Tube light rose, RHS 55B, medium length and thickness. *Sepals* light rose, long, held well out from the corolla. *Corolla* light burgundy (RHS 71B), ageing to cerise (RHS 57B). Overlapping petals, and long, bell-shaped bloom. *Foliage* pale yellowish green, medium-sized bloom. *Growth* trailer, self-branching, bushy, vigorous, free-flowering. Basket.

'Sundown'
FUCHSIA FOREST/CASTRO 1961
AFS Registration No 472
Double
Tube red, short and thick. *Sepals* red, short, broad and completely reflexed. *Corolla* dark lavender, streaks of pink on the outer petals, and at the base. Loose, medium to large bloom. *Foliage* medium green, medium-sized leaves. *Growth* upright, bushy, free-flowering. Bush.

'Sunkissed'
TIRET 1957
Double
Tube white, short and thick. *Sepals* white on top with green tips, flushed pink on the underside. Short, broad and slightly reflexed. *Corolla* dark red with pink marbling, medium-sized, fairly compact bloom. *Foliage* mid-green, medium-sized, ovate, serrated leaves. *Growth* upright, vigorous, rather lax, free-flowering. Bush or half-basket.

'Sunny Smiles'
GADSBY 1968
Registered 1971
AFS Registration No 967
Double
Tube pink, medium length, slightly thick. *Sepals* reddish pink on top, salmon pink on the undersides, long, narrow and held well out, curling slightly. *Corolla* crimson, paler at the base of the petals, medium-sized, bell-shaped bloom. *Foliage* light green, small to medium-sized, serrated leaves. *Growth* bushy, lax, vigorous, free-flowering. Needs early pinching to train it to shape. Bush or half-basket. *Parentage* 'Pink Galore' × 'Athela'.

'Sunray' (24)
MILNER 1872
Single
Tube red, short, medium thickness. *Sepals* dark pink on top, deeper shade on the undersides, reflexed. *Corolla* purplish-cerise, small and compact. *Foliage* light green with creamy white edges and flushed cerise. The foliage does vary considerably depending on the conditions under which it is grown. A very good foliage cultivar with few insignificant blooms. *Growth* upright, bushy, fairly vigorous. Bush.

'Sunset'
NEIDERHOLZER 1938
Single

Tube pink, short, medium thickness. *Sepals* pink on top, deeper pink on the undersides, tipped green. Short, broad and reflexed slightly. *Corolla* orange-cerise, small, open bell-shaped bloom. *Foliage* mid-green, with reddish veins, small to medium-sized, serrated leaves. *Growth* upright, bushy, self-branching, fairly vigorous and free-flowering. Bush. *Parentage* 'Rolla' × 'Aurora Superba'.

'Sunshine'
NEIDERHOLZER 1948
Single
Tube pale rose pink, short, thin. *Sepals* pale rose pink with green tips, short, broad, held well out. *Corolla* geranium lake, small and compact. *Foliage* mid-green, small to medium-sized leaves. *Growth* upright, bushy, self-branching and free-flowering. Bush.

'Sunshine Belle'
THORNE 1959
Single
Tube flesh pink, medium length and thickness. *Sepals* flesh pink, broad and reflexing. *Corolla* orange, fading to pinkish-purple. *Foliage* medium green, medium-sized, very finely serrated leaves. *Growth* upright, bushy, self-branching and fairly free-flowering. Bush.

'Susan'
NEIDERHOLZER 1948
Double
Tube ivory, short, medium thickness. *Sepals* pale rose pink, held well out from the corolla. *Corolla* pale blue, tinged campanula violet and splashes of mauve. Medium sized, compact bloom. *Foliage* mid-green, medium-sized, finely serrated leaves. *Growth* upright, bushy, free-flowering. Bush.

'Susan Allen'
ALLEN 1974
AFS Registration No 1215
Single
Tube crimson, short and of medium thickness. *Sepals* crimson, short, broad. *Corolla* cyclamen purple, medium-sized bloom. *Foliage* dark green with reddish stems, medium-sized leaves. *Growth* upright, bushy, free-flowering. Easy to grow. Bush. *Parentage* 'Albion' × 'Rosedale'.

'Susan Ford'
CLYNE 1974
AFS Registration No 1176
Double
Tube neyron rose, short and thin. *Sepals* neyron rose, crepe effect on the underside, and reflexing, short and broad. *Corolla* Imperial purple (RHS 78B), fading to cyclamen purple RHS 74B, rosette shaped. Compact, medium size. *Foliage* dark green, medium-sized leaves, serrated. *Growth* upright self branching, bushy and free-flowering. Will make a good exhibition plant. Bush. *Parentage* 'La Campanella' × 'Winston Churchill'.

'Susan Travis' (78)
TRAVIS 1958
Single
Tube pink, medium length and thickness. *Sepals* pink with green tips, short, broad and upturned. *Corolla* rose-pink, paler shade of pink at the base of the petals. Medium-sized, compact bloom. *Foliage* mid-green, dull, medium-sized, serrated leaves. *Growth* upright, bushy, free-flowering. Bush or garden hardy.

'Susan Young'
YOUNG 1975
AFS Registration No 1261
Double
Tube white, medium length and thickness. *Sepals* white RHS 155D, white tips RHS 155A, flushed pink and recurving over the tube. *Corolla* purple lilac RHS 76C, divided into four quarters, each of four petals. *Stamens* pink, anthers red. *Pistil and stigma* white. *Foliage* medium green. *Growth* upright, bushy, free-flowering. Bush. Sport of 'Blue Pearl'.

'Susie Olcese'
MARTIN 1960
AFS Registration No 447

Double
Tube white, medium length and thickness. *Sepals* white, long, broad, upturned. *Corolla* pale blue, very full and compact. *Foliage* medium green, medium-sized leaves. *Growth* trailer, free-flowering. Basket.

'Susie Tandy'
WHITEHOUSE 1980
AFS Registration No 1537
Double
Tube dark rose pink, medium length and width. *Sepals* waxy pink tipped green, deeper pink undersides. *Corolla* cream, flushed pale pink, small and compact. *Foliage* light to medium green, ovate, serrated leaf margins, small to medium in size. *Growth* natural trailer, self-branching and bushy, very floriferous. Basket. Shade for best colour.

'Suzy'
CARLSON/WESTOVER 1977
AFS Registration No 1430
Double
Tube medium pink, short. *Sepals* pink, tinged salmon, crepe-like, 2 in (5 cm) long, flaring upwards on maturity. *Corolla* lilac to pink, very loose, petals folding into each other. *Foliage* dark green, large, and long with red stems. *Growth* semi-trailer, will trail with weights. Basket. Sport of 'Bonanza'.

'Swan Lake'
TRAVIS 1957
Double
Tube eau de nil, short, medium thickness. *Sepals* white, flushed pink at the base, long and broad. *Corolla* chalk white, flushed pale pink in the centre. Medium-sized, compact bloom. *Foliage* mid-green, medium-sized leaves. *Growth* upright, bushy, free-flowering. Bush.

'Swanley Gem' (170)
CANNELL 1901
Single
Tube scarlet, medium length and thickness. *Sepals* scarlet, short, broad and reflexing. *Corolla* violet with reddish veins, and paler shade of scarlet at the base of the petals. Opens saucer-shaped, becoming paler as the bloom ages. *Foliage* mid-green, small leaves. *Growth* upright, bushy, self-branching and free-flowering. A good exhibition variety. Bush.

'Swanley Yellow' (178)
CANNELL 1900
Single
Tube orange-pink, long, medium thickness. *Sepals* orange-pink, medium length, narrow and upturned. *Corolla* rich orange-vermilion, small and compact, long and slender blooms. *Foliage* bronzy green, medium to large, serrated leaves. *Growth* upright, vigorous and free-flowering, but needs early pinching to make it into any sort of shape.

'Sweet Dreams'
FIELD 1980
AFS Registration No 1561
Double
Tube phlox pink (RHS 62B), short and thin. *Sepals* phlox pink, $1\frac{1}{4}$ in (3 cm) in length. *Corolla* phlox pink RHS 62B, with six phlox pink petaloids $\frac{1}{2}$ in (13 mm). *Pistil* pink. *Stigma* black. *Foliage* light green, leaves $2\frac{1}{4}$ in (6 cm) in length by $1\frac{1}{4}$ in (3 cm) wide. *Growth* upright, bushy and self-branching. Basket or bush.

'Sweetheart' (43)
VAN WEIRINGEN 1970
Single
Tube white, long, medium thickness. *Sepals* white, pink flush on the undersides, green tips, short, broad, and reflexing. *Corolla* pinkish-cerise, shaded white at the base of the petals. Medium-sized, slightly bell-shaped bloom. *Foliage* medium green, small, serrated leaves. *Growth* upright, vigorous, self-branching, bushy and very free-flowering. Good exhibition variety, but rather prone to *Botrytis*. Bush.

'Sweet Leilani'
TIRET 1957
AFS Registration No 296

Double
Tube pale pink, short and thick. *Sepals* pale pink with green tips. Short, broad and curling up over the tube. *Corolla* pale lavender-blue, very full and ruffled, with pink markings on the outer petals. *Foliage* light to medium green, medium-sized, serrated leaves. *Growth* upright, bushy, very free-flowering. Bush.

'Sweet Mystery'
GORMAN 1970
AFS Registration No 932
Double
Tube pale pink, medium length and thickness. *Sepals* pale pink, long, broad, recurving. *Corolla* waxy white, tinged with pink at the base of the petals. Very full, large bloom. *Foliage* bright green, medium-sized leaves. *Growth* upright, bushy, rather lax, free-flowering, Bush or basket.

'Sweet Red Eyes'
SOO YUN 1979
AFS Registration No 1494
Single
Tube crimson red, short, medium thickness. *Sepals* crimson red, $1\frac{7}{8}$ in (48 mm) long, crepe effect underneath, curling up and outwards to horizontal. *Corolla* white with red veins and at the base of the petals, forming a tight bell with petaloids forming cups. *Stamens* pink, pistil dark pink with white tip. *Foliage* medium green with red veins and stems. Leaves $1\frac{3}{4}$ in (44 mm) long. *Growth* upright, bushy but will trail if weighted. Blooms on tips of branches. Needs frequent pinching, blooms freely and early.

'Sweet Revenge'
GADSBY 1975
AFS Registration No 1315
Double
Tube neyron rose, medium length and thickness. *Sepals* neyron rose RHS 55A, broad. *Corolla* hyacinth blue RHS 91A, shading to wisteria blue RHS 92A. Petaloids neyron rose. *Foliage* medium green, long and narrow. *Growth* upright, bushy, free-flowering. Bush or standard. *Parentage* 'Rose Bower' × 'Magenta Flush'.

'Sweet Sixteen'
WALKER AND JONES 1951
Double
Tube pale pink, medium length and thickness. *Sepals* pink, medium length, broad, held slightly down from the horizontal. *Corolla* rich pink, with rose pink veins. Very full and compact. *Foliage* mid-green, medium-sized, serrated leaves. *Growth* trailer, very free-flowering, but requires pinching early to get it into shape. Basket.

'Swingtime'
TIRET 1950
AFS Registration No 66
Double
Tube scarlet, medium length and thickness. *Sepals* scarlet, broad and reflexing. *Corolla* pure white with scarlet veining. Very full, fluffy bloom. *Foliage* medium to darkish green, red veins, medium-sized, finely serrated leaves. *Growth* upright, but rather lax, very vigorous, bushy and free-flowering. Basket, bush (if well pinched and staked) or summer bedder.

'Swiss Miss'
FUCHSIA FOREST/CASTRO 1963
AFS Registration No 570
Semi-double
Tube pink, medium length and thickness. *Sepals* pink with green tips, long, broad and reflexed. *Corolla* white, flushed pink and with pink veins, very open, loose-petalled, fluffy bloom. *Foliage* mid-green, medium-sized, serrated leaves. *Growth* trailer, bushy, free-flowering. Half-basket.

'S' Wonderful'
CASTRO 1961
AFS Registration No 473
Double
Tube bright pink, medium length and thickness. *Sepals* bright pink, flaring out then curling up and under. *Corolla* inner petals pale lavender, outer petals orchid pink. Medium-sized, fairly compact

bloom. *Foliage* medium green, medium-sized, serrated leaves. *Growth* natural trailer, long, willowy, branches, vigorous and free-flowering. Requires pinching hard to form a good plant. Basket.

'Sylvia Barker'
BARKER 1973
AFS Registration No 1077
Single
Tube waxy white, long, medium thickness. *Sepals* waxy white with green tips, held well out. *Corolla* scarlet with a slight smoky cast, small bloom. *Foliage* dark green with outstanding veins, small to medium-sized, serrated leaves. *Growth* lax, bushy, vigorous, free-flowering. Bush.

'Sylvia Young'
YOUNG 1980
AFS Registration No 1573
Double
Tube white, short and thick. *Sepals* white (RHS 155A), with green tips on top, pale rose pink on the undersides, broad and medium length. *Corolla* pale mauve RHS 84A, medium to large, flared. *Stamens* pink. *Pistil* white. *Foliage* medium green, RHS 137D, medium-sized. *Growth* upright, free-flowering, bushy. Bush or standard. *Parentage* 'Susan Young' × 'Arthur Young'.

'Symphony' (103)
NEIDERHOLZER 1944
Semi-double
Tube pale pink, medium length and thickness. *Sepals* pale pink, long, narrow and curling upwards. *Corolla* pale violet-blue, fading slightly with maturity. Medium-sized very compact bloom. *Foliage* mid-green, longish, medium-sized, serrated leaves. *Growth* upright, bushy, vigorous, self-branching and free-flowering. A beautifully shaped fuchsia, not difficult to grow and shape. Bush.

'Tabu'
PASKESEN 1974
AFS Registration No 1187
Double
Tube pale pink, medium length and thickness. *Sepals* pale pink on top, salmon-pink on the undersides, held well out from the corolla but reflexing as the bloom matures. *Corolla* magenta rose fading to smoky-rose, with pale pink marbling at the base of the smaller outer petals. *Stamens* rose-pink. *Foliage* mid-green, medium-sized leaves. *Growth* upright, bushy, fairly vigorous and free-flowering. Bush or standard.

'Taddle'
R. GUBLER 1974
Single
Tube deep rose pink, short, thick. *Sepals* rose pink, short, broad and reflexing completely. *Corolla* white with pinkish veins, compact, medium-sized blooms. *Foliage* light to medium green, medium-sized leaves. *Growth* upright, bushy, vigorous and very free-flowering, makes a very good exhibition plant. Bush.

'Taffeta'
KENNETT 1962
AFS Registration No 536
Double
Tube white, medium length and thickness. *Sepals* white on top, flushed pale pink, undersides, pink. Short broad, reflexing. *Corolla* violet-purple, very full, and compact bloom. *Foliage* medium green, medium-sized leaves. *Growth* trailer, bushy, free-flowering. Basket.

'Taffeta Bow'
STUBBS 1974
AFS Registration No 1196
Double
Tube pink, short, medium thickness. *Sepals* carmine rose RHS 52C, broad and long, crepe effect on the undersides, opening flat when reflexing. *Corolla* purple-violet, RHS 82A with serrated petals, opens compact and flares on maturity. Very attractive, medium to large-sized bloom. *Foliage* dark green with crimson veins, medium-sized, serrated leaves.

Growth trailer, self-branching, bushy, vigorous and free-flowering. Basket.

'Taffy'

MARTIN 1961

AFS Registration No 467

Single

Tube white, flushed pink, long, medium thickness. *Sepals* pink on top with a stripe running down the centre, deeper shade of pink on the underside, tipped green. Long, narrow and pointing downwards over the corolla. *Corolla* salmon-pink, bright pink overlay, long and with serrated petals. An untidy, very open bloom. *Foliage* light green, medium-sized, heavily serrated leaves. *Growth* natural trailer, fairly vigorous and free-flowering. Inclined to be very rampant and very difficult to train to any recognised shape.

'Tahiti'

SCHNABEL 1963

AFS Registration No 583

Double

Tube white, flushed pale pink, medium length, thick. *Sepals* very pale pink on top with green tips and a deeper shade of pink on the undersides, long, broad and reflexing. *Corolla* bright rose pink, very full and compact, medium-sized bloom. *Foliage* medium green, large, finely serrated leaves. *Growth* upright, bushy, self-branching and free-flowering. Easy to grow, and worthwhile. Bush.

'Tahoe'

KENNETT 1964

AFS Registration No 615

Semi-double to double

Tube white, flushed pink, short, medium thickness. *Sepals* white with green tips, long, narrow and curving upwards. *Corolla* light blue with shades of lavender blue and orchid, with pink shading at the base of the petals. Medium-sized, fairly loose bloom, opening flat. *Foliage* medium green, large and serrated leaves. *Growth* upright, tending to be rather lax, vigorous and fairly free-flowering. Bush.

'Tamalpais'

NEIDERHOLZER 1951

AFS Registration No 99

Single

Tube white, medium length and thickness. *Sepals* white, faintly flushed pink, long, narrow and curling upwards. *Corolla* rose-pink, medium-sized, compact bloom. *Foliage* mid-green, medium-sized, serrated leaves. *Growth* trailer, long-branching, fairly vigorous and free-flowering. Needs early pinching to form a good shape. Basket.

'Tammy'

ERICKSON 1962

AFS Registration No 542

Double

Tube waxy white, medium length, thick. *Sepals* pink on top, deeper shade of pink on the undersides, long, broad spreading and twisting outwards then upturned. *Corolla* lavender purple with streaks of rose-pink, numerous petaloids. Large, open, loose-petalled bloom. *Foliage* medium green, small to medium-sized, finely serrated leaves. *Growth* upright, vigorous, rather lax, bushy. Free-flowering. Bush or basket.

'Tamworth'

HANDLEY 1976

AFS Registration No 1372

Single

Tube pure white, medium length and thickness. *Sepals* pure white with green tips, reflexing slightly. *Corolla* white at the base, then a band of salmon-pink turning to rich purple at the edge of the petals, medium-sized, fairly compact bloom. *Foliage* light green, medium-sized leaves. *Growth* upright, vigorous, bushy and free-flowering. Bush.

'Tangerine'

TIRET 1949

Single

Tube dark flesh-pink, long, medium thickness. *Sepals* greenish, flushed carmine with green tips, short, medium width. Held well out from the corolla. *Corolla* brilliant salmon-orange, small to medium size, fairly compact. Longish bloom of a distinctive colour. *Growth* upright, vigorous, very free-flowering. One requiring pinching early in order to get it into shape, but well worth any effort expended on it. Bush. *Parentage F. cordifolia* ×.

'Tanhouse'

ROYLE 1979
AFS Registration No 1525
Single
Tube light red, medium length and thickness. *Sepals* light red, with white tips. *Corolla* lilac, medium-sized. *Stamens* pink. *Pistil* pink. *Stigma* yellow. *Foliage* medium green, oval. *Growth* vigorous, self-branching, tall, upright. Free-flowering. Will make a good bush or standard.

'Tanie Balasam'

PENNISI 1969
AFS Registration No 859
Double
Tube white, short and thick. *Sepals* white, short, broad, reflexing. *Corolla* pink, very full, medium-sized bloom. *Foliage* mid-green, medium-sized leaves. *Growth* trailer, bushy, free-flowering. Basket.

'Tanu Lo Bue'

PENNISI 1969
AFS Registration No 858
Double
Tube red, short, medium thickness. *Sepals* red, short, broad, standing straight out from the corolla. *Corolla* pink with white variegations. Paler at the base of the petals. Large, compact blooms. *Foliage* dark green, small to medium leaves. *Growth* trailer, bushy, free-flowering. Basket.

'Tanya'

MRS E. HOLMES 1975
Single
Very pale pink self. Medium-sized, fairly compact bloom. *Foliage* mid-green, medium-sized leaves. *Growth* upright, bushy, free-flowering. A very delicate pink cultivar. Bush.

'Tanya Bridger'

BRIDGER 1958
Double
Tube white, long and thin. *Sepals* white, long, broad and reflexed. *Corolla* pale lavender with pink tinge on the outer petals. Medium-sized, compact bloom. *Foliage* pale green, medium-sized, ovate, finely serrated leaves. *Growth* upright, bushy, self-branching and free-flowering. Bush. Described by the raiser as a double 'Melody'.

'Tarantella'

NEIDERHOLZER 1946
Single
Tube red, medium length and thickness. *Sepals* red, long, broad, recurving. *Corolla* magenta, medium-sized, open blooms. *Foliage* mid-green, medium-sized leaves. *Growth* upright, bushy, free-flowering. Bush.

'Ted's Rainbow'

ZERLANG 1977
AFS Registration No 1404
Single
Tube pink, thin, medium length. *Sepals* pink, short and flaring. *Corolla* medium purple, short and round. *Stamens* pink. *Pistil* white. *Foliage* variegated lemon yellow, light to dark green, red veins. Oval, serrated edges. Leaves more yellow in full sun. *Growth* upright, self-branching, bush. Bush, basket.

'Teepee'

TOLLEY 1974
AFS Registration No 1232
Single
Tube dull, dark red, long, medium thickness. *Sepals* dull red, long, narrow, twisting. *Corolla* Indian red, shaped like an Indian teepee with the sepals lying on the corolla. Medium-sized bloom. *Foliage* mid-green, dull, ovate, serrated leaves,

reddish stems. *Growth* upright, self-branching, bushy, free-flowering. Bush.

'Television'

WALKER AND JONES 1950

Double

Tube white, medium length and thickness. *Sepals* white on top, pale pink on the undersides. *Corolla* deep orchid, splashed fuchsia pink, medium-sized, fairly compact bloom. *Foliage* mid-green, medium-sized leaves. *Growth* lax upright, bushy, fairly vigorous, free-flowering. Bush.

'Temptation'

PETERSON 1959

AFS Registration No 376

Single

Tube white, flushed pink, long, thickish. *Sepals* white with pink flush, long, broad and held well out from the corolla, medium-sized, compact bloom. *Foliage* darkish green, small to medium-sized, longish, serrated leaves. *Corolla* bright reddish-orange, shaded white at the base of the petals. Medium-sized compact bloom. *Growth* upright, bushy, free-flowering. Bush.

'Tennessee Waltz' (165)

WALKER AND JONES 1950

Semi-double

Tube rose madder, medium length and thickness. *Sepals* rose madder, long, broad and curving upwards towards the tube. *Corolla* lilac lavender with splashes of rose on the petals, fairly loose, uneven petal length. Medium-sized bloom. *Foliage* medium green, medium-sized, serrated leaves. *Growth* upright, vigorous, self-branching, and very free-flowering. One of the easiest fuchsias to grow, and the one with which every beginner ought to start. It shapes well and makes an excellent exhibition plant. Bush or standard.

'Teresa'

TAYLOR 1969

AFS Registration No 911

Double

Tub sepals and corolla pink. Medium-sized, compact bloom. *Foliage* darkish green, medium leaves. *Growth* trailer, bushy, free-flowering. Basket.

'Terracotta'

NEIDERHOLZER 1946

Single

Tube turkey red, medium length and thickness. *Sepals* turkey red, recurving. *Corolla* magenta, paler at the base of the petals, medium-sized, compact bloom. *Foliage* mid-green, medium-sized leaves. *Growth* lax upright, bushy, free-flowering. Bush.

'Tessie'

KEASTER 1973

AFS Registration No 1078

Single

Tube light pink, short, medium thickness. *Sepals* light pink on top, deeper shade of pink on the underside, reflexing. *Corolla* light rose pink, deeper rose at the edge of the petals, medium-sized compact bloom. *Foliage* dark green, medium-sized leaves. *Growth* semi-trailer, self-branching, vigorous, and free-flowering. Bush or basket.

'Tetrad'

BROWN AND SOULES 1951

AFS Registration No 77

Double

Tube red, short, medium thickness. *Sepals* red, short, broad, cupped over the corolla. *Corolla* dark blue, square shaped, medium-sized bloom. *Foliage* medium to darkish green, medium-sized leaves. *Growth* upright, vigorous, bushy and free-flowering. Bush.

'Texas'

HAZARD

Single

Tube white, medium length and thickness. *Sepals* white with pink tips, long, narrow and reflexing. *Corolla* reddish violet, medium-sized bloom. *Foliage* light green, medium-sized leaves. *Growth* trailer, vigorous, free-flowering, Half-basket.

'Texas Longhorn' (132)
FUCHSIA LA 1961
Double
Tube scarlet, long, fairly slender. *Sepals* scarlet, very long, narrow, drooping downwards. *Corolla* white with cerise veins, long blooms. *Foliage* mid-green, with reddish veins, medium-sized leaves, very finely serrated. *Growth* trailer, not an easy cultivar to grow, and for the few blooms which it normally produces it is hardly worth the effort. Trailer.

'Thalia' (15)
TURNER 1855
Triphylla type
Tube deep flame red, long and very slender. *Sepals* flame red, very small and pointed. *Corolla* orange-scarlet, small, compact. *Foliage* dark olive green with magenta veins and ribs. *Growth* vigorous, upright and very free-flowering in terminal racemes. Requires pinching early to form a good shape. 'Bush'.

'Thanet'
BENNETT 1975
AFS Registration No 1262
Single
Tube rose pink, medium length and thickness. *Sepals* cardinal red on top, rose opal on the underside, reflexing over the tube. *Corolla* camellia rose in the centre to royal purple. Edges of the petals royal purple. Opening flat with wide petals. Large blooms. Royal purple petaloids. *Pistil* rose opal. *Foliage* spinach green, medium size. Lanceolate leaves, slightly serrated. *Growth* upright, vigorous, free-flowering. Bush or standard.

'That's It'
FUCHSIA LA 1968
AFS Registration No 809
Semi-double
Tube smoky orange-red, thick, medium length. *Sepals* orange-red, deeper on the undersides. Long, broad and curling upwards. *Corolla* orchid purple, shaded pink at the base of the petals and veined reddish. Longish, compact bloom. *Foliage* mid-green, medium-sized, finely serrated leaves. *Growth* upright, bushy, very free-flowering. One which will need staking to support the large blooms, but well worth growing. Bush or half-basket.

'The Aristocrat'
WALTZ 1953
AFS Registration No 165
Double
Tube creamy white, long, medium thickness. *Sepals* pale rose pink with white tips upturned. *Corolla* centre petals creamy white, veined rose pink. Outer petals pale rose pink. Edges of the petals serrated, and the corolla flaring. *Foliage* mid-green, medium-sized leaves. *Growth* upright, vigorous and free-flowering. Bush or standard.

'The Continental'
MARTIN 1962
AFS Registration No 521
Double
Tube carmine, medium length and thickness. *Sepals* carmine, long, broad and reflexing. *Corolla* purple, very full and compact. Medium-sized bloom. *Foliage* bright green, medium-sized, serrated leaves. *Growth* lax bush, fairly vigorous and free-flowering. Bush or basket.

'The Diplomat'
KUECHLER 1962
AFS Registration No 505
Double
Tube carmine, medium length and thickness. *Sepals* waxy carmine, long, broad and reflexed. *Corolla* purple, very full and faintly compact, medium-sized bloom. *Foliage* bright green, medium-sized leaves. *Growth* lax bush, vigorous, free-flowering. Bush or basket.

'The Doctor' (192)
CASTLE NURSERIES
Single
Tube pale flesh pink, long and broad. *Sepals* flesh pink on top, slightly darker on the undersides. Broad, medium length, held well out from the corolla. *Corolla*

rosy-salmon, compact, medium-sized bloom. *Foliage* mid-green, medium-sized, ovate serrated leaves. *Growth* upright, fairly lax, bushy and free-flowering. This is a very attractive cultivar which needs pinching in its early stages to form a good bush, but can be used equally successfully as a standard or basket. Bush or half-basket.

'The Dowager'
REITER 1949
Double
Tube magenta red, medium length and thickness. *Sepals* magenta red, long, broad and reflexing. *Corolla* bluish-purple, large, full and compact. *Foliage* mid-green, small to medium-sized, serrated leaves. *Growth* upright, bushy, vigorous and free-flowering. Bush.

'The Franciscan'
SCHNABEL-PASKESEN 1960
AFS Registration No 460
Double
Tube pink, medium length and thickness. *Sepals* pink, long and broad, held well out from the corolla. *Corolla* bright pink with rose-pink veins. Full, flaring and medium-sized blooms. *Foliage* mid-green, medium-sized leaves. *Growth* trailer, free-flowering. Basket.

'The Jester'
TIRET 1972
AFS Registration No 1073
Double
Tube pale red, thick, medium length. *Sepals* white, reflexing. *Corolla* dubonnet red, full and compact. *Foliage* medium green, medium to large, serrated leaves. *Growth* upright, bushy, vigorous, free-flowering. Bush or standard.

'Thelma'
SAYERS 1974
AFS Registration No 1161
Semi-double
Tube creamy white, flushed pink, thick and of medium length. *Sepals* creamy white, flushed pink. *Corolla* ruby red, fading to lavender blue as the bloom matures. Shaded and splashed pink at the base of the petals. *Foliage* medium green, large serrated leaves. *Growth* trailer, bushy, free-flowering. Basket.

'The Madame'
TIRET 1963
AFS Registration No 576
Double
Tube pale red, medium length and thickness. *Sepals* pale red, short, broad and reflexed. *Corolla* burgundy red, full and compact, medium-sized bloom. *Foliage* mid-green, medium-sized, serrated leaves. Bush.

'The Marvel'
VICARAGE FARM NURSERIES 1969
Single
Tube white, medium length and thickness, slightly bulbous. *Sepals* white with green tips, broad and reflexing. *Corolla* pink with a lavender sheen, medium-sized, compact bloom. *Foliage* medium green, medium to large, serrated leaves. *Growth* upright, bushy, vigorous and free-flowering. Bush or summer bedder.

'The Monster'
GORMAN 1970
AFS Registration No 939
Double
Tube light green, small and of medium thickness. *Sepals* rose pink with a green stripe down the centre of each, and with green tips. Long, broad and recurving. *Corolla* opens bluish-purple and fades to magenta. Large, fairly compact bloom. *Foliage* mid-green, medium to large leaves. *Growth* trailer, bushy, vigorous and free-flowering. Basket.

'The Oregonian'
YORK 1952
AFS Registration No 140
Double
Tube white, medium length and thickness. *Sepals* white with pink tips, upturned. *Corolla* white, flaring open bloom.

Foliage mid-green, medium-sized, serrated leaves. *Growth* upright, bushy, vigorous and free-flowering. Bush.

'The Patriot'
TIRET 1971
AFS Registration No 995
Double
Tube pink, medium length and thickness. *Sepals* white with green tips and flushed pink. Medium length, broad and reflexing. *Corolla* white, very loose, open bloom with numerous petaloids. *Foliage* medium green, large serrated leaves. *Growth* trailer, fairly vigorous, free-flowering. Basket.

'The Phoenix'
TIRET 1967
AFS Registration No 737
Double
Tube pink, long, medium thickness. *Sepals* rosy pink, long, narrow and recurving. *Corolla* lilac, full and compact, medium-sized bloom. *Foliage* mid-green, medium-sized leaves. *Growth* trailer, vigorous, bushy and free-flowering. Basket.

'The Queen'
BROWN AND SOULES 1953
AFS Registration No 173
Single
Tube white, short, medium thickness. *Sepals* white on top, pink on the undersides. *Corolla* light blue with scalloped petals. Medium-sized blooms. *Foliage* mid-green, medium-sized leaves. *Growth* upright, vigorous and free-flowering. Bush.

'The Rival'
WALKER 1970
AFS Registration No 882
Double
Tube white, long and fairly thick. *Sepals* white with a pink flush on top, deeper shade of pink on the undersides. Long, broad and curling outwards and up. *Corolla* lavender, pink and deeper pink shades. Long petals, fairly compact, medium to large bloom. *Foliage* medium green, medium to large, finely serrated leaves. *Growth* lax bush, vigorous, free-flowering. It can be grown as a bush if well pinched in its early stages and staked to support the heavy weight of the blooms. Bush or basket.

'Theroigne de Mericourt'
LEMOINE 1903
Double
Tube pale cerise, short, medium thickness. *Sepals* rich cerise, broad, short and held horizontally. *Corolla* pure white, with slight red veining at the base of the petals. Very full and fluffy, medium-sized bloom. *Foliage* dark green, with cerise veins. Medium-sized leaves. *Growth* upright, bushy, very free-flowering. Bush or standard.

'The Small Woman'
WAGTAILS 1969
Double
Tube pale pink, medium length and thickness. *Sepals* pink with green tips, medium length, broad, horizontal with the tips slightly upturned. *Corolla* lilac pink, very full and fluffy, compact, small to medium-sized bloom. *Foliage* medium green, splashed gold. Small leaves. *Growth* trailer, fairly bushy and vigorous. Half-basket. Sport from 'Lovable'. Named after the British missionary, Gladys Aylward, whose exploits in crossing the mountains from China into Thailand in 1940 with 100 children were immortalised on film.

'The Tarns' (106)
TRAVIS 1973
AFS Registration No 1148
Single
Tube pale pink, short, medium thickness. *Sepals* pale pink on top, rose pink on the undersides, long, narrow and reflexing. *Corolla* violet-blue with rose pink shading at the base of the petals. Long, compact blooms. *Foliage* dark green, small, narrow, heavily serrated leaves. *Growth* upright, vigorous, self-branching and bushy. Free-flowering. Bush or garden hardy. *Parentage* 'Unknown' × 'Venus Victrix'.

'Thetis'
WALKER AND JONES 1949
Double
Tube red, medium length and thickness. *Sepals* red, medium length, recurving. *Corolla* dark red, fairly compact, medium-sized blooms. *Foliage* mid to darkish green, medium-sized, serrated leaves. *Growth* upright, bushy, vigorous, free-flowering. Bush.

'Thornley's Hardy'
THORNLEY 1970
Single
Tube white, slender, medium length. *Sepals* white, narrow and upturned. Green tips. *Corolla* cerise, shaded white at the base of the petals. Small. Compact bloom. *Foliage* mid-green, small, finely serrated leaves. *Growth* trailer, vigorous, bushy and free-flowering. Hardy. Half-basket or garden hardy.

'Thots of You'
SOO YUN 1967
AFS Registration No 729
Double
Tube light red, long, medium thickness. *Sepals* light red, broad and reflexed. *Corolla* white with red veins and a reddish flush on the petals. Large, fairly compact bloom. *Foliage* mid-green, medium to large leaves. *Growth* lax bush, vigorous, free-flowering. Bush or Basket.

'Three Cheers'
GREER 1969
Single
Tube bright red, long and slender. *Sepals* bright red, long, narrow and reflexing. *Corolla* dark blue, veined red, and with a white mark at the base of each petal. Opens flat. Medium-sized bloom. *Foliage* mid-green, medium-sized, finely serrated leaves. *Growth* upright, bushy, very free-flowering. Bush. *Parentage* 'Swanley Gem' seedling.

'Three Counties'
Found at the Three Counties Show and introduced by H.A. BROWN in 1947
Single
Tube scarlet cerise, medium length and thickness. *Sepals* scarlet cerise, short and broad. Reflexing to the tube. *Corolla* bluish violet, compact, medium size. *Foliage* mid-green, medium-sized leaves. *Growth* upright, bushy, free-flowering. Bush.

'Thunderbird'
TIRET 1957
AFS Registration No 292
Double
Tube neyron rose, long and slender. *Sepals* neyron rose, long, narrow and held well out from the corolla. *Corolla* vermilion, paler rose shading at the base of the petals. Long, compact, medium-sized blooms. *Foliage* medium green, medium-sized, serrated leaves. *Growth* trailer, vigorous and free-flowering. A very attractive cultivar. Basket.

'Tiara'
MARTIN 1965
AFS Registration No 632
Semi-double
Tube pale pink, medium length and thickness. *Sepals* pale pink, long and recurving. *Corolla* pale salmon pink in the centre. Outer petals lavender blue. Medium-sized, rather open bloom. *Foliage* mid-green, medium-sized leaves. *Growth* lax, bushy, vigorous and free-flowering. Bush or basket.

'Tiffany'
REEDSTROM 1960
AFS Registration No 424
Double
Tube white, medium length and thickness. *Sepals* white on top, pale pink on the undersides. Long, broad and upturned. *Corolla* pure white, very full and fluffy, large blooms. *Foliage* dark green, medium-sized leaves. *Growth* trailer, bushy, vigorous and free-flowering. A very beautiful cultivar. Basket.

'Tiki'
BARTON 1970
AFS Registration No 914

Double
Tube scarlet, medium length and thickness. *Sepals* scarlet, broad and reflexed. *Corolla* bright pink, very full and compact, medium-sized bloom. *Foliage* dark green, medium-sized leaves. *Growth* upright, bushy, free-flowering. Bush.

'Tillmouth Lass'
RYLE 1975
AFS Registration No 1254
Single
Tube pink RHS 62C, striped. *Sepals* rhodamine pink RHS 62A on the undersides, slightly paler on the top. Twisting and curling around the tube. *Corolla* lavender, fading to purple with slight veining at the base of the petals. *Foliage* mid-green, medium-sized leaves. *Growth* upright, bushy, free-flowering. Bush or standard.

'Timlin Brened'
BAKER/DUNNETT 1974
AFS Registration No 1200
Single, triphylla type
Tube flamingo pink, long, medium thickness. *Sepals* shell pink with green tips. Short. *Corolla* coral pink, short, oval petals. *Foliage* deep olive green with red veins and a satin sheen. Large leaves. *Growth* upright, bushy, vigorous and free-flowering. Self-branching. Bush.

'Timothy Hammett'
HAMMETT 1966
Registered 1972
AFS Registration No 1026
Single
Tube scarlet, medium length and thickness. *Sepals* scarlet, long and reflexed. *Corolla* purple, short and fairly compact. *Foliage* deep green, medium-sized leaves. *Growth* trailer, self-branching, bushy and free-flowering. Half-basket.

'Ting-a-Ling' (27)
SCHNABEL-PASKESEN 1959
AFS Registration No 381
Single
Tube white, thick, medium length. *Sepals* white, long and narrow, curling upwards. *Corolla* white, medium-sized, open, bell-shaped bloom. *Foliage* mid-green, medium-sized serrated leaves. *Growth* upright, bushy, vigorous and free-flowering. Bush or standard. A very nice cultivar which will make a good exhibition plant. It has two faults, however: it tends to mark easily, and it is prone to *Botrytis*.

'Tinkerbell'
HODGES 1955
AFS Registration No 244
Single
Tube white, flushed pink, long and slender. *Sepals* white with green tips, pink on the undersides. Long, narrow and reflexed over the tube. *Corolla* white with pink veins. Medium-sized compact bloom. *Foliage* pale green, medium-sized, serrated leaves. *Growth* lax, bushy, free-flowering. Bush or half-basket.

'Tinker Toy'
FOSTER 1973
AFS Registration No 1088
Semi-double
Tube pale tyrian rose, short and thin. *Sepals* pale tyrian rose with white tips, short and broad. *Corolla* lavender blue, rose pink at the base of the petals. The flowers have a lavender cast as they mature. Small, flaring blooms. *Foliage* light green with red stems. Small serrated leaves. *Growth* trailer, bushy, free-flowering. Basket.

'Tiny Tim'
GAGNON 1967
AFS Registration No 708
Double
Tube rose red, long, medium thickness. *Sepals* rose red, long, narrow and recurving. *Corolla* medium blue fading to lavender and ageing to fuchsia pink. Medium-sized blooms. *Foliage* mid-green, medium-sized leaves. *Growth* trailer, bushy, free-flowering. Basket.

'Tiny Tots'
PANCHARIAN 1975
AFS Registration No 1295
Single
Tube red, short and thin. *Sepals* red on top, rose pink on the undersides, 1 in (2.5 cm) in length. *Corolla* blue, marbled light pink at the base of the petals. Each of the four petals has two petaloids at the base. *Foliage* medium green, small and oblong in shape. *Growth* upright, self-branching, bushy and free-flowering. Colours best in the sun. Small bush.

'Titania' ('Queen of the Faeries')
TRAVIS 1976
Single, breviflora type
Tube cerise. *Sepals* cerise, long, medium width. *Corolla* deep coral with frilled edges. *Foliage* deep green, medium-sized, serrated. *Growth* upright, self-branching, bushy and free-flowering. Bush or quarter standard. *Parentage F. microphylla* × 'Golden Dawn'.

'Titania'
EVANS AND REEVES 1948
Carmine self with a long tube and sepals. Medium-sized bloom. *Foliage* mid-green, medium-sized serrated leaves. *Growth* upright, bushy, free-flowering. Bush.

'Toby Bridger'
BRIDGER 1958
Double
Tube white, short and fairly thick. *Sepals* pale pink with green tips. Short, broad and held over the top of the corolla. *Corolla* pink with darker pink veins. Very full and fairly compact, medium-sized bloom. *Foliage* dark green, medium-sized, finely serrated leaves. *Growth* upright, bushy, self-branching and free-flowering. Bush.

'Tolling Bell' (121)
TURNER 1964
Single
Tube scarlet, short and thick. *Sepals* scarlet, medium length, broad and recurving. *Corolla* white with cerise veins. Longish, bell-shaped bloom. *Foliage* mid-green, medium-sized, serrated leaves. *Growth* upright, bushy, vigorous and free-flowering. Bush or standard.

'Tom H. Oliver'
PENNISI 1972
AFS Registration No 1046
Double
Tube rose pink, short and thick. *Sepals* claret rose on top, pale rose pink on the undersides. Long, broad and held straight out from the corolla. *Corolla* dark ruby red with serrated edged petals, and shaded light rose pink at the base. Box type, medium-sized bloom. *Foliage* mid-green, medium-sized leaves. *Growth* trailer, self-branching, bushy and free-flowering. Basket.

'Tomico'
HAZARD
Date unknown
Single
Tube flesh pink, medium length and thickness. *Sepals* flesh pink, long, broad and reflexed. *Corolla* orange-red, medium-sized, compact bloom. *Foliage* bright green, medium-sized leaves. *Growth* upright, bushy, free-flowering. Bush.

'Tom Pacey'
PACEY 1964
Double
Tube white, flushed pink. Short, medium thickness. *Sepals* white with a pink flush on top, deeper shade of pink on the undersides and tipped green. Medium length, broad and pointing downwards over the corolla. *Corolla* pale pink, very full and compact, Medium-sized bloom. *Foliage* medium green, medium-sized, serrated leaves. *Growth* upright, long-branched, free-flowering. Needs pinching to shape in its early stages of growth. Bush.

'Tom Thorne'
BRIDGER 1959
Semi-double
Tube white, thin, medium length. *Sepals*

white on top with green tips. Undersides flushed pink. Medium length, broad and reflexed. *Corolla* white with pale pink veining. Medium-sized, rather loose bloom. *Foliage* medium green, medium-sized, serrated leaves. *Growth* upright, bushy, self-branching, free-flowering. Bush.

'Tom Thumb' (164)
BAUDINAT 1850
Single
Tube carmine, short and thin. *Sepals* carmine, short, medium width, held down from the horizontal. *Corolla* mauve-purple, small and very compact. *Foliage* medium green, small, finely serrated leaves. *Growth* upright, bushy, self-branching and free-flowering. A good exhibition cultivar. Bush, quarter standard or garden hardy.

'Tom West'
MEILLEZ 1853
Single
Tube red, small and of medium thickness. *Sepals* red, short, broad, held well out. *Corolla* purple, small and compact. *Foliage* variegated pale greyish green and cream, medium-sized leaves. *Growth* upright, lax growing, fairly vigorous. Half-basket.

'Topaz'
KENNETT 1961
AFS Registration No 478
Double
Tube white, flushed coral pink, medium length and thickness. *Sepals* white, flushed pale coral pink on top, deeper shade on the underside. *Corolla* centre petals violet-purple with topaz marbling. Outer petals and petaloids coral pink and topaz, marbled violet-purple. Medium-sized blooms. *Foliage* dark green, medium-sized ovate leaves. *Growth* trailer, bushy, vigorous and free-flowering. Basket.

'Topper'
BROWN AND SOULES 1952
Semi-double
Tube red, medium length and thickness. *Sepals* red, broad and reflexing. *Corolla* dark blue with a white flush in the centre of the petals. Medium-sized, compact blooms. *Foliage* dark green, small, narrow leaves. *Growth* upright, vigorous, bushy and free-flowering. Bush or standard.

'Top Score'
HANDLEY 1980
AFS Registration No 1542
Semi-double
Tube cerise, short, medium thickness. *Sepals* brilliant cerise. Long, thick and reflexing to the tube. *Corolla* cerise at the base of the petals, shading to rich violet at the edges. *Foliage* dark green with maroon veins and stems. Large leaves. *Growth* vigorous, tall growing, self-branching and bushy. Free-flowering. Bush or summer bedder.

'Top Secret'
PRENTICE 1967
AFS Registration No 717
Double
Tube white with a reddish tinge, long, medium thickness. *Sepals* white, flushed reddish, recurving. *Corolla* lavender blue centre petals, surrounded by numerous pastel shaded petaloids. *Foliage* mid-green, medium-sized leaves. *Growth* trailer, bushy, fairly vigorous and free-flowering. Basket.

'Topsy'
HAZARD
Date unknown
Single
Tube carmine, short and thin. *Sepals* carmine, short, narrow and held well out from the corolla. *Corolla* deep purple, small and compact. *Foliage* mid-green, small to medium-sized leaves. *Growth* dwarf upright, bushy and free-flowering. Bush.

'Torch'
MUNKNER 1963
AFS Registration No 566
Double

Tube pinkish white, medium length, thick. *Sepals* pink on top with green tips. Salmon pink on the underside. Broad and reflexing. *Corolla* centre petals reddish purple with the outer petals marbled and splashed salmon-orange and pink. Medium-sized, fairly compact, blooms. *Foliage* light to medium green, medium-sized, ovate, serrated leaves. *Growth* upright, vigorous, free-flowering. Needs pinching to shape. Bush.

'Tosca'
BLACKWELL 1965
Double
Tube deep rose pink, short and of medium thickness. *Sepals* deep rose pink, long, broad with crepe effect on the undersides. Reflexed to the tube. *Corolla* pink with cerise veining and shaded cerise at the base of the petals. Medium-sized, rather open, ragged blooms. *Foliage* mid-green, medium-sized, finely serrated leaves. *Growth* trailer, vigorous, bushy and very free-flowering. Basket.

'Tosson Bell'
RYLE 1975
AFS Registration No 1255
Single
Tube rose red, short, medium thickness. *Sepals* china rose on top, slightly deeper shade on the underside. Medium-sized and carried slightly below the horizontal. *Corolla* pinkish plum purple, shading to a paler shade at the base, fading on maturity to imperial purple. Bell-shaped. *Foliage* lettuce green RHS 144A. *Growth* upright, vigorous, bushy and free-flowering. Bush or standard.

'Touch of Frost'
SOO YUN 1969
AFS Registration No 851
Single
Tube white, medium length and thickness. *Sepals* white on top with green tips, pink on the underside. Long and recurving. *Corolla* old rose with white variegations at the base of the petals and a frosty look on the outside. *Foliage* bright green, medium-sized leaves. *Growth* lax bush, fairly vigorous and free-flowering. Bush or basket.

'Touch of Pink'
SOO YUN 1979
AFS Registration No 1495
Semi-double
Tube white with pink stripes, medium length and thickness. *Sepals* pale pink with pink edges and green tips. Underside flushed pink. Sepals smooth on top, creped below. Held well out and slightly twisted. *Corolla* white with pink veining, flared. Several petaloids. *Stamens* pink. *Pistil* white with a yellow tip. *Growth* vigorous, bushy, medium-sized upright. It will make a good bush or standard. Very free-flowering. Bush or standard.

'Tour Eiffel' (186)
DE GRAAF 1976
Single
Tube Salmon pink, bulbous. *Sepals* salmon pink, short and broad. *Corolla* rosy-purple, shaded salmon pink at the base of the petals. Medium-sized bloom. *Stamens and style* rose-pink. *Foliage* bronze-green, medium-sized leaves with red stems and centre vein. *Growth* lax bush, fairly, vigorous and free-flowering. Bush or basket. *Parentage* 'Alice Hoffman' ×.

'Tourtonne'
VAN SUCHTELEN 1968
Single
Tube red, long and thick. *Sepals* red, short and pointed. *Corolla* red, with touches of purple. *Foliage* darkish green, medium-sized leaves. *Growth* very vigorous, upright, free-flowering. Prefers sun for best results and will not withstand frost. Bush. *Parentage* 'Leverkusen' × 'Waternymph'.

'Tracy Wilson'
PRENTICE 1975
AFS Registration No 1300
Single
Tube rose pink, short. *Sepals* white on top, pink on the undersides with green tips.

Curling back over the tube. *Corolla* deep pink, four petals forming a tube, not flaring. *Foliage* dark green, small. *Growth* natural trailer, branches small and wiry. Very showy. Basket.

'Trail Blazer' (111)
REITER 1951
AFS Registration No 83
Double
Tube crimson, long and slender. *Sepals* crimson. Long, narrow and reflexed. *Corolla* rosy-mauve, paler at the base of the petals. Medium-sized, compact bloom. *Foliage* mid-green, medium-sized, serrated leaves. *Growth* trailer, vigorous, self-branching and very free-flowering. Basket.

'Trailing Queen'
Raiser and date unknown
Single
Tube red, fairly thin, medium length. *Sepals* red, narrow, held well out from the corolla. *Corolla* dark red, compact, medium-sized bloom. *Foliage* reddish-bronze, long branching and free-flowering; needs a lot of pinching to bring it into shape, but will make a very good half-basket.

'Tranquility'
SOO YUN 1970
AFS Registration No 909
Double
Tube white, medium length and thickness. *Sepals* white on top, flushed pink on the undersides. Green tips. Curling back over the tube. *Corolla* shades of purple and pink, changing to ruby-red and pink. Large, fairly compact bloom. *Foliage* mid-green, medium-sized leaves with red stems. *Growth* trailer, vigorous, bushy and free-flowering. Basket.

'Trase'
DAWSON 1956
Double
Tube carmine, medium length and thickness. *Sepals* carmine, short, broad and upturned. *Corolla* white, veined carmine and with a carmine flush at the base of the petals. Fairly full and compact, small to medium-sized bloom. *Foliage* medium green, small, finely serrated leaves. *Growth* upright, bushy, self-branching and free-flowering. Bush or garden hardy.

'Traudchen Bonstedt' (17)
BONSTEDT 1905
Triphylla type
Tube light rose, long, medium thickness. *Sepals* light rose pink. *Corolla* light salmon-pink, short and compact. *Foliage* light sage green, paler veins and ribs, reddish tinge underneath. *Growth* upright, free-flowering. Bush.

'Treasure'
NIEDERHOLZER 1946
Double
Tube pale rose pink, medium length and thickness. *Sepals* neyron rose, long, broad and reflexing. *Corolla* pale silvery violet-pink, very full and compact bloom. *Foliage* medium green, medium to large leaves. *Growth* upright, bushy, vigorous, free-flowering.

'Tresco'
TRESCO ABBEY GARDENS
Single
Tube pale red, short and very thin. *Sepals* red with green tips. Short, thin and held down from the horizontal. *Corolla* purple, shaded pink at the base of the petals. Very small, compact bloom. *Foliage* medium green, medium-sized, longish leaves. *Growth* upright, bushy, vigorous and free-flowering. Bush.

'Trewince Twilight' (36)
JACKSON 1972
AFS Registration No 1048
SINGLE
Tube white, short and fairly thick. *Sepals* white, short, broad and reflexing. *Corolla* pale mauve-pink, very compact, medium-sized bloom. *Foliage* medium to darkish green, small to medium, serrated leaves. *Growth* upright, bushy, self-

branching and free-flowering. Bush. It makes a very good exhibition plant, although the colour is not as outstanding as its parent. Sport of 'Marin Glow'.

'Trinket'
GAGNON 1965
AFS Registration No 620
Double
Tube pale pink, medium length and thickness. *Sepals* rosy-red, upturned and curling back to the tube. *Corolla* dark blue with red veins. Outer petals spreading out wide. *Foliage* medium green, medium-sized leaves. *Growth* trailer, self-branching, bushy and free-flowering. Basket.

'Trisha'
ANTONELLI 1965
AFS Registration No 636
Double
Tube white, medium length and thickness. *Sepals* white with green tips. *Corolla* burgundy, splashed rose and magenta. Medium-sized, compact bloom. *Foliage* mid-green, medium-sized leaves. *Growth* upright, vigorous, free-flowering. Bush.

'Tristesse' (146)
BLACKWELL 1965
Double
Tube pale rose pink, medium length and thickness. *Sepals* rose pink with green tips. Short, broad and reflexed. *Corolla* pale lilac-blue, fairly compact, small to medium-sized bloom. *Foliage* medium green, small to medium-sized, serrated leaves. *Growth* upright, bushy, self-branching and free-flowering. A very easy cultivar to grow and one which will make a good exhibition plant. Bush. *Parentage* 'Lilac Lustre' seedling.

'Triumphant'
NIEDRHOLZER 1946
Single to semi-double
Tube turkey red, medium length and thickness. *Sepals* turkey red, long and upturned. *Corolla* amethyst violet, large, loose bloom. *Foliage* mid-green, medium-sized leaves. *Growth* upright, very vigorous and free-flowering. Bush or standard.

'Troika'
DE GRAAF 1976
Semi-double
Tube rose red, medium length and thickness. Paler in colour when grown in warm conditions. *Sepals* white, broad, held well out. *Corolla* light blue, shading to lilac rose. Medium sized, compact bloom. *Stamens* pink. Style white. *Foliage* mid-green, medium-sized leaves. *Growth* lax upright, bushy, vigorous and free-flowering. It will make a good bush if pinched well in its early stages. Bush or basket.

'Tropicana'
TIRET 1964
AFS Registration No 596
Double
Tube greenish-white, tinged pink. Long and thin. *Sepals* rosy pink with green tips, darker on the underside. Short, broad and upturned. *Corolla* orange, full and fairly compact with numerous petaloids. *Foliage* light green, medium-sized, longish, serrated leaves. *Growth* trailer, vigorous, free-flowering. Half-basket.

'Tropic Sunset'
ANTONELLI 1965
AFS Registration No 635
Double
Tube carmine, short and of medium thickness. *Sepals* carmine, short and broad, pointing downwards. *Corolla* dark purple, paler at the base of the petals and splashed pink. Small to medium-sized, compact bloom. *Foliage* reddish-bronze, tipped green. Small ovate, serrated leaves with red stems. *Growth* trailer, self-branching, bushy, very vigorous and free-flowering. Basket or half-basket. *Parentage* 'Autumnale' ×.

'Troubadour'
WALTZ 1963
AFS Registration No 588

Double
Tube crimson, short, medium thickness. *Sepals* crimson, long, narrow and reflexing. *Corolla* dark lilac purple with splashes of crimson at the base of the petals. Medium to large, compact bloom. *Foliage* dark green, medium-sized leaves. *Growth* trailer, bushy, vigorous and free-flowering.

'Troutbeck'
THORNLEY 1972
AFS Registration No 1064
Single
Tube salmon pink, short and fairly thick. *Sepals* creamy white, flushed pink on top and on the underside, green tips. Short and slightly reflexed. *Corolla* aster violet RHS 87C, small and compact. *Foliage* medium green, small to medium-sized, serrated leaves. *Growth* upright, vigorous, bushy and free-flowering. Bush. *Parentage* 'Dorothea Flower' × 'Hawkshead'.

'Trubell'
GADSBY 1970
Registered 1971
AFS Registration No 968
Single
Tube reddish pink, short and thick. *Sepals* reddish pink, long, narrow and reflexing to the tube. *Corolla* purple, long and bell-shaped, with cerise veins. Paler shaded at the base of the petals. *Foliage* medium green, medium to large, long, serrated leaves. *Growth* upright, bushy, vigorous and free-flowering. Bush. *Parentage* 'Bishop's Bells' ×.

'Trudy'
GADSBY 1970
AFS Registration No 969
Single
Tube pale pink, medium length and thicnkess. *Sepals* pink on top, slightly darker shade of pink on the undersides. Short, medium width, recurving to the tube. *Corolla* cyclamen-pink, compact, bell-shaped bloom. *Foliage* mid-green, medium-sized, ovate, serrated leaves. *Growth* upright, bushy, fairly vigorous and free-flowering. Bush or garden hardy. *Parentage* 'Chillerton Beauty' ×.

'True Love'
SOO YUN 1967
AFS Registration No 731
Semi-double
Tube reddish white, medium length and thickness. *Sepals* white with reddish veins, long and broad. *Corolla* dark blue, variegated pink and blue at the base of the petals, and the petals are corrugated. A very attractive bloom. *Foliage* mid-green, medium-sized leaves. *Growth* trailer, vigorous and free-flowering. Basket.

'Trumpeter'
REITER 1946
Single, triphylla type
Tube pale geranium lake, long, thick. *Sepals* pale geranium lake, short and pointed. *Corolla* of the same colour, short and fairly compact. Long blooms which darken as the flower matures. *Foliage* bluish-green, long branches, wiry stems. *Growth* a natural trailer. Basket or half-basket.

'Tumbler'
TOLLEY 1974
AFS Registration No 1233
Single
Tube flesh pink, long and of medium thickness. *Sepals* flesh pink, long and twisting. *Corolla* geranium and rose pink, barrel shape, medium-sized bloom. *Foliage* medium green, small to medium-sized, ovate leaves. *Growth* trailer, long and thin branching, free-flowering. Half-basket.

'Tuonela' (175)
BLACKWELL 1969
Double
Tube reddish pink, medium length and thickness. *Sepals* reddish pink, long, broad and reflexing. *Corolla* pale lavender blue with reddish veins, and reddish shading at the base of the petals. Medium-sized, compact bloom. *Foliage* medium green, medium to large-sized,

serrated leaves. *Growth* upright, bushy, vigorous and free-flowering. Easy to grow. Bush.

'Turquoise Lady'
PLUMMER 1952
Double
Tube red, medium length and thickness. *Sepals* red, broad and reflexing. *Corolla* dark blue, paler at the base of the petals. Medium-sized, compact bloom. *Foliage* medium to darkish green, medium-sized leaves. *Growth* upright, vigorous and free-flowering. Bush or standard.

'Tutone'
MACHADO 1963
AFS Registration No 563
Double
Tube pink, short and of medium thickness. *Sepals* pink, broad and reflexing. *Corolla* greyish-blue and pink, full, compact bloom. *Foliage* dark green, medium-sized leaves. *Growth* lax bush, fairly vigorous, free-flowering. One that needs pinching as a young plant to form a good bushy shape. Bush or basket.

'Tutti-Fruitti'
SCHNABEL-PASKESEN 1966
Double
Tube pink, medium length and thickness. *Sepals* pink, reflexing. *Corolla* magenta-rose in the centre, with the outer petals and petaloids marbled rose pink. Full, compact bloom. *Foliage* mid-green, medium-sized leaves. *Growth* trailer, long-branching, free-flowering. Basket.

'Tutu'
REITER 1952
AFS Registration No 131
Double
Tube greenish white, short and of medium thickness. *Sepals* greenish-white on top, flushed pale pink on the underside. Long and spreading. *Corolla* pale rhodamine purple, flecked with aster-violet. Medium to large, open, flat bloom. *Foliage* mid-green, medium-sized, serrated leaves. *Growth* upright, bushy, low-growing, free-flowering. Bush.

'Twinkling Stars'
HANDLEY 1976
Single
Tube pale rosy-pink, short and thick, curved. *Sepals* pale pink on top, slightly deeper shade of pink on the underside. Short, narrow and pointed. *Corolla* fuchsia pink, short, held well out. *Foliage* medium green, small to medium-sized leaves. *Growth* upright, bushy and free-flowering. Bush. A plant which more often than not throws multiple-sepalled blooms, an unfortunate trait which, whilst giving it the star shape to which its name alludes, makes it unsuitable and unreliable for use as an exhibition plant.

'UFO'
HANDLEY 1972
AFS Registration No 1059
Single
Tube white, flushed pale pink, short and thick. *Sepals* white, long and narrow, reflexing right up the tube. *Corolla* lilac-lavender RHS 74B/C, white at the centre of the petals which open almost completely flat, saucer-shaped. *Stamens* pink. *Anthers* red. *Foliage* mid-green, small to medium-sized, serrated leaves. *Growth* upright, vigorous, self-branching, and free-flowering. An easy cultivar to grow. Bush.

'Ullswater'
TRAVIS 1958
Registered 1973
AFS Registration No 1149
Double
Tube pale pink, long and of medium thickness. *Sepals* pale pink, long, broad and upswept. *Corolla* orchid blue fading to orchid purple, paler at the base of the petals, large and compact. *Foliage* mid-green, medium-sized, ovate, serrated leaves. *Growth* upright, bushy and free-flowering. Bush.

'Ultramar'
REITER 1956
AFS Registration No 274
Double

Tube white, short and thick. *Sepals* white, long, broad and recurving slightly. *Corolla* pale lavender blue with numerous petaloids of a pinkish-white shade. Very full, medium to large bloom. *Foliage* medium green, reddish veins. Medium-sized, serrated leaves. *Growth* upright, bushy, vigorous and free-flowering. Bush.

'Ulverston'
THORNLEY 1978
AFS Registration No 1470
Double
Tube flesh pink, medium length and thickness. *Sepals* flesh pink on the top, rose bengal RHS 61D, on the underside. *Corolla* violet purple RHS 77A, distinct grey watermark on the edge of the petal. *Foliage* medium green. *Growth* bushy, vigorous, upright. Makes a good bush. Best colour if grown in sun. When cold, a small green bar appears on the tube causing it to bend slightly. *Parentage* 'Berkeley' ×.

'Uncle Charley'
TIRET 1949
Semi-double
Tube rose red, thin, medium length. *Sepals* rose red, long, narrow, curling up towards the tube. *Corolla* lilac lavender, open, bell-shaped bloom, medium-sized. *Foliage* mid-green, medium-sized, serrated leaves. *Growth* upright, bushy, vigorous and free-flowering. Bush.

'Uncle Jeff'
TIRET 1962
AFS Registration No 528
Double
Tube dark red, medium length and thickness. *Sepals* dark red, long, broad, recurving. *Corolla* deep purple, large, compact blooms. *Foliage* darkish green, medium-sized, serrated leaves. *Growth* upright, bushy, fairly vigorous and free-flowering. Bush.

'Uncle Jules'
REITER 1947
Double
Tube crimson, medium length and thickness. *Sepals* crimson, long, broad, reflexed. *Corolla* campanula violet, paler at the base of the petals. Very large, compact bloom. *Foliage* medium green, small to medium-sized, serrated leaves. *Growth* upright, vigorous, long, arching branches, free-flowering. Bush or standard.

'Uncle Mike'
TIRET 1962
AFS Registration No 531
Double
Tube white, medium length and thickness. *Sepals* white, broad, reflexed. *Corolla* lipstick red, ageing to reddish purple. Full, compact medium-sized bloom. *Foliage* mid-green, medium-sized, serrated leaves, *Growth* trailer, bushy, vigorous and free-flowering. Basket.

'Uncle Steve'
TIRET 1962
AFS Registration No 530
Double
Tube pale pink, medium length and thickness. *Sepals* pink, long, broad and outswept. *Corolla* plum purple, large, compact bloom. *Foliage* mid-green, medium-sized, serrated leaves. *Growth* natural trailer, vigorous, free-flowering. Basket.

'Unfinished Symphony'
BLACKWELL 1961
Semi-double
Tube carmine, medium length and thickness. *Sepals* carmine, short, broad, reflexing. *Corolla* clear blue with carmine veins. Medium-sized bloom. *Foliage* mid-green, medium-sized, serrated leaves. *Growth* upright, vigorous, free-flowering. Bush.

'Unique'
HAZARD/HAAG AND SON
Semi-double
Tube white, faintly tinged pink, short and thick. *Sepals* white on top, pink on the underside, short, broad and slightly upturned. *Corolla* rose madder, paler at the

base of the petals, and marginally darker at the edges. Small, fairly open bloom. *Foliage* light green, medium-sized, serrated leaves. *Growth* upright, bushy, vigorous and free-flowering. Bush.

'Upward Look' (168)
GADSBY 1968
AFS Registration No 870
Single
Tube carmine, short, medium thickness. *Sepals* carmine, short, broad, held well out from the corolla. *Corolla* pale roseine-purple RHS 68C, paler at the base of the petals. Blooms held erect, pointing upwards from the foliage. *Foliage* dull medium green, medium-sized, serrated leaves. *Growth* upright, bushy, fairly vigorous, very free-flowering. Bush. *Parentage* 'Bon Accorde' × 'Athela'.

'Vagabond'
SCHNABEL 1953
AFS Registration No 186
Double
Tube brilliant carmine, short, medium thickness. *Sepals* bright carmine, long, broad and upturned. *Corolla* magenta with the outer petals splashed carmine. Medium to large compact bloom. *Foliage* mid-green, medium-sized, serrated leaves. *Growth* trailer, vigorous, free-flowering. Basket.

'Valencia'
SCHNABEL-PASKESEN 1962
AFS Registration No 533
Semi-double
Tube rose-pink, medium length and thickness. *Sepals* rose-pink, long, broad, recurving. *Corolla* vivid pink, fairly loose, medium-sized bloom. *Foliage* dark green, medium-sized, serrated leaves. *Growth* upright, bushy, vigorous, and free-flowering. Bush or standard.

'Valentine'
REITER 1948
Semi-double
Tube white, flushed rose-pink, medium length and thickness. *Sepals* white, flushed rose pink, long, curling upwards. *Corolla* very dark imperial purple, lighter at the base of the petals, medium-sized bloom. *Foliage* mid-green, medium-sized, leaves, serrated. *Growth* trailer, bushy, vigorous, free-flowering. A very beautiful cultivar. Basket or half-basket.

'Vale of Belvoir'
GADSBY 1973
AFS Registration No 1127
Single
Tube neyron rose RHS 55B, thick, medium length. *Sepals* neyron rose with green tips, curling back towards the tube. *Corolla* spectrum violet RHS 82B, flushed rose, and fading to imperial purple RHS 78B. Medium-sized, open bell-shaped bloom. *Foliage* mid-green, medium-sized, serrated leaves. *Growth* semi-trailer, vigorous, free-flowering. If well pinched in its early stages it will make a nice bush. Bush or half-basket. *Parentage* 'Rosedale' × 'Lady Isobel Barnett'.

'Vance Wells'
GAGNON 1967
AFS Registration No 707
Double
Tube white, thick, medium length. *Sepals* white, long, broad and upturned. *Corolla* dark mulberry shade, paler at the base of the petals. Medium-sized compact bloom. *Foliage* dark green, medium-sized, serrated leaves. *Growth* trailer, vigorous, free-flowering. Half-basket.

'Vanessa'
COLVILLE 1964
Double
Tube white, flushed pale pink, medium length and thickness. *Sepals* pale pink on top, darker pink on the undersides with green tips. Long, broad and reflexed to the tube. *Corolla* pale pinkish lilac, very full and fluffy, loose-petalled, medium-sized bloom. *Foliage* light green, medium to large-sized, long, serrated leaves. *Growth* upright, vigorous, free-flowering. Bush.

'Vanessa Jackson'
HANDLEY 1980
AFS Registration No 1547
Single
Tube salmon red RHS 43C, medium length and thickness. *Sepals* salmon orange RHS 41C, 2 in (5 cm) long, held well out from the corolla. *Corolla* salmon-orange (RHS 41C) shading to orange-red RHS 40C, then to cardinal red, RHS 45C at the edges. The edges of the petals flare out sharply and overlap. *Pistil* salmon red, long. *Foliage* medium green tinged bronze and slightly serrated, leaves 3 in (7.5 cm) long by 2 in (5 cm) wide. *Growth* natural trailer which will make a good basket, very free-flowering and a large, distinctive bloom. Basket.

'Vanity Fair'
SCHNABEL-PASKESEN 1962
AFS Registration No 534
Double
Tube white, tinged pale green, long, medium thickness. *Sepals* white with green tips, flushed pink on the underside, short, broad and reflexing. *Corolla* pale pink, very full and fluffy, medium-sized bloom. *Foliage* medium green, large, serrated leaves. *Growth* upright, vigorous, bushy and free-flowering. Bush.

'Vee Jay's Torment'
VEE JAY 1979
AFS Registration No 1490
Single
Tube red, short and thin. *Sepals* red, flaring in pinwheel fashion. *Corolla* violet with red stripes, rose at the base of the petals. Although registered as a single, will occasionally throw blooms with 5 or 6 petals. *Foliage* yellowish green in the shade, greener if grown in the sun. *Growth* free-flowering, self-branching, natural trailer. Best grown as a basket.

'Velma'
ADAMS 1979
AFS Registration No 1522
Single
Tube off white, short. *Sepals* off white, maturing to deep pink, turning right back over the tube. *Corolla* deep pink, changing to purple as it ages, petals short and round. *Foliage* light green, leaves large. *Growth* free-flowering, medium upright. Bush. *Parentage* 'Serena Blue' × 'Fancy Flute'.

'Ventura'
EVANS AND REEVES 1951
AFS Registration No 100
Single
Tube coral pink, medium length and thickness. *Sepals* coral pink, short, broad, held well out. *Corolla* rose madder, medium-sized, bell-shaped bloom. *Foliage* mid green, medium-sized leaves. *Growth* upright, bushy, fairly vigorous, flowering in clusters. Bush.

'Venus Victrix'
GULLIVER 1840
Single
Tube white, very small and thin. *Sepals* white, green tipped. Very small, narrow, held well out. *Corolla* violet-purple, shaded white at the base of the petals. Very small, compact bloom. *Stamens and style* very long. *Foliage* medium green, small, longish and serrated leaves. *Growth* upright, very slow and difficult to grow. Not a free-flowering cultivar either. Believed to be a chance seedling found by Mr Gulliver, gardener to the Rev Marriott. The first white-sepalled fuchsia known.

'Vera'
NEIDERHOLZER 1946
Single
Tube bright red, medium length and thickness. *Sepals* bright red, long, broad, outswept. *Corolla* tyrian rose, large, loose bloom. *Foliage* mid-green, medium-sized, serrated leaves. *Growth* upright, vigorous, bushy and free-flowering. Bush.

'Verda Evelyn'
KUECHLER 1963
AFS Registration No 548
Double
Tube deep pink, short, thick. *Sepals* deep

pink, long, broad and upturned. *Corolla* pink with deeper pink petaloids at the base. *Foliage* dark green with reddish stems, medium-sized leaves. *Growth* trailer, bushy, vigorous, free-flowering. Basket.

'Vibrato'
SAYERS 1974
AFS Registration No 1162
Single
Tube salmon red, flushed orange, short, medium thickness. *Sepals* salmon red, short, broad, slightly upturned. *Corolla* rich claret red, small and compact. *Foliage* dark green, medium-sized, serrated leaves. Young stems red. *Growth* trailer, bushy, free-flowering in terminal clusters. Basket.

'Vicki Putley'
PUTLEY 1964
Single
Tube white, medium length and thickness. *Sepals* white, flushed pink, reflexing. *Corolla* crimson red, medium-sized bloom. *Foliage* mid-green, medium-sized leaves, slightly serrated. *Growth* bushy, lax, free-flowering. Needs early pinching. Bush.

'Victorian'
PASKESEN 1971
AFS Registration No 957
Double
Tube pink, short, medium thickness. *Sepals* pink, broad, upturned. *Corolla* pink, fairly full and compact, medium-sized bloom. *Foliage* medium green, medium-sized leaves. *Growth* upright, bushy, free-flowering. Bush.

'Vienna'
NEIDERHOLZER/WALTZ 1950
AFS Registration No 56
Double
Tube bengal rose, short, medium thickness. *Sepals* bengal rose, long, broad, recurving. *Corolla* lilac-blue, medium sized, compact bloom. *Foliage* mid-green, medium-sized, serrated leaves. *Growth* upright, bushy, fairly vigorous and free-flowering. Bush.

'Vienna Waltz'
NIX NURSERY 1971
AFS Registration No 942
Double
Tube darkish pink, medium length and thickness. *Sepals* dark pink broad, reflexing. *Corolla* rich lavender, splashed with pink and red. Medium to large flaring bloom. *Foliage* dark green, medium-sized leaves. *Growth* trailer, bushy, vigorous and free-flowering. Prefers to be grown in shaded conditions. Basket. Sport of 'Dusky Rose'.

'Vindolanda'
RYLE 1975
AFS Registration No 1256
Single
Tube crimson, short and thick. *Sepals* crimson RHS 52A, short, broad, slightly upturned. *Corolla* violet RHS 87 fading to cyclamen purple RHS 74A, small. *Foliage* lanceolate, serrated, medium green with pink vein. *Growth* upright, self-branching, bushy, and vigorous. Short-jointed, and floriferous. Bush. Colours best in shaded conditions.

'Vinegar Joe'
HAZARD
Single
Tube pink, long, medium thickness. *Sepals* pink, long, broad, upswept. *Corolla* rosy-purple, medium to large, compact bloom. *Foliage* mid-green, medium-sized leaves. *Growth* trailer, bushy, vigorous, free-flowering. Basket.

'Viola'
DALE 1950
Single
Tube pink, short, medium thickness. *Sepals* pink, held well out from the corolla, medium length. *Corolla* bluish mauve, compact, medium-sized bloom. *Foliage* mid-green, medium sized, serrated leaves. *Growth* upright, bushy, low-growing, free-flowering. Bush.

'Violacea'
FUCHSIA LA 1968
AFS Registration No 804
Double
Tube white, short, medium thickness. *Sepals* white, long, upturned. *Corolla* orchid-pink, full and compact, medium-sized blooms. *Foliage* mid-green, medium-sized leaves, slightly serrated. *Growth* natural trailer, fairly vigorous, free-flowering. Basket.

'Violet'
NEIDERHOLZER
Double
Tube scarlet, medium length and thickness. *Sepals* scarlet, short, broad and held well out. *Corolla* bishops violet, compact, medium-sized bloom. *Foliage* mid-green, medium-sized, serrated leaves. *Growth* upright, bushy, self-branching and free-flowering. Bush.

'Violet Adams'
BARTON 1970
AFS Registration No 917
Single to semi-double
Tube pale red, short, medium thickness. *Sepals* pale red, reflexing slightly. *Corolla* white with red veins, rather open, loose-petalled bloom. *Foliage* yellow to lettuce green, medium-sized leaves. *Growth* upright, bushy, self-branching and free-flowering. Bush.

'Violet Bassett-Burr' (55)
MRS E. HOLMES 1972
Double
Tube pink, short, medium thickness. *Sepals* white, flushed pink and with green tips. Long, narrow and recurving completely to the tube. *Corolla* pale pinkish lilac, full, rather loose-petalled bloom. *Foliage* darkish green, medium-sized, serrated leaves. *Growth* upright, vigorous, free-flowering, needs early pinching to shape. Bush.

'Violet Flush'
HOWARTH 1980
AFS Registration No 1579
Double
Tube red, medium-sized and thickness. *Sepals* bright red, broad. *Corolla* blue violet, splashed deep pink, small, petaloids pale pink. *Pistil* red, long. *Stamens* red. *Foliage* medium green, small and wiry, lanceolate with serrated leaf margins. *Growth* trailer, or bush, self-branching, free-flowering. Bush or basket. Prefers sun for the best colour. *Parentage* 'Masquerade' × 'Pink Ballet Girl.'

'Violet Gem'
WALTZ 1949
Semi-double
Tube carmine, short, medium thickness. *Sepals* carmine, long, broad, held well out. *Corolla* deep violet-purple, very full, spreading. *Foliage* medium to darkish green, medium-sized leaves. *Growth* upright, fairly vigorous, free-flowering. Bush.

'Violet Nymph'
CROCKETT 1966
AFS Registration No 822 (1969)
Double
Tube carmine rose, small, thin. *Sepals* greenish-white on top, pure white on the undersides, reflexing to the tube. *Corolla* shades of campanula violet, fading to petunia purple. Lighter at the base of the petals. Small, fairly compact blooms. *Foliage* medium green, small leaves. *Growth* upright, self-branching, bushy and free-flowering. Bush.

'Violet Rosette'
KUECHLER 1963
AFS Registration No 549
Double
Tube bright carmine, long, medium thickness. *Sepals* bright carmine, long, broad, reflexed straight up to the tube. *Corolla* deep violet purple, shaded red at the base of the petals. Very full, fluffy, medium-sized blooms. *Foliage* bright green, medium-sized, finely serrated leaves. *Growth* upright, bushy, fairly vigorous and free-flowering. Bush.

'Violet Roth'
PENNISI 1967
AFS Registration No 711
Double
Tube greenish-white, short and thick. *Sepals* greenish-white, recurving. *Corolla* green, fading to light green, medium-sized bloom of a most unusual colouring. *Foliage* medium green, medium-sized leaves. *Growth* upright, bushy and free-flowering. Bush.

'Violetta'
SCHNABEL 1952
AFS Registration No 114
Single
Tube ivory white, thin, medium length. *Sepals* ivory white, long and curving upwards. *Corolla* bishop's violet with a paler blotch at the base of each petal. Medium-sized, bell-shaped blooms. *Foliage* bright green, medium-sized leaves, slightly serrated. Growth upright, vigorous, bushy and free-flowering. Bush.

'Violette Szabo'
HOLMES 1980
AFS Registration No 1557
Single
Tube blush white, medium length and thickness. *Sepals* blush white RHS 62D on top, creped rhodamine pink RHS 62A on the undersides, long and slender with green tips, reflexing. *Corolla* rose purple RHS 75A, rhodamine purple RHS 68D at the base of the petals and roseine purple RHS 68A on the edges, the whole fading to roseine purple on maturity. *Pistil* blush white with yellow style. *Foliage* medium green with paler veins, heavily serrated, lanceolate. Leaves have pink petioles and part of the main vein is the same shade. Growth upright, self-branching and bushy. Flowers borne in terminal nodes. Very free-flowering. Bush or standard. Will stand either sun or shade.

'Virginia Chiles'
CHILES 1953
AFS Registration No 160
Double
Tube neyron rose, short and thick. *Sepals* neyron rose, long, broad and upturned. *Corolla* hyacinth blue. Petals splashed with lilac and phlox pink. Medium-sized bloom. *Foliage* mid-green, medium-sized, serrated leaves. *Growth* trailer, bushy, free-flowering. Basket.

'Virginia Lund'
TIRET 1966
AFS Registration No 689
Double
Tube pink, medium length, thin. *Sepals* pink, narrow and upturned. *Corolla* pure white. Petals have scalloped edges and give this cultivar a most attractive look. *Foliage* mid-green, medium-sized leaves. *Growth* upright, bushy and free-flowering. Bush.

'Visitor'
PALKO/SOO YUN FIELD 1978
AFS Registration No 1448
Semi-double
Tube spiraea red, short and thin. *Sepals* spiraea red, long and curving upwards. *Corolla* dark aster violet, fading to light cyclamen, very loose. *Foliage* light green, medium-sized leaves with reddish stems. *Growth* semi-trailer, free-flowering and bushy. Half-basket.

'Vivace'
NESSIER 1952
AFS Registration No 119
Semi-double
Tube turkey red, medium length and thickness. *Sepals* turkey red, broad and upturned. *Corolla* maroon red with the serrated edges of the petals turkey red. Medium-sized, compact bloom. *Foliage* bright green, medium-sized, serrated leaves. *Growth* upright, very vigorous, free-flowering. Needs a lot of pinching to keep it in check. Bush or standard.

'Viva Ireland'
NESSIER 1956
Single
Tube pale pink, thin, medium length.

Sepals pale pink, long, narrow and recurving. *Corolla* lilac-blue, lighter at the base of the petals. *Foliage* medium to darkish green, medium-sized, long and narrow, serrated leaves. *Growth* bushy, rather lax, self-branching and very free-flowering. A most beautiful cultivar which does well as a summer bedder. Bush or half-basket.

'Vivien Harris'
HARRIS 1978
AFS Registration No 1484
Single
Tube turkey red, long and thick. *Sepals* turkey red, short, and held well out. *Corolla* deep turkey red, small and compact. *Foliage* medium to darkish green, medium-sized serrated leaves. *Growth* bushy, upright and vigorous. Free-flowering with blooms resembling, the triphylla type. Bush. *Parentage* 'Leverhulme' × 'Rufus'.

'Vivien Lee'
NIEDERNOLZER 1947
Single
Tube, sepals and corolla pale pink. Small blooms. *Foliage* medium green, small to medium-sized, serrated leaves. *Growth* upright, bushy and free-flowering. Bush.

'Vobeglo'
DE GROOT (Netherlands)
Single
Tube rose pink, short and thick. *Sepals* rose red, held well out from the corolla. *Corolla* lilac purple, darker at the edges of the petals. *Stamens* rose. *Style* pale rose pink. *Foliage* medium green, very small leaves. *Growth* dwarf growing with short branches, upright, fairly free-flowering with flowers standing out erect. *Parentage* 'Pallas' (*F. regia typica* × 'Bon Accorde') × 'Henriette Ernst'. Dwarf bush or rockery plant.

'Voltaire'
LEMOINE 1897
Single
Tube scarlet, thick, medium length. *Sepals* scarlet, short, broad and slightly reflexed. *Corolla* magenta purple with reddish veins, medium-sized bloom. *Foliage* mid-green, medium-sized, ovate, serrated leaves. *Growth* upright, bushy, vigorous, free-flowering and easy to grow. Bush or summer bedder.

'Voodoo'
TIRET 1953
AFS Registration No 157
Double
Tube dark red, short, medium thickness. *Sepals* dark red, long, broad and upturned. *Corolla* dark purplish-violet, very full and fluffy bloom. *Foliage* medium to darkish green, medium-sized leaves. *Growth* upright, vigorous, self-branching and free-flowering. A very attractive cultivar. Bush.

'Vulcan'
PUGH 1975
AFS Registration No 1238
Semi-double
Tube china rose RHS 58D, medium length and thickness. *Sepals* neyron rose RHS 58C on the underside, china rose on top. Pale green tips. *Corolla* neyron rose at the base, shading to ruby red RHS 64A at the tips. *Stamens and pistil* neyron rose. *Foliage* lettuce green RHS 144A with red veins, medium-sized leaves. *Growth* upright, self-branching, vigorous and bushy. Free-flowering. Requires tight pinching. Bush or standard.

'Wagtails White Pixie'
See 'White Pixie'.

'Waldfee'
TRAVIS 1973
AFS Registration No 1150
Single, breviflora type
Tube soft lilac pink, long and thin. *Sepals* soft lilac pink, broad, spreading. *Corolla* soft lilac pink, squarish and reflexing. Small blooms. *Foliage* matt forest green RHS 136A with a silky sheen, small to medium-sized, serrated leaves. *Growth*

self-branching trailer or bush, vigorous free-flowering. Bush *Parentage F. michoacanensis* ×.

'Waltz Time'

WALTZ 1959
Double
Tube pure white, medium length and thickness. *Sepals* white, long, broad and upturned. *Corolla* pale pink, very full and fluffy, compact bloom. *Foliage* mid-green, medium-sized leaves. *Growth* trailer, bushy, fairly vigorous and free-flowering. Basket.

'War Paint'

KENNETT 1960
AFS Registration No 431
Double
Tube white, short and thick. *Sepals* white on top, flushed pink on the undersides, broad and curling up to the tube. *Corolla* dianthus purple, marbled coral pink and fading to reddish purple. Paler at the base of the petals. Compact, medium-sized bloom. *Foliage* medium green with reddish veins. Large, finely serrated leaves. *Growth* upright, bushy, vigorous and free-flowering. Bush.

'Warton Crag'

THORNLEY 1973
AFS Registration No 1100
Single
Tube flesh pink, short, medium thickness. *Sepals* creamy white with green tips. Broad, opening to show the creamy white, thick sepaloids. *Corolla* pink RHS 72A, rather uneven petals. *Foliage* dark green, medium-sized leaves. *Growth* upright, bushy, free flowering. Bush. 'Jamboree' seedling.

'Wave of Life'

HENDERSON 1869
Single
Tube scarlet, thin, medium length. *Sepals* scarlet, short, broad and upturned. *Corolla* magenta purple, small and compact. *Foliage* greenish-yellow and gold, small to medium-sized, serrated leaves. *Growth* bushy, lax, not very vigorous, and, like most variegated leaved cultivars, not a prolific bloomer. Bush.

'Waverley'

STEWART 1971
AFS Registration No 961
Single
Tube pinkish white, long, medium thickness. *Sepals* light pink, tipped green. Long, narrow and pointed. *Corolla* orange-magenta, medium-sized, compact bloom. *Foliage* bright green with red veins. Large, ovate, serrated leaves. *Growth* upright, bushy, vigorous and free-flowering. Bush or standard.

'Wawona'

NIEDERHOLZER 1946
Single
Tube pale crimson, medium length and thickness. *Sepals* crimson, medium length, slightly reflexed. *Corolla* peony purple with a crimson stripe on the petals, opening up wide. Medium-sized bloom. *Foliage* mid-green, medium-sized leaves. *Growth* upright, very vigorous, free-flowering. Bush or standard.

'Waxen Beauty'

CLYNE 1975
AFS Registration No 1287
Double
Tube greenish-white with rose pink shading. Short and thick. *Sepals* greenish-white, waxy, arched and slightly reflexed. *Corolla* white with pale pink shading in the centre. *Foliage* spinach green, medium sized, almond-shaped leaves. *Growth* vigorous, bushy, upright. Strong growing and free-flowering. Makes a very good exhibition plant up to a $6\frac{1}{2}$ in (16.5 cm) pot. Bush or standard. *Parentage* 'Ting-a-Ling' × ('La Campanella' × 'Flirtation Waltz').

'Wedgewood'

SCHNABEL 1951
AFS Registration No 82
Double
Tube white, thin, medium length. *Sepals*

white, long, shiny, narrow and upturned. *Corolla* bluish-violet, paler at the base of the petals. Open and spreading, medium-sized bloom. *Foliage* mid-green, medium-sized leaves. *Growth* upright, fairly vigorous, free-flowering. A very attractive 'blue' shaded cultivar. Bush.

'Wee Lass'
GADSBY 1975
AFS Registration No 1283
Single
Tube red, short and thick. *Sepals* cardinal red RHS 53B, short and thick. *Corolla* bluebird blue RHS 94, lighter at the base, to spectrum violet RHS 82B, very small, $\frac{2}{5}$ in (1 cm). *Foliage* medium green, small leaves. *Growth* dwarf, upright, bushy, self-branching and free-flowering. Ideal for small pot culture or rockery use. *Parentage* 'Gambit' × 'Upward Look'.

'Wee One'
TIRET 1954
AFS Registration No 209
Double
Tube pale pink, short, medium thickness. *Sepals* pale pink on top, pink on the underside, short, broad and upturned. *Corolla* soft pink, small to medium-sized, compact bloom. *Foliage* medium green, small to medium-sized leaves. Growth upright, long-branched, fairly vigorous and free-flowering. Bush.

'Welsh Dragon'
BAKER 1970
Double
Tube rose pink, long, medium thickness. *Sepals* rose pink, long, broad and upturned. *Corolla* magenta rose, petals falling in layers. Medium-sized bloom. *Foliage* mid-green, medium-sized, finely serrated leaves. *Growth* upright, bushy, free-flowering. An easy one to grow and very worthwhile. Bush.

'Wennington Beck'
THORNLEY 1973
Double
Tube reddish brown RHS 47A, short, medium thickness. *Sepals* pink, flushed green on top, clear soft pink on the undersides. Reflexing back to the tube. *Corolla* soft violet-blue RHS 85A, flushed pink at the base of the petals which have serrated edges. Medium-sized bloom. *Foliage* mid-green, small to medium-sized leaves. *Growth* trailer, lax, bushy, fairly free-flowering. Bush or half-basket. 'Dorothea Flower' seedling.

'Westlake'
NESSIER 1952
AFS Registration No 120
Double
Tube rose madder, medium length and thickness. *Sepals* rose madder, long, broad and reflexing. *Corolla* bishop's violet, marbled solferino purple, with shades of fuchsia purple at the base of the petals. Medium-sized, compact bloom. *Foliage* mid-green, medium-sized, serrated leaves. *Growth* natural trailer, vigorous, free-flowering. Basket.

'Whirlaway'
WALTZ 1961
AFS Registration No 494
Semi-double
Tube white, medium length and thickness. *Sepals* white with green tips. Faintly tinged pink. Long, narrow and curling upwards. *Corolla* white with a faint tinge of pink as the bloom matures. Medium-sized, very loose-petalled bloom. *Foliage* mid-green, long, medium-sized leaves with finely serrated edges. *Growth* lax upright with long, willowy branches. Vigorous and free-flowering. A cultivar which needs pinching to form a good shape. Bush.

'Whirligig'
CROCKETT 1969
AFS Registration No 857
Single
Tube rose opal RHS 51A, medium length and thickness. *Sepals* rose opal, long and reflexing. *Corolla* violet-purple RHS 77A, overlaid plum purple RHS 79C, and veined rose opal. Medium-sized blooms

with twisted petals. *Foliage* medium green, long, wavy leaves. *Growth* upright, villowy, fairly vigorous, free-flowering. Bush.

'White Ann'
WILLS 1972
Registered 1973
AFS Registration No 1130
Double
A sport of 'Heidi Ann', identical to 'Heidi Weiss' (q.v.).

'White Bride'
GADSBY 1970
AFS Registration No 868
Double
Tube white, medium length and thickness. *Sepals* white, flushed pink, tipped green and slightly upturned. *Corolla* white, long and full. *Foliage* medium green, large and roundish. *Growth* upright, self-branching and free-flowering. Prefers to be grown in the shade. Bush.

'White Fairy'
WALTZ 1963
AFS Registration No 589
Double
Tube pure white, medium length and thickness. *Sepals* pure white. *Corolla* snowy white, full and fluffy, medium to large blooms. *Foliage* light green, small to medium-sized leaves. *Growth* upright, self-branching and bushy. Free-flowering. Bush or semi-trailer.

'White Falls'
TOLLEY 1974
AFS Registration No 1234
Semi-double
Tube baby pink, short, medium thickness. *Sepals* baby pink with green tips, short and broad. *Corolla* creamy white with pink veins. *Stamens and pistil* pink. *Foliage* medium green, bright, crinkled, ovate. *Growth* self-branching, vigorous, tending to be rather lax and requiring early staking to form a good bush. Free-flowering. Bush or basket.

'White Gigantea'
WALKER AND JONES 1952
Double
Tube red, medium length and thickness. *Sepals* red. *Corolla* white, large and full. *Foliage* mid-green, large leaves. *Growth* upright, self-branching, vigorous and free-flowering. Very heavy bloomer, and a large showy plant. Bush (requires staking).

'White Gold'
YORK 1953
AFS Registration No 190
Single
Tube white, flushed pink. Short, medium thickness. *Sepals* white with green tips. Long, narrow and curling upwards. *Corolla* creamy white with pink veining. Medium-sized, loose-petalled blooms. *Foliage* green, variegated golden yellow. Small, serrated leaves. *Growth* bushy, lax, low-growing, fairly free-flowering. Low Bush.

'White King' (25)
PENNISI 1968
AFS Registration No 753
Double
Tube white, short and fairly thick. *Sepals* white, long, broad, held over the corolla and turning up at the tips. *Corolla* pure white, very large with pleated and folded petals. Full, fluffy blooms. *Foliage* mid-green, medium-sized, finely serrated leaves. *Growth* natural trailer, vigorous and fairly free-flowering, but one that required pinching in its early stages to get it into shape. A superb cultivar, well worth growing. Basket.

'Whiteknight's Amethyst'
J.O. WRIGHT 1980
AFS Registration No 1595
Single
Tube red-purple. *Sepals* shading from pale red-purple at the base, through greenish white to yellow-green at the tips. Slightly triangular-shaped. *Corolla* violet RHS 83A, ageing to red-purple. Tubular with

heart-shaped petals. *Style and stamens* purple-red with blue pollen. *Foliage* dark green, small leaves. *Growth* upright, vigorous. Will take full sun.

'Whiteknight's Blush'
J.O. WRIGHT 1980
AFS Registration No 1592
Single
Tube pale pink, medium length and thickness. *Sepals* pale pink, spreading, green tips. Lanceolate. *Corolla* clear pink, rather like *F. magellanica* var. *molinae* but much larger. *Foliage* dark green with green veining on the leaves and branches. Small leaves. *Growth* upright, small, self-branching. Hardy. Bush.

'Whiteknight's Cheeky'
J.O. WRIGHT 1980
AFS Registration No 1593
Single
Tube dark tyrian purple, triphylla type. *Sepals* dark tyrian purple, small and spreading. *Corolla* dark tyrian purple, very small. Flowers are borne in erect terminal racemes, horizontally and clear of the foliage. *Foliage* dark and velvety with red veining. *Growth* upright, small, bushy. Bush. *Parentage* 'Whiteknight's Ruby' × *F. procumbens.*

'Whiteknight's Gem'
BRIGHT 1910
Single to semi-double
Tube soft pink, short, medium thickness. *Sepals* soft pink, short, broad, held well out. *Corolla* bluish mauve, small to medium-sized, compact bloom. *Foliage* mid-green, medium-sized, serrated leaves. *Growth* upright, vigorous and free-flowering. Bush. Similar to 'Constance'.

'Whiteknight's Glister'
J.A. WRIGHT 1980
AFS Registration No 1594
Single
Tube red RHS 53C, medium length and thickness. *Sepals* red RHS 52A at the base, shading to near white at the tips, small and spreading. *Corolla* red purple RHS 66A, with rounded petals. Small and tubular. *Foliage* green with a cream border, strongly variegated. *Growth* upright, fairly vigorous but rather slow growing. Occasionally throws green shoots. Bush. Sport of *F. magellanica* var. *molinae* × *F. fulgens.*

'Whiteknight's Pearl'
J.O. WRIGHT 1980
AFS Registration No 1591
Single
Tube white, thin and of medium length. *Sepals* pale pink with small green tips. *Corolla* clear pink with roundish petals. Resembles *F. magellanica* var. *molinae*, but larger. *Foliage* dark green, small. *Growth* upright, bushy, fairly free-flowering. Bush. *Parentage F. magellanica* var. *molinae* × (*F. magellanica* var. *molinae* × *F. fulgens*).

'White Pixie' (124)
Sport of 'Pixie' introduced by RAWLINS 1967, and by WAGTAILS NURSERY as 'Wagtails White Pixie'
Single
Tube red, short and thin. *Sepals* red, short, broad and upturned. *Corolla* white with reddish pink veins. Small and compact. *Foliage* yellowish-green, red veins. Medium-sized, serrated leaves. *Growth* upright, bushy, free-flowering and hardy. Bush or garden hardy.

'White Queen'
DOYLE 1899
Single
Tube creamy white, long, fairly thick. *Sepals* creamy white, short, broad and held well out from the corolla. *Corolla* salmon-orange. Fairly long blooms. Small, compact corolla. *Foliage* mid-green, medium-sized, ovate, serrated leaves. *Growth* upright, vigorous but rather lax. Very free-flowering. Bush.

'White Queen'
PENNISI 1970
AFS Registration No 885
Double

Tube white, short, medium thickness. *Sepals* white, short and broad, upturned and with green tips. *Corolla* white, fairly full and compact. Medium-sized bloom. *Foliage* mid-green, medium-sized, finely serrated leaves. *Growth* upright, bushy, free-flowering. Prefers to be grown in the shade to keep the white colouring. Bush.

'White Spider' (88)
W.R. HAAG 1951
Single
Tube pale pink, long and thin. *Sepals* pinkish with green tips. Long, narrow and curling upwards. *Corolla* white with pink veins. Long petals, fairly compact. *Foliage* medium green, small to medium-sized, serrated leaves. *Growth* upright, vigorous, free-flowering. Not an easy cultivar to shape, but very easy to grow. Bush or quarter standard.

'Wigwam'
PASKESEN 1966
AFS Registration No 663
Double
Tube pale rosy-pink, medium length and thickness. *Sepals* rosy-pink, broad and upturned. *Corolla* pale magenta, fading to rose-bengal. Medium-sized, full and compact bloom. *Foliage* dark green, leathery, medium-sized leaves. *Growth* upright, bushy, vigorous and free-flowering. A cultivar that needs early pinching to form a good shape. Bush or standard.

'Wild and Beautiful'
SOO YUN 1978
AFS Registration No 1452
Double
Tube white, short and thick. *Sepals* pale neyron rose on the outside, darker neyron rose on the undersides. Longish, slightly upturned. *Corolla* dark amethyst violet, fading to china rose at the base of the petals. Medium-sized bloom. *Pistil and stamens* neyron rose. *Foliage* light green, large leaves. *Growth* semi-trailer, bushy, very vigorous and free-flowering. Bush or basket.

'Wild Fire'
HANDLEY 1972
AFS Registration No 1060
Semi-double
Tube rose pink RHS 52C, short and thick. *Sepals* bright rose pink on top, deeper shade of pink on the undersides. Long, broad and curling up over the tube. *Corolla* cardinal red RHS 53C, ageing to crimson-scarlet, with salmon red shading at the base of the petals. Medium-sized, compact bloom. *Foliage* mid-green with reddish centre veins, medium to large, heavily serrated leaves. *Growth* upright, spreading, lax, free-flowering. Low bush or basket.

'Wild 'n' Wonderful'
SOO YUN 1977
AFS Registration No 1409
Double
Tube red, short and of medium thickness. *Sepals* pink to red, long with green tips curling up towards the tube. *Corolla* white with red stripes. Large, loose, and flaring, with serrated-edged petals. *Foliage* medium green, long, serrated leaves. *Growth* semi-trailer, vigorous, very free-flowering. Basket or bush.

'Wilf Tolley'
GADSBY 1974
AFS Registration No 1225
Semi-double
Tube pale pink, short and thick. *Sepals* china rose RHS 58D, waxy with green tips. Held well out from the corolla. *Corolla* purple-violet RHS 80B, pale pink at the base and changing to cyclamen purple RHS 74B on maturity. Medium-sized, bell-shaped bloom. *Foliage* medium green, small serrated leaves. *Growth* upright, bushy, self-branching, vigorous and free-flowering. Bush.

'William Braas'
TIRET 1951
AFS Registration No 97
Double
Tube white, medium length and thickness. *Sepals* white, flushed pale pink on

top, deeper on the underside, and upturned. *Corolla* rose-madder, medium-sized, compact bloom. *Growth* lax, bushy, free-flowering. Basket.

'Williamette'
PEPPER 1952
AFS Registration No 126
Double
Tube rose pink, short, medium thickness. *Sepals* rose pink, long, broad and upturned. *Corolla* white, splashed fuchsia pink, very full and compact. *Foliage* mid-green, medium-sized leaves. *Growth* trailer, bushy, free-flowering. Basket. Sport of 'San Pablo'.

'William Silva'
WEISEL 1950
AFS Registration No 73a
Double
Tube red, short and thick. *Sepals* red, short, broad and recurving. *Corolla* red with lavender and pink stripes on the petals. Paler reddish pink at the base of the petals. Small to medium, compact bloom. *Foliage* medium green, small, serrated leaves. *Growth* upright, bushy, vigorous and free-flowering. Bush.

'William van Orange'
HAAG 1952
Single
Tube light apricot, medium length and thickness. *Sepals* light apricot, broad and reflexing. *Corolla* clear orange, compact, medium-sized bloom. *Foliage* pale to medium green, medium-sized, serrated leaves. *Growth* upright, bushy, vigorous and free-flowering. Bush.

'Wilson's Joy'
J.W. WILSON 1974
Single
Tube white, short and fairly thick. *Sepals* white on top, flushed pink on the undersides. Short, broad and held well out from the corolla. *Corolla* bluish-cerise, shaded cerise at the base of the petals. Medium-sized, fairly compact blooms. *Foliage* mid-green, medium-sized, slightly serrated leaves. *Growth* upright, bushy, vigorous and free-flowering. Bush. *Parentage* 'Mrs Marshall' ×.

'Wilton Gem'
RAPLEY 1974
Semi-double
Tube cerise, short and thick. *Sepals* cerise, short and broad, reflexing towards the tube. *Corolla* pinkish cerise with cerise veining, medium-sized bloom. *Foliage* light green, medium-sized, serrated leaves. *Growth* upright, bushy, vigorous and free-flowering. Bush.

'Wilton William'
RAPLEY 1974
Double
Tube cerise, short and of medium thickness. *Sepals* cerise, short, broad and held out over the top of the corolla with the tips upturned. *Corolla* pinkish mauve with cerise veining. Small, untidy bloom. *Foliage* medium green with reddish veins, small serrated leaves. *Growth* upright, vigorous, bushy and free-flowering. A rather open, loose-petalled and untidy flower with little to commend it. Bush.

'Wilton Winkie'
RAPLEY 1974
Single
Tube crimson, short and thick. *Sepals* crimson with green tips. Short, broad and upturned. *Corolla* violet-purple with crimson veining. Shaded pale reddish at the base of the petals. Small, compact bloom. *Foliage* dark green with crimson veining, medium-sized, finely serrated leaves. *Growth* upright, vigorous, bushy and free-flowering. Easy to grow, and a rather attractive, if not unusual, bloom. Bush.

'Windmill'
PASKESEN 1967
AFS Registration No 727
Single
Tube red, short, medium thickness. *Sepals* red, short, held well out from the corolla. *Corolla* deep blue, paler at the base of the

petals. *Foliage* medium green, small leaves. *Growth* lax upright, self-branching and very free-flowering. Bush or summer bedder.

'Wine and Roses'
WALKER 1969
AFS Registration No 834
Double
Tube pale pink, short and thick. *Sepals* pale pink on top, darker on the undersides with green tips. Short, broad and curling upwards. *Corolla* wine purple in the centre, shaded pale pinkish white at the base of the petals and with long pink petaloids on the outside. A most unusual, rather untidy bloom. One for the connoisseur. *Foliage* light green, medium-sized, ovate and finely serrated leaves. *Growth* trailer, vigorous, free-flowering. Requires a lot of pinching when small to form the basic shape. Basket.

'Wings of Song'
BLACKWELL 1968
Double
Tube rose pink, medium length and thickness. *Sepals* rose pink, long, broad and upturned to the tube. *Corolla* lavender pink with pink veins. Fairly compact, medium-sized bloom. *Foliage* mid-green with reddish veins. Medium-sized, ovate, heavily serrated leaves. *Growth* natural trailer, very vigorous, self-branching and free-flowering. Basket.

'Winner's Circle'
PANCHARIAN 1975
AFS Registration No 1296
Double
Tube red, short and medium thick. *Sepals* cranberry red, smooth on top and with a crepe effect on the undersides. Broad, spoon-shaped. *Corolla* cyclamen purple with red at the base of the petals, changing to rose-red as the flower matures. Small petaloids of the same colour. *Foliage* medium green, medium-sized leaves. *Growth* semi-trailer, vigorous, free-flowering. Not an easy one to grow. Bush or basket.

'Winnie'
SOO YUN FIELD 1966
AFS Registration No 685
Single
Tube pink, medium length and thickness. *Sepals* pink, long and upturned. *Corolla* blue, fading to light orchid. Paler at the base of the petals. Medium-sized, compact bloom. *Foliage* bright green, medium-sized leaves. *Growth* upright, bushy, free-flowering. Bush.

'Winsome'
HAZARD
Single
Tube white, short and of medium thickness. *Sepals* white, long, broad, recurving. *Corolla* white, faintly tinged pink. Medium-sized blooms. *Foliage* mid-green, medium-sized leaves. *Growth* upright, fairly vigorous, bushy and free-flowering. Bush.

'Winston Churchill'
GARSON 1942
Double
Tube pink, medium length and thickness. *Sepals* pink on top, darker on the undersides, green tipped. Short, broad and reflexed. *Corolla* lavender blue with pinkish veins, and splashed pink on the outer petals. Small to medium-sized, fairly compact blooms. *Foliage* medium green, small to medium-sized, longish, serrated leaves. Growth upright, bushy, self-branching and free-flowering. It will make a good exhibition plant but can be rather unreliable in its flowering time. Bush or quarter standard.

'Wonder Blue'
NIEDERHOLZER 1946
Double
Tube phlox pink, short and of medium thickness. *Sepals* phlox pink, long, broad and reflexing. *Corolla* deep blue, very full and compact, large bloom. *Foliage* medium green, medium-sized, serrated leaves. *Growth* upright, vigorous, bushy and free-flowering. Bush.

'Wood Violet'
SCHMIDT 1946
Double
Tube red, short, medium thickness. *Sepals* red, short and broad, held well out then turning upwards. *Corolla* violet blue, small but very full and compact. *Foliage* medium to darkish green, small to medium-sized, serrated leaves. *Growth* upright, bushy and free-flowering. Small bush.

'W. P. Wood'
WOOD 1954
Single
Tube scarlet, short and thick. *Sepals* scarlet, short, broad and held well out from the corolla. *Corolla* purple, reddish purple at the base of the petals. Small compact bloom. *Foliage* dark green, small, heavily serrated leaves. *Growth* upright, bushy, low growing, free-flowering. Bush or garden hardy.

'Wyandot'
FUCHSIA LA 1972
AFS Registration No 1022
Double
Tube rose madder, short, medium thickness. *Sepals* rose madder, long, broad and reflexing. *Corolla* pale violet-purple in the centre, with the outer petals streaked tyrian rose. Fairly compact, medium-sized bloom. *Foliage* dark green, medium-sized leaves, serrated. *Growth* upright, vigorous, bushy, free-flowering. Bush.

'Xenia'
HAZARD
Date unknown
Single
Tube white with pink flush, medium length and thickness. *Sepals* white, flushed pink. *Corolla* pale violet purple, petals edged pink, with pink at the base. *Foliage* medium green, medium-sized leaves. *Growth* very lax trailer, vigorous, free-flowering. Basket.

'Xenia Field'
THORNE 1960
AFS Registration No 455
Double
Tube pale pink, small of medium thickness. *Sepals* pale pink, short. *Corolla* pink with bright pink splashes on the petals, small and compact. *Foliage* medium green, small leaves. *Growth* dwarf, upright, bushy and compact. Bush.

'Xtra Nice'
PRENTICE/VEE JAY 1978
AFS Registration No 1487
Double
Tube rose pink, short, medium thickness. *Sepals* rose and white on top, salmon rose on the underside, folding back over the tube. *Corolla* lavender with salmon rose at the base of the petals. *Foliage* medium green. *Growth* natural trailer, which will make a good basket.

'Yankee Clipper'
SOO YUN 1971
AFS Registration No 945
Double
Tube short, medium length, red. *Sepals* carmine red, short and medium width. *Corolla* ruby red and carmine, large flowers. *Foliage* medium green, long leaves. *Growth* upright, vigorous, self-branching and free-flowering. Easy to grow. Bush.

'Yankee Doodle'
HODGES 1953
AFS Registration No 152
Sinlge
Tube red, short and medium thickness. *Sepals* deep red, reflexed. *Corolla* very unusual colour combination which can be white or white with purple-blue blotches of irregular shape. Opens flat. *Foliage* medium green. *Growth* vigorous, upright, bushy and free-flowering. A most unusual coloured fuchsia. Bush.

'Yelena Suzanne'
TRAVIS 1980
AFS Registration No 1586
Single
Tube wine purple, thin, medium length. *Sepals* wine purple, narrow and slightly reflexed. *Corolla* lavender to lilac, longish.

Flowers axillary in loose terminal spikes. *Foliage* light green, obovate. *Growth* upright, vigorous, self-branching. Bush. Will take full sun, but the best colour develops in the shade. *Pollen parent F. arborescens.*

'Yonder Blue'
TIRET 1954
AFS Registration No 210
Double
Tube rose red, medium length and thickness. *Sepals* rose red, long and broad, upturning. *Corolla* deep blue, full and very compact, large flowers. *Foliage* medium green, medium-sized leaves. *Growth* upright, vigorous, bushy and free-flowering. Bush.

'Yosimet'
Raiser unknown
Double
Tube white, medium length and thickness. *Sepals* white, long and slightly reflexing. *Foliage* medium green. *Growth* upright, bushy, vigorous, free-flowering. Bush.

'Yuletide' (122)
TIRET 1948
Double
Tube crimson, medium length and width. *Sepals* crimson. *Corolla* creamy white, full, large. *Foliage* medium to darkish green. *Growth* upright, vigorous, bushy and free-flowering. Bush or standard. A nice flower, large and showy.

'Yum Yum'
ERICKSON 1961
AFS Registration No 487
Double
Tube pale pink, medium length and width, flushed green. *Sepals* pale pink, short and upturned. *Corolla* rose pink with orchid pink shading. *Foliage* medium green. *Growth* low growing, bushy, free-flowering. Bush or stiff-branching trailer. Beautiful plant, very heavy bloomer.

'Yvonne Holmes'
R. HOLMES 1974
AFS Registration No 1210
Single
Tube crimson RHS 52A, medium length and thickness. *Sepals* crimson RHS 52A, green tips. Medium length and width, curving slightly upwards. *Corolla* cyclamen purple RHS 74B, carmine RHS 52B at the base, veined cherry red RHS 45C, bell-shaped. *Stamens and style* pink, stigma pale yellow. *Foliage* pale to medium green, with veins paler green. Foliage lanceolate, serrated, medium size. *Growth* upright, self-branching, bushy and very free-flowering. Branches red, shoots light green. Very easy to train, will do well out of doors. Bush. *Parentage* 'Percy Holmes' × 'Mr A. Huggett'.

'Zenobia'
HAZARD
Single
Tube pink, medium length and thickness. *Sepals* pink, slightly upturned. *Corolla* deep pink, large blooms. *Foliage* medium green, medium to large. *Growth* trailer, vigorous, free-flowering. Basket.

'Ziegfield Girl'
FUCHISA FOREST 1966
AFS Registration No 671
Double
Tube pink, medium length and thickness. *Sepals* pink on top, deeper pink on the undersides, green tips. *Corolla* pink, very full. *Filaments* pink. *Style* pink. *Foliage* medium to dark green with crimson veins, very slightly serrated. *Growth* natural trailer, very free-flowering, but difficult to grow well. Grows best in the shade. Basket.

'Zody's Dante'
Semi-double
Tube bright cerise. *Sepals* bright cerise, recurving. *Corolla* purple with rose pink marbling. *Foliage* medium to dark green, slightly serrated. *Growth* upright, self-branching and bushy. Bush. A very attractive flower and easy to grow.

GLOSSARY

Anther	The pollen-bearing part of the stamen.
Axil	The angle formed by the junction of leaf and stem from which new shoots or flowers develop.
Berry	They fleshy fruit containing the seeds; the ovary after fertilisation.
Break	To branch or send out new growth from dormant wood.
Calyx	The sepals and tube together, the outer part of the flower.
Cordate	Heart-shaped.
Corolla	The collective term for the petals, the inner part of the flower.
Cultivar	A cultivated variety, a cross between two hybrids or a species and a hybrid. Normally written cv.
Cyme	An inflorescence where the central flowers open first, as in *F. arborescens*.
Double	A fuchsia with eight or more petals.
Filament	The stalk of the stamen.
Hybrid	A cross between two species.
Hypanthium	The correct term for the tube.
Lanceolate	Lance- or spear-shaped.
Node	Part of the stem from which a leaf arises, or a bud. When taking cuttings, roots form most readily at this point.
Ovary	The part containing the ovules which, after fertilisation, swells and encloses the seeds.
Ovate	Egg-shaped.
Pedicel	The flower stalk.
Petal	A division of the corolla.
Petaloid	Normally used to describe the smaller outer petals of the corolla.
Petiole	The leaf stalk.
Pinch	To remove the growing tips.
Pistil	The female part of the flower, consisting of the ovary, stigma and style.
Semi-double	A fuchsia with five, six or seven petals.
Sepals	Normally four, which, with the tube, form the calyx, the outermost part of the flower.
Single	A fuchsia with four petals only.
Sport	A shoot different in character from the typical growth of the parent plant, often giving rise to a new cultivar, and which must be propagated vegetatively.
Stamen	The male part of the flower comprising the filament and anther.
Stigma	The part of the pistil to which the pollen grains adhere.
Stop	To remove the growing tips.
Style	The stalk carrying the stigma.
Tube	The elongated part of the calyx, correctly called the hypanthium.
Variety	Botanically a variant of the species, but formerly used to denote what is now correctly termed a cultivar.

BIBLIOGRAPHY

Great Britain

Boullemier, L.B., *Fascinating Fuchsias*, privately published 1974
Goulding, E.J., *Fuchsias*, Bartholomew 1973
Jennings, K. and Miller, V.V., *Growing Fuchsias*, Croom Helm 1979
Proudley, B. and V., *Fuchsias in Colour*, Blandford Press 1981
Puttock, A.G., *Lovely Fuchsias*, John Gifford 1959
Puttock, A.G., *Pelargoniums and Fuchsias*, Amateur Gardening Handbook 34, Collingridge 1959
Thorne, T., *Fuchsias for all Purposes*, Collingridge 1959
Travis, J., *Fuchsia Culture*, privately published
Wells, G., *Fuchsias*, Wisley Handbook No. 5, Royal Horticultural Society 1976
Witham Fogg, H.G., *Begonias and Fuchsias*, John Gifford 1958
Wilson, S.J., *Fuchsias*, Faber & Faber 1965
Wood, W.P., *A Fuchsia Survey*, Benn 1950

USA

The New A to Z on Fuchsias, published by the National Fuchsia Society Inc. 1976
The Third Fuchsia Book, published by the American Fuchsia Society 1962

South Africa

Tomlinson, Val, *Growing Fuchsias in Southern Africa*, Galaxie Press 1976

The Netherlands

van der Laan, J.E., *Fuchsias het hele jaar door*, Thieme & Cie 1974

Germany

Fessler, A., *Fuchsien fur Haus und Garten*, Kosmos 1980

France

Cesar, J., *Les Fuchsias*, Editions Dargauld 1981

APPENDIX

PRINCIPAL FUCHSIA SOCIETIES

AUSTRALIA
Australian Fuchsia Society Inc.
Box No 97
PO Norwood
South Australia 5067

BELGIUM
Les Amis du Fuchsia
rue de l'Esperance 62
4000 Liège

CANADA
British Columbia Fuchsia Society
2175 West 16th Avenue
Vancouver 9 British Columbia

DENMARK
Dansk Fuchsia Klub
Secretariat
V/Merete Printz
Frugtparken 1
2820 Gentofte

ETHIOPIA
Horticultural Society of Ethiopia
PO Box No 1261
Addis Ababa

FRANCE
Section Fuchsia de la S.N.H.F.
14 rue Brossement
Villeloy s/Yvette
Palaiseau 91120

GERMANY
Deutsche Dahlien, Fuchsien und
Gladiolen Gesellschaft,
674 Landau i.d. Pfalz,
Den Altes Stadhaus,
Köln.

GREAT BRITAIN
The British Fuchsia Society
The Bungalow
Brookwood Military Cemetery
Brookwood, Woking, Surrey, England.

HOLLAND
Nederlandse Kring van Fuchsia Vrienden
Graaf Floris V straat 6
Geertruidenberg

NEW ZEALAND
Canterbury Horticultural Society
Fuchsia Circle
25 Albert Terrace
St Martins
Christchurch 2

NEW ZEALAND
New Zealand Fuchsia Society
c/o PO Box 8843
Symonds Street
Auckland 1

SOUTH AFRICA
South African Fuchsia Society
Box 193
Hilton 3245
Natal

UNITED STATES OF AMERICA
American Fuchsia Society
Hall of Flowers
Garden Center of San Francisco
Golden Gate Park
San Francisco
California 94122

National Fuchsia Society
6121 Monero Drive
Rancho Palos Verdes
California 90274

ZIMBABWE
Fuchsia Society of Zimbabwe
PO Box GD 115
Greendale
Salisbury

INDEX OF COLOUR PLATES

'Abbé Farges' 152
'Achievement' 173
'Aintree' 41
'Alaska' 29
'Alice Ashton' 102
'Alice Hoffman' 125
'Alice Travis' 154
'Alison Ewart' 100
'Alwin' 128
'Andenken an Heinrich Henkel' 18
'Andrew Ryle' 118
'Andromeda' 96
'Angela Leslie' 69
'Annabel' 31
'Auntie Jinks' 57
'Aurora Superba' 177
'Autumnale' 22

'Baby Blue Eyes' 160
'Beacon' 140
'Billy Green' 12
'Bittersweet' 179
'Bland's New Striped' 141
'Blue Waves' 144
'Blush of Dawn' 53
'Bon Accorde' 54
'Border Queen' 97
'Bouffant' 131
'Bountiful' 84
'Bow Bells' 45
'Brutus' 161
'Burning Bush' 22
'Buttercup' 49

'Cascade' 48
'Celia Smedley' 44
'Chang' 191
'Chillerton Beauty' 107
'Citation' 129
'Clair de Lune' 188
'Cliff's Unique' 104
'Cloth of Gold' 21
'Cloverdale Pearl' 167
'Coachman' 190
'Collingwood' 40
'Coquet Bell' 101
'Coquet Dale' 98
'Cotton Candy' 34
'Court Jester' 151
'Crinoline' 35
'Curtain Call' 91

'Daisy Bell' 184
'David Alston' 133
'David Perry' 162
'Derby Imp' 169
'Display' 136
'Dollar Princess' 172
'Dutch Mill' 143

'Eleanor Leytham' 81
'Empress of Prussia' 112
'Estelle Marie' 59
'Evensong' 26

'Falling Stars' 117
'Fiona' 58
'First Kiss' 89
'Flirtation Waltz' 39
Fuchsia arborescens 1
F. boliviana 2
F. b. var. *luxurians* 4
F. b. var. *luxurians* 'Alba' 5
F. cordifolia 3
F. denticulata 11
F. fulgens 'Rubra Grandiflora' 6
F. hemsleyana 7
F. magellanica var. *macrostema* 'Tricolor' 23
F. m. var. *macrostema* 'Variegata' 9
F. procumbens 10
F. serratifolia 11
F. splendens × *F. fulgens* 8

'Gartenmeister Bonstedt' 16
'General Monk' 156
'Genii' 19
'Golondrina' 93
'Grasmere' 66
'Gruss aus dem Bodethal' 163

'Happy Fellow' 189
'Heidi Ann' 145
'Heidi Weiss' 126
'Heron' 159
'Howlett's Hardy' 158

'Impudence' 130
'Isle of Mull' 63

'Jack Shahan' 65
'Joan Hurd' 51
'Joe Kusber' 60
'Joy Patmore' 46
'Julie Horton' 73

'King's Ransom' 56
'Koralle' 13
'Kwintet' 94

'La Campanella' 50
'Lace Petticoats' 33
'Lady Isobel Barnett' 148
'Lady Thumb' 123
'L'Arlesienne' 85
'Le Berger' 30
'Lena Dalton' 108
'Leonora' 74
'Liebriez' 134
'Lilac Lustre' 149
'Loeky' 137
'Lye's Unique' 47

'Macchu Picchu' 180
'Margaret' 157
'Margaret Brown' 80
'Margaret Roe' 176
'Marin Glow' 61
'Marinka' 116
'Mary' 14
'Mary Poppins' 183
'Mephisto' 113
'Mieke Meursing' 139
'Miss California' 83
'Monsieur Thibaut' 174
'Mountain Mist' 52
'Mr A. Huggett' 166
'Mrs Lovell Swisher' 77
'Mrs Popple' 155
'Mrs Rundle' 182

'Nicola Jane' 138
'Nina Wills' 75

'Ocean Beach' 181
'Orange Crush' 185

'Pacquesa' 120
'Papa Bleuss' 105
'Paula Jane' 109
'Peppermint Stick' 171
'Pink Bon Accorde' 67
'Pink Cloud' 76
'Pink Darling' 99
'Pink Fairy' 70
'Pink Jade' 79
'Pink Marshmallow' 82
'Pink Quartette' 68
'Pixie' 147
'Powder Puff' 72
'President Margaret Slater' 42
'Preston Guild' 62
'Prince Syray' 92
'Put's Folly' 37

'Queen of Derby' 142

'R.A.F.' 135
'Red Rum' 119
'Red Spider' 110
'Rev. Doctor Brown' 86
'Ridestar' 150
'Ron Holmes' 90
'Rose Churchill' 64
'Rosecroft Beauty' 20
'Royal Purple' 153
'Rufus' 115

'Santa Cruz' 114
'Sea Shell' 38
'Shy Lady' 32
'Sleigh Bells' 28
'Snowcap' 127
'Sophisticated Lady' 87
'Southgate' 71
'Stardust' 187
'String of Pearls' 95
'Sunray' 24
'Susan Travis' 78
'Swanley Gem' 170
'Swanley Yellow' 178
'Sweetheart' 43
'Symphony' 103

'Tennessee Waltz' 165
'Texas Longhorn' 132
'Thalia' 15
'The Doctor' 192
'The Tarns' 106
'Ting-a-Ling' 27
'Tolling Bell' 121
'Tom Thumb' 164
'Tour Eiffel' 186
'Trail Blazer' 111
'Traudchen Bonstedt' 17
'Trewince Twilight' 36
'Tricolor' 23
'Tristesse' 146
'Tuonela' 175

'Upward Look' 168

'Violet Bassett-Burr' 55

'White King' 25
'White Pixie' 124
'White Spider' 88

'Yuletide' 122